Books are to be returned on or before
the last date below.

LIBREX-

METAMAUS

ART SPIEGELMAN LOOKS INSIDE
HIS MODERN CLASSIC, MAUS.

PLUS

THE COMPLETE MAUS, a hyperlinked DVD of MAUS
with an in-depth archive of audio interviews with his
father, photos, notebooks, drawings, essays and more.
(See detailed description overleaf.)

MAUS

MY PARENTS SURVIVED HELL and moved to the suburbs.

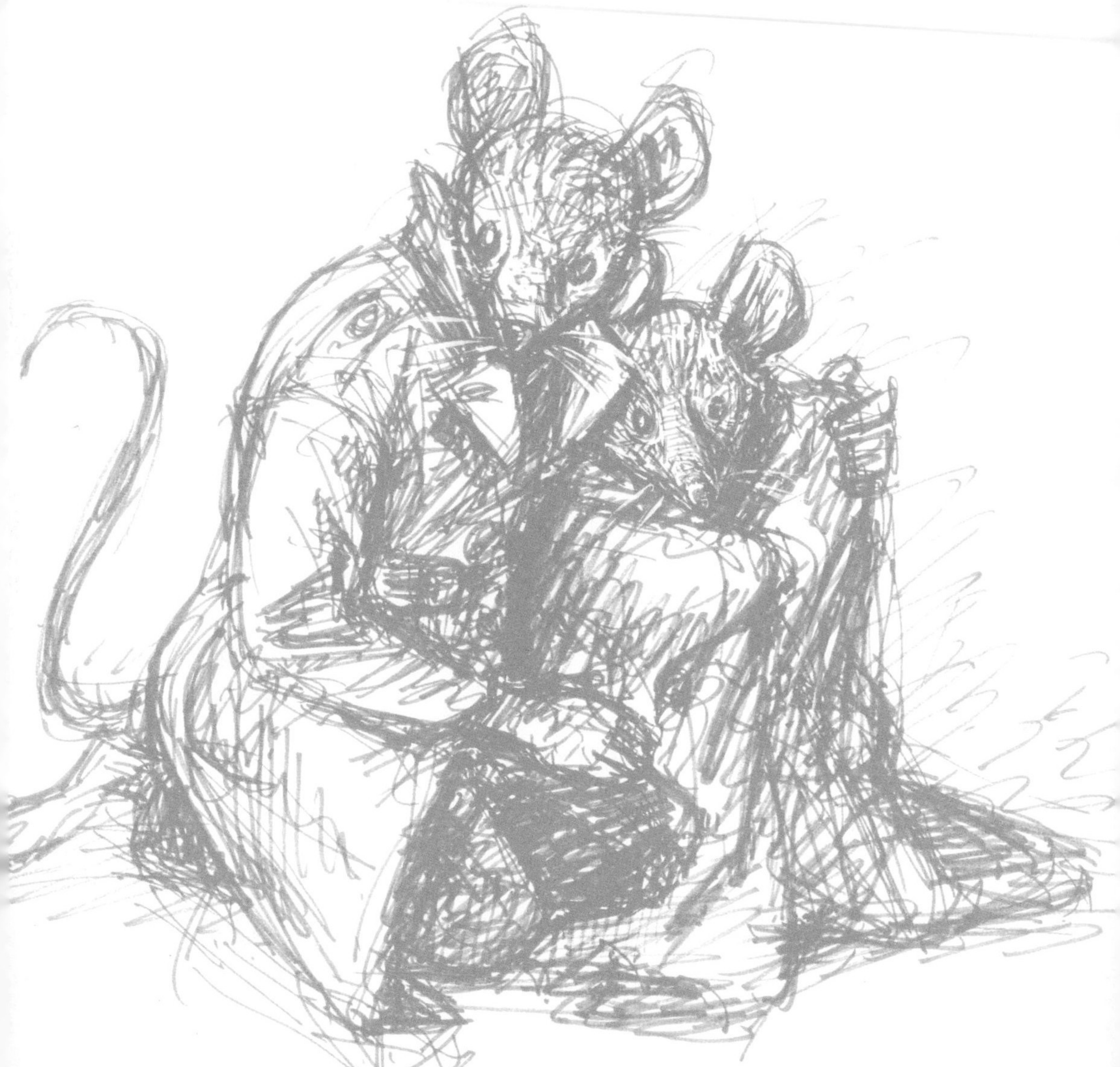

MetaMaus

FOR DASHIELL, NADJA & FRANÇOISE

THANKS to my associate editor, Hillary Chute, and to Bill Kartalopoulos for the indispensable help in shaping and realizing this project; to Jonathan Bennett for lending his design skills; to Si Spiegelman and Andrew Zelby for sharing family history; and to Jesse Fuchs for help in curating my sketches. Special thanx to Pantheon's crackerjack head of production, Andy Hughes; to Dan Frank, my editor at Pantheon, as well as his assistant, Jillian Verrillo...and to Françoise, my muse and lifelong editor.

I'm overwhelmed by the generous dedication and expertise of Ryan Nadel (and his cohorts at 8Leaf Digital, Ian McDonald and Tony Cheung) who made the DVD possible against all odds. Thanks as well to the Vancouver Centre for Digital Media (and of course to Bob Stein and his crew at Voyager for their original Maus CD-ROM).

VIKING
PUBLISHED BY THE PENGUIN GROUP
PENGUIN BOOKS LTD, 80 STRAND, LONDON WC2R 0RL, ENGLAND
WWW.PENGUIN.COM
FIRST PUBLISHED IN THE UNITED STATES OF AMERICA BY
PANTHEON BOOKS
AND IN CANADA BY RANDOM HOUSE OF CANADA LTD. 2011
FIRST PUBLISHED IN GREAT BRITAIN BY VIKING 2011
1
COPYRIGHT © ART SPIEGELMAN, 2011

ISBN: 978–0–670–91683–2

META

CONTENTS

MAUS

VIKING

an imprint of

PENGUIN BOOKS

M ETAMAUS is built around a series of taped conversations with Hillary Chute. (She is currently Neubauer Family Assistant Professor in the English Department at the University of Chicago and was previously a Junior Fellow in Literature in the Society of Fellows at Harvard University.)

In 2006, after reading her lucid takes on my work and that of others I gave her free access to my rat's nest of files, archives, artwork, notebooks, journals, books, and dirty laundry. She soon became my chief enabler and associate editor in a project I kept resisting. (It was hard to revisit *Maus*, the book that both "made" me and has haunted me ever since; hard to revisit the ghosts of my family, the death-stench of history, and my own past.) Her relentless enthusiasm, diligence, and intelligence allowed this project to happen.

—a.s.

(Page references to Maus in the interview and captions refer to The Complete Maus published in one volume.)

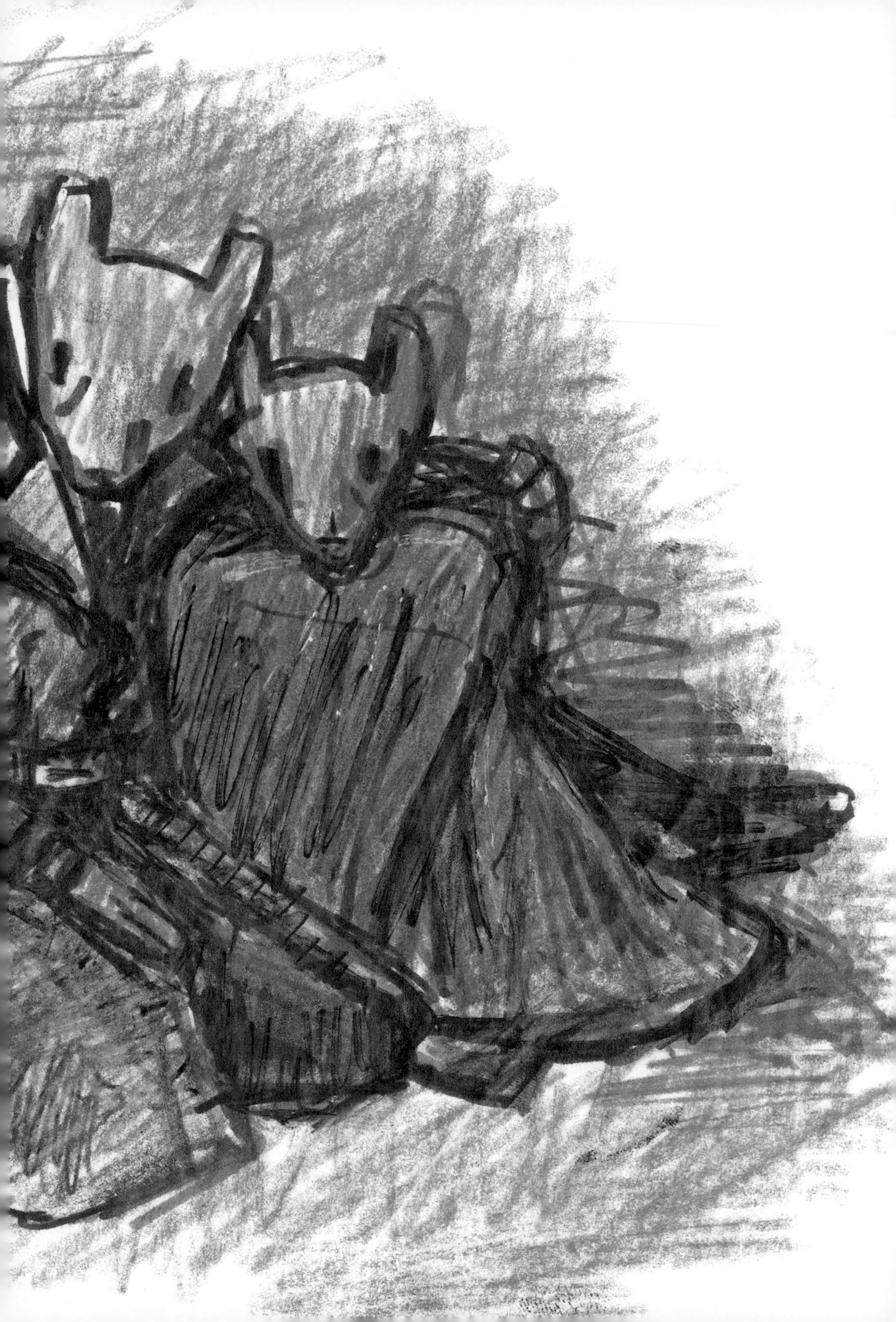

INTRO

Y'KNOW, *MAUS* HAS HAD A *FAR* LARGER IMPACT IN THE WORLD THAN I EVER EXPECTED!

25 YEARS AGO I'D ONLY HOPED IT MIGHT BE DISCOVERED SOMETIME AFTER I DIED.

IT'S SWELL TO GET RECOGNITION... BUT IT'S KINDA *HARD* TO BE SEEN BEHIND A MOUSE MASK!

THE BOOK SEEMS TO LOOM OVER ME LIKE MY FATHER ONCE DID.

JOURNALISTS AND STUDENTS *STILL* WANT ANSWERS TO THE SAME FEW QUESTIONS...

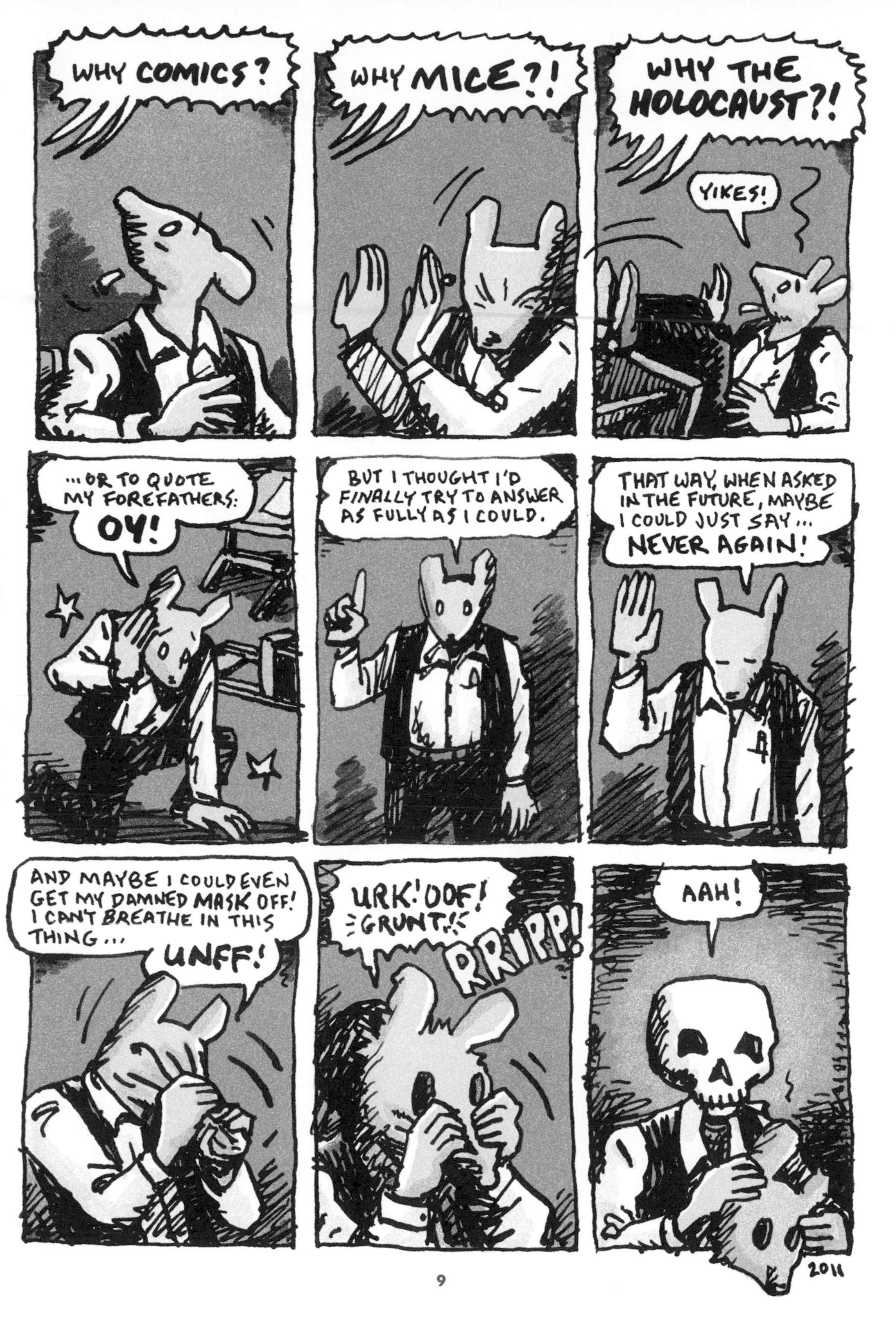
WHY COMICS?
WHY MICE?!
WHY THE HOLOCAUST?!
YIKES!
...OR TO QUOTE MY FOREFATHERS: OY!
BUT I THOUGHT I'D FINALLY TRY TO ANSWER AS FULLY AS I COULD.
THAT WAY, WHEN ASKED IN THE FUTURE, MAYBE I COULD JUST SAY... NEVER AGAIN!
AND MAYBE I COULD EVEN GET MY DAMNED MASK OFF! I CAN'T BREATHE IN THIS THING...
UNFF!
URK! OOF! GRUNT!
RRIPP!
AAH!
2011

Study for *Maus II* contents page.

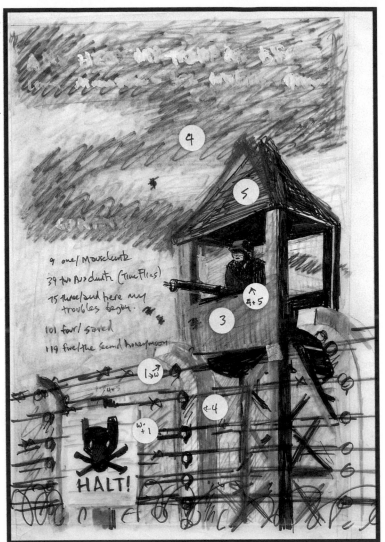

The *New Yorker*, 3/15/99.

WHY THE
HOLOC

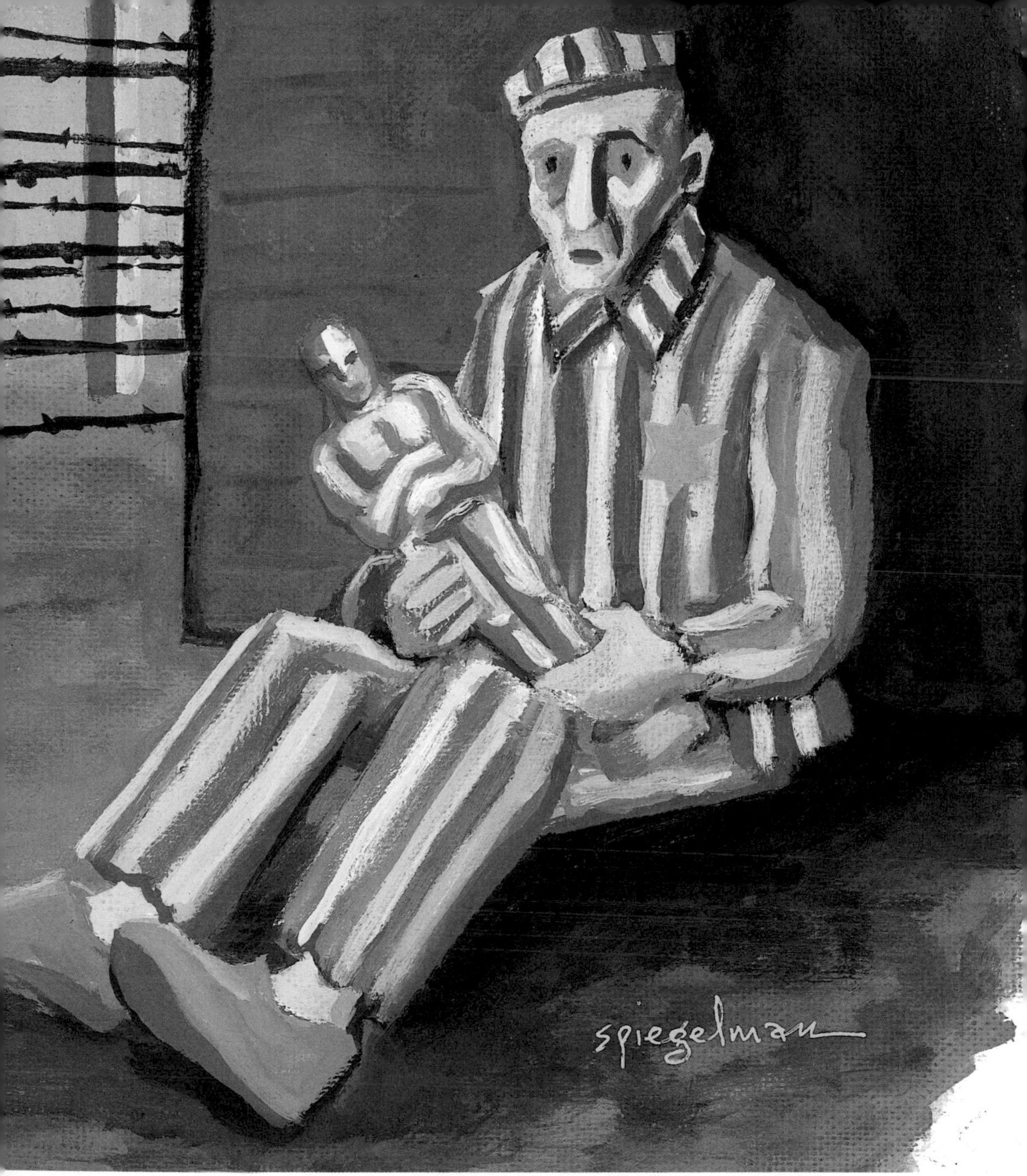
spiegelman

AUST?

When did you become aware that your parents had survived the Holocaust?

My parents didn't talk in any coherent or comprehensive way about what they had lived through. It was always a given that they had lived through "the War," which was their term for the Holocaust. I don't think I even heard the word "Holocaust" till the late '70s, but I was aware of "The War" for as long as I was aware of anything, just from passing

references in our home. You know, "Oh, we're going to stay with Yulek, and Yulek, I helped him very much when we were in the camps, and we'll go stay with him for a while." Even when I was four years old, there was an awareness that these people were part of some fraternity. And I certainly was made aware that they weren't American the way other people around us were Americans.

ABOVE: "Mein Kampf," *New York Times Magazine*, 5/12/96 (special issue on literary memoir).

I'm sure—without even being able to identify it as anxiety. When I was little, there was a lot of: "Go play with Sol while we visit with Esther. Sol's father died in the War. It was really terrible," blah-de-blah. Nobody had the phrase "second generation" in their vocabulary back then, but most of the kids my parents set me up to play with were like Sol, not American Jews let alone from any other tribe. There would be these absolutely unconnected moments that invaded my daily life at random. Like, when I was ten or eleven, Anja's taking me on an errand to do some grocery shopping in our Queens neighborhood, and she has to go to the bathroom. She's fidgeting, and she's debating whether she can make it to the store and use the shopkeeper's bathroom, or whether she should turn around and go home. We ended up heading back home. And as we're walking she's reminiscing, distracting herself from needing to pee. She says, "You know, during the War, I remember when I had to piss in the fields while I was working"—she didn't use that word, but whatever way she said it—"and you know, if the kapos would find you pissing when it wasn't a moment where they specifically were telling you to go piss, they could beat you and kill you. And I didn't know what to do and some friends stood in a circle around me so that I couldn't be seen by the guards."

Anja would tell me about some things that happened to her in the camps—that example is the one that stays with me most clearly—but she'd refer to things without giving me any context or background, and they mostly served to terrify me as a kid. I don't remember Vladek ever telling me much of anything when I was younger about what he went through. But when I asked as a young adult and he finally did slow down to tell me his story, he seemed to respond like it was my birthright to know these things.

Still, his first response was: "People don't want to know about such stories." To him, it was really a matter of brushing it all aside to survive in the new postwar universe he had walked into. He did describe trying to tell Herman and Helen, my mother's brother and his wife—the only close relatives that I knew growing up—what he and Anja had gone through after moving in with them after arriving in America in about 1950. They just had no clue about

Was that something that caused you anxiety?

ABOVE: From *Ravensbrück*, a Ukrainian booklet of drawings on Anja's bookshelf, published c. 1946.
RIGHT: Original art from "Portrait of the Artist as a Young %@&*!"

the enormity of what had happened, and whenever my parents would try to talk about it, they would interrupt and squelch the details. When Anja would talk about starving, they would talk about food shortages in America during the war. The way I picked up any sense of their stories was eavesdropping in the Polish I supposedly didn't know when they talked with their survivor friends.

You could understand Polish?

I had a kind of passive Polish that allowed me to know what was going on. It had to do with trying to know what they were planning for me. If they said, like, "Oh, we're going to make Artie go with us to so-and-so's house," knowing I wouldn't want to go, they would say it in Polish. Cracking the code was a "survival mechanism" for me, but it was a passive Polish that never got any use. Otherwise I'd have blown my cover and they would have switched to Yiddish.

Do you remember how you got a clearer sense of what your parents had lived through?

During the Eichmann trials, in 1961, like most Americans. I was thirteen. My parents followed the extensively televised trials closely and I got wind of the history that way. And I discovered a well-worn paperback book around that time, while sneaking through my mother's private shelves, right near *Lady Chatterley's Lover.* I think it was *Minister of Death: The Adolf Eichmann Story,* and it had a few pages of pictures, my first exposure to the atrocity photos. And by burrowing around that bookshelf in my parents' den, I found some other books and pamphlets published in Polish and Yiddish right after the war. Some of those had photographs and drawings too—these gave me my first full and conscious realization that something enormous and devastating had hit my family. Some of those booklets actually were the models for the *Maus*

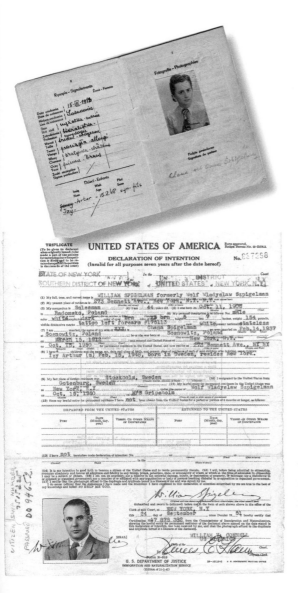

booklets included in *RAW* magazine when *Maus* was presented as a work in progress. Something about their humble graphic design and printing was important to me.

Let's clear something up which can be confusing. Can you clarify Anja, Anna, Vladek, Willie—can we set this straight?

Vladek was actually born Zev Spiegelman. His Hebrew name was Zev ben Abraham. He was brought up in a rather Yiddish household, but his Polish name was Wladislaw with a "W." Wladec was a diminutive of Wladislaw. When his part of Poland, Silesia, was controlled by Russia, it was Vladek with a "V." When the Germans took over—it was part of the Polish tug-of-war—he had a German name, Wilhelm, but was also called "Wolf." And then when he came on the boat to America he became William. I settled on the one people could pronounce, which is not W-l-a-d-e-c, but V-l-a-d-e-k. The Russian spelling is just easier to locate for American eyes. Anja was born "Andzia Zylberberg." Her Hebrew name was Hannah, though in her assimilated household that wasn't something she was called regularly. She became Anna Spiegelman when she moved to America.

TOP LEFT: Anja's Polish passport, 1946.
LEFT: Vladek's U.S. naturalization application, 1951.
BELOW AND FACING PAGE (counterclockwise): Booklets from Anja's bookshelf: *How I Survived the Nazi Hell; Auschwitz; Arsonists' World; Smoke Over Birkenau; We, the Ukrainians (Buchenwald); The Underground Movement in the Ghettos and Camps; Maus* insert booklets in *RAW*.
FACING PAGE, CENTER: Chapter 4 insert in *RAW*, vol. 1, no. 5.

MAUS

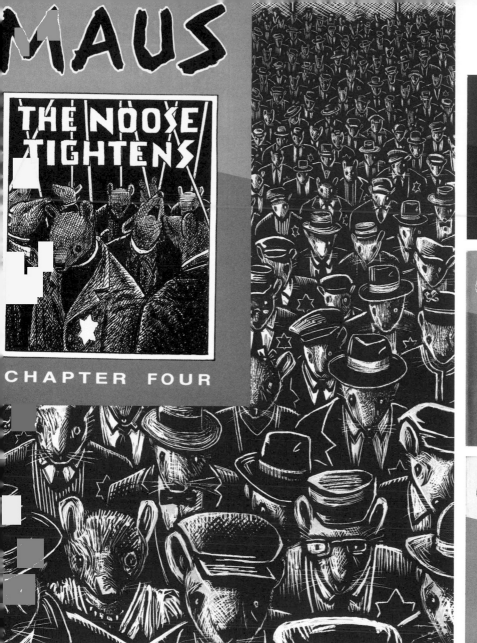

THE NOOSE TIGHTENS

CHAPTER FOUR

MAUS

The HONEYMOON

CHAPTER TWO

MAUS

MOUSE HOLES

CHAPTER FIVE

MAUS

MOUSE TRAP

CHAPTER SIX

В. Коваль

Ми U
Українці

BUCHENWALD

1 9 4 8

RUCH
PODZIEMNY
w
GHETTACH
i
OBOZACH

MATERIAŁY
i
DOKUMENTY

1 9 4 6

MAUS

PRISONER of WAR

CHAPTER THREE

One other note about names and spellings is my phantom brother, Richieu. I only found out later that I'd totally misspelled his name, but I'm glad I did. I thought of it as some kind of Frenchified version of Richard, but actually in Polish, it's R-y-s-i-o, Rysio, and I just had never seen it written down until well into the process. I probably would have wanted to change it anyway, because to my American eyes that would look more like some Japanese name than anything else. I guess it's all part of the fluid nature of the Jewish immigrant experience. I was born Itzhak Avraham ben Zev, after all. An immigration official decided Arthur Isadore would be more American when we got off the boat. I adamantly changed it to Art on my official papers as soon as I could.

We learn more about Anja's family than Vladek's in *Maus*. What was his family like, and what was it like for him growing up?

At one point I toyed with having a chapter in *Maus* called "Little Father," including what I'd gleaned about his early years, but it seemed to distort the shape of the book and I abandoned it. He was the third of nine children. One younger brother got scalded to death in early childhood—an accident in which he tipped over a cauldron of boiling laundry. The fates of the rest are summarized on page 276, but

Vladek was always called "Little Father" by the rest of the family because of his practical disposition. The family was quite poor and Vladek began working at a very early age. One anecdote involved Vladek's father who had some sort of small seltzer factory and once got involved in a failed get-rich-quick scheme. As I understood it, my grandfather partnered with someone who had forged government liquor stamps and he sealed the bottles to make bootleg liquor cheap. They got caught eventually and my grandfather took the fall for the rich guy who was fronting the money for the operation. Vladek, who was very, very young at the time, volunteered for the job of regularly walking to the prison several miles away to bring news from the family. Vladek described how he would talk to his father in the prison yard while being observed by the guards, and he would have covert

LEFT: Unused early chapter title draft. ABOVE and FACING PAGE, TOP: Late '70s character sketches. RIGHT: Draft, page 59.

messages from the lawyer hired by his father's wealthy partner about how the trial was going. Vladek would write the news inside his Hasidic-style hat, and then just hold the hat so his father could read the important stuff while they pretended to talk about other things.

My father was brought up as a very religious Jew. He was very proud that his father, though not a rabbi, would always house important rabbis whenever they came through his village. They could always be sure that it was kept really kosher and appropriate for an Orthodox Jew. That was obviously one of the things that differentiated his side of the family from Anja's. Her family was relatively worldly as well as wealthy.

In fact, when I asked my cousin Lolek, Anja's nephew, to describe my father's father, he was very dismissive. In a conversation I taped with him in July 1982 he said:

I knew Willie's father. I met him once, a bearded kind of thing. Because he was like many very religious Jews, he would be mumbling to himself. Not an articulate individual. That's about all I remember. And I think that I did meet one of your dad's brothers. But they were very religious. And religious in the Southern Baptist sense, that they would stick to the letter without really understanding what it said . . . And I had been weaned differently. So that I, even as a youngster, I just didn't have much patience with that kind of thinking.

The more secular Zylberberg family just couldn't relate. (That phrase—the "bearded kind of thing"—made me try to find a way to indicate some sort of a beard on Vladek's father without deviating too far from the almost anonymous mouse masks I was drawing.) So Vladek goes through this yeshiva childhood and then is moving

ONE NIGHT I HAD A DREAM...

DON'T WORRY

A VOICE WAS TALKING TO ME. IT WAS, I THINK, MY DEAD GRANDFATHER...

DON'T WORRY MY CHILD!

IT WAS SO REAL, THIS VOICE.

YOU WILL COME OUT OF THIS PLACE-FREE! ON THE DATE OF PARSHAS TRUMA.

I WOKE UP RIGHT AWAY. AND WHEN I WENT TO SLEEP AGAIN IT WAS "PARSHAS TRUMA, PARSHAS TRUMA."

toward a much more secular life when he meets up with Anja. By the time he comes through the death camps—though he never said this in so many words—it's as if he lost all faith, but for someone brought up so Orthodox, he couldn't become an atheist. He moved as far as he could on the spectrum of apostasy by becoming a Conservative Jew.

There are some mystical episodes in *Maus,* which are treated very respectfully.

I didn't want to impose my cynicism on events so significant to my parents' understanding of what they went through. By allowing the mouse in the dream sequence of Parshas Truma on page 59 to be drawn more mouselike—with the crosshatching and indications of fur, and to have the hand be as human as I was able to draw it, rather than the little abstracted banana-bunch hands that figure elsewhere—it had an otherworldly quality. Referencing Parshas Truma allowed an indication of what Vladek's religious upbringing was like. And on page 188 the Polish priest provided a window into a numerological mysticism that I don't buy into, but Vladek did. And for my mother there was that oddly analogous moment of going to a fortune-teller against her own better judgment and taking it in. If I was making this story up, I'd never have come up with those particular anecdotes, but they seem central to my parents' stories.

Was this anecdote about the gypsy fortune-teller on page 293 of *Maus* one that Anja had mentioned to you?

Yes. A number of times. You know, these things that give life meaning, whether they're fictional constructs or not, are important.

How do you understand your parents' relationship with each other? Even before the war begins, you show that their relationship is complex.

Once, after criticizing something about Vladek, my cousin, Lolek, who didn't hold him in high regard though he adored my mother, said of them, "But, you know, it was a real marriage." And I would agree with that as the bottom line. They were wrapped up around each other in ways that were inextricable. It wasn't necessarily something that made them happy, but it was something that made them.

In *Maus* we learn about how Vladek escapes the camps, but we don't get much information on how Anja escapes the camps.

I found out from interviews with others what I could find out,* but without, perhaps, what was in the notebooks, and without a mother who survived long enough to be able to tell me her story— which is possibly, arguably the one I would have told if all else were equal in an alternate universe— all I can know is that she was fortified and helped by Vladek at a certain point, but survived quite a while without contact with Vladek, both before he was able to relocate her

Study, page 293.

*See "Memories of Anja," pages 278–288.

in the camp and certainly after their ways parted. She certainly didn't commit suicide at that time; she managed to get through in ways very different from the ways Vladek got through. From what I could figure out, the strategies included something that comes up in *Maus* only en passant where she takes the bread she gets

Anja and Vladek for Art's bar mitzvah album, 1961.

from Vladek and shares it with her hungry friends as if she wasn't hungry. If one tries to understand survival strategies—if that's not too cold-blooded to say—I think that she instinctively moved toward the version that had to do with creating a fabric of interdependent people who helped each other, more so than Vladek, who was a rather self-sufficient person. Sharing food with others made them protective of her.

I have relatively few anecdotes from Anja, but even that story about her pissing in the field indicates somebody who was woven into a life with other people who she helped, and who helped her. I heard something similar from Pavel, the shrink who appears in volume 2. He told me about his own experiences in Birkenau; he was in a barrack with a number of other guys from Terezín, and they got through together. As I remember it, there was a period where he, or maybe it was a friend, temporarily lost his vision. After some days it came back, but while he was blind, the others sort of faked it for him, guiding

him around, and got him through. I've tried to understand how people made it through their impossible situations. There were those who, like Vladek, were resourceful in figuring things out for themselves, and others who followed his lead: "I'm with him. Whatever he's doing I'm going to try to do that because he seems to have figured something out," and there were other people who really got through another way. I know a survivor's son who told me about his father who survived very specifically because he was part of a whole group taken to the camps from his small village at the same time. They stuck together throughout the entire camp experience and they all kept each other alive. That's a way of making it through that is in some ways counterintuitive to the American notion of the individual who triumphs. There really was a kind of identification with their whole group that got them through, and insofar as I can glean anything from the clues about Anja, that was how she survived.

Do you know if your parents discussed with each other their stories of exiting the camps?

They knew each other's stories. Though when I would ask Vladek about Anja's story, he didn't seem to have a clear memory of her specifics. Possibly there are

21

Slightly. I'd heard from Anja a bit about how she grew up in a well-off household, and that somehow related to the fact that my uncle and aunt had a hosiery mill. And my father would tell me stray bits... I asked him once about how come he had this weird scar, a chunk of his skin out on his finger, and the answer had to do with chopping wood as a young man, and the ax hitting his finger. Several times he glowingly told me about once seeing Siegmund Breitbart perform when he was a kid. Breitbart was a famous Jewish strongman from Lodz who could straighten out iron horseshoes with his teeth and stuff like that. These were, to me, really fascinating glimpses of their prewar life, a magical world before I was in it.

Were there any parts of the story that you knew already?

Yes, the three-page "Maus" story I did in 1972 [see pages 105–107] was based on what I knew before I knew anything; one of those free-floating shards of anecdote I'd picked up. But even there, I didn't know the part about Vladek burying the Jew who discovered his bunker and turned the family over to the Nazis until I went back home and asked him to verify what I was drawing while I was in the middle of working on it. It was only then that I proceeded to try to find anything out more systematically.

I had come back to the city while working on that

things he had heard from her, but didn't want to tell me, but what I was aware of when I was interviewing Vladek was that he had created a narrative by having told it. As a result when he was telling what he had told before, it had a kind of clarity to it. When he was telling things that nobody had asked him about before, or things that he hadn't thought about before, it was much harder for him to tell. I'm not saying anything about him that isn't true of everybody, I suppose. But he'd never told Anja's story, and therefore when I would ask, "Well, where was Mom? What was she doing?" he would say, "Well, she was like me, and she did this and that," but it was vague; there wasn't a sense of her as having had a separate orbit that I could get from my probings and questioning of him.

When you started formally taking notes on Vladek's testimony and taping it, were you aware of your parents' prewar lives?

> LIKE, HERE'S WHERE SOME GUY FOUND YOUR HIDING PLACE AND TURNED YOU IN TO THE GERMANS...

> YAH. I BURIED THAT GUY...

> I CAME TO BE ON A WORK DETAIL AFTER, AND I BURIED HIM!

> GOD! I'VE GOTTA CHANGE MY STRIP AND ADD THAT IN!

strip, showed it to my father, and he immediately started telling me the rest of the story, past the point that I had drawn. And then, all of a sudden, I was off to the races wanting to know more. So I extended my stay in New York City. I stayed for about four days and taped as much as I could. He told me most of the story in *Maus*. Although I later went back and would interview him over and over again to get more detail, texture, and other facets, the essence of it was really this one set of conversations that took place in '72.*

Those first interviews mostly took place on the little terrace of our house in Queens, outdoors, with a reel-to-reel tape recorder. They rather astonishingly end with Vladek

grabbing the microphone and making his statement to posterity after being totally oblivious through everything—which is why I always am suspicious of my own take on anything. He really didn't seem to know he was being interviewed for any purpose at all. But at the end he grabbed the microphone as if he was broadcasting on the radio, and said: "So now you can know what happened, and God forbid we must never let this should never happen again!" It was like a public statement after following through all that intimate material. He gave his testimony a shape. I wasn't aware of him having any special need to bear witness at

See the 1972 transcript,
MetaMaus *pages 237–277.*

FACING PAGE, TOP LEFT: Rough draft, *Maus*, page 263. ABOVE: Panels from "Portrait of the Artist as a Young %@&*!," 2008. BELOW: Panel from 1972 first version of "Maus" and two studies from *Maus*, page 119.

all—but at the end he kind of planted that flag in it. It seemed to come from a more ritualized part of his brain; it was like his rabbi was talking.

So that was the first round. And then, back in '77 or even a little bit before, I began to make forays to see him, taping him again and again almost until he died in '82. We'd go through it all, and I'd say, "OK, we finished, let's start again!" Partially, it was just a way to spend time with him, so there are lots of tapes that are very repetitive of the earlier information, but sometimes little details or facets would get re-remembered and retrieved.

What was interviewing him like for you?

The irony is just that the safety zone in my relationship with my father took place in discussing the moments when he was least safe, and where there were just such high stakes and disaster everywhere. Yet for both him and me there was a certain kind of familial coziness on some level of having something to talk about other than our disappointment with each other. So the problem in the book was to communicate that: this isn't just images of Art and his father talking into a tape recorder that make up one little fragment of a relationship; this is three-fourths of that relationship. It gave us a site on

which we could have a relationship, let's say. When I first came back to New York in '75, I didn't tell him I had moved back. For the first six months or a year, I'd put a towel over the phone and pretend to be talking to him from San Francisco! (I think I'd read that trick in a *Dick Tracy* comic as a kid.)

I had made a half-hearted stab at getting closer to him right after my mother died in 1968, but I was about as far out and far gone as I could be. Even before she killed herself, I was barely out of the mental hospital myself. We were unable to offer each other any solace. At that point I was still in some kind of deep rebellion, mainly hanging out at a commune in Vermont. We just weren't able to have a conversation; it would always end up with nasty arguments over something or other, with demands being placed on me that I couldn't possibly live up to. Our generation gap was a Grand Canyon–sized chasm.

After Anja's suicide, the rabbi from the Rego Park Jewish center made a condolence call to Vladek; coming over to talk unctuously about her death in the most fatuous clichés, not knowing Anja at all, but about how it's spring and there are flowers and life renews itself. Hopeless. In wild contradistinction, my hippie girlfriend's father, Irving Fiske—the Mister Natural of the commune I was involved with—came

LEFT: Art c. 1968; ABOVE: Panel from "Spiegelman Moves to NY. Feels Depressed," 1975; RIGHT: *Maus* notes, c. 1978.

by and tried to convince Vladek that what he oughta do now is come stay up at the commune and screw some of the beautiful young hippie chicks who were up there. Mercifully, Vladek couldn't register a word Irving was saying.

I remember Vladek saying something in the immediate aftermath of my mother's death. He said, "Maybe I made a mistake with you." I said, "What's that?" And he said, "Well, I always let Anja have her way with you." In other words, he allowed her to be my parent rather than him being a parent. And now it was clearly just too late for us to have that with each other. He was just a distant and authoritarian figure.

In early treatments of *Maus*, one episode is about you and Vladek playing baseball…

It has to do with the pathos of Vladek being marched out to play ball even though he had no idea what a baseball was. I barely had an idea myself, and insofar as I did have an idea I didn't like the idea. So all of a sudden Vladek and Art are standing in a Rego Park sidestreet tossing a baseball back and forth. Neither of us would have any predisposition toward this, it was some kind of manufactured occasion for us to try to bond as father and son because my mother thought it would be a good idea. But Vladek was never supposed to end up on a Rego Park street throwing a ball. It's only the displacements of history that dropped him from outer space to there.

What were some of the difficulties in interviewing him?

There really was no barrier to our discussions except his own memory or ability to articulate, and my ability to know what questions I might ask. So that

MY FATHER—
he used to call me "Butch" when he wanted to be affectionate. I was anything but a Butch. I don't know how the idea first entered his head, but there was something very touching about his attempt to be American and I reciprocated by calling him "Pops."

Once, we decided to play baseball in front of the house like other kids did with their fathers. It didn't work at that well: my father had no idea how to throw a ball and, personally, I was terrible at baseball and therefore hated it. The fiasco only lasted about fifteen minutes — most of the time spent with one or the other of us chasing the ball. I think I remember other kids — catholics who lived across the street — looked on us with contempt. At any rate we silently gave it up and went back in the house. We never tried anything like that again.

OXO. Baseball and dads again. From a 2004 sketchbook.

Oxo had always detested playing ball. It was one of the strong arguments against becoming a father....

Ex-Oxo had never seen a ball back in the old country. Oxo's catholic neighbors' had laughed themselves silly.

was a kind of intimacy, and it was more than I could achieve elsewhere with him. Every once in a while, I'd find that I'd been pushing him too far, and he would obviously be either physically tired from being on that Exercycle while talking, or something would be a bit too emotional for him to be able to go further at that particular moment. But I don't remember anything like: "No, don't turn on the tape recorder."

Was your anger at Vladek about burning your mother's notebooks something that affected your interview process with him?

No, my anger against him was so free-floating and easy to access—whether it had to do with something absolutely picayune or whether it had to do with something as major as that—it was just our leitmotif. When he'd do or say something too painful or exasperating or sad, it was just hard to go back for more, so maybe I'd just skip a couple of weeks. It wasn't any more than that.

Were there any specific parts of Vladek's story that you particularly related to?

The anecdote where Vladek is almost caught by Polish children calling him a Jew when he was in hiding was a source of nightmares

for me. It appears on page 151. It was vivid for me even before I drew it—one of those places where I could enter into Vladek's story and feel it viscerally. The vulnerability of being the other, that made even little children lethally dangerous.

You have indicated, in *Maus* and elsewhere, the problems of memory.

I remember my frustrations when he would recite almost word for word an event he'd told me before. I guess that's how memory works though—it gets replaced by language. When I was asking him stuff that he hadn't ever talked about, he'd have a difficult time locating it and telling me about it. I wasn't angry at him for it, but I would just be exasperated when going back to transcribe what I'd gone through, and finding that it would be close to verbatim as something he had told me before. I'd have to tease out the differences between versions of a story to try to locate some very specific bit of information. And when I could, then that would become part of the next round of interviewing. I certainly don't blame him for it as I sit here trying to figure out, like: did I go back to look at Auschwitz two times or three times?

Memory is a very fugitive thing. And I was aware of it at the time as part of the

ABOVE: *Maus*, page 151. Drafts, studies, and final panel.

ABOVE: Mieczylaw Kościelniak, from the cycle "The Prisoner's Day," 1950 (courtesy Auschwitz Museum).

problem and part of the process. It wasn't like there was a text and he'd only be willing to read certain parts of it to me at certain moments. I felt that I was being given fairly good access to what he could get access to himself.

And you show that process in the book, like with the scene where you and your father wrestle over whether or not there was an orchestra in Auschwitz.

There were some things that would just come out in the interviews that had to be structured—things had to be suppressed, pulled forward, and shaped to make the narrative. But it was obvious to me, doing my homework, that Vladek's memory didn't jibe with everything I read. I knew I had to allude to that somewhere. And for a while that was troublesome to me. And as is often the case, the things that are troublesome lead to the more profound

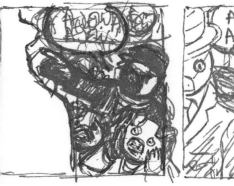

solutions. So, I specifically asked Vladek about the orchestras in Auschwitz in order to have the sequence at the top of page 214 happen. I was trying to figure out where the elision should be: do I just correct errors based on other people's authority? Or do I ignore other people's authority and go strictly with Vladek's memory as if it was an objective correlative that could be drawn?

That's such an important issue.

It's so basic. I wrestled with it for a long time. In matters of firm historical record—that is, with lots of different independent witnesses—I tended to triangulate the event and allow his memory to be subsumed in the grander memory. But if there was any kind of personal reason for him to remember differently—because it was something he specifically says he saw, or because of the importance and weight it seemed to have in the conversation—then I went with his version and tried to make a visible correction if necessary. The closer it came to his personal story, the less I would interfere. But I thought there ought to be at least one place in the book where that process is made explicit. And the Auschwitz orchestra is about as well-documented as anything in Auschwitz might have been. Enough of those musicians

survived, wrote memoirs. There are photographs of the orchestra taken by Nazis. There are so many different descriptions of it happening that I knew I wasn't veering off into Holocaust-denier Heaven: "Oh, he's just making this stuff up, spreading the big lie!" So, when I asked Vladek about the orchestra and he didn't remember one, I thought: "OK, that's the moment!"

On the top half of page 214, the orchestra's shown playing, the prisoners are being marched past the orchestra, I ask about it, and my father thinks for a moment and says, "An orchestra? No, I remember only marching, not any orchestras. From the gates guards took us to the workshop. How could it be there an orchestra?"

What's really important here was allowing Vladek to say that—because the actuality is, he probably didn't walk out through the main Auschwitz gate when he'd go to work in a tin shop. He went out through one of the work gates on the side and presumably didn't march past the orchestras. He may not have even seen or heard it when he first came into the camp, since he was brought in a truck with a few others, not in one of the massive relocations by train. It's very possible that for him the orchestras didn't exist, and I don't want to deny that. I just want to

ABOVE: Study for page 214. TOP RIGHT: Auschwitz orchestra at camp gate, SS photo, 1941 (Auschwitz Museum). RIGHT: Top of page 214.

insist that it was there even though he's asking how it could be. So I say, "It's very well documented." And he says, "No, at the gates I heard only guards shouting." Fine.

But the way it is drawn is a complex visual dialogue because A: I could have left the whole damn thing out. B: I could have just had him say that he doesn't remember an orchestra in a scene in the present and not shown anything. But instead, as the cartoonist, I opted for C: I show the orchestra, then have Vladek say that he doesn't remember seeing one. Then I have the orchestra being blotted out by the people marching because that's all he remembers. And finally—I get to "win" this argument since I set it up—I show the little bits of the cello and the silhouettes of the musicians behind the marching figures to insist that they were there. And to top off this interchange, because of my compulsive need to make formal things that nobody will notice, the bit of wall that's covered up by the marching prisoners becomes a musical staff with notes on it.

Funny how memory works. I'm certainly as vulnerable as Vladek was to the inevitable warping of memory. On page 216, where Vladek manages to talk to Anja in Birkenau, I was saved from what would have been a terrible error. I began sketching a sequence in which Vladek is actually talking down from the roof he's mending to Anja and—is there something about her head being shaved there?

**No, it doesn't actually come up
in the text of the book. I've only
noticed it in your notes.**

Good. Because that wasn't in my father's
tapes. I had elided an anecdote in Tadeusz
Borowski's *This Way for the Gas, Ladies
and Gentlemen,* which took place in the
same exact camp with a very similar situation. The protagonist talking to his lover
about her hair. And Vladek had told me
how unhappy Anja was about how she
looked in the camps; she was ashamed.
But the specific anecdote, talking to a
loved one from a distance and finding out
about her shame, allowed the character
in Borowski's autobiographical fiction to
say, "Don't worry, you'll have hair
and our children will have
hair," or whatever—it was
not Vladek talking, it was

Tadeusz Borowski's protagonist. If I hadn't
been scouring my notes over and over
again I could have slipped into having that
re-entered into my father's story in an act
of unconscious plagiarism.

**You have some notebook pages from
around '86–'87 that are about how you
feel that even though Vladek was really
frustrating and you were wrestling with
him, in the process of making the book
you came to kind of identify with him.**

Well, tell me more. You know, I put it in a
notebook so I'd never have to think about
it again.

**You wrote: "I'm really like Vladek,
agonizing over *Maus* the way he agonized
over his repair jobs." So there's this
identification/disidentification.**

TOP: Art and Vladek in Fort Tryon Park, 1955. TOP RIGHT: Vladek, 1946. RIGHT: Sketchbook, 1983.

32

I'm sure that's at the center of what made our relationship so fraught. Being rebellious and resistant to Vladek, but finding aspects of him well embedded into my character formation. I remember a moment back when I was incarcerated in Binghamton State mental hospital back in my psychedelic days, wandering around the dayroom, gathering up pieces of string or something, just to have something to do and, in that sense, unconsciously reenacting the kinds of scavenging Vladek always did reflexively: "Oh, this piece of paper could come in handy sometime; this scrap on the ground, maybe I could use it as toilet paper." There were so many ways in which I didn't want to model myself after Vladek; it was very hard for me to acknowledge aspects of myself when I'd see him acting out in exasperating ways. I try to understand how I function as a parent to my kids and I'm positive I've done some things that are equally god-awful.

Can you talk about your concerns about how to represent Vladek as a character?

I was trying to not sentimentalize: it never had occurred to me to try to create a heroic figure, and certainly not to create a survivor who's ennobled by his suffering—a very Christian notion, the survivor as martyr. And that meant a warts-and-all relationship that included me being really unpleasant. When I read the story back, I think, "Yeah, he was a pretty ungrateful schmuck, that kid. And not especially sympathetic to real suffering." I was trying to catch those aspects of myself without turning them into a caricature, or turning Vladek into a caricature. I allowed myself permission to portray my father in ways some would see negatively, but I recognized that despite his impossible flaws and the ways he whacked me up as a father, there is something kind of endearing about him as a character. It was all a matter of calibration.

There's a phrase Ren Weschler used in a beautifully written essay about *Maus**. The phrase delighted me as a concise acknowledgment of what I strived so hard for in telling the story. He talked about the book's "crystalline ambiguity." If I

---

*See MetaMaus *DVD* supplements.*

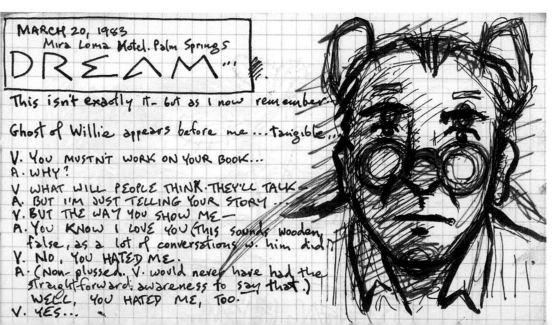

MARCH 20, 1983
Mira Loma Motel. Palm Springs
DREAM...

This isn't exactly it — but as I now remember

Ghost of Willie appears before me ... tangible...

V. YOU MUSTN'T WORK ON YOUR BOOK...
A. WHY?
V WHAT WILL PEOPLE THINK. THEY'LL TALK
A. BUT I'M JUST TELLING YOUR STORY...
V. BUT THE WAY YOU SHOW ME—
A. YOU KNOW I LOVE YOU (THIS sounds wooden, false, as a lot of conversations w. him did)
V. NO, YOU HATED ME.
A. (Non-plussed. V. would never have had the straightforward awareness to say that.) WELL, YOU HATED ME, TOO.
V. YES...

couldn't ultimately determine a character's motives, it wouldn't have been correct to imply those motives, but rather to just explain what happened and allow one to make one's own determination. To what degree did Vladek actually help Anja? To what degree was Mala a sympathetic presence, to what degree not? To what degree did I ultimately love my father or hate him? All of those ambiguities had to just be presented without being spun for the sake of catharsis—that was essential.

All kinds of elisions and ellipses and compressions are a part of any shaped work, and my goal was to not betray what I could find out or what I heard or what I knew but to give a shape to it. But giving shape also involves, by definition, the risk of distorting the underlying reality. Perhaps the only honest way to present such material is to say: "Here are all the documents I used, you go through them. And here's a twelve-foot shelf of works to give these documents context, and here's like thousands of hours of tape recording, and here's a bunch of photographs to look at. Now, go make yourself a *Maus*!"

Are you ever struck by how people conflate the Art character with you, in the sense that they don't pick up on some of the self-critique that's going on?

Well, I was made painfully aware of it when Harvey Pekar went into several years of attack mode in *The Comics Journal* back in the '80s; what he was saying included the fact that he'd have been a lot

ABOVE: Study, page 95. BELOW: Draft, page 42. TOP RIGHT: Draft, page 106. BOTTOM RIGHT: Study, page 100.

better of a son than I was. Basically all of the information that he had about my father's life and mine was, obviously, from my book. The fact that, as an autobiographical author, he didn't seem to grasp that there was some distance, some degree of objectification going on was staggering. Pekar was like: "[Gasp!] I found Spiegelman out! He was being insensitive to his father!" Well, yeah.

If anything, I would say that the process of doing the book was very useful for getting in touch with the other side of the story, because in making this kind of work, one has to inhabit and identify with each character. You have to act out their poses, you have to think them through. So, in that sense, even though I am very resistant to the notion of my work being dismissed or understood as a therapeutic exercise, it is true that there is a kind of gestalting necessary just to be able to inhabit each character. The very process of giving voice and visual gesture to Vladek was a way of inhabiting his point of view so he could be more than I might have otherwise reduced him to.

That key panel at the end of the first volume, where Art walks off and calls his father a murderer, was one of the places where I assumed

anyone who identified me too directly with the character in my book might have had a clue that I would not have done that if I wanted to portray myself with any kind of *amour-propre,* self-respect. Still, I didn't originally intend that to be the end of the volume. It was just the end of part 1, never meant to be the cliffhanger it became when it was released as a separate volume before I finished part 2.

In the sequence when the two of you are discussing "Prisoner on the Hell Planet," Vladek does say to you: "It's good that you got this outside your system"...

I naturally assumed Vladek would never see or read "Hell Planet" since it appeared in a small print-run underground comic, *Short Order,* and he did not browse head shops looking for comic books. He just didn't read any of my work, unless I read it to him. But, as he explains, it was because he saw the photo of Anja at the beginning of the strip, after Mala got a copy through a friend's son, that he wanted to see what it was. Narratively, this discussion of "Hell Planet" is rich—the characters aren't allowed to reduce themselves to cartoon types. Mala's sympathy toward the work, and her capacity to verify that this emotional piece of work actually had a kind of objectivity to it—that it was accurate to the way she experienced the days after my mother's death, being in the same living room, sitting where everybody was sitting shiva—allows a moment for Mala to become more dimensional as a character.

And then, Vladek displays himself to be a much more complex character than I'd, literally, have imagined. I wouldn't have given Vladek the credit for being sensitive enough to say, "It's good that you got this outside your system." He didn't tend to acknowledge my needs and feelings, and I would have been prone to think of him as responding with hurt and anger that I revealed something too intimate. In a sense it's like when people talk about a friend and say, "He's not himself today." Well, we're reduced down for convenience's sake to a series of tropes and twitches, but we are none of us ourselves. And that's what makes us a self, and that was the process of doing *Maus*—finding Vladek as more multifaceted than what would happen with my more meager imagination if I was creating fiction. The advantage to using the stuff of real life is that one really is left with people who are far more interesting than what one could ever make up.

Notes toward *Maus II*, chapter 3, c. 1989.

The episode where he acts in a racist way toward a black hitchhiker feels like a crucial one, especially coming toward the end of the book.

It was important for me to present Vladek's casual racism in the book. The non-reflective nature of calling black folks "shvartsers," the assumption that they would steal from him, and all of that stuff was indicated here. And it was an attitude widely shared by his survivor friends. This is a place where it should be noted, "Look, suffering doesn't make you better, it just makes you suffer!" It's not meant to be excoriatingly condemning. It is part of Vladek's impossible nature. It is also, though, what festered into becoming the Final Solution; and it is what allows our current immigration debates to take certain kinds of appalling coloration now. It is what allows us to call Arabs "ragheads," it's what allows Arabs to think of Jews and Americans

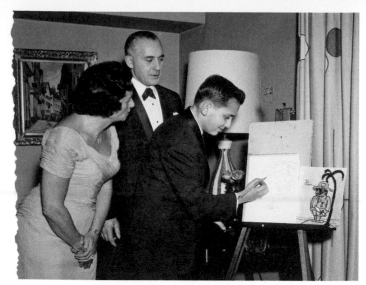

ABOVE: Staged photo for bar mitzvah keepsake album, using a borrowed easel as Vladek and Anja feign interest, 1961.

and it gave me a zone of safety from them, in that sense. Doing *Maus* in cartoon form was probably abetted by the fact that I knew it would be opaque to Vladek. I could do what I needed to do and not have him question it because it was all alien turf to him.

"Portrait of the Artist as a Young %@&*!"—the strip that functions as an introduction to the recent re-release of my 1970s collection, *Breakdowns*—begins with my memories of playing the "scribble" game with my mother when I was very young. One of us would make random marks on a piece of paper, and the other would have to add lines to turn it into something. It encouraged me to exercise my visual imagination, and it's among the warmest childhood memories I have. For Anja, becoming an artist was a relatively reputable activity. Although she shared some of Vladek's economic anxieties, it wasn't as horrifying to her that one would become a maker of

as wearing targets around their necks so one can kill them, it's that whole process of dehumanization. I'm not exempting myself, my culture, my father, or the Nazis or Poles from it; it seems to be a basic aspect of how tribes organize themselves.

Interestingly, Françoise didn't have those specific prejudices about African Americans deeply implanted in her DNA. She inherited cultural prejudices against Algerians and Moroccans, but was perfectly comfortable—almost insanely so—going to the crack-drenched ghetto in Bed-Stuy in the '70s to take a vocational course in offset printing. I quaked when I once went out to pick her up after class, but she seemed to have made friends with some of the dealers and addicts she saw daily on the streets.

You said your father never read any of your work. I'm wondering to what degree your parents were involved in how you decided to become a cartoonist.

My impulse to become a cartoonist had something to do with finding a zone that was not my parents' zone. It was my assimilation into the American culture in ways that were closed to my parents,

LEFT: Study, page 258.
RIGHT: Scripting/lettering, *Maus*, page 99.

HE LOVED SHOWING OFF HOW "HANDY" HE WAS... AND PROVING THAT ANYTHING THAT I DID WAS ALL WRONG. HE MADE ME COMPLETELY NEUROTIC ABOUT FIXING STUFF

HE LOVED SHOWING OFF HOW "HANDY" HE WAS... AND PROVING THAT ANYTHING I DID WAS ALL WRONG. HE MADE ME COMPLETELY NEUROTIC ABOUT FIXING STUFF.

I THINK ONE OF THE REASONS I BECAME AN ARTIST WAS THAT HE THOUGHT ART AND LITERATURE WAS IMPRACTICAL, AND HE DIDN'T COMPETE WITH ME—HE ALWAY THOUGHT

I THINK ONE OF THE REASONS I BECAME AN ARTIST WAS THAT HE THOUGHT THAT ART WAS AN IMPRACTICAL WASTE OF TIME. IT WAS AN AREA WHERE I WOULDN'T HAVE TO COMPETE WITH HIM.

YOU ARE GOING TO QUEENS ARE YOU? ARE YOU GONNA GO HELP HIM?

NAH—I GOT TOO MANY DEADLINES. I'ED RATHER FEEL GUILTY.

cultural artifacts. And of course her mandate to perhaps make something out of her wartime diaries had everything to do with the specific cartoonist I became.

Then there was the fact that they didn't rip up my comic books, as I've heard some American parents did. The entire comic-book-causes-juvenile-delinquency madness passed them by totally. They didn't know a thing about it. From my mother's side there was a willingness to look benignly on my subversive reading. From my father

A.S. roughs for Topps' Wacky Package stickers, c. 1975.

there was just: "Why waste money on this frippery?" Since he was able and willing to buy me cheaper used comic books, from before the Comics Code–sanitized moment—comics that were much more interesting and fraught than the ones I could get on the newsstands—he had a big influence on my tastes and development.

And as I both have said and now drawn in that introduction, there is an efficiency that comes with Vladek's territory that had to do with packing. "Well, we're gonna have to go somewhere, and you have to get as much as you can into a suitcase" is certainly part of the aesthetic that informs the

kind of comics I make. *Maus* could have been ten times longer if I'd just not tried to pack it as tightly. Drawing doesn't come easily to me—maybe I'm lazy like my father always told me I was—but nevertheless everything is tightly packed.

If I objectify myself enough, I can see both that there is this ornery impulse of just wanting to follow my own muse, and yet a certain kind of pragmatism that has followed me through my work life that has not been shared by some cartoonist pals who are totally baffled by how on earth you get the rent paid every month. It allowed me to have Topps Bubble Gum as a Medici for a long time and be happy for it; it allowed me to try to figure out how to apply the comics I was making in such a way that they could get published; it probably is even in my decision to turn away from the comics that would find me with a smaller and smaller audience.

I suppose I could have sought out a gallery audience, and only needed several patrons. That wasn't a first choice for me, because I wanted to find a way to be in contact, in communication. My father's pragmatism tugging against my mother's more intellectual disposition shaped my notions of what an artist might be.

If anyone else drew this, it would make me very tense.

You touched on it when you talked about your mother's notebooks, but aside from the obvious fact that your parents were survivors, was there anything about your relationship with them that made you want to do a book about the Holocaust?

I didn't know that I did want to do a book about the Holocaust. If anything, I was in allergic reaction to my own Jewishness. I don't know that I'd go so far as to talk about it as self-hating (even though some people were angry at *Maus* for my lack of Zionist zeal), but when I was a kid I wasn't sure being Jewish was such a great idea—I'd heard they killed people for that. *Maus* somehow involved coming out of the closet as a Jew (it now strikes me as risible that anyone might have mistaken me for, say, Nordic... I was, after all, born in Stockholm). The legacy of great secular Jewish cartoonists consoled me somewhat—"Oh, Al Capp is really named Alfred Caplin! And Stan Lee is Stanley Lieber! Cool!"— but I signed my very first comics Art Speg when I was twelve.

The earliest three-page version of "Maus" deracinated the races. Yes they're mice, yes they're cats, but we're not even sure if they are Jews or Nazis unless we know our history. So there wasn't movement toward that kind of ethnic cultural embrace that is a given for certain Jewish American writers, certain black American writers. Somewhere there was this "write what you know" dictum that must have been in there. But neverthe-less really the impulse to work with this was finally made clear to me only as I was working. It wasn't even clear that I was operating out of my mother's mandate to do something with the notebooks. These were necessary enzymes in the soil, but I wasn't aware of them until much later. I was moving through other things in the front of my brain.

What was Vladek's reaction to the comics work of yours he saw? Did it change before he died?

He really had wanted me to become a dentist after I proved I had no aptitude for becoming a doctor. He consoled himself by saying, "Okay, even dentists were made doctors in Auschwitz." I'd have economic security, and if I wanted to make my stupid cartoons at night, fine. He did get some very abstract pleasure in the fact that I could actually earn a living, which I had started doing even at fifteen, by having my first cartoons paid for: I got a regular freelance position as a cartoonist for a local Queens weekly, *The Long Island Post.* That was a good thing; getting a check is a good thing. And when I got a steady job with Topps Bubble Gum

TOP RIGHT: *Maus* notebook, 1989. ABOVE: Photo of the artist exhibiting "Blowing Bubbles," 1970.

he looked incredibly relieved and wanted me to keep it for life. I got the gig as a summer job when I was eighteen, and one way or another, the relationship lasted twenty-three years.

When I was going through my full-fledged adolescent rebellion in my early twenties, I remember showing him an elaborate porno drawing that I'd made—intending to just make him unhappy, I guess. I had made a picture called "Blowing Bubbles," this woman riding on a giant penis that I had done as a commissioned drawing, and it had all these little elves and gnomes fucking all over it, and I said, "Oh, look at what I just finished." I show him this picture—this was after my mother's death. And his response was very unfazed. It was: "Oh, from this you make a living?" And that was it! It was the wonderment of, "Oh, America, the streets are paved with gold. He does this and he gets money for it." But it wasn't genuine shock.

I was quite satisfied with my life as a cartoonist, since it wasn't about money, but rather about making certain kinds of things that I liked and needed to do. I was trying to make things on my own terms. But I never had the degree of worldly success that would have made him say:

"My son, he made Mickey Mouse!" Or anything like that. That success was all after both my parents were gone.

Are you sad about that? That it was after they died?

I guess, but it probably would have made him as unhappy as happy. Finding out that he was perceived by some readers as an impossible and insufferable person might have left him distressed. It's all so hypothetical, I can't figure that one out. I do think that my mother would have been rather proud of it, and I would love to have had that as something I could experience directly rather than just know.

How did you decide you wanted to make a longer version of *Maus* in the first place?

Well, when I did that long set of interviews with Vladek, it wasn't with the idea of making anything more than that three-page strip. It was just: "Oh, I really need to know this. I just need to know it." At that moment the intrinsic formal "stuff" of comics was more compelling for me than any given narrative, but I had these tapes. I played parts of them for a few friends in Binghamton one evening, and I was surprised at the intensity of their response, with one friend, Barbara, just breaking down in inconsolable tears. And I think, in my divorced-from-my-feelings way, I thought: "Oh, this is something I should remember! I have an emotional response to this, and so do others." It planted some seed that this was something I'd need to return to, though it didn't come to the foreground again until I'd moved from Binghamton to San Francisco and then back

1/40   Mom and me in the park, 1951 (Maus Revenge)   spiegelman

79

ler, boss of the SS
s, who are the only
at attitude toward
ude toward these
our own blood to
ls'' were the non-
ho fell into Nazi
ttitude'' found its
urder.
d open in 1945,
ird Reich was an
prisoners of war

from the U.S. and the British Empire were the best off,
being kept in life if not in health by Red Cross packages.
Russian POWs were worked like cattle and died like flies.
Worst off was the mass of miserable humanity herded into
the concentration camps: Jews, political prisoners, underground fighters, gypsies, hostages, black-market dealers
and miscellaneous thousands who ran afoul of Himmler's
police. Flogged and starved behind the barbed wire of
scores of camps, they worked in quarries and mines and
underground factories making V-bombs for Hitler. Six million and more of them went up in black smoke in the tall
crematorium chimneys that clouded the skies of Germany.

"Worst off was the mass of miserable humanity herded into the concentration camps: Jews, political prisoners, underground fighters, gypsies, hostages, black-market dealers and miscellaneous thousands who ran afoul of Himmler's police."

— Jews makes a cameo appearance on pages 550–551 of the magisterial *The Second World War* by Winston S. Churchill and the editors of *Life*. © 1959 by Time Inc.

of the Bulge,
come to res-
prison camp.

Gross Germans, SS guards in the Belsen concentration camp where some 80,000 people died, are put to work by the Allies stacking starved bodies of their victims after the arrival of the troops.

to New York City. I had to somehow have ongoing contact with Vladek, and finding a way to do that became part of the decision to make his story into a longer work.

I'd conceived of making some long comic book that needed a bookmark . . . and had to find something actually worth doing. I didn't have the stamina to devote myself to a one-hundred, two-hundred, three-hundred-page book just to serve up a lot of yuks or escapist melodrama. And after the three-page "Maus" I realized I had unfinished business, something to go

back to. We weren't then as we are now, in a culture saturated with Holocaust stories that feel safely in the past to most Americans—and can seem like a genre, even, to be dipped into for its pathos and historical lessons.

Did you have any doubts either going into the three-page story or the longer project?

Beyond the usual every-strip-is-a-plunge-into-the-unknown and I didn't know if I'd come out on the other side of it, no. In the first one I didn't have doubts that I could

LEFT: Photograph by George Rodger//Time Life Pictures/Getty Images.

somehow make something happen in those three pages, maybe because I didn't fully understand all the issues and problems. With the long work, I knew I was taking on something enormously difficult.

And from the get-go I was trying to give shape to it without knowing what that final shape would be, while simultaneously trying to figure out how my relationship with my father in the present would inform that work. It never seriously occurred to me to try to do it without that relationship as an aspect of the book.

Were the people around you supportive of the project from the get-go?

I would say Mala was quite supportive. Vladek seemed to be willing to cooperate, though it seemed mainly because it got me coming out and visiting every week. Françoise was bedrock solid in her support. A few of my artist-filmmaker friends were behind me while I was shaping it, but they insisted I should just publish my rough sketches. On the other hand, with my peers in general—maybe I'm being harsh—I think that it was totally invisible to them. There was neither encouragement nor discouragement. There wasn't the same degree of interest as when I was pursuing paths closer to what theirs were. On the other hand, my pal at

Topps Gum, Len Brown, who tended to like mainstream comics and movies, was very much behind this book in progress—and it made me realize that *Maus* wasn't as rarefied as my previous work, that it was conceivable there could be an actual audience!

Once you decided you were going to do this longer *Maus* project, how did you start going about it? Did you want to do research on the war first, and then interview your father, or the other way around?

When I took the plunge I knew I was in for a really long project—meaning two years. Ah, the naiveté of youth: I really thought that was an infinitely long time. So I started by just interviewing him again, and found that there was no way to understand what he was telling me unless I began to really immerse myself and read.

I guess I've always preferred research to writing or drawing. During the long immersion in *Maus* I was open to all readings, obsessively, that had to do with what happened. Back when I worked on the three-pager, I remember being able to do all my research in a couple of weeks through inter-library loans; there really wasn't that much to read, in English, at least. Now it would take several lifetimes to absorb the existing literature—but finishing the book made it feel a lot less urgent for me to keep up with the proliferating fiction, nonfiction, cinema, and whatever that now surrounds the Hitler period. I find myself not exactly resistant to it, but not often compelled to immerse.

What was the climate like in terms of how people talked about the Holocaust when you started?

I had been shocked when, as a kid, I looked at the definitive, two-volume

picture history of World War II with text by Winston Churchill, published by Time-Life Books in 1959. My parents probably regretted the purchase. It was one of the heaviest things in the house: over six hundred luxuriously oversized pages, boxed with an LP record of Churchill's speeches. It was filled with sumptuously printed war photographs and color war paintings but the reference to Jews and concentration camps was a damn cameo—less than a footnote—mentioned in passing among other victims of "Nazi Barbarism" on one spread. Churchill's war seemed to have very little to do with the one my parents went through.

The Holocaust just wasn't part of the public conversation. As a kid, I can remember my friends asking my mother about the number on her arm, and her saying it was a phone number she didn't want to forget. And I somehow knew that some of my American friends' parents said: "Tch, tch, tch, oh, they had such a hard life," but I didn't quite have any sense of what that was, and I didn't know what those friends did or didn't know. The Eichmann trial was a watershed in public awareness, not just for my thirteen-year-old brain, but for the culture at large having to think about what the world did to its Jews. I'd been aware of the Anne Frank diary, of course—that seemed to have been the alpha and omega of books about the Holocaust when I was growing up—but I didn't slow down to read it until '71 or '72. Only a generation later did it become a standard middle-school text, and I remember my daughter getting excited about it as a coming-of-age love story and being inspired to briefly keep a diary.

Which books were most significant for you?

In the mid-'70s I started to amass what eventually became hundreds of books on the subject. Among the ones I referred to repeatedly were Raul Hilberg's meticulous *The Destruction of the European Jews* and Lucy Dawidowicz's *The War Against the Jews*. Though I was wary of her neocon

tendencies, her scrupulous history of how the Final Solution played out in different countries and its central place in the Nazi project was invaluable, an important corrective to that Churchill Time-Life book. I became addicted to survivor memoirs and I reread Primo Levi's *Survival in Auschwitz* a number of times, blown away by its humanism and generosity of spirit. *The Drowned and the Saved,* the heartbreaking book of essays published shortly before Levi's suicide, is deeply laced with despair and may be the most profound work I read by any survivor— though Tadeusz Borowski's short stories, *This Way for the Gas, Ladies and Gentlemen,* is right up there too. It was written in the kind of hard-boiled style

'HOLOCAUST'
Powerful miniseries
starts this week

TV GUIDE

Local Programs April 15-21
30¢

History of Jewish Life in Poland—I grabbed that as soon as it was published in 1977. I'd already discovered Roman Vishniac's photos of shtetl life in '71, and I studied them even more closely when I realized I would need to reconstruct a Vanished World. I wore my first copy of his book to pieces. I also had my handful of family photographs from Anja's side of the family that I certainly scrutinized, but I couldn't really associate those with much beyond the mystery of not having a family.

There was a cultural Zeitgeist shift around that time though. I'd already launched into *Maus* when the *Holocaust* three-part television miniseries came out in 1978, and that "docu-drama" or whatever they call that sort of thing brought about a major heightening of public awareness of what had happened. For me it was sort of a mind-blowing moment: I remember watching one night of the *Holocaust* drama on television—this was before VCRs—and being rather distressed by its glibness. Anyway, I was watching it with Robert Crumb who was visiting and Jay Lynch, my earliest cartooning crony, who was our houseguest at the time. Lynch was staying in a makeshift tent in our open loft. While Crumb was making wisecracks about the tackiness of the show, Jay and his girlfriend—who had just arrived from Chicago for a conjugal visit—went off and screwed in the tent. So this whole other event was distracting me from trying to understand how America was assimilating the Holocaust.

that I admire, though it makes Chandler and Hammett look like romantic wimps. There was a detailed objectivity to his prose, as if his eye was a camera trained on a world that stopped at the barbed wire fence, and it gave me some indispensable help in trying to envision life in a death camp. And, because of the nature of my book, I needed lots and lots of photos and images, of course. Picture books, like one called *The Hitler File,* that I found myself looking at to find out "What did those uniforms look like, exactly?" Wartime magazines, like *Signal,* the Nazi equivalent of *Life,* collections of photos of Eastern European shtetl life before the war and things like that.

Were you able to find things like that in the '70s when you started your research?

Well, I've always scoured flea markets and used bookstores here and in Europe. And there were a couple of collections like *Image Before My Eyes: A Photographic*

And then, the night after, I went out to visit Mala and Vladek, to watch part two of the show with them. Vladek didn't want to watch it, saying, "Oh, I know those stories already." I watched it with Mala, and every once in a while, Vladek would

ABOVE: *TV Guide,* April 15–21, 1978. A wartime drawing by Leo Haas, a survivor of Terezín and Auschwitz. *TV Guide* cover © 1978. RIGHT: A.S. 1977 Sketchbook page.

come in and say, "Ah yes, well, this, you know, when he was there, I was here," you know—that kind of kibitzing the story, so I got bits of it from him that way. And Mala entered into it as if it was one more soap opera on TV that had nothing to do with her own life (just like most of the intended audience): "Oh, I wonder what this character's going to do when they shut down the ghetto," or whatever. So I had two diametrically opposite screenings in two days, virtually getting the bends somewhere between my cartoonist gang and my survivor family. The third night I think I just watched it with Françoise and we were able to assimilate what had happened the other two nights. I was appalled by the ersatz acting, the stupidity of the narrative choices being made, but was still fascinated that somebody had woven something together intended for

— HASID IN CRACOW. 1938 · from photo by R. Vishniac

MARCH 1939 – A Jewish family flees Memel following the German Annexation

Typical Polish Jew. circa 1923

P circa 1943.

Polish Market Place – from photo by R. Vishniac

a mass audience. I'd read the Gerald Green book that accompanied the mini-series and it certainly set off cautionary flares: Don't go through the maudlin conventionalization of narrative, you don't wanna be anywhere near this shit. Still, I was impressed by the impact it had as a harbinger of the flood of other literature that followed. And ultimately I was knocked out when it was screened on German television and created a kind of national crisis, a reassessment of what had happened in Germany. It was the first time people my age seemed to be asking their parents about what had happened in the war—and it was directly responsible for extending the statute of limitations on bringing Nazi war criminals to justice. It was really important beyond its kitsch.

Let's talk more about research . . . So you mentioned your parents had some books about the war around the house when you were growing up. How did they inform your thinking?

Well, there were the small-press books I told you about, and one called *The Black Book,* a cataloguing of the atrocities— and one paperback on the same hidden shelf of forbidden knowledge that was about Aleister Crowley and Satanism called *The Beast 666.* Anyway all of it kind of sat together as a kind of semi-pornography for me. In fact, I think *House of Dolls,* a sleazily unhealthy fiction/memoir by a survivor that was a widely read paperback book in the fifties about the whorehouses of Auschwitz, might have been on that shelf too. Many years later I read *Shivitti,* a memoir by the *House of Dolls* author, Ka-Tzetnik, about his LSD therapy and revisiting Auschwitz on acid, and trying to come to terms with an incestuous relationship with his sister who died in the camps—what an astounding character! Anyway I read part of *House of Dolls* as pornography, which, I guess, is the way most people read it: as part of the whole leather-bondage sexy-Nazi pathology. As a kid, the connection between the pornographic aspect of the death camps— the forbidden, the dangerous and fraught— was all one big stew that I couldn't separate out.

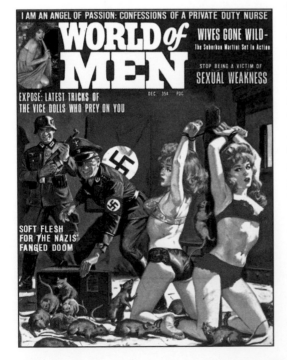

LEFT: *World of Men,* Dec. 1964. ABOVE: *House of Dolls,* Pyramid Books, 1957. RIGHT: From *Auschwitz: Album of a Political Prisoner* by Paladij Osynka, 1946.

To say those books informed my thinking, or even to say I was thinking about this at all in my early teens, would give me too much credit. It was all just part of The Big Taboo. I hadn't even read Elie Wiesel's *Night* until I began the "Maus" strip in '71 or '72. I'd just avoided the whole can of maggots. It occurs to me right now, though, that perhaps the whole taboo-smashing ethos of the underground comix scene did allow me to stir up the buried connections to the unspeakable that my mother's secret bookshelf opened up. Till this conversation, when I thought of that handful of books, I was more prone to remember those small Polish and Yiddish pamphlets.

Why were you particularly attracted to the small-press pamphlets?

These pamphlets were so clearly not part of a mass-cultural production, that they had a kind of fanzine-like magic to me and really struck me hard. I couldn't understand the words in those pamphlets, but pored over the two that had pictures. Anything at all with cartoon-like drawings had an immense pull on me, especially those from before my own childhood. There was one booklet that had just little watercolor drawings of Ravensbrück, printed very badly out of register. One booklet of pamphlets basically consisted of badly drawn gag cartoons by a Russian inmate about Auschwitz—stuff like "Ha, ha! You didn't get any soup!"

When did you first come across drawings by survivors—or drawings by people who didn't survive—and how did you find them?

Before embarking on *Maus* I consciously set about looking for material that could help me visualize what I needed to draw. The few collections of survivors' drawings and reproductions of surviving art that I could get my hands on were essential for me. Those drawings were a return to drawing not for its possibilities of imposing the self, of finding a new role for art and drawing after the invention of the camera, but rather a return to the earlier function that drawing served before the camera—a kind of commemorating, witnessing, and recording of information—what Goya referred to when he says, "This I saw." The artists, like the memoirists and diarists of the time, are giving urgent information in the pictures, information

1. "Арбайт махт фрай" – праця визволює. Іронія. Визволює від життя. За стягнення однієї брукви чекає виголодженого в'язня "гандбінда" – одна з найжорстокіших кар.

1) „Arbeit macht frei." — Labor makes free. Irony. It makes free from life. For steeling of one turnip the starved prisoner will be punished by "Hand-binde" — one of the most painful punishments.

that could be transmitted no other way, and often at great risk to their lives. For someone like me, who was trying to visually reconstruct what they lived through—or didn't—their images were invaluable.

At one point in the book Vladek says they didn't have watches at Auschwitz. They didn't have cameras either, for the most part, in Auschwitz. So one is left with the remains, the ruins that are sifted over endlessly by Claude Lanzmann in *Shoah*. There were some contemporary photographs to look at, but most of what happened was not photographed. There aren't really a lot of photographs of inmates in Auschwitz being beaten. But there are drawings by people who were beaten of what was happening to them. And those drawings range in levels of craft and skill from rather primitive—people who had virtually no graphic art training—to people who were incredibly skilled artists who even had access to art supplies in Auschwitz.

Some of the often anonymous art I found could simply help me understand what, say, a barrack looked like. One drawing, for instance, shows a kapo beating up a prisoner. One gets to see that the beating is being done with a stick, while in the background there are prisoners who are made to squat and watch and just keep their hands raised to the point of exhaustion, and it's all taking place in front of one of these Birkenau-style barracks. There's just enough information for you to see wooden shoe versus leather shoe, what kind of patches were put on the uniform. It's very convincing as a drawing, and it's very touching as a drawing because it's not drawn well. And one can only imagine what lengths the artist had to go to bury that drawing somewhere and not be caught with what would have been a death sentence. The drawings that were less skillful kept me in mind of just how, whatever my skill-set is, it wasn't something to get hung up over, that I should keep moving after doing the best I could, because the drawings had a purpose.

Some of the drawings that were among the most important to me were by an artist named Mieczyslaw Kościelniak. He was a very skilled, academically trained Pole, not Jewish, and therefore was able to get a job in the art barrack, basically, doing genealogies, signage, portraits of SS men in Auschwitz. There was a poster in Auschwitz that I've often seen reproduced, that says, "One Louse Means Death." Incidentally, the louse on page 251 of *Maus* is collaged into the page, swiped from his poster. That was his day job. But then secretly he went back into that studio and did several suites of drawings, one called "The Prisoner's Day, Auschwitz," another one called "The Prisoner's Day, Birkenau." And there aren't that many images, maybe twenty pictures in each suite of drawings—rather detailed, really well represented drawings of the roll call, hauling the cans of soup, the quotidian moments of life in the camp presented very convincingly, and with a clarity beyond most photography. They were as close as one could get to seeing it directly. So, inevitably, I pored over those things and whatever photos I could dig up. Kościelniak's drawings had the detailed content I needed to re-abstract back toward my simple comics panels.

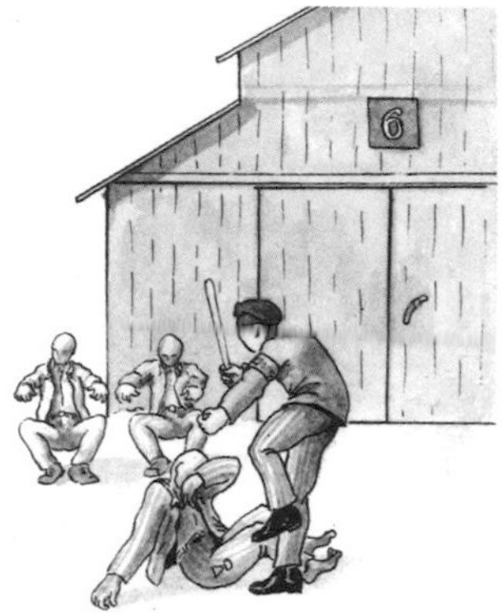
6

Alfred Kantor was also an amazing resource. Kantor was a teenager in Terezín and Auschwitz, evidently drawing to keep himself sane, drawing what was around him. He destroyed most of the drawings he made while in Auschwitz, but reconstructed them while he was in a DP camp right after the war. At that point, now that the drawings would no longer cost him

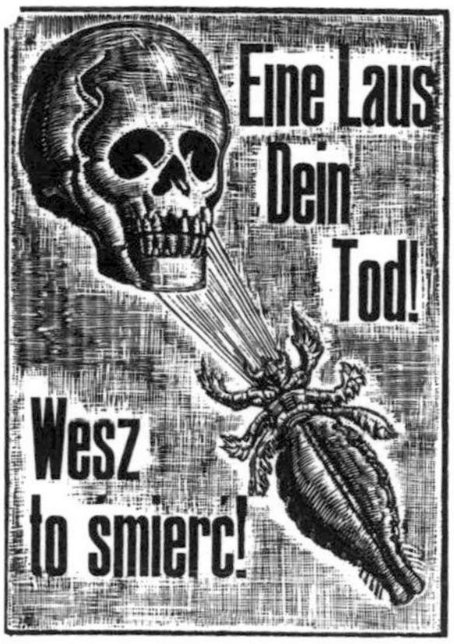
Eine Laus
Dein
Tod!
Wesz
to smierc!

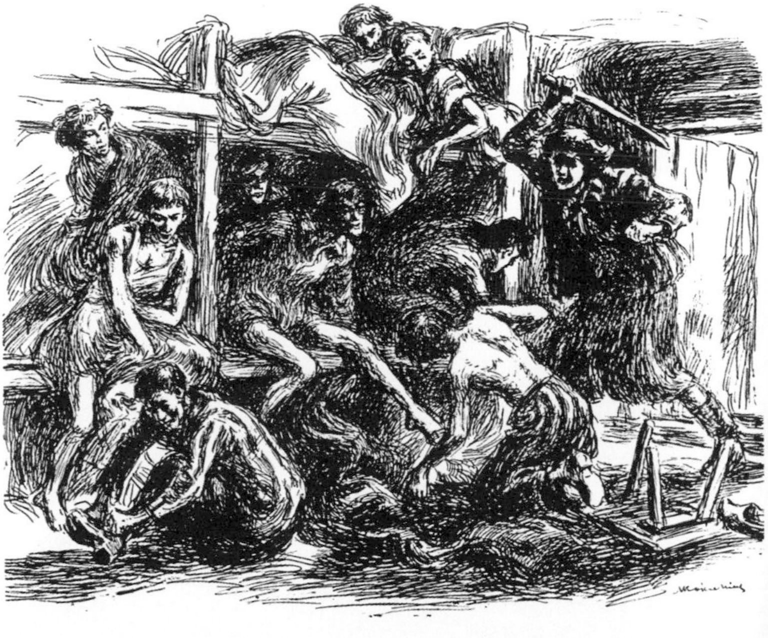

18 year olds looked like 30 year olds.

Serving dinner means a few minutes rest.

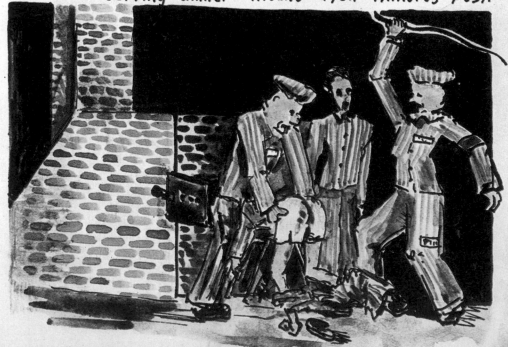

Punishment for theft of soup.

his life, he redrew a visual diary of what he'd just gone through. He went on to a successful career in advertising. Late in his life a friend saw it and encouraged him to publish *The Book of Alfred Kantor,* which—for somebody with my double-track disposition toward reading and looking—was an important clue to the moment-to-moment texture of life in a death camp. Kantor was drawing many of the same places and situations my parents were in, so his book became indispensable.

Now what about researching the parts of the book that have very specific information, like how to repair shoes?

Ah, yes, the survival skills that were passed along include, on page 220 of *Maus,* how to fix a shoe, even if you're not a shoemaker but have to learn fast because your life genuinely depends on it. Vladek was rightly proud of the skills that he had. I'll insist alongside Pavel that it was all luck, but still—insofar as a human has some capacity to interact with his environment rather than give in to the despair that strikes me as the "reasonable" response to ending up in Auschwitz— Vladek's focus on using what skills he could master to get himself through was really significant.

I'm such an idiot about practical stuff, maybe in rebellion against Vladek putting such a high premium on it. He probably explained it all rather well, but I just couldn't figure out how he did that damn shoe repair, so I had to find books on the subject to understand how it would be done without elaborate machinery. The good old New York Public Library had

LEFT: From *The Book of Alfred Kantor.* With permission Alfred Kantor. BELOW LEFT: Detail from 1987 *Maus* notebook, with inset from an old shoe repair manual. BELOW RIGHT: Detail from *Maus,* page 220, penultimate draft.

some very out-of-print books on shoe repair that came to my rescue. It was satisfying to find out, though I probably still couldn't fix a shoe if I ended up in a death camp, and it allowed me to insert a Melville moment into the book: "Oh, so that's how whaling is whaled," you know? I wouldn't have wanted to stop the whole book dead every ten pages to show off my research, but my overt use of the "how-to" aspects of comics-making on that page, the diagramming that allows one to see exactly how something's done, also allowed me to literally illustrate what Vladek repeatedly told me: "You must know every-thing to survive."

Were there any films or specific photographs that became part of your research?

While in the middle of *Maus*, I devoured documentaries on Hitler and on the camps, from *Night and Fog* to the kinds of things PBS would show during fund-raising drives. I'd videotape them and freeze frames to draw from. Claude Lanz-mann's nine-hour *Shoah* came out just as I was starting what became the second volume of *Maus*. Its sobriety and respect for what could be shown and what couldn't had a very strong impact on me.

Specific photos? Well, that ubiquitous photo by Margaret Bourke-White of prisoners at the liberation of Buchenwald was the

ABOVE: Auschwitz burning pits, clandestine photo, 1944. BELOW LEFT: Jew paraded through village in occupied Poland. CENTER: Detail, *Maus*, page 35. RIGHT: "The Jews Are Our Misfortune" streamer over Brucken, Germany. Photo from *Der Stürmer*, mid-1930s. FACING PAGE, TOP: Detail, *Maus*, page 232. BELOW: Allied Reconnaissance photo of Birkenau, August 25, 1944.

splash panel of my 1972 strip.

I was reading desperately to understand the history of the period, and some of the anecdotes,

THE OTHERS HAD TO JUMP IN THE GRAVES WHILE STILL THEY WERE ALIVE...

that I found in an obscure book of photo-documents of the Holocaust.

And there was a chilling out-of-focus snapshot secretly taken by prisoners in Auschwitz of the Hungarian Jews being thrown into burning pits in 1944. It was smuggled out to England during the war to try and convince the British to intervene. I drew a version of it into the second part of *Maus*.

in addition to those my father told me, came from sources where I could document events that were emblematic.

Page 35, for instance, is filled with emblematic panels. And there are occasionally photographs that correspond to specific panels, like a Jew being barred from going into a store in panel two and the mocked Jewish man in panel three

There's a battered copy of an aerial photo of Auschwitz from some magazine that I saw in your files . . .

Yes, I found that while working on the long book—a reconnaissance photo, one of the essential references. It showed the entire killing apparatus in Auschwitz that the Allied planes wouldn't deign to waste a bomb on. You know, it was

Abschrift!

Geheime Staatspolizei
Stapoleitstelle Kattowitz
Außendienststelle Bielitz
— IV B 4 - 691/44 -Ow.—

Bielitz, den 16.3.44

Personalakt

An das
KL-Auschwitz
— Pol.t. Abteilung —
in Auschwitz

Betrifft: Flüchtige Juden
Vorgang : Ohne

Die tieferstehend genannten Juden werden über Vfg. der Stl. Kattowitz am heutigen Tage der dortigen Dienststelle zwecks Umsiedlung überstellt:
1.) Eibuschütz, Liba S., geb.7.6.1924 zu Wolbrom
2.) Mandelbaum, Blima,Golda S., geb.8.7.1929 zu Sosnowitz
3.) Mandelbaum, geb.Rosmarin,Riwka S.,geb.10.12.1899 zu Sosnowitz
4.) Mandelbaum, Alter Isr., geb.6.8.1896 zu Pils, Krs.Ilkenau
5.) Spiegelmann,geb.Silberberg,Anna S.,geb.15.3.1912 zu Sosnowitz
6.) Spiegelmann, Wilhelm Isr., geb.11.10.1906 zu Dombrowa.

I.A.
Unterschrift (unles.)

damnably difficult to visualize even the most rudimentary things, like the layout of Auschwitz. Just studying maps and that photo over and over again, trying to figure out where it all took place—"I'll be damned, my father grew up pretty close to where Auschwitz was!"—it wasn't that clear to me until I found certain artifacts like that photo. It all got a little less hazy when I went to Poland in the late '70s, and again in '87.

One baffling thing I saw on my second trip was one of the wooden barracks in Birkenau; they were originally built for about fifty horses but held up to eight hundred prisoners each. On my first trip I looked for those, and they were all rubble—local Poles had cannibalized most of the wood for heating right after the war, so all that was left were the remains of the stables' chimneys, marking where each one had been. I didn't understand how come I hadn't noticed this building in perfect condition on my first trip, so I asked. Turns out it was a brand-new reconstruction, built as a set for some on-location Holocaust movie and the Polish authorities were happy to leave it standing as part of their museum since it looked so accurate. It was useful for me to be able to walk through and photograph it to draw from, but it was also crazy-making: the idea of a Hollywood reconstruction of a death camp eventually replacing the haunted ruins just seemed deeply wrong. Maybe I was just jealous of how easy it was for movie-makers to deploy an army of researchers with an unlimited budget to reconstruct that building when

every scrap of information I needed for
Maus was so hard-won.

So you made two research trips to Poland?

Yes. The first time was before the first
Maus volume was finished. And I was
able to get some books from the Auschwitz
Museum store that were incredibly useful. In 1987 I went back with a German
ZDF television documentary crew, and
through their clout got a hold of a lot of
important material—even a copy of the
records of when my parents were brought
to Auschwitz.

**Did you travel anywhere
else to do research?**

I did go to Dachau to look around. That
was on a separate trip to Munich when
the German edition of *Maus I* came out.
And certainly when I'd visit France it
was easy to find World War II reference
images and pick up all these Pétain-era fan
magazines for a song.

**What were some of the things you
researched specifically in Auschwitz?**

I really needed to know exactly where
things were: seeing the crematoria, the
scale of the camps, and getting copies of
the museum's maps and diagrams made
the work possible...and I was able to see
what a bathroom in Auschwitz I looked
like. I knew I needed to draw that.

On page 227 of *Maus*, first there's a
collagelike graphic of workers silhouetted
in the foreground with the repeated figure

TOP LEFT: Vladek and Anja's Auschwitz arrest record, March 16,
1944. LEFT: A.S. at the gates of Auschwitz, Oct. 1979 (photo:
Françoise Mouly). RIGHT: A 1992 visit to Germany when *Maus II*
was published there (*The New Yorker*, 12/07/92). See also "A Jew
in Rostock," *MetaMaus* pages 156–157.

of mice hauling boulders to depict the concept of "Black Work" as efficiently and emblematically as possible; it's followed, at the bottom of the page, with a very specific image of Vladek hiding from a *selektion* in the toilet. It was a very vivid moment for me in his story; I think I may have heard about it long before the more formal sessions on tape. As an American boy, my notion of hiding in the toilet had more to do with masturbating than with surviving a *selektion*, but anyway, whenever I tried to envision it, I had a problem since I didn't know what the damn toilets in his barrack looked like. The only photos I could find showed the long boards with holes in them like an endless outhouse setup—the Birkenau version of a toilet. But no reference for the Auschwitz I toilets where Vladek hid. So when I was at the Auschwitz museum with film crew in tow, I asked the museum official about these and he said, "Oh, well, everything's been remodeled here, but there's one barrack that hasn't been touched." He brought me over there with keys, and was able to unlock the door and show me the actual toilets that were identical in each of these buildings. Now since Auschwitz I had been a soldiers' garrison in World War I, and wasn't built specifically as a death facility, it had real toilets. And plumbing. So I was able to take photographs of that and get it right.

An oral historian took me to task in some academic journal for getting the toilets wrong, saying they were just long planks. I was proud of getting it more right than that historian, though, inevitably, I must

TOP LEFT: Toilets in Auschwitz I (A.S., 1987).
CENTER LEFT: Panel from penultimate draft, *Maus*, page 227.
LEFT: Page from *The Book of Alfred Kantor*. With permission Alfred Kantor.
TOP RIGHT: Panel study, *Maus*, page 227.
RIGHT: Penultimate draft of *Maus*, page 230.

obligation to present these pages in detail and it involved documentation that was relatively hard to find at the time, though it became more accessible a few years later. It's strange, I originally assumed I'd draw all the Auschwitz parts of the book in a more deliberately sketchy mode, sort of like the image on page 63, in the first part of *Maus,* where some Jews are taken off into the woods and shot. The large panel there was made to look like a journalist illustrator's sketch, and I always somehow assumed that, since I couldn't visualize Vladek's life in Auschwitz—to the point of being paralyzed by the prospect—the drawings would be more tentative, seen through a fog of scribbled lines. Oddly

have been off in some details despite all my research. When my father says he was walking down a street in Sosnowiec, I couldn't know what street. When I started, I might have imagined one that looked like a small street in, say, Binghamton, New York. Research and travel got me to at least know what a small street in Silesia might have looked like in the '30s and '40s, but a quest for ersatz verisimilitude might have pulled me further away from essential actuality as I tried to reconstruct it. Here, because I had the information and was trying so hard to know what to draw, I was able to show the flush mechanism on the toilet, even though I presented it simply. But it actually stands out—and it stood out for this historian—because of its very specificity. It's the opposite of the montage panel above it of mice carrying boulders.

There is a very detailed sequence in book 2 of the crematoria . . .

Because Vladek witnessed the crematoria, because he described dismantling them when he worked as a tinman, it became my

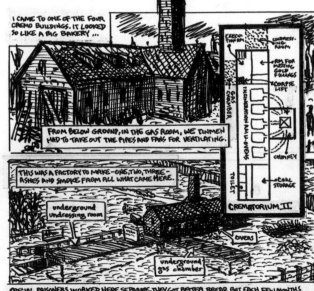

enough, things got more and more precise as I went along. I had learned how to draw more precisely in my small-scale panels and tried to get everything in focus. Maybe as a way of getting past my own aversion I tried to see Auschwitz as clearly as I could. It was a way of forcing myself and others to look at it.

The clinical, dehumanized representation of the crematoria with almost no figures seemed appropriate to the book, especially when immediately followed by a page with the panel that I had to wrestle with more than any other: the screaming mice in the flaming pits. To follow that objective photographic representation—the extreme suppression of just showing architecture— with a much more subjective image made sense. But trying to make that drawing—a direct depiction of physical anguish—risked melodramatic trivialization of their suffering. I did everything I could to draw it with conviction, drew it dozens of times.

Can you say more about your experience of going to Auschwitz with the film crew? You were trying to conduct your own research and at the same time you were the subject of a documentary.

When Françoise and I made our first foray into Poland in 1979, it was still behind the Iron Curtain. We went without much preparation—I only brought some crazy old prewar Polish-English dictionary that my parents had gotten in Sweden. It's the zaniest dictionary I've ever seen. It was all wrong. It would have the word "men," and tell you how to say "men" in Polish, but then it would have certain suffixes of "men," like "-ingitis" and "-struation." Poland was the first Soviet-bloc country I'd visited and that became as interesting as researching my own past history. I hadn't a clue as to how to find the places my father had been telling me he grew up in, and he wasn't of much help except to tell us not to go at all because they kill Jews there. Using the present tense: "They kill Jews there. Don't go!" He was afraid for us. And the Auschwitz Museum was a resource that I visited as just one more tourist.

I knew so little on the first trip, all I knew was: Birkenau is near, but there was not any signage to help me find it. And after we had gone through the sanitized and cleaned up Auschwitz Museum, which is in Auschwitz I where my father was, I realized we hadn't seen the killing center.

TOP: Thumbnail of breakdown for page 230, actual-size detail from *Maus* notebook, 1986–1989 (see "Maus notebooks" in accompanying *MetaMaus* DVD). ABOVE: Birkenau, the Death Gate. Auschwitz tourist photo. RIGHT: Study for *Maus*, page 199 (near actual size).

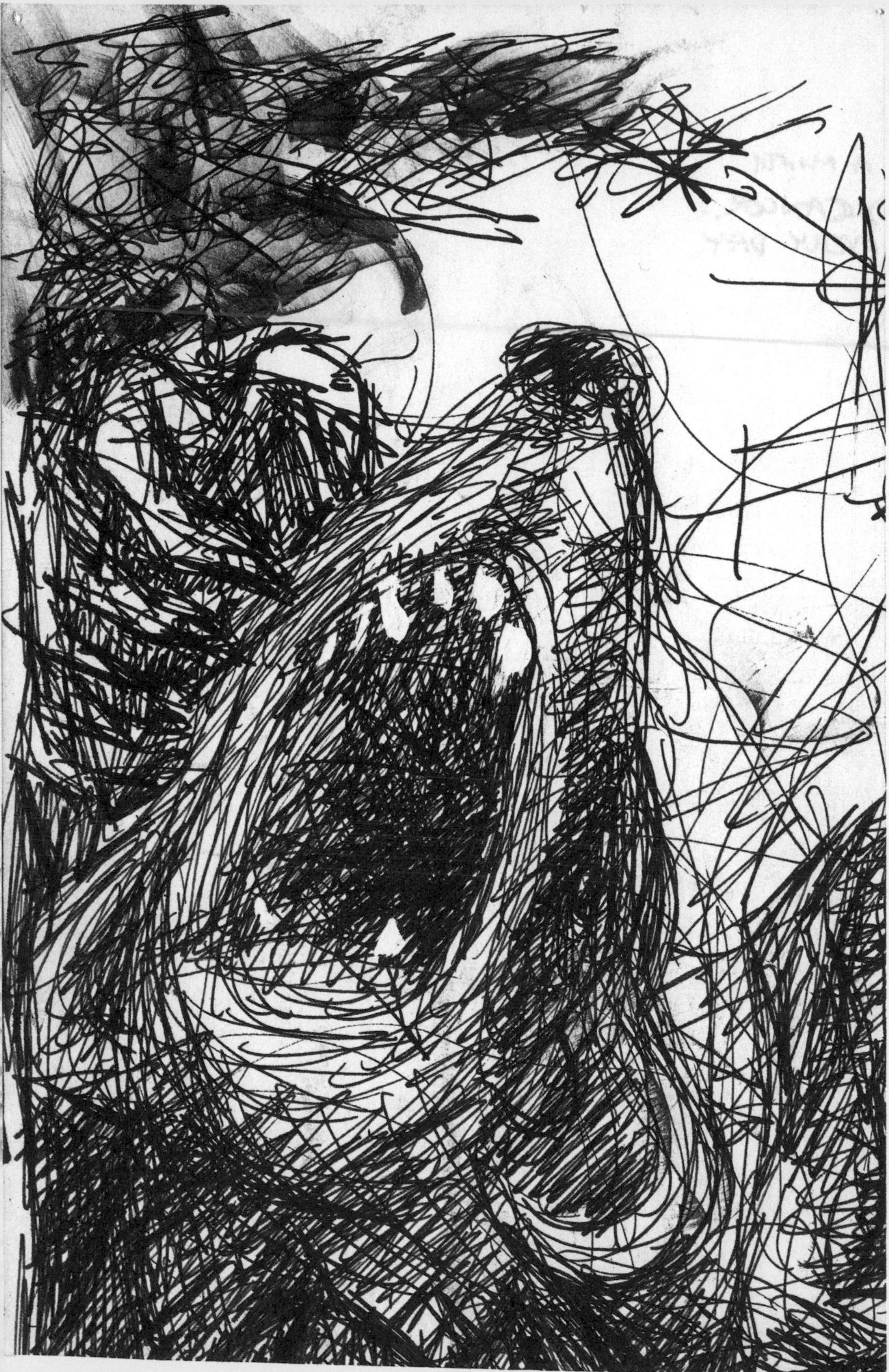

It was really hard to find, and by the time we did, it was almost dusk. We had to walk to the gates of Birkenau and it wasn't set up as much of a museum—it was just rubble. And it was vast. Françoise and I went into the falling remains of one of the endless wooden stables originally intended for about fifty horses, turned into barracks for seven hundred to one thousand prisoners—not like the brick buildings in Auschwitz I. And we're walking through it and it's really eerie. It was getting dark, there was no illumination from electricity or anything, and it really felt like walking on bones. And by the time we came out on the other side of this, this long warehouse-like place with little multilevel bunk-beds, bunk-pallets—we're sort of looking around and it's dark. Pitch black. And it's dark everywhere. We can't even see lights in the distance.

It was a fairly moonless night. We were outside now in one of the most haunted places on the planet. And we couldn't find our way out. What we did is walk till we got to barbed wire and then try to find a place to get through. And we finally found some tracks; we could

see the tracks. We followed the tracks out, again, in total darkness, and we're following the tracks back trying to figure out which way we'd come from. And we're walking and then all of a sudden we see some guys with lanterns. And I have almost no Polish, they had no English, and I ask, *"Co się stało?"* "What happened?" And there's a one-word answer from this guy with the lantern, who says: "Brezhnev!" Evidently there was a power outage in this part of Poland. A common occurrence. There were no lights in the town of Oświęcim, there were no lights anywhere except for these guys' lanterns. We had been walking down the

tracks to get out, and it was all terrifying.

When we found our way back there with a film crew six or seven years later, everything was paved. The Auschwitz Museum directors and curators had already done the research of finding my parents' papers that they had been given when they entered Auschwitz. And the film people looked up the exact spot where my parents' house had been, based on the information I'd given them in advance. A really major amount of research was being done on my behalf in order to facilitate what turned out to be an incredibly lame documentary, though the only reason I'd accepted doing the documentary was for that exact research that they did for me. The filmmaker, Georg Stefan Troller, was a German Jew whose main interest, it seemed, was trying to go one-on-one with his friend, Claude Lanzmann, but he had a rather heavy-handed aesthetic. One of my stipulations was that they take Françoise with me, and that they take my daughter.

In the film, there are images of Nadja sitting on the train . . . this tiny baby . . .

Nadja was under a year old, maybe six months or something. So we had a nanny who was taking care of her who called her Nadinka, and we had diapers, which were impossible to get in Poland in 1987. They had a van full of diapers for us to use while we were on the trip. Everything was made possible for me. And we had translators, and there were people mistranslating for me because they didn't want to hurt my feelings. I remember being in the archive where I was getting copies of certain photographs of drawings made by prisoners in Auschwitz that hadn't been available. And the archivists doing it for me were talking to one another and saying, "Oh, yes, he made this book where Poles are pigs, it was disgusting." And my translator turns to me and says, "Oh, they've heard of your book!" So my little bits of Polish were very useful to just get a sense of what was going on.

TOP LEFT: Birkenau barracks, no date. Auschwitz Museum. LEFT: Birkenau barracks, 1945. ABOVE: Home movie, trip to Auschwitz, 1987. Polish nursemaid with baby Nadja and Françoise at the gates of Auschwitz and RIGHT: in Birkenau.

AND SO WE CAME OVER TO GROSS-ROSEN. HERE WAS A SMALL CAMP, WITH NO GAS.

Breslau
GROSS-ROSEN
POLAND
1 INCH = 90 MILES
GERMANY
Czestochowa
SUDETEN-LAND
Krakow
AUSCH-WITZ
CZECHOSLOVAKIA

IT WAS THOUSANDS OF PRIS-ONERS FROM ALL AROUND BEING PULLED BACK INTO GERMANY.

Your "passive Polish."

Yes. The problem with the actual documentary was how manipulative the whole damn thing was. One of the sites for this thing was Gross-Rosen, where my father passed through just for a night in the death march out of Auschwitz. At some point I got them to take me. And Troller positions me in the middle of this field, and they're shooting on real film, not on video, so everything's very planned out in advance. Troller says: "Art! Do you know where we are?" I say, "Yeah, we're at Gross-Rosen where my father came through." And he says: "How does it feel to be here, right where your father could not have come out from?" Well, I don't know what to say. "Well, I'm glad to be able to retrace some of this material. I need to know it." He says: "Yes, but how do you feel about it?" I

say, "Well frankly right now I don't feel much of anything, except I wish I wasn't being photographed." And at some point I say, "Well, it was amazing that my father actually made it through here. You know? He was already beginning to get sick with what turned into typhoid when he got to Dachau, which is where he was taken to next." And Troller says: "Can you say that again, but cry?" I said, "No, I absolutely can't." Then I got to see this footage, which was included in the film, and I'm in the middle of the field, but way at the other end of the field there's a gallows, and he had positioned me so I was standing right under the gallows, and that's all you need to know about the manipulative intentions of that documentary.

I think most of the budget on this film that wasn't spent on diapers was blown on hiring a locomotive to drive up to the gates of

TOP: Panels 1 and 2, *Maus*, page 244.
ABOVE: Entrance gate to Gross-Rosen, 1987 (photo: Françoise Mouly).
RIGHT: Documenting the ZDF-TV documentary. A bearded translator for ZDF-TV haggles with local residents and representatives over the right to film a locomotive crossing their property at the Birkenau gate (home movie).

Auschwitz. So we show up one morning and the train is there to be driven to the gates of Auschwitz so that Troller can film it as a cutaway in his film, even though my parents had been brought to the camp by truck. And the place is surrounded by angry, toothless Polish peasants. They look like they're straight out of some old *Li'l Abner* strip—the Scragg family or something—and they're all really angry and they won't get off the tracks. They had learned from various other projects that had been shot there that they could get paid for letting this train go over their land, and that was the only thing they were interested in. This was interesting to me in a way that nothing else that was being shot that day was interesting. I said, "Could you please film this?" And then the crew explained, "No, no, we don't have that much film to shoot with." I said, "Well, you're gonna have a lot of film because I'm going back home if you don't film it. This is the most interesting thing that's happened since we've been here." And then there was a discussion between the cameraman and Troller and they finally agree to shoot it, and I said, "And you can't use 'English film,'" meaning when they pretend to shoot something. The

cameraman is not holding it up to his eyes because he doesn't want to be stopped by the angry peasants, but he does at least shoot the transaction. Troller, though, almost cut it out of the final footage, and I had to lobby for it with the BBC co-sponsors to get it put back into the film.

Another moment: Françoise and I were somewhere in some other haunted spot in Birkenau, and we were both crying and, all of a sudden, there was a cameraman I really liked who popped up from out of nowhere, shooting us crying and hugging each other inside a barrack. It was such a violation, it was so horrifying, and it was strictly to make this kind of TV moment—the reason that TV news always covers people at fires, because you can get the cameras there, and won't cover waterboarding, because you can't. The problem was that for the most part Troller was making a film to make sure Germans felt guilty about what had happened, to be shown on German television. He certainly didn't seem much interested in the fact that I was a cartoonist. I could have been a shoe salesman whose father had gone through Auschwitz, if that would have worked as a hook to let him do this thing.

ABOVE: 14k gold lady's compact and cigarette case (photo: Steven Chu).
BELOW: Art, with the German TV crew at Birkenau, reading a reprint of postwar Basil Wolverton horror comics.

So the film was a mess, but it was incredibly important for me as a way to research what had happened. To be taken to the place where Vladek and Anja have their reunion after the war—that Jewish center in Poland my father finally works his way back to; to be able to see where Anja's house had been; what a street looked like. And

some things were just mind-blowing, like being taken to a place where in all good intentions the Auschwitz Museum had set up a little graveyard with crucifixes where the Jews had rebelled against the Germans and had been shot down. In a sign of what was intended as respect there were these little crosses to mark the graves. It was a Catholic Polish country that wasn't that sensitive to what the hell this Jewish thing was about, trying to honor and mark what had happened. There was a lot to digest from that trip.

And Françoise made her own movie...?

We had our own video camera, and one can recognize the footage shot by Françoise rather than me since it tended to be in focus and coherent. It was ultimately much more of a document than the Troller documentary. I was supposed to sign a separate agreement for the Troller film to be shown in America, but I just never signed it—it was too embarrassing.

ABOVE: Early draft, *Maus*, page 86. BELOW: Studies for page 86.

You mentioned some archival material surfaced in Poland, like your parents' arrest record. What other archival family material was part of your research?

Just that uncanny scrap of bureaucratic paperwork that showed when they arrived at Auschwitz, their arrest record.

What about your parents' passports?

I found their Swedish ID papers for emigrating from Poland, and a lot of that stuff, in my father's safety deposit box after he died. The other thing I found there was this gold lady's compact and a gold cigarette case that he'd hidden in the ghetto and retrieved after the war. It's told in *Maus*, when he takes me into the bank. We're looking into that safety deposit box, and he shows me those gold pieces he'd hidden

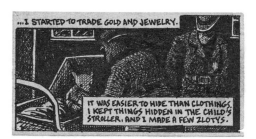

in Srodula. I asked, How can you possibly still have them? "When the Gestapo found us, I dropped quick a few things into the chimney. If they found the rest of my jewels at least these might remain." After he got out of the camps, in 1945, he snuck back to Srodula and at night, while the people inside slept, dug those things out from the bottom of

the chimney. So that survived him, and it's the most significant legacy I got from Vladek in terms of what I inherited from him: a woman's gold compact and cigarette case—the distillation of all that was left of whatever fortunes were built up over generations by various Spiegelmans and Zylberbergs. Last year we gave the cigarette case to Dash and the compact to Nadja as graduation gifts.

Who did you interview besides your father to get information?

I certainly interviewed Mala to find out a little bit about where she was during the war. And I interviewed a woman, Hadassah Rosensafdt, who had known Anja, and helped my father find her after the war. She was an important figure among the survivors who formed various Jewish organizations after the war, and she had been useful to my mother to a degree, during the period in Auschwitz when Vladek and Anja were separated from

each other, though she didn't tell me anything very specific. One or two other friends of my mother who survived were able to give me some scraps of information. I interviewed David and Ita Kracauer, nominally my godparents, refugees who had become friends of my parents in Sweden and then followed them to America after. I knew them when I was a young kid, and then went to talk to them as old people in Miami. They were very useful in terms of giving me insights into my father that both verified and expanded some of my own intuitions about my parents. I think the most hilarious one was this: after bad-mouthing Vladek for a while, David Kracauer said, "But one thing about your father, he was always faithful to Anja." And then Ita Kracauer blurts out, "Yes, why would he pay for something he could get for free?"

He was considered kind of a skinflint even among other Jewish survivors. This led to that tortured soliloquy in *Maus* when I'm worrying about portraying some kind of stereotyped Jewish miser. Not everybody was like Vladek, y'know? His frugality was sort of amusing to some of his other survivor pals.

Another survivor, your therapist, Pavel, seems like a central part of *Maus*, even though he only appears for a few pages.

A PHONE CALL TO PAVEL WHILE WORKING ON CHAPTER ~~VII~~ p.8

- Hi Paul, sorry to bother you at work... I'm working on a sequence where somebody smuggles a gold watch out of Auschwitz and wants to trade it for food — How much is it worth approximately? Like, can he ask for a kilo ~~pound~~ of butter? ~~oh~~ Is that too low? Too high.

~~Hi Ii~~ It's not a ROLEX, right.

Naw. More like a "Polex"

- Well — not butter, it would melt, unless it was winter — say a pound of salami and maybe a loaf of bread.

- Thanks. ~~I guess~~ Sorry if this call was weird for you to get while working — I guess it's like questions from outer space.

Outer space — yah... I read the novel you lent me by Goebbels — He wrote it while he was going but it was terrible — why would anyone want to read it?

P — I guess he's a name brand author

P — Yah, but he was better as a minister of propaganda.

A — Uh-Huh.. too bad Hitler never illustrated it — then it would've been a best seller... well see you next wednesday

P okay. Bye bye.

Well, he was a real presence for me. My sessions with him would often take place late at night. They would go on for hours. He was not that interested in the forty-five-minute session. He'd often fall asleep—I got at least forty-five minutes of him being awake—but our meetings took place after a long day that started with him training social workers for the city, and then included a private practice day and night, often dealing with AIDS patients, at the very beginnings of the AIDS epidemic.

He saw AIDS as death taking place in a surrounding life that was rushing by heedless—analogous to how he experienced Auschwitz. In the midst of all this, he was game to see me at sessions that would start at ten thirty p.m. We'd then go on for an hour and a half or two hours, and I would just wake him up for the interesting parts. Somehow in the course of all that it was quite effective. He served up nuggets of wisdom that still reverberate in my head many years later, like his definition of "neurosis." He said a neurosis is just a solution that has become a problem.

After our sessions were over I'd often go downstairs and accompany him on a chore he took on every night: he'd take all the food scraps he could gather and feed the stray cats that lived in Central Park, across the street from his office. (He really did have photographs of cats in his hovel of an office as

TOP: *Maus* notebook page, 1988. ABOVE: Paul Pavel.

reported in *Maus*.) So the same way that he identified with his AIDS patients—their death in life—he identified with these stray cats. He had several in his house/office. He was not one of those pristine two-hundred-dollars-an-hour shrinks. At a certain point I had to beg him to take more money, because I felt that this was all insanely low-budget, but it just wasn't an issue for him.

One night, we're going down to feed the cats after one of our snooze-and-probe sessions, and he's carrying those scraps downstairs and he says, apropos of I don't remember what, that basically he's a nihilist. And I ask him how this involves getting up in the middle of the night to talk to dying AIDS patients, and being so available to patients way past the point of it being good for his health, and he says something that one might take as just an off-the-cuff remark, but I found profound: "Well, I decided that behaving ethically was the most nihilistic thing I could do." It delighted me as an idea, as a way of living one's life.

Is that something that is reflected in the book at all?

It's part of what helped me find the tone of the book. I remember a line from *Shoah*. A Jewish commander of the 1943 Warsaw ghetto uprising says, "If you could lick my heart, it would poison you." It indicates just how complete the absence of sunlight can be. To find a tone that could be informed by that bleakness and not be an inevitable prescription for suicide was difficult. A lot of popular culture about the death camps turns into Holokitsch. It sentimentalizes—it allows people a facile route back to just how life-affirming life is or something.

To avoid that and still allow for the small moments that are what make a life worth

living demanded a tone that I needed to find in *Maus*: how to avoid despair or cynicism without becoming fatuous. And Pavel's discussion of what it means to soberly take stock of just how fucking meaningless everything is and what one nevertheless does from moment to moment was very useful for me—not just as a cartoonist, but as a model to aspire to.

Why do you think that Holokitsch, as you call it, is so prevalent, and has *Maus* ever been accused of being it?

I coined the term quite a long time back: *somebody* must have accused me of it by now. But why is it so prevalent? There's a kind of kitschification in our culture in general. It's that thing of trying to always go for the sentimental money shot whenever one can that informs our debates about abortion, informs our presidential races, informs much of our popular culture. It's all got to be reduced to Good Guys and Bad Guys. After the fall of the Berlin Wall, Communists ceased to be as attractive as villains. I guess interest in the Holocaust really metastasized at that point: "This is the perfect hero/villain paradigm for movies." It's replaced cowboys and Indians. Maybe it's convenient to have genocides displaced into the old country.

The Holocaust has become a trope, sometimes used admirably, as in Roman Polanski's *The Pianist*, or sometimes meretriciously, like in Roberto Benigni's *Life Is Beautiful*. Almost every year there's another documentary or fiction film up for some Academy Award in this category. Then there are lots of sentimentalized documentaries about life in the shtetl or

RIGHT: Comment on "Mirroring Evil," an exhibit of contemporary art using Nazi-era imagery at the Jewish Museum (*The New Yorker*, 3/25/02).

Duchamp Is Our Misfortune

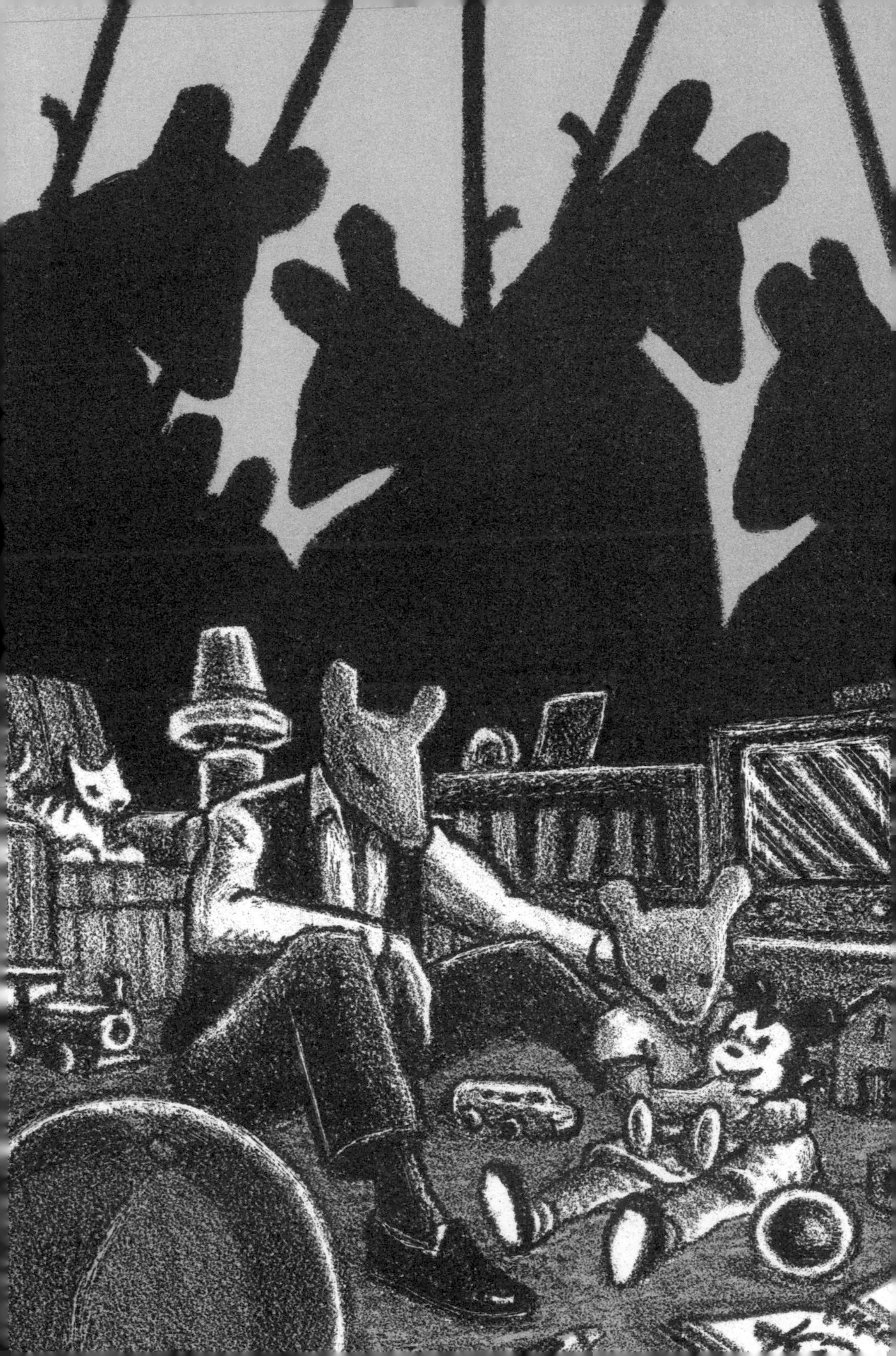

World War II that keep appearing every time there's a fundraiser on WNET to get the Jewish patron vote. Ultimately it becomes ripe for horrific parody, like Paul Verhoeven's *Black Book* and Tarantino's *Inglourious Basterds*. Nazis are fun. But maybe now that history stopped ending we can have Russian villains again, and Arab terrorists can be the Nazis.

You said you were working on some other project, and then you decided to turn your attention to *Maus* because it seemed harder. Can you explain why?

My work life has mostly consisted of finding the hardest thing I'm capable of doing to placate the Hanging Judge within. I wanted a challenge worth meeting as I turned thirty, and *Maus* qualified. It was difficult for me to have to think about my past, and it was difficult for me to have to be in the presence of my father, both metaphorically and quite actually.

So all of those things led me toward taking on a history too big for me to understand—rather than taking on the other big project I was toying with, "A Life in Ink," focusing on the century through a meta-fiction. It was going to be a history of comics in the form of a fictional cartoonist's biography, made up of documents and booklets in a box, all to be printed on the multilith printing press Françoise had moved into our lives and loft.

There's a page in a 1985 notebook of yours in which you're speculating explicitly on what you would say if someone asked you about the premise of *Maus*. You write: "There's more to survival than bringing the body through its ordeal unscathed. There's the building of a personality with depth and understanding, something difficult enough to achieve even without
passing through the center of history's hell. Survival is having children even if they hate you. Vladek believes that kaddish is immortality, survival. The son says kaddish once and stops but he draws *Maus*." What do you think about this now?**

I think I was a very articulate younger man! I suppose an exteriorized response to that question about my premises would be, "Well, *Maus* is about the Holocaust and its impact on the survivors and those who survive the survivors." This paragraph is about the importance of trying to talk about Vladek, rather than about the sub-clause of that quote, which is the center of history's hell. I wasn't grandiose in that sense. My focus really had to do with trying to understand how damaged Vladek was, and whether he had been as damaged before the war or not, and what the implications of those psychological issues might be.

The real story in *Maus*, at its most basic level, is probably something that goes further than that quote from my old notebook about degrees of survival. The subject of *Maus* is the retrieval of memory and ultimately, the creation of memory. The story of *Maus* isn't just the story of a son having problems with his father, and it's not just the story of what a father lived through. It's about a cartoonist trying to envision what his father went through. It's about choices being made, of finding what one can tell, and what one can reveal, and what one can reveal beyond what one knows one is revealing. Those are the things that give real tensile strength to the work—putting the dead into little boxes. So, say, the more successful an illusionistic, cinematic experience a *Maus* movie would be, the more of a lie it would be.

LEFT: "The Past Hangs Over the Future," from *4 Mice*, a portfolio of lithographs, 1992.

You've gotten lots of offers to turn *Maus* into a film, right?

Endless—they've been pouring in ever since the first volume came out! If I could only have been sure it wouldn't actually get made I'd have been glad to sell the option. As it is I keep a copy of *Maus* in a glass bookcase with a sign that says: "In Case of Economic Emergency, Break Glass!" But, as Françoise succinctly put it: "Next to making *Maus*, your greatest achievement may have been not turning *Maus* into a movie."

Do you think you succeeded in what you set out to do?

Maus changed the face of the way the medium I work in is perceived. It demonstrated for many that comics could be a serious art form, and that's swell, but it also generated a lot of confusion because of its subject matter. If somehow *Maus* could have attracted the attention it did without being about the central trauma of the twentieth century, it would have been easier to approach the work as comics. In fact, from the get-go there were attempts at moving *Maus* out of its category: "Is it comics . . . or is it tragics?" as a *New York Times* reviewer put it. The subject matter so overwhelms interest in the (relatively speaking, trivial) formal aspects of the book that the assumption winds up being: "Well, it's pretty rudimentary as comics, but boy, that subject matter! If

you can take on this subject matter, you can do anything in a comic." But the formal aspects, I believe, are what has kept the book compelling in ways that other "Holocaust comics" that have come along in its wake aren't.

I built the book to last, and it was the highly articulated structure that sustained me and the work. It wasn't just, "Oh God, it's too hard to think about Auschwitz, I'll do it tomorrow," that made it take thirteen years. I had to subsume my formal interests in service to my narrative. It involved wrestling with the limitations and possibilities of comics to figure out how to translate the narrative.

In terms of it being a text about the Holocaust, were you thinking about what the tone would be like? For example, there are some amusing moments in the text…

I didn't think in terms of making a text about the Holocaust. (I'm sorry, I keep wanting to put the word Holocaust—and Graphic Novel too—in quotation marks to disown them. The word Genocide was coined to refer to what happened to my family, and is free of the odd religious implications of "Holocaust," a burnt offering.) The book was a text about my . . . my struggle, "*mein kampf.*" And within that context I was just trying to tell the story without falling into the two pits on either side of the project: either coming off as a cynical wisenheimer about something that had genuine enormity, or being sentimental, a form of trivialization on the other side of that road. Finding that tone in a sense was an essential part of the task at hand.

I was grateful for the anecdote I was able to use on page 121, about Vladek's cousin peddling some cake in the ghetto that made everyone ill. Although it would have been a bummer to be one of the starving people who bought a slice of cake made with laundry soap, my father told it as if it was a big yuk. And I thought that leaving it as that was great. It allows humor that's situational that could come about even in these dark situations, without betraying the narrative itself, without turning it into some kind of "Holocaust comic book" and whatever that might mean to somebody

LEFT: Original art, page 121. ABOVE: Study for page 121.
RIGHT: Studies for page 71.

who didn't know what I was up to…and as a bonus, it reveals an aspect of my father's sense of humor.

I laugh out loud at the part in the book where your dad throws out your coat and gets you a naugahyde Windbreaker instead. I love the scowl on the mouse face.

This anecdote has been useful when I've needed to justify why it was useful to insert myself into the story. Not everybody had a father who lived through Auschwitz, but everybody had a father who got them a naugahyde Windbreaker, you know? Those parent-child tensions seem to be relatively universal and, I now realize, have allowed for an empathic identification early in the book.

You say the book is about memory for you, but to what degree has this book now become a replacement of memory and an extension of memory for you?

I think like all written language it's a replacement for memory. That's what the

invention of the alphabet did to us apes. I remember sitting with a shrink I saw briefly after Pavel died. She'd ask, "So when did your father die?" And I'd say, "Well, I'll get back to you on that." And then I'd have to—basically, I'd have to go home and find out because I'd written it down in *Maus*, on the gravestone, but I didn't carry it in my head anymore. And so she very witheringly said, "So you've replaced your memory with a book." And I said, "Well, I did, but I didn't remember doing it."

That line that Vladek used after he saw the "Prisoner on the Hell Planet" sequence, saying "It's good you got this outside your system," is what I was hoping to do: not so much to expunge it, but to give it shape and thereby be able to put it aside. Another bit of naïveté, because that is just not how things work. You travel with your baggage wherever you go.

It's almost twenty-five years since the first volume of *Maus* appeared, and thirty or more years after you started working on it. How did *Maus* first get published?

The chapters first appeared as a work-in-progress in *RAW,* the avant-garde comix magazine that Françoise and I started in 1980. Since we published it biannually— and never knew whether that meant twice a year or once every two years—I had flexible deadlines I could actually meet. At some point a foreign rights agent from the Scott Meredith Agency, Jonathan Silverman, told us that a Greek publisher had looked into reprint rights to *RAW,* but lost interest when they found out it wasn't a porn magazine. The agent, now that he'd seen a few of my *Maus* booklets, wanted to offer the book to U.S. publishers. Scott Meredith said, "If anybody buys that, I'll eat my hat!" Rejections came from almost

---

R, STRAUS & GIROUX, INC.

HILL & WANG

OCTAGON BOOK

October 19, 1983

Mr. Jonathan Silverman
Scott Meredith Literary Agency
845 Third Avenue
New York, NY 10022

Dear Jonathan:

Thank you for the chance to see Art Spiegelman's MAUS: A SURVIVOR'
TALE. It's a very interesting piece of work, but I don't think it
for us.

Sincerely,

Michael di Cap

MDC/bc
Enclosure

ARts spiegelma

ST. MARTIN'S PRESS, Incorporated

175 FIFTH AVENUE, NEW YORK, N.Y., 10010

Telephone: (212) 674-5151

CABLE AI
TWX: 710-

Mr. Jonathan Silverman
Scott Meredith Literary Agency
845 Third Avenue
New York, NY 10022

September 28, 1983

Dear Jonathan,

I must admit I've had a real battle with myself over MAUS.
I found it quite affecting, and reminiscent of my own grandparents'
stories of European pasts--though their stories don't even approach
the drama of this one. I enjoyed the novel-in-comic-form, and got
involved enough in the story to read it through to the end. But
I'm sure you realize the difficulty of publishing this one--a novel
about the Holocaust in comic book form? You can imagine the response
I've gotten from the sales department. No matter how many other editors
I can get to be curious about this unusual creation, I can't see how
to advance the thing into bookstores. This is not to say that we
haven't done sad books; our recent A PARTING GIFT was about dying
children, and I don't know what could be sadder than that. But in order
to sell A PARTING GIFT, we had to take a major position on the book,
and I don't think, from what I've heard so far, that we'd be able to
do the same for MAUS. Perhaps a publisher of illustrated books would
do this properly because Art Speigelman is who he is--or perhaps
Schocken would be able to do it based on their history of publishing
serious Jewish history.

Anyway, thanks very much for thinking of me, and I'm sorry I
can't be of more help.

With all best wishes.

Sincerely,

Bob Miller
Editor

MORROW & COMPANY, INC. | PUBLISHERS

backs   Morrow Junior Books
           Lothrop, Lee & Shepard Books
           Greenwillow Books

JE, NEW YORK, NEW YORK 10016

September 8, 198

Literary Agency, Inc.
Avenue
ork, N.Y. 10022

Jonathan:

so much for sending along MAUS: A SURVIVOR'S TALE by Art
elman. The idea of a comic strip novel is quite intriguing,
iegelman is certainly an impressive talent. Sadly, however, des-
s setting. I just didn't find the story here to be sufficiently com-
or enveloping, especially for a book that will be among the
f its kind (if not the very first). I won't, therefore, be
an offer for the book, and am returning the manuscript herewith.

gain though, for giving us the chance to consider it.

Regards,

James Landis

PENGUIN BOOKS

VIKING PENGUIN INC.
40 WEST 23 STREET
NEW YORK, N.Y. 10010
(212) 807-7300

ber 21, 1983

an Silverman
Meredith Literary Agency
ird Avenue
rk, NY 10022

onathan:

going to pass on Art Spiegelman's Maus, but not without a lot of thought and
sion. In part my passing has to do with the natural nervousness one has in
hing something so very new and possibly (to some people) offputting. But
rucially I don't think Maus is a completely successful work, in that it seems
e way conventional. (Which is not for one second to suggest that the horror
ignance of the story are not as real as possible.) In putting such charged
al material into comic strip form, one would expect something very new, and
oesn't really happen in Maus; in contrast, I would say that Raymond Briggs'
the Wind Blows does seem like something new in the world.

this doesn't come off as rationalization. Something doesn't work for me--
r another editor here-- in Maus, and it is very hard to get a handle on what
y it is. But Mr. Spiegelman has a lot of artistic nerve, and I wish you good
n finding another editor and house with a different viewpoint.

ely,

Howard

W. W. NORTON & COMPANY · IN

25 October 1983

Jonathan Silverman
Scott Meredith Literary Agency, Inc.
845 Third Avenue
New York, NY 10022

Dear Jonathan Silverman:

Thank you for letting me see MAUS. The idea behind
it is brilliant, but it never, for me, quite gets on
track. The cover is a wonderful image, nightmarish
and moving, but very little inside lives up to its
promise. The general tone of the narration is more
like that of a situation comedy than seems right for
the book. The Nazi-cats, for example, have almost no
presence in the comic book frames. I had hoped to find
the same threatening presence as in the cover drawing.

I offer another quibble for what it's worth. The contemporary scenes are fine as a framing device, but their
constant use is jarring and it trivializes the harsh
scenes of Poland during the war. Perhaps Mr. Spiegelman
needs to be less faithful to the letter of his parents'
experience, in and out of Poland, in order to get
closer to its spirit.

I am sorry not to be able to take this further, but
I am indeed grateful for the look. Best wishes.

Yours sincerely,

Hilary Hinzmann

---

much for including me in the submission for Art Spiegelman's
ascinating project, and I wish I felt on surer ground as to
rket would be for a book-length and book-format version of
might attract a considerable following, but then again few
ve done well in the past. I'm afraid I must take the coward's
no, but I'll watch the book's progress with interest.

thinking of me.

August 12, 1983

Jonathan Silverman
Scott Meredith Literary Agency
845 Third Avenue
New York, NY 10022

Dear Jonathan:

With true regret I'm writing to tell you that we will not be making an offer for MAUS. I think it is an exciting and important project, and I have tremendous admiration for Art, but after a great deal of discussion which involved a large proportion of the Holt staff, in the editorial, sales, and marketing departments, I have had to conclude that there is not enough support here for us to consider launching what would be a publishing campaign of some complexity.

Response to MAUS was strong and mixed. Some people did not like it at all: felt the graphics were undistinguished and the telling of the Holocaust story added nothing we have not had in other forms, many times over. But there was a strong chorus of admiration, some from surprised readers who had not expected to like the story (because the very idea of a "cat and mouse comicstrip" account of the Holocaust horrified them), but found themselves very moved by it. And some found the graphics perfectly suited to the purpose -- graceful, simple, dynamic. But both those who liked it and those who didn't (and some who didn't still thought we should consider publishing it), were in agreement that publishing it would be a complex undertaking with many obstacles to overcome. This is also my opinion, and though I can see strategies for overcoming each obstacle, in the end I felt there was not enough enthusiasm among the group for making the effort

In a way publishing MAUS would be like publishing several different books at once, in that it appeals to various audiences. Its being a graphic novel is a distinctive trait, and certain people would be attracted to it on that basis. The RAW readers and Art's fans would be in this group. But for Holt to undertake the book we would have aim at a much broader audience. I think a younger-reader group coul be attracted by the graphic-ness -- perhaps high school kids who wou not sit down and read THE MURDERS AMONG US might pick up MAUS. But w would be in that case a strength -- its being "cartoon" -- becomes a weakness when trying to attract the interest of many of those whose chief concern is the Holocaust. The contrast between the seriousnes of the subject and the apparent frivolity which "a cartoon with Jews as mice and Nazis as cats" inspires is so great that I had in severa cases to talk for 5 minutes just to convince someone to even read th book. Once they read it they see that it is very serious, but this initial resistance is a serious hurdle. I believe to overcome this you would have to enlist the support of well-respected individuals many fields -- get strong quotes and endorsements from a variety of people (not "cartoon people") to catch the attention of those who w otherwise not be interested. There are organizations which should

PREVIOUS PAGES: Some *Maus* rejection letters.
RIGHT: A singular rejection letter from David Stanford (*RAW*'s editor six years later at Penguin Books).
BELOW: Reference photo for the cover of *Maus I* (models: Charles Wright and Françoise, circa 1979).
BELOW RIGHT: Early study for *Maus I* cover.

every reputable publisher. Many just sent dismissive "This does not meet our needs at this time" form letters, but I got some oddly clueless ones. One I wish I still had said my work was too much like a TV sit-com.

I was telling my rejection stories to Louise Fili, then the art director at Pantheon. She expressed surprise that her house had passed on it and showed it directly to the publisher, André Schiffrin. Fred Jordan of Grove Press was considering my book at the time, but one of the Pantheon editors, Tom Engelhardt, agreed to take it on. My agent literally gave his boss a hat for dinner.

Why did *Maus* come out in two volumes?

Pantheon had put up a tiny advance and was very patient. In 1985, somebody showed me an interview with Steven Spielberg that indicated he was producing a feature-length animated cartoon about Jewish mice escaping the anti-Semitic pogroms of Russia to set up

a new life in America. I believed that Don Bluth, the director, had seen the *Maus* chapters in *RAW* and I just imagined the story conference that led to *An American Tail:* "Okay. The Holocaust is kind of a bummer, you know, but maybe if we do a *Fiddler on the Roof* thing with cuter mice we could make a go of it." I was terrified their movie would come out before my book was finished. Fred Jordan of Grove Press tried to console me, saying, "Why are you so upset? All they stole is your high concept and, frankly, your high concept stinks." But the confusion could have left me being perceived as somehow creating a kind of twisted and gnarled version of a Spielberg production rather than what I'm be approached early on for support.

There is another MAUS -- the story of Art's relationship with his father, and the reconciliation of the generations through the telling of this story. Some readers found this something that resonated strongly for them. They felt that this story should be brought out more in the second half of the book. What did the entire experience mean to Art? How did it change him? How did he feel about his father and the whole saga, and about history and his place in it? Had we decided to make an offer, we would have wanted to talk with Art to see if he would be interested in working to develop this theme further, as it was felt this gave the book another dimension beyond the Holocaust story itself.

This, as I mentioned, was another area of concern -- that just being graphic in form and using cats and mice was not enough to make MAUS stand out among the many Holocaust stories. I myself don't feel that this is a problem, though I would like to see Art develop the theme I just mentioned.

Another concern was whether or not the book would receive the serious review attention which would be necessary to break it out and away from the Spiegelman-fan market into the larger literary world. Again, careful nurturing of support from a variety of public and literary figures, and a grand strategy for orchestrating review and publicity support (and perhaps being willing to spend the money to take Art out on tour), would be important.

I mention all these hurdles because I think they are all real. I obviously think they can be overcome, but it's clear that a lot of energy is involved. The publisher would need to be so excited about the book, and about its potential, that this effort would be a welcomed challenge. I'm afraid that here the balance came out on the other side -- the reservations were too many, and make the obstacles seem too high to attempt. One element of this is the expectation of sales. You intend a major auction and hope for large offers from major houses. Most here feel the book would do well to sell 15,000 copies in trade paperback, which puts a different sort of limit on the amount of energy and money which could be devoted to it. Again, it's a matter of attitude and enthusiasm; if you thought spending a lot of money in support could bring the book great success and high sales, then you might spend it.

I know this project means a lot to Art, and I feel it is an important book. For that reason I hope you find either a major house which will feel the thrill and carry the book onto the field with all flags flying (perhaps Knopf?), or a smaller house which can devote more time and detailed attention than a bigger house could to supporting the book and helping it find a large readership.

Thanks for giving me first crack at this project, and for being patient in waiting for my response. It didn't work out, but I feel satisfied that we fought the good fight and did everything possible. Though I am personally disappointed, I feel confident that you will find a good publisher for MAUS -- meaning a publisher which is in love and wants the whole world to know. When pub date comes, I'll be one of the

quite sure was the case: *An American Tail* was a sanitized reworking launched from the *Maus* concept. And just a few years ago my friend, Aline Kominsky told me that her mother had praised me: "That Art Spiegelberg, he's such a talented boy! Not only did he do *Maus*, but he did *E.T.*!"

An artist friend, Bruno Richard, suggested I publish the first half right away. But Pantheon had no interest in that until something unprecedented happened: A critic named Ken Tucker* wrote a glowing essay of *Maus* in the *New York Times Book Review*. They almost never covered work in progress, certainly not work in

---

See Ken Tucker's "Cats, Mice and History" on the MetaMaus DVD supplements.

progress being published in a small press magazine, and decidedly not a work in progress being published in comics format. The review described *Maus* as probably the most important literary event of our times, or something like that, and the result was a deluge of letters to Pantheon asking when the book was coming out. Pantheon reconsidered and—fortunately for me—*An American Tail* ran into union problems with its animators . . . so *Maus I* came out first.

How has the book's success affected you? How did it change your life?

Well, I never came dressed for success, so I just wasn't prepared for the overwhelming positive response to *Maus*. I'd been doing comics that required people to slow down and study rather than read. I'd arrogantly assumed my work would be appreciated posthumously.

The success of *Maus* called my bluff— "Okay, Okay! So you're a genius! So now what?!" I had actually thrived on the relative neglect; it made me get up and work. Neurotically, the anhedonic way I experienced the success of *Maus* was to spend the next twenty years trying to wriggle out from under my own achievement. The fact that *Maus* looms fairly large in

ABOVE: *The Wild Party* by Joseph Moncure March, 1994.
New Yorker covers, "Valentine's Day," 2/15/93, and
"Brief Encounter," 9/26/94.
Open Me... I'm a Dog!, 1997.
Little Lit: Folklore & Fairy Tale Funnies, 2000.

contemporary literature, and certainly in comics, is something that affects not just me but—in ways that I can imagine might be annoying—most other serious comics artists. I've tried to take heart from Joseph Heller, who was "stuck" with his looming achievement, *Catch-22*. No matter what he wrote, his later books were received with less enthusiasm: "Well, *Good as Gold* is interesting, but it's no *Catch-22*." His response made me grin. He said, "Well, yes, but what is?"

Maus brought financial security and recognition, opening more doors than I could ever walk through, but one thing I couldn't have predicted has been the weight of trying to not get in the way of the work that I'd spent so long doing. I'd incurred an obligation to the dead.

All I knew in the post-*Maus* moment was that there could be no *Maus III*. The war ended, the story was over, my father died. And as I have quipped many times before, I didn't want to become the Elie Wiesel of comic books and become the conscience and voice of a second generation. As a result, having to find my own place as a cartoonist has involved a lot of thrashing in the years since *Maus*. Resuscitating Joseph Moncure March's *The Wild Party,* a hot hardboiled poem from the 1920s, allowed me to try my hand at decorative and sexy illustration (impulses that had to be suppressed in *Maus*). Working for *The New Yorker* also helped me reinvent myself and find other aspects of my voice after *Maus*. Making picture books and comics for kids let me inhabit my role as a father.

How have your kids reacted to *Maus*?

Gee. The only reasonable way to answer that question is to let them answer it themselves.

ABOVE and OVERLEAF: A conversation about childhood with Maurice Sendak (published in *The New Yorker*, 9/27/93).

I'LL GIVE YOU AN EXAMPLE...MY FRIEND LOST HIS WIFE RECENTLY, AND RIGHT AT THE FUNERAL HIS LITTLE GIRL SAID, "WHY DON'T YOU MARRY MISS SO-AND-SO?" HE LOOKED AT HER AS IF SHE WERE A *WITCH*!

...BUT SHE WAS JUST BEING A REAL KID, WITH DESPERATE DAY-TO-DAY NEEDS THAT HAD TO BE MET NO MATTER WHAT.

HELP!

PEOPLE SAY, "OH, MR. SENDAK. I WISH I WERE IN TOUCH WITH MY CHILDHOOD SELF, LIKE YOU!"

AS IF IT WERE ALL QUAINT AND SUCCULENT, LIKE PETER PAN.

CHILDHOOD IS CANNIBALS AND PSYCHOTICS VOMITING IN YOUR MOUTH!

I SAY, "YOU ARE IN TOUCH, LADY— YOU'RE MEAN TO YOUR KIDS, YOU TREAT YOUR HUSBAND LIKE SHIT, YOU LIE, YOU'RE SELFISH...

THAT *IS* YOUR CHILDHOOD SELF!"

IN REALITY, CHILDHOOD IS DEEP AND RICH. IT'S VITAL, MYSTERIOUS, AND PROFOUND. I REMEMBER MY *OWN* CHILDHOOD VIVIDLY...

I KNEW TERRIBLE THINGS... BUT I KNEW I MUSTN'T LET ADULTS *KNOW* I KNEW...

IT WOULD SCARE THEM.

Maurice Sendak

art spiegelman

Nadja

Nadja Spiegelman was born in 1987. A 2009 graduate of Yale University, she has worked as a Web producer and is currently a freelance writer.

•

HC: When do you remember being aware of *Maus* as a thing in your life?

NS: One of my earliest memories is of being in a Chinese restaurant with my dad, shortly after he'd won the Pulitzer Prize. I was five years old and I didn't know what the prize meant. I remember going up to the waiter and telling him that my dad had won the Pulitzer Prize. He went over and congratulated my dad. My dad was angry with me. He scolded me for bragging. I was confused, because I didn't really understand what bragging was. But I realized what I had done was wrong. I was embarrassed and ashamed. Really deeply ashamed. I never volunteer information about who my dad is now. I don't know when exactly I first became aware of *Maus* as a book in the world. I didn't read the book for a really long time, until high school. But I tried a couple times. But it was really hard to read. Not difficult, just hard.

ABOVE: Nadja, 2010 (photo by Lindsay Nordell).

HC: Was it because it was something that your dad had written, or was it because it was about your family?

NS: My grandparents were this secret that I didn't know anything about. My dad never talked about his parents, and I knew that it was for a reason. I sensed that he had shut the difficult things into this book, and that it was all in there waiting for me whenever I was ready. So it scared me to read it. I have very little extended family on my mom's side, and none at all on my dad's. I'd always wished for a big family—doting grandparents, cool older cousins— but instead my family was in this book. A lot of people I knew had read it before I had, and they knew more about my grandparents than I did. I tried to pick it up sometimes but I think, maybe, it was easier to have my own made-up version of my paternal grandparents, a private and personal version.

HC: How did you decide that you were going to read it?

NS: I got part of the way through it a couple times. It's always been a presence, so I don't remember the exact first time I read it all the way through. I remember reading the "Prisoner on the Hell Planet" comic though. That was the way that I learned that my grandmother had killed herself. It made my connection to her death a personal and private one, almost unmediated by my father. Even though, of course, it was his telling, in his book.

HC: Did you just have a sense from when you were little that it wasn't something that you should ask about?

NS: I think my dad read too many books on the Holocaust when he was working on *Maus* and he just couldn't talk about it anymore. I think there was a part of him that wanted to protect Dash and me from the horrible things that he knew. For me, it meant feeling a little disconnected from my family and my history.

HC: What do you think about the book being dedicated to you and your brother?

NS: I feel like the gesture of it being dedicated to us is sort of like: this is for the new generation. It's a lot to carry forward. In the first printing, the book was dedicated to me and Richieu. Richieu was a specter-like presence in my dad's life, just a photograph on the mantel, but a photograph that carried all this weight. My own grandparents are like that for me: just characters in a book, but a book that's shaped my life.

HC: Do you remember when you first started realizing what World War II was?

NS: My elementary and middle school, the United Nations International School, covered a lot of African history and Indian history, and Asian history, and tried to shy away from the European and American history. So we only glanced over World War II, really. I don't really remember learning about it. It was from reading *Maus* that I got a grasp of how terrible the Holocaust had been. When I first got to college, I had a campus job working in the Fortunoff archives. I was transcribing video recordings of Holocaust survivors from French into English. I'd listen to the narratives in French and type them in English. It wasn't a random job; I felt like I was ready to engage with these stories.

But it was incredibly difficult to go back and forth from hearing about these things in a dark room of the library to the carefree partying of freshman year of college. Between hearing it in French, translating in my head, and typing it out—it was really seeping into my brain. For the most part, the people whose stories I was hearing had been on the peripheries of the war. French Jews who'd been relocated or escaped the country. But I transcribed this one narrative about someone who had been locked in a work camp. The Nazis left when they heard the Allies were coming but they left all the prisoners locked in there. It descended into mayhem, and people were eating each other. He described it in detail. I typed up that one and then I left, really shaken. I didn't feel like I could talk to my friends about it, it just seemed like a story that came from a different world. When I went back into work, I tried to tell the woman who was my immediate supervisor about it. She told me about people who had been exploring the Arctic and had gotten stuck and eaten each other as well. And I was like, "You know, this really isn't helping." I quit after that, and got a different campus job.

HC: Did you gravitate toward that job in part because of your family?

NS: Definitely. I thought that it was time for me to learn about it. But with war stories, I think there's an element of something almost pornographic about how horrible they are. You need to know why you want to learn, and you need to know your own limits. There's also my French side of the family, and what they were doing during the war. My great-grandmother got caught up with this Italian who had dealings with the Nazis, and when he died she was blamed for what he'd done, so she was in jail for being a Nazi sympathizer. Which was a very indirect way of being involved, but there's still this conflicting sense of my ancestry. Victims and perpetrators both.

HC: Do you identify as French?

NS: It depends on who I'm identifying myself to. In America, I feel French. In France, I feel like an American. I suppose I feel more like a New Yorker than anything else.

HC: Have you felt identified with the Jewish part of your family?

NS: On a religious level, no. I've always been an atheist. I had an anti-religious upbringing. "Religion is the opiate of the masses," was one of the first famous quotes I learned.

But still, when people ask me if I'm Jewish, I say yes. I can't say no. I know less about Judaism than most of my non-Jewish friends do. I've been to synagogues only for other people's bar mitzvahs. But I still say yes. A large part of my family was killed because of who they were. I can't deny that part of who I am.

HC: You've had a lot of adventures...

NS: I always felt like a sheltered kid and I didn't want to be. I did a lot of volunteer work, in high school and college. I went to Nicaragua and to Tanzania, and I worked with homeless people in New York and I spent a summer working at a camp for people with developmental disabilities. I've always felt the need to give back and to push myself to learn about the world.

LEFT: Art and Nadja (photo by Mariana Cook, © 1993).

HC: Do you think your interest in helping other people is in any way connected to your family history?

NS: Not consciously. But part of it comes from this inherited survivor's guilt—from my dad's parents to him to me: What have you done to deserve to be alive? Couple that with the fact that I was born into a very privileged life, and my guilt is huge. Maybe I'm more Jewish than I say, after all.

HC: How do people react to you when they learn who your father is?

NS: My dad says, "Being a famous cartoonist is like being a famous badminton player" and for the early part of my life, it felt like that was true. But that changed as I got older. When I did get into a good college, people in my high school weren't shy about telling me that it was only because of my father. I can be defensive about it. Once at college, I started getting a lot of Facebook messages from people I didn't know, at other schools, asking if my dad was Art Spiegelman, asking me to answer ques-

tions for essays they were writing, asking if we could be friends. For a while I wrote back politely with my dad's agent's contact information, then I didn't write back at all, and then I started writing back ridiculous things, to let off steam. I'm not my father, and while I'm incredibly proud of him, I need to carve out my own identity that's separate from his. It's strange for me, doing this interview, because I only talk about how I feel about my father with the people I'm very very close to.

HC: You did your senior project at Yale in creative writing. What did you focus on?

NS: I wrote my mom's story, from when she was thirteen to when she was my age. It's in part because my mom has had an interesting life that I wanted to learn more about and in part to figure out my own relationship with my mother. It's also because I like to write, and before I could really do anything else, I needed to find a way of addressing my dad's book. This was a way of doing what he did, but at the same time, something completely different.

•

ABOVE: Dash and Nadja, 1996. RIGHT: Dash, 2006 (photo: Nadja Spiegelman). OVERLEAF: Art's birthday, 1995 (photo: Françoise Mouly).

Dash

Dashiell Spiegelman was born in 1991. Currently a student at Brown University, he previously attended St. Ann's School and the United Nations International School. Among other activities, he's interested in parkour, mead-making, sculpture & Claymation, and apiculture.

•

HC: So how old were you when you actually read _Maus_?

DS: I'd say around anywhere from eleven to thirteen, maybe. I'd say more around eleven, but I'm not really sure. I didn't want to read it for a long time, because it had to do with the "ghost" side of the family, people I had never known. I knew it had to do with them, and I knew that my dad had told me stories of kids who had just gotten really freaked out by reading that book, because they were way too young. And I feel like, if other kids were getting freaked out, then... it was just something that was kind of daunting for me.

Recently, a kid from my high school said, "Oh! Your dad! Yeah, he wrote that book! I love that book! _Open Me...I'm a Dog!_" And, truthfully, that's the book I loved, too. I grew up with that book.

DS: No, not really. The conversations we've had that have related to *Maus* aren't necessarily so much about the book, but would be about, say, whether to send money to this Jewish thing that was performing rites for my late grandmother. Just stuff like that where my dad didn't want to do it, saying it was religious voodoo, but my mom did, actually, which is kind of an interesting situation.

I've heard a lot of stories about my grandfather, enough so that even though I can't visualize him, I can imagine who he was as a person. And when I try and visualize my grandparents on that side, I don't visualize them as mice. We've had enough conversations about them so that they're people who are formed through a ton of different anecdotes instead of through different pictures.

HC: So with *Maus*, you went and got it on your own from some bookshelf in the house or something?

DS: Yes. I feel like I wouldn't give *Maus* to anybody. If I had a kid, I would tell them that it's there, the same way my dad did for me. It sucks to have to choose for yourself, but it's something you have to be able to decide on your own. Because if you're not ready and somebody chose for you, that would breed so much resentment.

When I read *Maus*, it was in some ways a surreal experience. Just because I had been, in some ways, so afraid. It was just like there was a big stigma against it, because I was telling myself, "Just wait until you're ready," but how are you supposed to know when you're ready? I read it in one sitting. I didn't read it, I guess, in the circumstances that I would have wanted to read it, if I had read it in a removed way, where it wasn't talking about people I knew.... When it showed my mom as a mouse and it looked a lot like my mom? I was just like, OK, that's kind of hard to ignore. All of it was really moving and really scary.

HC: You said that you didn't ask your dad a lot of questions about it.

HC: So it made sense to you when you read it, the mice...?

DS: Of course, just because I grew up with comics.

HC: When you were reading *Maus*, did you at any point forget that this was your family?

DS: Oh yes, of course. There were definitely a lot of points where I forgot and there were definitely a lot of points where I empathized more with the mouse character of my grandfather than with the ghost, not-really-there character of my grandfather that was composed of anecdotes and the fact that I had a grandfather on my mother's side and so I should have one on my father's side.

HC: Did it ever disappoint you as a kid that you had no grandparents that you knew on your dad's side?

DS: Well, it would have, but the example of grandparents that I did have...? The relatives on my mom's side, they kind of drove her out of France. She was just like, "You guys are driving me crazy." And I just figured that's what relatives were, in some way. I wasn't thinking, "Let's get some of that!" Don't need another set.

HC: Does your mother's family ever talk about _Maus_?

DS: No.

HC: Do you think they've read it?

DS: I'm pretty sure they must have read it. I'm guessing and I'm not sure at all, but I've never had a conversation with them about it.

HC: You mentioned that when you were at the United Nations International School, you identified as French. You have such an interesting family background. Do you think of yourself as being "multicultural"?

DS: I was never really Jewish in the sense that I had to do Jewish stuff that was not fun. I didn't have to do anything that was a pain. And I also celebrated Christmas every year. It was just kind of like, take what you want, leave what you don't. But in the sense of being French, definitely, because there's a really big contrast between America and France, and they're very aware of one another.

HC: Have you ever felt put into a stereotype in France?

DS: It could be an issue for me, not because I'm Jewish, but because I'm American . . . but it's never really come up because I don't have an accent. In France though, they are really, really racist. I love France; that's like home away from home. And I always just kind of thought: "It has better food! And it's really pretty!" France had this kind of magical quality to it, and once I learned that there's this, like, rampant racism, that was just a hard, hard blow. (I mean, I can't be sure, and if you want to put this inside the book you might want to talk to my parents and confirm, but I'm pretty sure my grandfather was really unhappy that my mom was marrying a Jewish man. But wasn't once he became famous.)

HC: And it's funny because your dad's dad was bummed out that he was marrying a non-Jewish woman.

DS: Yeah, yeah. Nobody was happy with that relationship. Just them two. That's all that matters.

I think of myself as Jewish through heritage but not through culture. I also feel guilty about it a lot, just because a lot of times people are like, "Oh, that kid's dad wrote _Maus_ . . . Tell me, what Jewish holiday it is today?" And I'm like, "Fucked if I know." I'm not a religious person. Nobody in my family is. We were definitely raised as atheists. Which I think I'm thankful for. It also gave me something which I only recently acknowledged, and it's something that I'm also ashamed of about myself, but that I'm working on. In the same way that some people might have some kind of stigma against atheists, I have some generalizations that exist in my head and aren't rational, necessarily, about people who believe in religions in general. And it's hard for me to accept the fact that I really strongly don't believe in that, and that other people just as strongly do believe in that. At the same time I think it's also really interesting: I read _Paradise Lost_ this year in school; we read a lot of the Bible—it's stuff that's really fascinating to me.

HC: _Maus II_ is dedicated to you and your sister. Do you ever have any feelings about that?

DS: My parents told me at some point that these two people came up to them, and they said, "Oh my God, Art Spiegelman, we love you so much," and they just started talking and this couple had recently had a child, and they named their child Dash because they read the book and they saw it was dedicated to Dash and Nadja. That was a really cool story to hear because in a technical way, there's a kid named after me. That's just a really nice feeling. But having a book dedicated to me? In some ways it's really cool, in other ways I really don't think about it that often.

HC: Is there anything else that you want to say about how _Maus_ affected you and your family?

ABOVE: Nadja, Art, Dash, and Françoise, 2004 (photo: © Sarah Shatz).

DS: My dad redraws stuff and rewrites stuff until it's perfect to him, when other people reading it wouldn't have noticed anything in the first place. Which in some ways makes me think he's crazy—and it must be really hard for my mom sometimes, just because she has to deal with that—but in other ways it's really admirable because it shows that he's really doing the work for himself.

My dad also doesn't understand when I switch from liking English, to liking science, to liking martial arts, to liking all these different kinds of things, just because for him it's been: "Comics, that's just what I do." And that uncertainty about what you're good at isn't something he's ever felt. It's hard to have a dad who just doesn't know what that's like, but it's also really cool, because he's got some purpose; he had a message to give and he gave it.

I feel really bad for him, though, just because he did something really, really great, and it was in his medium, comics, but now, for the rest of his life, I feel like I'm going to be compared to him, and whatever he does is going to be compared to him. In the same way the person who I was when I was eight is a different person, the dad who did *Maus* is a different dad than the dad that I have now.

HC: He's been super-focused on comics from being a kid all the way through now...

DS: He's stepping out of it, though. The next logical step after comics, of course, is stained glass windows, and that's what he's doing now, designing a window for his old high school. That's such a really cool idea to me. That's a really concrete accomplishment.

•

90

Obviously Françoise is a character in the book. How would you describe her role in the project, in bringing it into being?

Well before I embarked on *Maus*, I indicated in a notebook entry that I needed to settle down. I needed to find a spouse in order to be able to do any long-term project, because otherwise I would just be too busy torturing myself to actually sit down and apply myself to the sublimated torture of making a long work. It's basically in the book as in my life: she was a stabilizing influence. With all the sturm und drang of our individual personalities, she is nevertheless a real stabilizing force who acts as the voice of reason in *Maus*. It wasn't premeditated as a story device, but the few times—and it has only been a few times—that I've re-read the work over the years, she clearly is the one who calls me out on my thrashings as we drive to see Vladek in the Catskills, laces into Vladek when he reacts badly when a black hitchhiker is picked up, but also was less exasperated by him than I was. Vladek never got to her the way he got to me; she

OUR LATEST ISSUE....

DASHIELL ALAN MOULY SPIEGELMAN
December 29, 1991. 6:23 A.M.

actually thought of him as kind of endearing. She liked him. And she was able to meet him halfway on things that were important to him in ways that I simply couldn't, ranging from converting to please him, to other times when they would just go over his accounting books together.

You would have loved that, huh?

They got along fairly well, you know. And those things reflect in the work throughout. As a character she doesn't come on stage nearly as often as Vladek, Anja, and Art do. But the central role that she has in my life was visually and emotionally present in the book. And she certainly allowed the book to happen in the sense of: "Oh, he's a puddle on the couch again, I'm going to have to scrape him off and get him upright." Just in that real basic way she was a factor in helping the book get made. And in the years since, I think she has been able to keep me in line, so that I don't just go either megalomaniacally nuts, or self-excoriatingly nuts; every once in a while she just nudges me back toward some kind of upright position to walk forward as best I can.

TOP: Nadja's birth announcement, 1987. ABOVE: Dash's birth announcement, 1991.

Françoise

HC: Can you talk a little about the early days of RAW, when Art was first starting on the long Maus?

FM: It's hard even for me to re-inhabit the world as it was before we did *RAW* because first *RAW*, and then *Maus* itself, had such an impact, and people's perceptions changed so much because of it.

When I met him in 1976, Art's worldview was already fully formed. When he delivered at the Collective for Living Cinema the full span of the lectures he would later give at SVA, he called the presentation an "idiosyncratic historical and aesthetic overview of comics" and it was just that. He had this vision of what comics could do, and of what he could do with the medium. He hadn't decided to do the long *Maus* yet, but it was clear that whatever project he was going to do would be extremely ambitious and would expand the possibilities of what could be done in comics in an exponential way. One of Art's traits that serves him well is that he's constitutionally unable to do something lightly (though it drives me crazy when it's about choosing yogurts). [Laughter.]

When I got together with him, he was gathering the work in *Breakdowns*. He was always extremely charismatic, but he also lived in complete isolation, intellectual and social: he had moved away from what was left of the underground comix milieu, and nobody in publishing in New York would give him the time of day. He experienced a deep sense of rejection—there were no reviews or sales for *Breakdowns*—but it didn't make him question what he believed in, quite the opposite. If anything, it made him gather his forces, a kind of quiet before the storm.

When *Arcade* petered out, it took his friendships with the other cartoonists down with it, so he didn't especially want to do another magazine. He wanted to be off on his own horse, not mired in editing other people's work. He wanted to do something that would demonstrate what he knew was possible but didn't yet exist.

HC: What were you doing at the time?

FM: I had a printing press in our loft. I was so excited by printing and publishing, I wanted

to do *RAW*. Art must have realized that this was as good a shot as he would ever get to give shape to his broader vision, so he humored me and we compromised, with me doing all the daily grind work for *RAW*, and him in his mousehole all day.

HC: How did the two of you think of the *Maus* project back then?

FM: I know it sounds silly now that *Maus* has been read by literally millions of people, but, at the time, a long literary comic book, a comic book that makes you laugh, cry, and empathize, whose characters stay with you the way characters in a novel do...that all sounded like the vision of a madman then. And there was such a scream of outrage when people heard that he wanted to do a comic book about the *Holocaust*! It was a taboo topic, and doing a "comic book" could only mean mockery, satire.

It's nearly impossible to recall, even for me, what he was up against when he made the decision to start that book: the scorn and fury with which the idea was received, especially

LEFT: Françoise in the *RAW* office, 2006. Photo by Sarah Shatz. ABOVE: At her press, c. 1980.

from survivors and families of survivors; the intractability of the subject matter; the difficulty in researching even the practical aspects of the project: what do the toilets look like, how do you deal with moral ambiguities such as the Jewish police, or the kapos?

Whenever he stalled or despaired, which was erratic throughout but inevitable every time he finished a chapter, it was painful to see him deeply depressed, and just as tough when he dove back into it. I read maybe only a tenth of what he read, but I know more about the death camps than anyone would ever want to know.

Back then, Art was a *génie incompris,* and we're now both pining nostalgically for that moment, at least I know I am: it's a lot easier to be *incompris,* not understood, than to be *mécompris,* misunderstood. What I mean is, just because it now exists, and because it's so universally known, everyone assumes that *Maus* was inevitable, was always meant to exist. The world behaves as if *Maus* is an exotic animal, and Art a clever biologist who "discovered" it, named it, and brought it out to everyone's attention.

HC: What's the effect of that?

FM: He's the handler who has to feed the beast, which has turned into a big bag of obligations. Art now gets told by anyone and everyone what he should do or not do, owing to his perceived obligations as the author of that phenomenal success—and, as you know, he doesn't like being told what to do. So, now, all these years later, the man who likes to complain finally has a legitimate grievance: he gets to complain about the success of *Maus.* [Laughter.]

HC: Do you remember what you thought of Art when you first met him?

FM: I first met him casually through our common friends, Ken and Flo Jacobs. (Ken was a filmmaker whose work interested me, and who I had met after arriving in New York in 1974 at the age of nineteen when I was on a sabbatical from studying architecture in Paris.) I asked Ken and Flo for comics, because I was trying to speak English better, to learn more English. I had gone to the newsstand to find some, but there was virtually nothing there. Anyway, they gave me a couple of issues of *Arcade,* and they introduced me to Art when he moved back to New York in 1976. Art gave me more comics and that's when I remember first realizing who Art was, when I read "Prisoner on the Hell Planet." That work blew my mind in a way that few things ever had... I just couldn't let go of it. So I did something that I had never done before: I picked up the phone and called him. I don't call people. I hate the telephone, especially given that I barely spoke English. But if I had access to the author, I just had to ask him some of the questions that were twirling in my mind. The main thing I couldn't get over was: How could he acknowledge feeling sorry for himself rather than feeling sorry for his mother?

HC: So it was in a sense a criticism?

FM: No, it wasn't, it was total puzzlement. I realized this was someone with a unique mind, a ruthlessly clear mind—someone who didn't shy away from saying what everyone else would have hidden. I just—I needed to know. I had felt some of the power of the handwritten confession in Justin Green's work, but "Hell Planet" went further. It is also a "confessional" work, but it takes resolute chances with going against conventions, with portraying the author/hero in a negative light. How did Art manage to talk publicly about how he felt rather than how he was expected to feel, how he should have felt? What the rest of the world was trying to impose on him was overwhelming—it was telling him, "Oh, feel guilty, feel guilty!" Where did he find the strength to acknowledge that pressure but also say, "Wait, what about me?"

HC: Yes, that's a big leap...

FM: To me it was inconceivable. I mean, there

was such discordance: he's supposed to feel guilty, and instead, he's calling his mother a murderer! He's actually cursing his mother. I just had to know, so we ended up spending about eight hours on the phone. And eventually I realized, "I actually want to spend more time with this person." It was really in reading that strip that I first got a sense of how extraordinary Art is. Brutally, ruthlessly honest, which is one way to get at the truth and, to me, the mark of a true artist.

Also, in Art's comics, I had found something that was challenging and rewarding, but was also entertaining without being contemptuous or condescending to its audience. "Hell Planet" has wit as well as pathos—all of Art's work wasn't just formally interesting, it actually communicated. It was as challenging and interesting intellectually as the independent cinema I was seeing at the Anthology Film Archives, but without the snooze. That's the part with which I had a hard time—the kind of pedestal on which those artists put themselves.

Frankly, at the time I met Art, I had been keeping away from men, including a few who were courting me, because I didn't want to fall under the sway of anybody. I was really upset when I fell in love with Art, because it was the opposite of what I had vowed to do, and I fought tooth and nail. On the other hand it was inescapable. The guy is charming, he's entertaining, he's as smart as anybody could be, and he doesn't have the slightest ounce of pretension. I now realize, after thirty-something years of life together, there have been times when I've cursed Art, but never have I felt, "Oh my God, he's so pretentious!" He's just anything but that. And clearly that, to me, meant a lot.

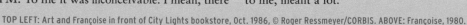

TOP LEFT: Art and Françoise in front of City Lights bookstore, Oct. 1986, © Roger Ressmeyer/CORBIS. ABOVE: Françoise, 1980.

HC: In a way, did you fall in love with comics and with Art at the same time?

FM: I fell in love with the possibilities of the medium the way he was using it. We had our first date-date when he called me before Thanksgiving 1976—and asked, "What are you doing for Thanksgiving?" When I said, "What's Thanksgiving?" he was thrilled and took me to Chinatown for a duck dinner.

HC: Did you meet Art's family?

FM: Yes, when we got married I knew Vladek and Mala. And Art was somewhat concerned about his father.

HC: Because you weren't Jewish?

FM: Because I wasn't Jewish. But I knew that Vladek really liked me. He always knew that I wasn't Jewish, but he also really liked me.

HC: So you and Vladek kind of hit it off.

FM: Yes, I liked him and he liked me. I understood very well how Art could be driven mad by him, but Vladek and I appreciated qualities in each other. And he couldn't drive me crazy the way he drove Art crazy.

HC: I think you can see that in *Maus*, that you and Vladek have a certain rapport that Art doesn't necessarily have with him.

FM: Art constantly got irritated by him. Mala also was not exactly amused. Vladek was exactly as Art portrays him, in terms of being unbearable, so cheap, and complaining all the time. But the point of entente between Vladek and me is that he knew that I would also do everything I could to fix the toaster before throwing it out.

HC: Right, right, he knew that you have practical skills and are a practical person and get things done...

FM: Yes. We recognized the highly developed practical side in each other. That was some-

Vladek and Françoise, 1978 (photo by Ken Jacobs).

thing he appreciated in a daughter-in-law. The not-Jewish part, he knew that there wasn't much that I could do about it.

HC: Right, like it wasn't your fault...

FM: It wasn't my fault. His father was saying to him, "Oh, she's really nice, but you know, you have to be careful." "Why?" said Art. "Well, you know, you shouldn't get too involved with her because she might want to get married, and she's non-Jewish."

But we already were married by then. I was going to be forced to leave the U.S. because of visa problems. We'd gone to a young pro bono lawyer who turns to Art and says, "You know, there are not too many ways for her to get a work permit, or to get the right to stay in this country, but since you two are together couldn't you get married?" And brutally honest Art said, "Is there any way other than that?" [Laughter.]

So, Art just dropped it on Vladek as a bomb: "Well you know what? We are married."

HC: With no preparation?

FM: None! But after his first shock Vladek just said, "Well, would she convert?" Not so much for his own sake as much as for "What will people say?" He lived in a very, very small community.

HC: So you didn't mind converting?

FM: No, actually. Once Art told Vladek that we were already married, Vladek's response made sense to me: "Would she mind converting, because I want to be able to tell people." "People" only meant Aunt Helen, cousin Max—about five people. Still, to him it mattered. And I said to Art, "Absolutely."

I felt I could totally empathize with this man. He had so few social interactions. Because he went through the camps, when he would announce, "Hey, my son got married"—which should be a joyous occasion, something that he should be happy about and proud of— immediately he would be asked, "Oh, is she Jewish?" And he wanted to be able to say, "Yes." That's all he wanted. It's not like he cared much about my soul being saved, or me actually being Jewish or not. He wanted his grandchildren to be Jewish and he wanted not to have to lie when he was going to be asked. I saw no reason to put him through the agony of "Is she Jewish?" and he would have to say, "Actually, she is not."

HC: So you were totally respectful of that; that makes a lot of sense.

FM: Well, to me it made a lot of sense.

HC: Did Art mind?

FM: Yes.

HC: He didn't want you to convert?

FM: He really didn't want me to. We were in complete disagreement there.

HC: So what happened?

FM: I am the one who insisted. I said, "I don't want your father to be miserable because you got married." And I said to Art that I wanted to do whatever it'd take...And especially because Vladek understood that it wasn't a matter of my religious belief or lack of religious belief. If he had wanted me to actually believe in God that would have been much harder to deliver because I couldn't have done that.

HC: You couldn't convert easily to belief...

FM: No. But I knew enough to know that it mattered, especially because Art is an only son and because he is one of the only surviving members of two very large families. And I wasn't even thinking in terms of having kids then, but to me it was a no-brainer.

So Art reluctantly called Vladek's rabbi and said, "What can you do to convert my wife?" so we could have a Jewish wedding. The long and short of it is Art came back and said, "This is ridiculous." It was going to be a long, complicated process with this Conservative rabbi out in Queens. Art had asked, "How many sessions are we going to have to do, to come and see you?" And the rabbi said, "Well, nine months to a year." And then Art protested, "That's way too long." And the rabbi said, "Well, it takes nine months to make a baby, it should take nine months to make a Jew."

After Art hung up, we went from Conservative to Reform. Art did the footwork and found this conversion mill, a program where they'd convert the Japanese boyfriend so that he could marry the Jewish girl. It was a summer program and by the end of August the whole thing was done. But the catch for Art was that we both had to go. It was a ridiculous course because you had to learn everything about being a Jew in something like ten sessions.

So we got to the conversion ceremony. We're standing in this shul, in this Reform synagogue on the Upper West Side, and it turns out that the rabbi is a woman. And Art asks, "Well, if you sign the certificate could you please not use your first name, not sign it as Sally?"

HC: Because Vladek would freak out?

FM: Art said, "Oh my God, if my dad finds out the rabbi is a woman, then the whole thing is for naught!" All I remember is standing in this darkened shul, and then Art and I are on stage with the rabbi, and all of a sudden this woman goes into this lengthy speech: "Do you realize what you are getting into? It takes GUTS to be a Jew!" I was listening to her talk: "And centuries of persecution!" Out of nowhere she

looking the other way, and they're at polar opposites of each other. And all that Vladek could say, over and over again, and he really meant it, is: "This is the most beautiful day of my life. This is the most beautiful day of my life."

HC: Oh, this is so sad, actually...

So then, twenty years later, I said to Art, "You're going to turn fifty, what can I get you?" And then, he asked for my hand. That's when he asked for me in marriage, in 1998. He wanted me and he wanted to get married. So we staged a wedding for his fiftieth birthday. We had time to plan; we finally did it for our friends, for ourselves, and we had children by then. The wedding was absolutely gorgeous. I went to buy a wedding dress with Nadja. Lawrence Weschler was our "rabbi," performing a ceremony that we wrote. Robert Crumb and his band provided the music. Dash stunned the room when he read a poem of his. And it was the most beautiful day of my life. It was our...

HC: Third wedding.

FM: Yes, we had three weddings. But all with each other.

•

has this prepared speech, and I'm thinking, "You know, maybe you're right—maybe I didn't really think this through."

But I got inducted, and then she signed the certificate, though not at all the way Art had asked her. She actually did sign "Sally." Fortunately, it didn't occur to Vladek to actually study the signature to see if it was a man or a woman. He only saw a signed certificate and he immediately scheduled a Jewish wedding. His rabbi still wouldn't officiate at our wedding because I wasn't properly converted in a way that he could recognize. So Vladek had to take a Reform rabbi in Queens.

We ended up getting married in a gym that wasn't even in a synagogue, but where they held services. It smelled like wet socks and Lysol, and it was as tawdry a ceremony as you can imagine. Nobody was very tearful at that wedding. But Aunt Helen was there and cousin Max was there, and afterwards we went to a local diner and then to Vladek's house.

HC: And was he happy?

FM: Yes. Somewhere I have a photo of Vladek looking in one direction, very happy, and Art

ABOVE: The wedding cake, 1998 (advice to wedding planners: If you are not certain you have enough cake for all your guests, decorate with a pair of taxidermically stuffed mice wearing veil and top hat). RIGHT: Françoise's hand in marriage, with *Maus* ring and watch (photo by Jürgen Frank).

Have you stayed in touch with Mala in the years since you finished Maus?

I guess the main thing we had in common was our shared difficulty with Vladek, and we slowly drifted out of contact after he died. I had assumed she's still in Florida, but met an old friend of hers at a talk I gave in Vancouver in 2008 who told me she'd died a couple of years before.

Though you've said you don't want to be the Elie Wiesel of comic books, you have participated in conferences about the Holocaust. You have some notes in your notebook about a Holocaust conference in L.A. in 1988. Tell me about what happened there, and your experiences at other conferences.

Well, that was one of a small handful of exceptions. This particular conference lured me in because it was set up to have children of survivors and children of perpetrators in conference together. It took place at the Simon Wiesenthal Center's Museum of Tolerance. I was interested because I hadn't met any children of Nazis. I was there to meet whatever swinging single daughters of SS men I could, but the actuality was only one poor traumatized young German woman showed up to represent her entire species among a whole bunch of mouse-folk like me. And she was just so guilt-ridden and weighed down by a history far vaster than her own personal history that it made me realize only Germans and Jews could get together comfortably to wail about the past, because the conjoined history weighs so heavily on both sets of psyches.

The people who attended the conference were primarily survivors, very old retired Jews who were fans of this place. *Maus* was not as well-known as it has become since, and the audience consisted of about two hundred Vladek Spiegelmans, you know, all glaring at me. They certainly never read it, but they all knew it was something about Jews as mice, and they knew it was a comic book. And comic books were so far beneath contempt that it was by definition an insult. During the Q&A, I was asked by an old man, "Couldn't you wait until we were dead before you would make such a thing?" I then tried to explain about how "comics" was a misnomer for my medium, because it implies that it's humor, and though there actually are, on some level, things that happen in the course of my conversations with my father that are funny, none of the humor was at the expense of the victims, but just situational. And then I tried to explain the sobriety of the project, the issues I was grappling with, why I did it in comics form and so on, but I was still met with a glaring and opaque hostility. So all I could really do was say, "Well, I'm finishing the project up, and I promise I'll never do it again." This was as close as I could get to an apology.

At another point in that conference, I was part of a Theodor Adorno–inspired "Can there be art after the Holocaust?" panel with a couple of historians and Harry Mulisch, a Dutch novelist

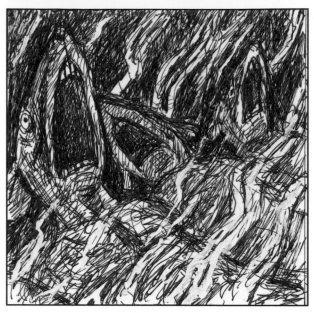

who wrote a book called *The Assault* that evokes life in Holland during the Occupation. He explained the difference between his novel and journalism: in journalism it makes a difference if a fire happened, in a novel it's just how well one can describe a fire. Therefore, as a novelist, he felt he couldn't deal with what happened in Auschwitz because it was too indescribable—that it's best left to the Raul Hilbergs and other historians of the world. There were a lot of historians on the panel and in the audience, and they were happy with Mulisch's answer, but I took it as a personal challenge. I felt we need both artists and historians. I tried to explain that one has to use the information and give shape to it in order to help people understand what happened—that historians, in fact, do that as much as any artist—but that history was far too important to leave solely to historians.

Have you ever disagreed with the ways that people have wanted to use or reference *Maus*?

Too often to remember them all. Once the Anne Frank House proposed an exhibit and book that would create timelines and charts of where Vladek was and where Anne Frank was at the same moment. They had a well-mounted show of my *Maus* drawings a few years before but this idea struck me as wrongheaded and somewhat exploitative. Next time I went to Holland and walked by there, I saw a poster for an exhibit about where Oskar Schindler was at various moments in time compared to where Anne Frank was. It seemed to have as much to do with franchising and marketing as sober reflection.

On the comics side, I remember a book on graphic novels from Phaidon that used *Maus* and other art without permission. They blew up the most horrific panels of *Maus* to full art book size. The mice screaming in agony being burned alive in a pit had been turned into something very graphic and totally decontextualized. It led to my one foray into litigation. I had

ABOVE: Panel study, *Maus*, page 199. RIGHT: *Maus* notebook, 1988.

been upset by other versions of *Maus* that enlarged the artwork. It is meant to be printed the size it is drawn. There is something graphically appealing about blowing it up, but I'm wary. It violates something really important about the integrity of the work to allow it to be gestural and decorative beyond its actual scale.

What about the Holocaust Museum in D.C.? Have you had any interaction with them?

There was some tentative discussion of showing *Maus* art there, and it struck all concerned as outside the museum's core mandate. I thought *Maus* doesn't really need the Holocaust Museum, and the Holocaust Museum really doesn't need *Maus*, or other contemporary art made about the Holocaust. But if they were willing to expand the mission of the museum to show contemporary work, it seemed important that they do a show about contemporary genocide. The war in the Balkans was raging at the time, and they were remarkably receptive to the idea.

Did the show ever happen?

A show happened, but not the show I proposed. I was just trying to find some way of signaling attention to the connectedness between the two events and suggested a show of contemporary artists' responses to the Balkans. We corresponded about it and I suggested a title: "How about if we call it 'Never Again and Again and Again'?" They had no use for that title, so I came up with "Genocide Now." They said they couldn't call it a genocide because the UN doesn't. I figured if it walks, talks, and quacks like a genocide, it's a genocide. But they didn't want to step on every possible funding land mine they could find. They said, "Maybe we should

Thoughts triggered by:
LA Holocaust conference (Kristalnacht '88)
"Holocaust" has become the secular sacrament of JUDAISM
its defining feature.
∴ Doing "MAUS" has made me overtly Jewish to the world
I brood because I think of the "Holocaust" as a World issue not
one of parochial interest only.
Even Jews force this issue — insisting on the "uniqueness" of
the Holocaust (wasn't the Khmer Rouge Cambodian killings
also unique? For that matter wasn't Jonestown?) Not to minimize
the horror of the Genocide or deny its Jewish character
but to try to come to grips with it all somehow in a
meaningful way without reducing it to the rationale for
the existence of Israel means remembering 11 million and
the result of dehumanizing any other.

just do a show of news photos from Time-Life photographers." I had zero interest in curating an art show, but was pleased my proposal could prod some show there about the Balkan nightmare.

Have Holocaust deniers ever responded to the book?

No burning crosses on the lawn that I can remember, though I imagine the book's form proves to them that the death camps never happened. Lurking on one Holo-hoax site I saw a thread citing the Auschwitz orchestra page we talked about as proof that I'm subconsciously acknowledging that my father's a liar and made the whole thing up.

At my most deliriously generous, I believe Holocaust denial is an understandable response to trying to wrap one's brain around the scale of the crime; then I come to my senses and realize it's just more of the mindless anti-Semitic venom that wiped out my family in the first place.

Y'know, back in 2006, in revenge for the Danish Draw Mohammad cartoon stunt, Iran held an International Anti-Semitic Cartoon contest with big cash prizes, look-

ing especially for Holo-hoax cartoons. I figured it was right up my alley and tried my hand at a few, but finally just submitted them to *The New Yorker* and *Harper's*.

Can you sum up some of the different ways that people received the book?

The fact that the book was really genuinely received at all outside the shtetl of comics was very gratifying. Even my very supportive first editor at Pantheon, Tom Engelhardt, braced me before publication by saying that Pantheon published lots of books that only sold three thousand copies, and if they were good books, by God, they were proud of them. The fact that *Maus* became a phenomenon, a crossover hit, was beyond any expectation.

There was also the misguided notion that *Maus* was some kind of "Auschwitz for Beginners." I had no faith that one could make the world better by telling someone what happened in the past, but there has been a kind of secondary life for the book as a didactic tool. "Well, it's a comic, it's a sugarcoated pill"—a sugarcoated cyanide pill that we can get people to swallow to understand the horrors of history. I had a much narrower goal: tracing my parents'

"No more Palestinian blood, thanks. It's bad for my cholesterol."

'HA! HA! HA! WHAT'S REALLY HILARIOUS IS THAT NONE OF THIS IS ACTUALLY HAPPENING!'

can be considered children's books, I can settle for *Maus* being on those shelves. It's also on countless college syllabi, used in history and Holocaust and postmodern lit classes, and at least once in a psych course on Dysfunctional Families and even in a course in Native American Studies(!).

The work seems to have found itself useful to other people in my situation, meaning children of survivors (even though I resist terribly being part of any group other than "cartoonists"). The mere idea of a child of survivors resenting and resisting his parents was breaking a taboo that I hadn't expected. I was clueless enough to not realize that that wasn't how everybody reacted, that mine wasn't a universal response. For some other children of survivors, *Maus* in a sense offered permission to reconfigure their own thoughts about what they'd gone through. So that was part of the response that I'm not unhappy—it's hard for me not to talk in triple negatives when I want to say something's OK. That was OK! On the other hand, I didn't want to be contained in the notion of a Jewish-American artist, and all of these hyphens are issues.

How do you feel about having a well-known cartoon character named Art Spiegelman out in the world?

Well, at this point there's this thing that I call the "Spiegelmonster" that lives in the

experiences and thereby finding out how I came to be on the planet against all odds. It allowed me to focus without getting overwhelmed by the enormity of it all.

I remember being irrationally peeved when the first volume got some kind of Young Adult book award from librarians. I'd made something as mature as I was capable of making, and it seemed unfair that I was the victim of a prejudice against my medium: "Well, comics aren't really for grownups, so let's give it a Young Adult award." I have since come to terms with the fact that comics are an incredibly democratic medium. I've met some pretty stupid older readers and remarkably perceptive younger readers, and ultimately I reconciled to the fact that if *Gulliver's Travels* and *Huckleberry Finn*

LEFT: Two of my submissions for Iran's Anti-Semitic Cartoon Contest. *The New Yorker*, 2/27/06.
ABOVE: My Final Solution to Iran's Anti-Semitic Cartoon Contest. *Harper's*, 6/06.

house with us. I didn't calculate that into my equation. "Famous cartoonist" in many ways is an oxymoron because what you know is the work, rather than the person. But there is a way in which *Maus* presented this character named "Art Spiegelman," who people project on to, either with protective

camaraderie, or with hostility, and I don't recognize myself in those projections. We have been the beneficiaries of my minor fame in various ways. And there are also ways in which it is absolutely crushing because I often don't see myself in it—I haven't been able to, in the jargon, "own it." I had never calculated that *Maus* would be anything other than one work that would then be followed by a work after and followed by a work after.

I confess that I once had this notion that the great model for me as an artist was James Joyce. Joyce had three or four different incarnations of himself, each represented by works that were stylistically, thematically vaguely related to each other, but were almost the works of different creatures. *Portrait of the Artist* is a very different work than *Ulysses*, which ultimately is a much easier work to navi-

gate through, as difficult as it is, than *Finnegan's Wake*. It was to me the ideal model for an artist. I had this notion that my first collection of work, *Breakdowns,* was going to be a fractal, a paradigm of what I wanted to do in longer, larger terms. The pieces were all there in *Breakdowns.* One of the earliest works in there was the three-page version of "Maus," and there was also "Prisoner on the Hell Planet," so there would be one work that would be the autobiographical, narrative project writ large, in the sense of a much more textured and densely made, full-length thing. And then I felt that a later strip I did in 1974, "Ace Hole," might be the model for a second large work that could strive to be as densely woven as *Ulysses*. And then I'd move into what would be the work represented by "Malpractice Suite," that would then have to do with allowing the visual and elliptical connection of phrases from panel to panel to become a much more impenetrable work than anything I'd ever done before. Sigh— that was the naïve game plan. I didn't calculate how difficult it would be to get past the embrace that greeted the first step of a three-part plan. What has come since is much more fragmented and groping than the dreams of youth…

TOP: Rejected cover sketch to accompany an interview in *Heeb* magazine, fall 2008. ABOVE: Self-portrait, 1974, featuring Picasso woman, Ace Hole, Nancy, and Maus (modeled on a 1942 self-portrait of Ernie Bushmiller).

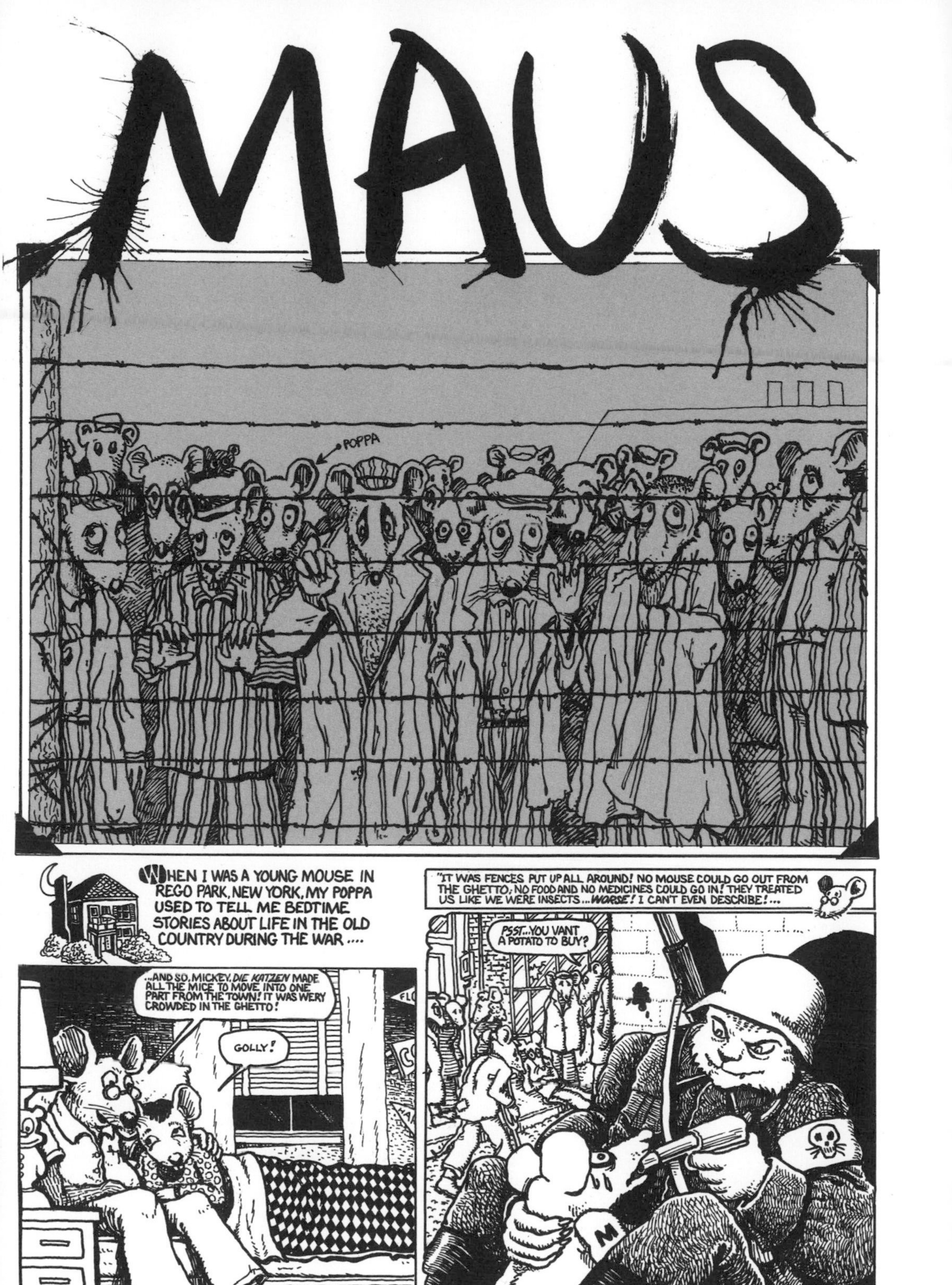
MAUS
POPPA
WHEN I WAS A YOUNG MOUSE IN REGO PARK, NEW YORK, MY POPPA USED TO TELL ME BEDTIME STORIES ABOUT LIFE IN THE OLD COUNTRY DURING THE WAR....
...AND SO, MICKEY, DIE KATZEN MADE ALL THE MICE TO MOVE INTO ONE PART FROM THE TOWN! IT WAS WERY CROWDED IN THE GHETTO!
GOLLY!
"IT WAS FENCES PUT UP ALL AROUND! NO MOUSE COULD GO OUT FROM THE GHETTO; NO FOOD AND NO MEDICINES COULD GO IN! THEY TREATED US LIKE WE WERE INSECTS... WORSE! I CAN'T EVEN DESCRIBE!...
PSST...YOU VANT A POTATO TO BUY?
M
©1972 art spiegelman

ABOVE and OVERLEAF: The original three-page version of "Maus" in *Funny Aminals*, 1972, published by Apex Novelties, San Francisco.

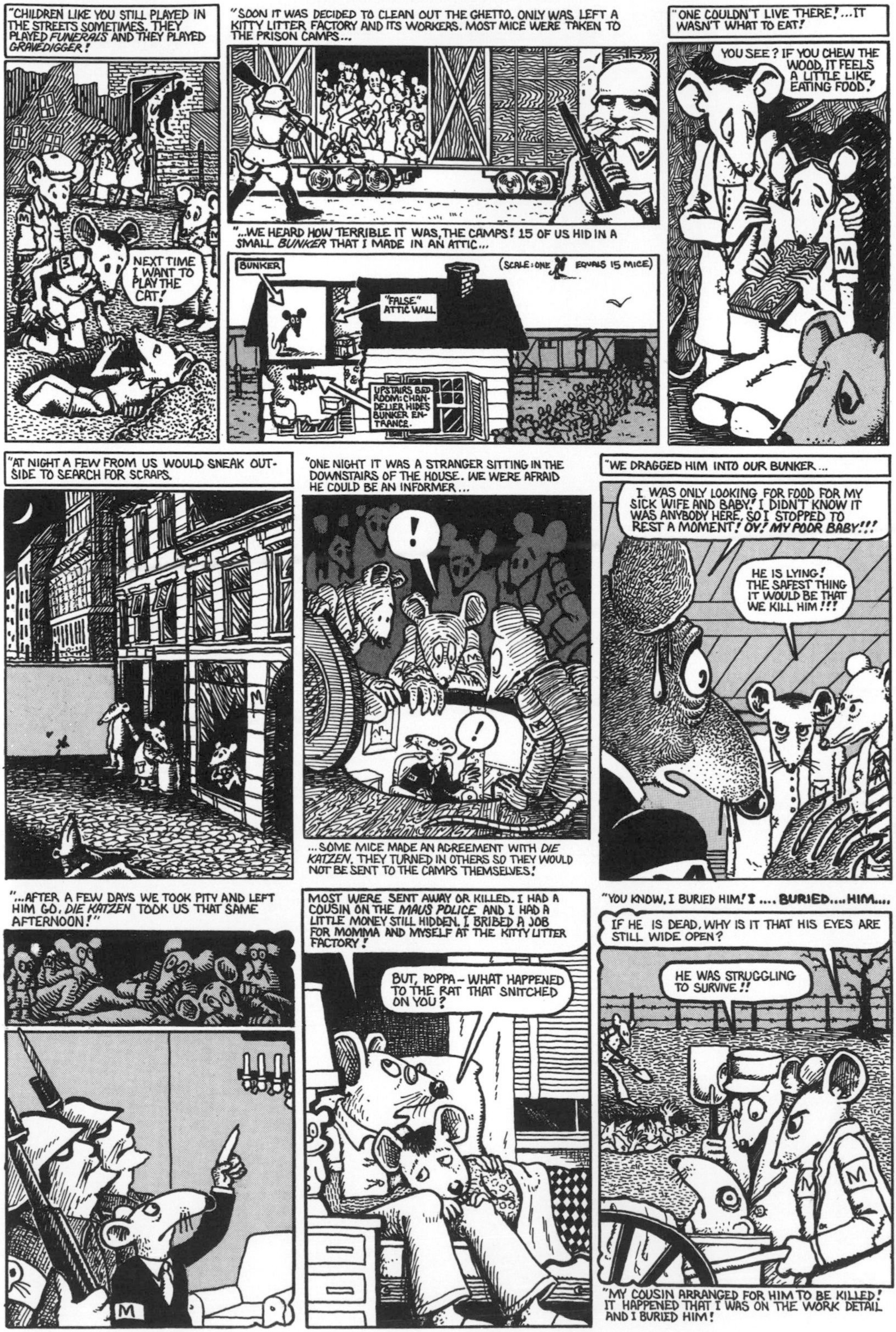
"CHILDREN LIKE YOU STILL PLAYED IN THE STREETS SOMETIMES. THEY PLAYED *FUNERALS* AND THEY PLAYED *GRAVEDIGGER*!
NEXT TIME I WANT TO PLAY THE CAT!
"SOON IT WAS DECIDED TO CLEAN OUT THE GHETTO. ONLY WAS LEFT A KITTY LITTER FACTORY AND ITS WORKERS. MOST MICE WERE TAKEN TO THE PRISON CAMPS...
"...WE HEARD HOW TERRIBLE IT WAS, THE CAMPS! 15 OF US HID IN A SMALL *BUNKER* THAT I MADE IN AN ATTIC...
BUNKER
(SCALE: ONE EQUALS 15 MICE)
"FALSE" ATTIC WALL
UPSTAIRS BEDROOM: CHANDELIER HIDES BUNKER ENTRANCE.
"ONE COULDN'T LIVE THERE!...IT WASN'T WHAT TO EAT!
YOU SEE? IF YOU CHEW THE WOOD, IT FEELS A LITTLE LIKE EATING FOOD."
M
"AT NIGHT A FEW FROM US WOULD SNEAK OUTSIDE TO SEARCH FOR SCRAPS.
"ONE NIGHT IT WAS A STRANGER SITTING IN THE DOWNSTAIRS OF THE HOUSE. WE WERE AFRAID HE COULD BE AN INFORMER...
!
!
...SOME MICE MADE AN AGREEMENT WITH *DIE KATZEN*. THEY TURNED IN OTHERS SO THEY WOULD NOT BE SENT TO THE CAMPS THEMSELVES!
"WE DRAGGED HIM INTO OUR BUNKER...
I WAS ONLY LOOKING FOR FOOD FOR MY SICK WIFE AND BABY! I DIDN'T KNOW IT WAS ANYBODY HERE, SO I STOPPED TO REST A MOMENT! *OY! MY POOR BABY!!!*
HE IS LYING! THE SAFEST THING IT WOULD BE THAT WE KILL HIM!!!
"...AFTER A FEW DAYS WE TOOK PITY AND LEFT HIM GO. *DIE KATZEN* TOOK US THAT SAME AFTERNOON!"
M
MOST WERE SENT AWAY OR KILLED. I HAD A COUSIN ON THE *MAUS POLICE* AND I HAD A LITTLE MONEY STILL HIDDEN. I BRIBED A JOB FOR MOMMA AND MYSELF AT THE KITTY LITTER FACTORY!
BUT, POPPA - WHAT HAPPENED TO THE RAT THAT SNITCHED ON YOU?
"YOU KNOW, I BURIED HIM! **I .... BURIED.... HIM....**
IF HE IS DEAD, WHY IS IT THAT HIS EYES ARE STILL WIDE OPEN?
HE WAS STRUGGLING TO SURVIVE!!
M
M
"MY COUSIN ARRANGED FOR HIM TO BE KILLED! IT HAPPENED THAT I WAS ON THE WORK DETAIL AND I BURIED HIM!

"SO... IN TIME THE FACTORY WAS LIQUIDATED TOO, AND THE WHOLE GHETTO WAS CLOSED! AGAIN SOME FROM US MANAGED TO HIDE IN A CORNER..."

DIE KATZEN MADE GUARDS AROUND TO STARVE OUT THOSE LEFT IN THE GHETTO ...

"AFTER SOME WEEKS THE GUARDS LEFT US FOR DEAD ..."

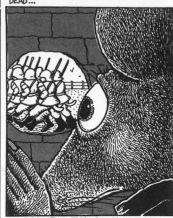

...WE SAW THIS FROM A TINY HOLE THAT WE MADE IN THE WALL WITH A SMALL PIECE WOOD AND OUR NAILS!

"THERE WAS NO FOOD AT ALL! WE LEFT THE *BUNKER*, BUT WHERE TO GO? **WHERE TO GO?**..."

"YOUR MOMMA AND I SNEAKED TO HER OLD HOME TOWN.... LOCAL CATS SHE KNEW BE-FORE THE WAR WERE AFRAID TO HIDE US!"

GO AWAY! QUICKLY!!!

"WITH MY LAST MONEY I MADE A DEAL WITH ONE CAT TO SNEAK US OUT FROM THE COUNTRY..."

OKAY— MEET ME HERE TOMORROW MORNING! I'LL HIDE YOU IN MY WAGON!

THANK YOU, THANK YOU!

"THE NEXT MORNING WAS ONLY WAITING *DIE KATZEN!* ...."

...THEY SENT US TO *MAUSCHWITZ* ....

"... MAUSCHWITZ ... "

...AND SO IT WAS.... I CAN TELL YOU NO MORE NOW....

...I CAN TELL YOU NO MORE .... IT'S TIME TO GO TO SLEEP, MICKEY!

UH-HUH... G'NIGHT, POPPA!

FLOR

CO

HAR

In 1977, about two years after Spiegelman moved back to NYC from San Francisco, he began visiting his father regularly and resumed the interviews with Vladek that he'd begun in 1972. In 1978, he made his first tentative stabs at drafting *Maus*.

RIGHT: 1980s *Maus* binder and earliest 1978 draft pages.

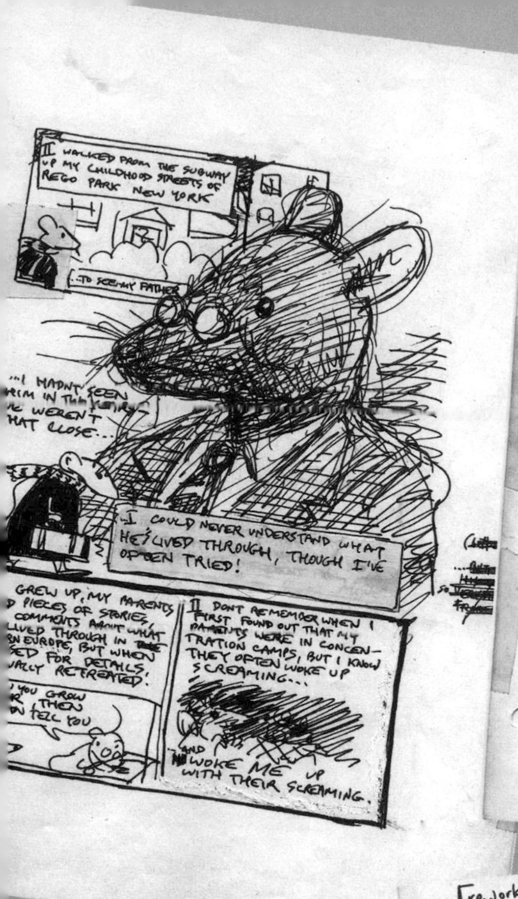

I WALKED FROM THE SUBWAY UP MY CHILDHOOD STREETS OF REGO PARK NEW YORK
...TO SEE MY FATHER
...I HADN'T SEEN HIM IN TWO YEARS. WE WEREN'T THAT CLOSE...
...I COULD NEVER UNDERSTAND WHAT HE'LIVED THROUGH, THOUGH I'VE OFTEN TRIED!
I DONT REMEMBER WHEN I FIRST FOUND OUT THAT MY PARENTS WERE IN CONCENTRATION CAMPS, BUT I KNOW THEY OFTEN WOKE UP SCREAMING...
...AND WOKE ME UP WITH THEIR SCREAMING.

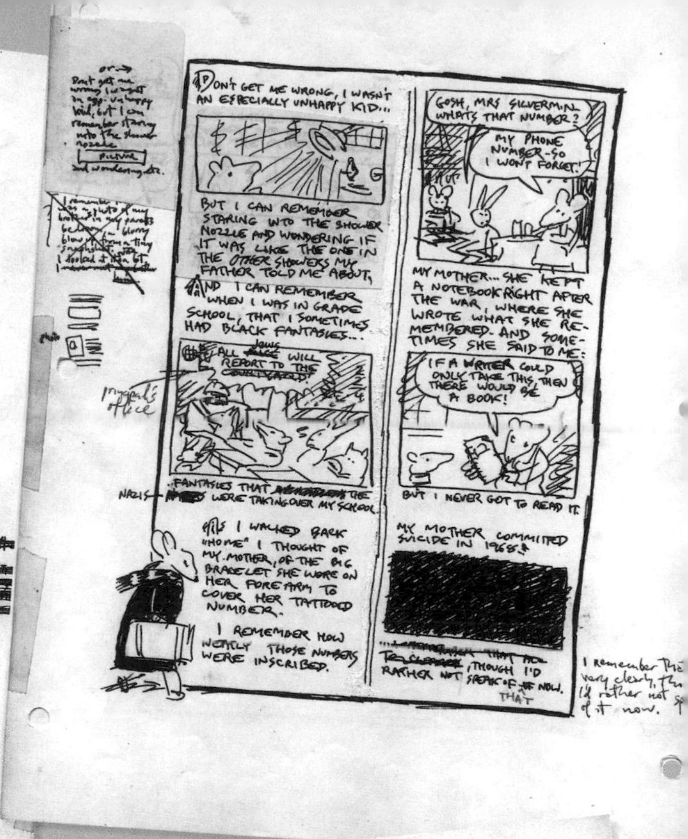

DON'T GET ME WRONG, I WASN'T AN ESPECIALLY UNHAPPY KID...
BUT I CAN REMEMBER STARING INTO THE SHOWER NOZZLE AND WONDERING IF IT WAS LIKE THE ONE IN THE OTHER SHOWERS MY FATHER TOLD ME ABOUT,
AND I CAN REMEMBER WHEN I WAS IN GRADE SCHOOL, THAT I SOMETIMES HAD BLACK FANTASIES...
FANTASIES THAT NAZIS WERE TAKING OVER MY SCHOOL
AS I WALKED BACK "HOME" I THOUGHT OF MY MOTHER, OF THE BIG BRACELET SHE WORE ON HER FOREARM TO COVER HER TATTOOED NUMBER.
I REMEMBER HOW NEATLY THOSE NUMBERS WERE INSCRIBED.
GOSH, MRS SILVERMAN, WHAT'S THAT NUMBER?
MY PHONE NUMBER-SO I WON'T FORGET!
MY MOTHER... SHE KEPT A NOTEBOOK RIGHT AFTER THE WAR, WHERE SHE WROTE WHAT SHE REMEMBERED - AND SOMETIMES SHE SAID TO ME:
IF A WRITER COULD ONLY TAKE THIS, THEN THERE WOULD BE A BOOK!
BUT I NEVER GOT TO READ IT.
MY MOTHER COMMITTED SUICIDE IN 1968.
...THOUGH I'D RATHER NOT SPEAK OF THAT NOW.
I remember that very clearly, tho I'd rather not speak of it now.

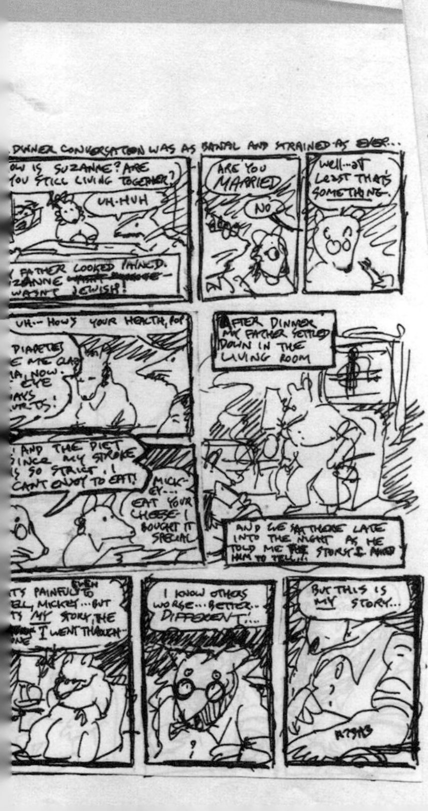

...DINNER CONVERSATION WAS AS BANAL AND STRAINED AS EVER...
HOW IS SUZANNE? ARE YOU STILL LIVING TOGETHER?
UH-HUH
ARE YOU MARRIED
NO
WELL... AT LEAST THAT'S SOMETHING.
MY FATHER LOOKED PAINED. SUZANNE WASN'T JEWISH!
UH... HOW'S YOUR HEALTH, POP
AFTER DINNER MY FATHER SETTLED DOWN IN THE LIVING ROOM
AND THE DIET SINCE MY STROKE IS SO STRICT, I CAN'T ENJOY TO EAT!
MICKEY... EAT YOUR CHEESE! I BOUGHT IT SPECIAL
AND WE SAT THERE LATE INTO THE NIGHT AS HE TOLD ME THE STORY...
I KNOW OTHERS WORSE... BETTER... DIFFERENT...
BUT THIS IS MY STORY...

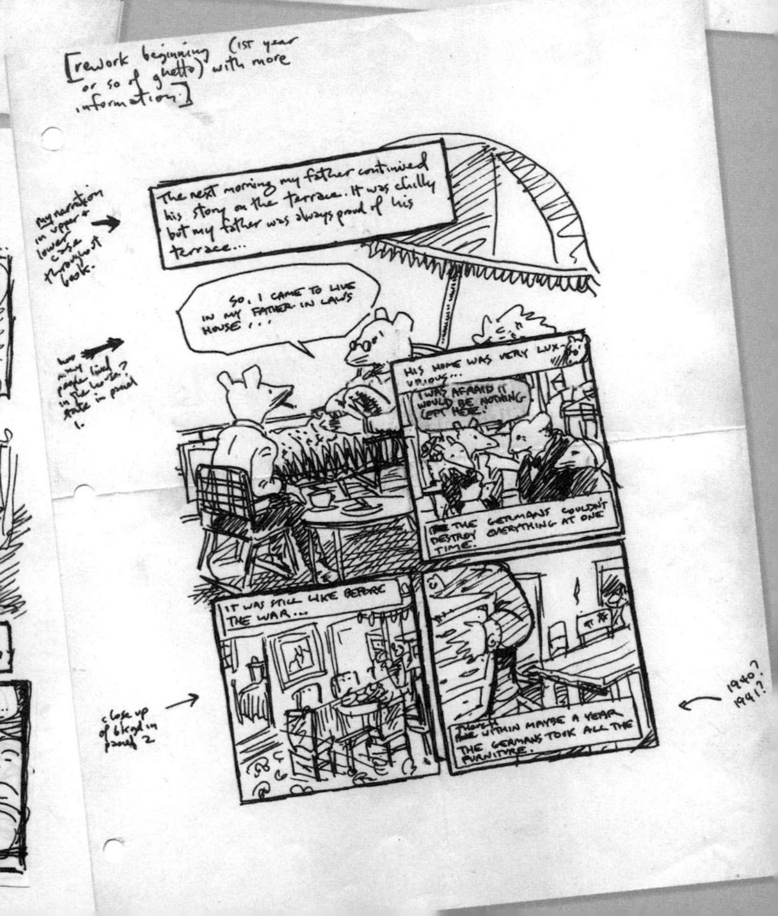

[rework beginning (1st year or so of ghetto) with more information]
my narration in upper & lower case throughout book.
The next morning my father continued his story on the terrace. It was chilly but my father was always proud of his terrace...
SO, I CAME TO LIVE IN MY FATHER-IN-LAWS HOUSE...
HIS HOME WAS VERY LUXURIOUS...
I WAS AFRAID IT WOULD BE NOTHING LEFT HERE.
THE GERMANS COULDN'T DESTROY EVERYTHING AT ONE TIME.
IT WAS STILL LIKE BEFORE THE WAR...
THOUGH WITHIN MAYBE A YEAR THE GERMANS TOOK ALL THE FURNITURE.
close up of bread in panel 2
1940? 1941?

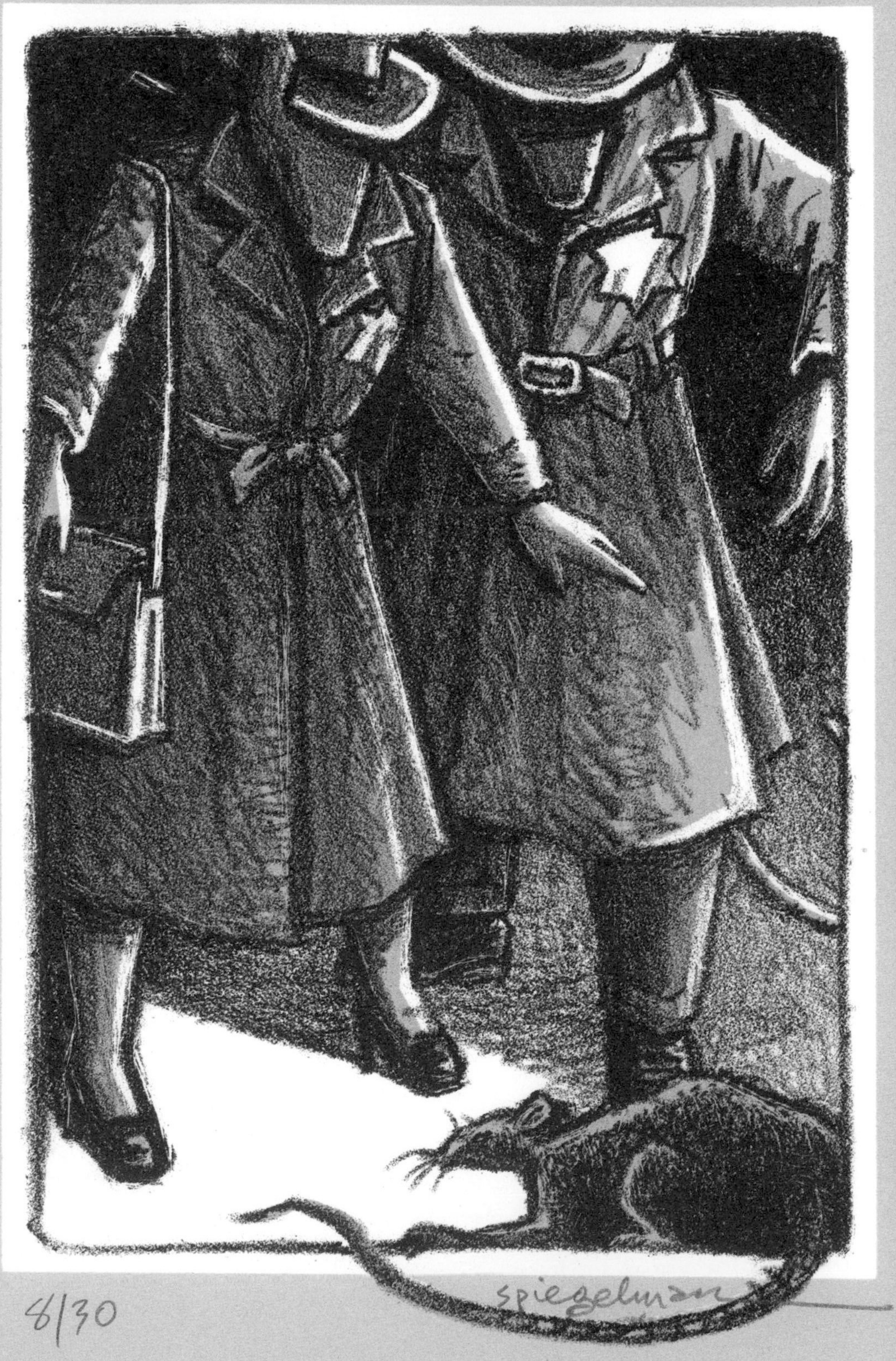
8/30
spiegelman

WHY  MICE?

So...how did you come across the idea of drawing mice, anyway?

AH, mice...
Actually, it all started with me trying to draw black folks. In 1971, when I was twenty-three, I was part of an extended community of underground comix artists centered in San Francisco, that had come together in the late '60s in the wake of R. Crumb's *Zap Comix*. A cartoonist pal, Justin Green, was put in charge of getting together a comic book called *Funny Aminals*. As I remember, Crumb had agreed to do the cover and lead story because Kathy Goodell, a girlfriend of his, and Terry Zwigoff (years later the director of the Crumb documentary) wanted to put out some kind of animal rights comic— you know, a mercy and respect for animals sort of thing. The tone changed as soon

FACING PAGE: "Mäuse + Mouse," from *4 Mice*, a portfolio of lithographs, 1992.
ABOVE: Cover of *Funny Aminals*, © R. Crumb, 1972.
TOP: Panel from "Portrait of the Artist as a Young %@&*!" in *Breakdowns*, 2008.

as Crumb did a story about a big-legged chicken woman being stalked by two little fox boys who lure her into a bedroom and eat her. Literally.

My first thought, to do something in the mode of an old EC horror comic like *Tales from the Crypt*, was kind of a bust. I wanted to do something in that melodramatic pulp illustration mode, complete with venetian blind shadows, but with animal faces in which the dénouement would have the protagonist getting crushed to death by a giant mousetrap that snaps shut on his body. I made some sketches but I was floundering when I went into a class that I'd been sitting in on at Harpur College (SUNY Binghamton), the school that had justifiably kicked me out a couple of years earlier (but granted me an Honorary Doctorate in 1995). A filmmaker I had become close friends with, Ken Jacobs, was teaching an introduction to cinema class. On this particular day, Ken showed a bunch of old racist animated

cartoons from the silent and early sound era. The blacks were cheerfully represented as subhuman, monkeylike creatures with giant minstrel lips—stereotypes stealing chickens, stealing watermelons, playing dice, all singin' & dancin', just the daily stock in trade of our racist cartoon heritage. In the same session he showed typical old Farmer Gray cartoons—animals frolicking on a farm, stuff like that, and I think he might have even shown "Steamboat Willie"—the first sound cartoon by Walt Disney. "Steamboat Willie" had come right in the wake of *The Jazz Singer* and essentially what we're looking at here is a jazzy Mickey Mouse—not the suburban and staid Mickey Mouse of later decades. He was a jazz age wiseguy—Al Jolson with large round circles on top of his head—and it all led me to my Eureka moment: the notion that I could do a strip about the black experience in America, using an animated cartoon style. I could draw Ku Klux Kats and an underground railroad and some story about racism in America.

its sting. I had actually drawn some excruciatingly clumsy and embarrassing comics emulating Crumb while looking for my own voice as an underground cartoonist, and it would have been very easy for my

That seemed really exciting for a couple of days until I realized that it could be received as one more example of the trope that Crumb had consistently mined with Angelfood McSpade and other willful racist caricatures: the return of the repressed—all that insulting imagery that had been flushed out of the mainstream culture but existed in the back of everybody's lizard brain—now brought back in a kind of Lenny Bruce "Is there anybody I haven't insulted yet?" spirit, with the hope that if you say the word "nigger" over and over again, you remove

notion to come off as one more racist "parody" even if I did bring in Ku Klux Kats and worked with honorable intent. It just felt problematic.

After my self-excoriating doubts settled in, I realized that this cat-mouse metaphor of oppression could actually apply to my more immediate experience. This development took me by surprise—my own childhood was not a subject for me. I hadn't been thinking about that at all, and my knowledge of what had happened in Hitler's Germany was actually very modest—and it wasn't clear to me then that there were echoes and precursors for this kind of imagery of Jews as vermin built into the Nazi project itself. The image of Jews as defenseless scurrying creatures was in there somewhere—I'd read Kafka's

FACING PAGE, TOP: Panel from "Portrait of the Artist as a Young %@&*!" in *Breakdowns*, 2008. LEFT: Original art from "Portrait . . ." TOP: Detail from "Phucked Up Phunnies" (drawn by Spiegelman in 1968, published in the Harpur College yearbook in 1970). BELOW LEFT: Acme School of Drawing ad, *Popular Mechanics*, 1908. BELOW RIGHT: Angelfood McSpade, *Zap Comix* no. 2 © 1968 by R. Crumb.

"Josephine the Singer, or the Mouse Folk," but I don't think I'd even focused on it specifically as a metaphor for the Jewish people back then. It was just one more Kafka fable I'd absorbed. But I did realize that if I shifted from Ku Klux Kats and anthropomorphized "darkies" to the terrain I was more viscerally affected by, the Nazis

chasing Jews as they had in my childhood nightmares, I was on to something. It became my three-page contribution to *Funny Aminals*.

You've said that Hitler was your collaborator on *Maus*. When did you become aware of the history of anti-Semitic caricature and stereotypes in creating your animals?

I began to read what I could about the Nazi genocide, which really was very easy because there was actually rather little available in English. So I did what research I could through interlibrary loans

"Just like Jews among mankind, rats represent the very essence of malice and subterranean destruction."

THE ETERNAL JEW,
A FILM BY FRANZ HIPPLER,
1940

and remembered some anecdotes from my father's life and began to transpose it into this animal form. The most shockingly relevant anti-Semitic work I found was *The Eternal Jew*, a 1940 German "documentary" that portrayed Jews in a ghetto swarming in tight quarters, bearded caftaned creatures, and then a cut to Jews as mice—or rather rats—swarming in a sewer, with a title card that said "Jews are the rats" or the "vermin of mankind." This made it clear to me that this dehumanization was at the very heart of the killing project.

In fact, Zyklon B, the gas used in Auschwitz and elsewhere as the killing agent, was a pesticide manufactured to kill vermin—like fleas and roaches. "Geno-cide" is a term that was invented after World War II to refer specifically to what had happened to the Jews because there was no label for that scale of crime: trying to kill an entire ethnic group. To accom-

plish that required totally dehumanizing one's neighbors—one murders people; one commits genocide on subhumans. I remember reading that most aboriginal tribes' name for themselves was synonymous with "the humans." In Rwanda, for example, Hutus referred to Tutsis as cockroaches.

Dehumanization is just basic to the whole killing project—America demonized the Japanese during World War II (it's what primed us for dropping the bomb on Hiroshima) and the Abu Ghraib torture photos suggest that the beat goes on. The idea of Jews as toxic, as disease carriers, as dangerous subhuman creatures, was a nec-essary prerequisite for killing my family.

FACING PAGE, TOP: Italian cover by A.S. (with apologies to Winsor McCay) for *The Complete Stories of Franz Kafka*, Einaudi, 2004.
FAR LEFT: Poster (Dutch version) and frames from *The Eternal Jew*, a German "documentary" by Franz Hippler, 1940.
TOP RIGHT: *The Poisonous Mushroom*, a children's book by Ernst Hiemer with color illustrations by Fips, *Der Stürmer*, 1938.
LEFT: "Rats. Destroy Them," a 1940s poster from occupied Denmark.

As I began to do more detailed and more finely grained research for the longer *Maus* project, I found how regularly Jews were represented literally as rats. Caricatures by Fips (the pen name of Philippe Rupprecht) filled the pages of *Der Stürmer*: grubby, swarthy, Jewish apelike creatures in one drawing, ratlike creatures in the next. Posters of killing the vermin and making

them flee were part of the overarching metaphor. It's amazing how often the image still comes up in anti-Semitic cartoons in Arab countries today.

An early review of *Maus* by Adam Gopnik, in *The New Republic*, compared your use of mice with the Bird's Head Haggadah. What do you think of that?

ABOVE: *Collier's* cover by Arthur Szyk, Dec. 12, 1942.

having any other god but God and did it by representing all of the figures as animals. I think the essay referred to it as a way of "drawing something too sacred to show" and in *Maus*, Gopnik described what I was doing as showing something too profane for depiction.

Despite my shoddy religious training, I was aware of this commandment, if only from looking through my mom's shelf of bestselling novels when I was growing up. There was a book by Chaim Potok called *My Name Is Asher Lev*, about a Hasidic boy who grows up to become a great painter, how he had to break away from his religion in order to become a figurative artist. So I was aware, even in my teens, that the project that was most consuming in my life was to make as many graven images as I could, and on some level, that probably helped fuse that mouse face onto my work even though I was totally unconscious of that aspect of what I was doing.

It's brilliant. I hadn't known about that Haggadah, but the reference seemed dead on. The same piece also academically traced my work back to the roots of Italian caricature, which was interesting to me but had no resonance with the junk culture I'd actually grown up with and avoided my actual influences as if they were inconvenient turds in the middle of the living room. But Gopnik's point about the Bird's Head Haggadah was a fundamental one: depicting humans was proscribed in much of Jewish tradition; like drawing Mohammad, it grew out of the commandment against making graven images of God. So some cagey medieval scribe had set out to decorate a Haggadah without breaking the commandment about

TOP: "The Vampire—Let loose in the world by the Devil, he incites and torments the people," by Fips for *Der Stürmer*, 1934.
LEFT: Detail from the Bird's Head Haggadah, Mainz, c. 1300 (© The Israel Museum, Jerusalem).
RIGHT: Drawing by Fips for *Der Stürmer*, 1937. (Label on sack: "Property of the people—Not for Jews.")

I solved the problem to my satisfaction, I'd minimized the disparity, so that the cats and mice became, more or less, overt masks. I liked working with a metaphor that didn't work all that well though I certainly didn't want my metaphor to work as an endorsement of Nazi ideology, or as an implicit plea for sympathy, like, "Aw, lookit the cute defenseless little mouse." To equalize them in scale didn't mean to give them equal power, but it didn't put the mice necessarily at the total biological disadvantage that the metaphor otherwise implies.

In the three-page "Maus" I was interested in class and racial oppression. It was my hippie self that first steered me toward the black rights thing and then eventually left me by default with the Nazi/Jew thing. What's most curious and interesting about that first attempt is that I managed to almost totally deracinate it. The references to the Jews are as *die Mausen*. The references to the Nazis are as *die Katzen*. The factory that my father works in, in the ghetto, is not presented as a shoe factory, but a kitty litter factory.

How did you decide to draw cats specifically and create the cat/mouse metaphor?

The cats and mice just came as a set, part of all the Tom and Jerry comics and cartoons that I grew up with. One problem I had was the disparity of scale of the creatures. Tom and Jerry are not, on any level, equal. Tom looms large and even if Jerry is a smart, crafty little creature, he only comes up to the top of Tom's paw. When I began work on the long *Maus* my first impulse had me drawing large cats and small mice. By the time

TOP: Sketchbook drawing, 1991. ABOVE: "Mouse, Tefillin, Cat, and Traps," a *RAW* postcard, 1979.

"Cat + Maus," from *4 Mice*, a portfolio of lithographs, 1992.

I pushed toward the metaphor of oppression, using my own history, my parents' history, but not owning it, not trying to get the texture of the actual details right. Only when I began working on the long book did I realize that, okay, I can use my cat and mouse heads but it would be fatuous to move in the direction of Aesop's Fables. The work would just turn fatuous and fake. Only through the specific could I imply the general.

How did you decide to use pigs in *Maus*? This particular choice has caused a lot of negative reactions...

In the first three-page "Maus," I only needed cats and mice. Once I had to deal with, say, my father's description of the Polish nanny that took care of Richieu... Well, what do I do with her? I couldn't make Poles mice and I couldn't make them cats. At that point my animated cartoon lexicon became useful. Look, Poles suffered terribly under the Nazis, but they were also often victimizers of Jews, and certainly left my father with a very, very frightened and angry response to his "fellow" Poles—anti-Semitism at that point in Polish history was rather virulent. There are still strains of it today, with almost no Jews to be virulent toward; though I hear that now Polish attitudes have begun shifting toward a kind of nostalgia, something like Americans' attitude toward Indians as somehow exotic and admirable. In earlier centuries, the Poles were the Jews' salva-

tion, so I wasn't necessarily trying to find a pejorative—but trying to find an animal outside the cat-mouse food chain, and I found Porky Pig—and the whole peaceable kingdom of funny animal comics—a useful model, since Porky's one of the toon gang, alongside Bugs Bunny and Daffy. Hey—Wilbur, the pig in *Charlotte's Web* is downright endearing and pigs, in their Snowball incarnation as well as Napoleon, were the absolute stars in *Animal Farm*! Those dualities of piggy/swine and mousie/rodent only enrich the simplemindedness of my basic conceit in *Maus*.

If I think of Hitler as my collaborator, in his plan for the Thousand Year Reich, the Slavic races, including the Poles, were not meant to be exterminated like the Jews but rather worked to death. They were slated to be the master race's work force

FACING PAGE: Drawing by A.S., late 1980s?
LEFT: *Ha-Ha Comics* no. 59, © 1948 Creston Publications.
ABOVE: One of the earliest draft pages, January 1978. Drawn before pigs entered the picture (and before mice were explicitly referred to as Jews), this draft eventually informed page 151.

of slaves. In my bestiary, pigs on a farm are used for meat. You raise them, you kill them, you eat them. If you have mice or rats on the farm, there's only one thing to do which is kill them before they eat all your grain. So my metaphor was somehow able to hold that particular vantage point while still somehow acknowledging my father's dubious opinion of Poles as a group.

There's one page, 138, in which the central image—the large image on the lower left—shows Vladek and Anja disguised as Poles by wearing overtly Woolworth-like pig masks over their more convincing mouse masks. Anja's seen with a long rat tail hanging out because it wasn't as easy for her with her Semitic features to pass for Polish as it might have been for Vladek. On this page, you have, essentially, a hub, which is the lower left-hand panel, and these spokes coming out, which are the surrounding material. So Vladek and Anja, in their overtly masklike masks with strings dangling in the back, are surrounded by two contrasting episodes. One has their former nanny, a Polish woman who had been an intimate of the family, opening the door when they're seeking shelter, then slamming it on them. Later on you find out that this is the woman who basically stole whatever property they had but returned just family photos because they were of no monetary value to her or anybody else. So that's on the one hand. On the

other, on this same page, they go to see the janitor of the building they had lived in when they were well-to-do—a lower-class Polish janitor named Mr. Lukowski. In desperation they go to their old building and knock on the door and Lukowski, at great personal risk, hides them in the barn. One succinctly gets the two sides of the pig mask on one page.

Maus was only translated into Polish in 2001, years and years after it had been translated into dozens and dozens of other languages.

Well, fairly early on *Maus* had been optioned for publication in Poland, but at least two or three times it seemed to fall through the cracks and it never happened. A very dedicated translator was eager to do it, but the publisher ran into, um, labor problems—which seemed especially appropriate in a country that was reshaped by Solidarity. They kept losing the plates and otherwise slowing things down so that it couldn't get printed. This was all in the wake of some Polish government official who came to America and went back home sputtering about the fact that there was a calumny against the Poles that existed in America in which the story of the Holocaust was told with Poles as pigs. And he was sure that such a thing would never be published in Poland because if it was, the Poles would rise up and

THIS PAGE and FACING PAGE: Studies, notes, and final art, page 138.

122

boycott the publisher. So that seemed to lead to more of these plates getting lost, and eventually it led to the translator—a journalist named Piotr Bikont who had been involved with *Gazeta*, the Solidarity newspaper—deciding to set up his own publishing house and to publish it himself. So when *Maus* was first published there, a demonstration was planned to protest the book; it consisted of some angry Poles carrying placards and burning the book in front of his newspaper offices. Accord-

ing to Piotr it was a very small demon-stration—just big enough to fill a small TV screen, which was the whole point of it, I suppose. Piotr had gotten wind of it beforehand and he actually came to the window wearing a pig mask and waved down at the protesters. As he described it to me, he said he felt like the King of Denmark who wore a yellow star out of solidarity with the Jews. He put on his pig mask in solidarity with the Poles who were burning this book.

The immediate response was actually quite intense—a number of Poles were eager to read this thing, in spite of the fact that they had very little comics culture to draw on to be able to make sense of it. But eventually the book receded to being the kind of book that I believe may still be available, but only if one asks for it. It's not on display. You have to kind of ask for it from behind the counter—this in an environment that includes the almost scary philo-Semitism I was referring to.

How did you react to the idea that people were demonstrating against the book?

Proud! It proves I succeeded in getting at a real issue, even if breaking a taboo incurs anger. I don't think, "Oh, man, I wasn't a good boy—I oughta apologize." Clearly in Poland—and among American Poles as well—the reaction to the pig thing is disproportionate to the offense. After all, Jews accommodated themselves to the idea of being portrayed as rodents of one kind or another. There seems to be something deeply problematic about the Polish ability to assimilate its past. It proves that the book actually hit something alive, a nerve

that needs to be cauterized. The tragic fate of the Poles under the Nazis has led to a kind of competition of suffering.

The Poles really did suffer in World War II, in great numbers, and it's not a contradiction to have an acknowledgment of Polish suffering and to understand that Jews were singled out for an even worse fate; a fate that was often meted out at the hands of the Poles the Jews ran into. It's a complex thought, but not an infinitely complex thought, that has led to a kind of bristling—a funny word to use for pigs!— when the perceived insult is recognized in the work, but then undercut by the actual anecdotes in that work. All the prejudices at play, including those of Polish Jewish survivors like Vladek, are indicated by those animal masks that conceal far more complex faces, that is, human ones.

In the eighties, my friend Ren Weschler introduced me to Helena Luczywo, one of the founders of *Gazeta*. Initially she was extraordinarily interested in *Maus*, and told me it was the first book her daughter had read in English. And as I talked to her further, I found that she was pinioned by the ambivalence that *Maus* created in her. It turned out that she's half-Jewish—or completely Jewish, I forget. Her grandmother, I believe, was killed in the Kielce pogrom right after the war, killed by Poles for being Jewish. Here was someone who is a very intense Polish patriot, stuck with the same legacy that informs my family, but with a genuine and fierce pride in Polish culture and achievement, and is left flummoxed by my book. I had real sympathy with her dilemma.

ABOVE: Anti-*Maus* protestors (photo by Anna Kaczmarz for *Dziennik Polski*, May 28, 2001). TOP: Piotr Bikont, the Polish translator and publisher of *Maus*, waves to the demonstrators from his *Gazeta* newspaper office window (photo by Stanislaw Makarewicz for *Super Express*, May 28, 2001).

You had a tough time getting a visa to go to Poland in the late '80s.

I applied and all of a sudden I'm called down to the consulate and an ambassador from Washington, D.C., comes up to see me, and tries to be very nice. He's explaining that it's a really big insult to call Poles pigs and points out that Hitler called the Poles *schwein*! And I say, "Exactly! And he called us vermin." So we were getting along just fine for a minute. I said, "I'm just making a book that uses Hitler's pejorative attitudes against themselves." And he's nodding, and I continue, "And considering the bad relations between Poles and Jews for the last few hundred years in Poland, it seemed right to use a non-Kosher animal." Then we stopped getting along quite as well.

A.S., unpublished drawing, 1996.

Have people in the Jewish community been uncomfortable with the animal metaphor?

When *Maus* was about to come out my editor at Pantheon suggested I just move to the country for a while and lie low, because there would probably be unpleasant repercussions from the Jewish community. It never happened. If anything, I guess my fellow American Diasporists could accept the self-deprecating image of Jews as cute fuzzy rodents. But I think that one of the reasons Israelis were never quite comfortable with the book is that the image of mice contains the stereotype of Jews as pathetic and defenseless creatures.

Shortly before the first volume was published in 1986, I was very grateful for the Jewish Museum's willingness to show original pages of *Maus*, when that still seemed risky. Early editions of *Maus* were proudly festooning a quote from Susan Goodman, then curator at the Jewish Museum, about how important the book was—it was the first sign of a legitimate Jewish community signing on for the book. I remember trying to convince the curator at the time to do a whole show about comic books and Jews. Her response was, "But there's a big difference between Jewish Art and Art by Jews!" so we dropped it. Now, as the medium becomes less disreputable, comic books have been embraced as part of the Jewish heritage, and shows about the People of the Comic Book are a hit on the Jewish museum circuit in the U.S. and across Europe.

So, why did you pull your work out of the "Masters of American Comics" show when it came to the Jewish Museum in New York in 2006?

Oy! Dun't esk! While I was proud to be part of a giant celebration of comics as art that concurrently spanned two Los Angeles museums, MOCA and the Hammer, I was blindsided to discover, only by reading an ad in the *New York Times*, that the show was slated to travel and end up on the East Coast as a joint show, with the comic strip art shown at the Newark Museum and the comic book and graphic novel work shown at the Jewish Museum in New York. I feared that the aesthetic and curatorial choices—I'd helped initiate and acted as a consultant for that Masters show—would be distorted into becoming a provincial show about the ethnography of comics. Doing a show about Jews and comics twenty years after my conversation with Susan Goodman, when the Masters show implied a genuine zeitgeist shift, seemed like a big step backward. Rather than try to reconstruct my reasons for pulling out, let me just quote from the letter I wrote to the L.A. museum directors:

Excerpts from a January 26, 2006, letter re:

MASTERS OF AMERICAN COMICS EXHIBIT

...The fact that the Jewish Museum will be the site within the NYC limits for the seven comic book artists to be exhibited there [makes] central a subtext that was invisible at MOCA: the early comic book (unlike its more upscale cousin, the comic strip) was a largely Jewish creation. Recently, as comics become more widely embraced in the higher precincts of American culture, these Jewish roots have occasioned several celebrations (most notably Michael Chabon's Pulitzer Prize-winning novel, *Kavalier and Clay*, and Gerald Jones' recent *Men of Tomorrow*) and even comic art exhibits...[Note: a 2005 show of superhero comics curated by Jerry Robinson was later added, in abbreviated form, as "Superheroes: Good and Evil in American Comics," by the Jewish Museum to their half of the Masters show.] I understand that only four of the seven artists in the Jewish Museum's portion of the show are card-carrying Jews... and that I'm the only one still living who carries that card. But since *Maus* looms so large in the public's perception of the comic book's recent apotheosis, the subject of the Holocaust can trump considerations of form in this museum's context. The statement intended by the Masters show, an exhibit formed to postulate that comics can actually be some sort of...Art, would be undermined by presenting the medium as some sort of "ethnic" phenomenon.

...I have an idea, one that sidesteps most of the pitfalls I've just outlined...It requires some curatorial rethinking, as does any transplanting of an exhibition, but I propose that EACH of these two venues present works by all fifteen artists. The hundreds of objects that have been gathered in L.A. are more than sufficient to allow two complete overviews in which works are allowed to reflect on and "talk" to each other, keeping the historical armature somewhat in place but emphasizing the cross-fertilizations between artists. (I'd love to see some McCays and Herrimans near my *No Towers* pages, some *Gasoline Alley*s and *Peanuts* near Chris Ware's...) Visitors to each city's museum could get an intimation of the medium's sweep and—safety in numbers—the Jewish artists, while present in NYC, no longer determine an overarching discourse...

When nobody but my friend John Carlin, one of the key curators of the original exhibit, was eager to implement that plan, I regretfully withdrew from the show, trying to just bite my tongue and not curse too loudly about a significant exhibit that had devolved into a confused mess.

There are many comics about the Holocaust now...

Yes, like Hollywood, comic books have now colonized the Holocaust. I hesitate to comment, since it might just seem like "slamming the competition." The most bizarre was a life of Anne Frank as told to Astro Boy, published by an outfit called Edu-Manga. And in 2007 the Anne Frank House published a fictionalized color series of graphic novels specifically as an international teaching aid about the Holocaust for schools. They're very earnest and drawn in a pleasant Tintin style. They met with enough success to have now put out their own Anne Frank graphic novel adaptation of the diary for schools. The subject is too vast to be limited to my one book, of course, but some of these projects strike me as if they were trying to set my work right by smoothing down the rough edges, by making a more didactic, more sentimental, more slickly drawn Holocaust comic book. It reminds me of a quote by Picasso talking about his paintings, saying he doesn't have time to make it pretty. He has to cut to the bone. What I'm seeing around me now are other works that try to make it pretty. This means they re-enter that maudlin sentimentalizing notion of suffering and how it ennobles and often insist on the primacy of Jewish suffering over other suffering, and so on. Some of them seemed to suggest, "Well, we'll do it with humans so we get rid of that whole stupid baggage of the animal masks." But I think it's those animal masks that allowed me to approach otherwise unsayable things. What makes *Maus* thorny is actually what allows it to be useful as a real "teaching tool," despite the non-didactic intent of my own book. *Maus* really only tried to teach me something, while at the same time telling a story to other people. It understands and acknowledges the pleasures of narrative without, I hope, pandering to it.

Does that make you feel uncomfortable?

What, being considered an apostate by my people? Well, I admired Philip Roth even back when he had lived through the *shonda* of confessing that Jews masturbate. The kind of Jewishness I was interested in was in that querulous, difficult Jew who continues to ask questions, even when it's a question of exactly how many nozzles are shooting out Zyklon B. The whole nature of Judaism as a process of questioning is actually interesting to me. The idea

that there should be midrashes and midrashes of commentary around commentary around commentary—that's swell. But when the focus is on questions about theological issues, I'm less interested than when the interrogations are focused on the "reality-based" world that a lot of us still live in.

Has anyone objected to your use of cats?

Well, I was once in the airport leaving a book tour in London, when I got a call from Paul Gravett, a comics scholar, who told me, "You know, you're missing Desmond Morris on the radio right now!" I never did hear the broadcast, but what he reported to me was that the zoologist was unhappy about my depiction of the Nazis as cats, saying that *Maus* set the case for ailurophiles back a thousand years to the Middle Ages, when cats were seen as witches' familiars.

The cats are actually the most lovable of the animals in the *Maus* zoo. Right? If you're given a choice of, "Would you rather be

a cat, a mouse, or a pig?" lots of people would say, "Oh, cats sound good." That of course has the advantage of making the reader, in this particular case, complicit with the murderers. Even in the way that they're drawn, the cats have the most human of the faces. The mice have the most abstracted and the least physiologically human representation: the nose is at the bottom, the eyes are at the midway point, and there's no room for that mouth. The pigs have those unsightly snouts. The reader has to reinterpret those signs that

seem to be in contradistinction to the story being told.

You draw many animals in the book besides mice, cats, and pigs. How did you make those other decisions?

Well, at a certain point I did feel enslaved by my metaphor. I couldn't just walk away and say, "So all other groups are just gonna have bland human faces, okay?" Each issue that came up required a different solution. One of the first problems was what to do about us Americans—I tend to identify myself more as an American than as a Jew—and in a melting pot like America it's hard to know what animal one might use. Turning again to my simpleminded ur-text of American popular culture: cats chase

mice, and dogs, by God, chase cats—it's a direct food chain. In fact, using pigs specifically allowed for a creature outside that food chain, because whatever other roles the Poles had in World War II as victims and as victimizers, they also were outside the food chain. They were there as witnesses. They didn't create the genocide. It was taking place on their farm, you know, on their turf, and since they were not immediately slated for the same destiny as Jews, they were there as witnesses.

But dogs were easy; it's almost the *Family Feud* answer to what animals come to mind and how do you perceive them. The dogs were the heroic vanquisher of cats, so there was that. Besides, as soon as you're a cartoonist drawing a dog, you've got lots of different kinds of dogs to draw. You've got Collies and Dachshunds and Cocker Spaniels and Chihuahuas and their

FACING PAGE, TOP LEFT: Discarded chapter title for what became "Auschwitz: Time Flies." TOP CENTER: Undated cat drawing, late '70s. TOP RIGHT: Sketchbook, 1978. LEFT: Sketchbook drawings, early '80s.

species or sub-species are much more clearly delineated than cats, even though cat fanciers will say otherwise. Here, the fact that there were so many possible dogs got me to actually verbalize to myself: "Oh, I get it. Americans are a mongrel race, a bunch of mutts." Bill Mauldin's panel cartoons of Willie and Joe—the "dogfaces" of World War II as GIs were called—came to mind as soon as I started trying to figure out what it might mean to draw a dog in an army uniform.

"Them wuz his exack words—'I envy th' way you dogfaces git first pick o' wimmen an' likker in towns.'"

We have British fish, Swedish reindeer, and a lot of others...

Right. As the book was coming to a close, I really couldn't have cared less about my metaphor, but I was stuck with it. People would ask me, "Oh, how would you draw us Italians?" and I was always stumped. I just had to deal with each of these issues as they came up, and it led to the whole

sequence in *Maus II* of talking to Françoise about how to represent her.

In a way I started reaching for the absurd to make sure one didn't take the ruling metaphor at, um, "face" value. When Vladek looks for Anja after the war, he goes to a large displaced persons center at Belsen. The British are in charge of that camp. I guess I could have avoided the whole issue since they just appear in the mise-en-scène for a panel or two, but I decided to give the Brits a walk-on part—or, as it finally resolved itself, a swim-on part. I thought about fish and chips, an island culture, fish out of water. All those things just seemed to lead me toward drawing fish without bicycles but with jeeps.

It echoed some panels in the first book when I first realized there are more than just Poles, Germans, and Jews in the world. When Vladek accompanies Anja to a sanatorium, there are other animals there. There was a goat, rabbits, reindeers

TOP LEFT: Bill Mauldin's WWII dogfaces, Willie and Joe. *Stars and Stripes*, Nov. 1944. TOP RIGHT: A.S. sketchbook, 1983.

or moose . . . I don't know, I think there was a giraffe in the background. It illustrated the possibility of that peaceable kingdom of different animals living side by side.

I vividly remember drawing the sequence where my mother went to see a fortune-teller—I was in a small cabin, deep in the woods of Connecticut that summer.

I prefer to work at night when I can, and these giant moths kept flinging themselves against the glass, trying to get in. Most of them looked like casting calls for Mothra. They were insane and enormous. I got really fascinated by what their faces looked like. And it was at precisely the moment I was trying to figure out how to draw the gypsy, so it was preordained that I'd use gypsy moths.

After the war, Vladek went to Poland, and from Poland to Sweden as a displaced person with Anja. Sweden was quite welcoming to refugees after the war. I thought of the Swedes as somehow far outside the loop of my Eastern European narrative and finding an animal so totally out of scale with mice, cats, and mutts—those large galumphing and gentle reindeer—struck me as amusing.

There's a point in the later part of the book (page 291) where, after they are free of their captors, Vladek and his friend, Shivek, go to visit Shivek's brother in Hannover. Vladek said that they had kids, and the brother, who is Jewish, was kept safe by his wife during the war. This was definitely a mixed marriage, so in my book that meant a cat and a mouse coupling. One of the many problems with visualizing Hitler's racist thinking by casting groups as different species, is that different species cannot, of course, reproduce. In fact, Nazi propaganda often depicted the Jew as the wicked seducer of German maidenhood, defiling the Aryan race. So here a Jew and a German have kids. At first I didn't know quite what to do, but drawing some creature that looked like something in

ABOVE (LEFT TO RIGHT): Studies. Fish, page 291; dogs, page 272; gypsy moth, page 293; reindeer, page 285. Detail of draft, page 291.

Die Spinne

Manch Opfer blieb im Netze hangen / Von Schmeicheltönen eingefangen
Zerreißt das Netz der Heuchelei / Ihr macht die deutsche Jugend frei

between a cat and a mouse highlighted the speciousness of demarcating groups of people as separate species.

In your article "Looney Tunes, Zionism, and the Jewish Question" published in *The Village Voice* in 1989,* you bring up Sartre's point that a Jew is someone whom others call a Jew. We see that reflected in the page where you draw a prisoner first as a mouse and then as a cat.

Yes. The racism was all so arbitrary, even the Nazis couldn't keep it straight. In the camps, different categories of prisoners were marked with different colored triangles on their uniforms. My father told me about a German who had gotten

---

*See MetaMaus *DVD supplements.*

dragged into Auschwitz as a "criminal" to be marked with a green triangle, but had somehow been classified as a Jew with a yellow triangle. My very first impulse was to avoid that anecdote—too complicated— but almost immediately I realized that it was better to race head-on into these issues of race and hierarchy. If I'd evaded the issue, one could still take comfort as a non-Jew reading *Maus* that it ain't you. One of the advantages of using these masked figures at all is that it creates a kind of empathic response by despecifying the faces—it allows one to identify, and then get stuck with having to embrace one's own corrupt and flawed humanity.

You're right to spot how important that Sartre quote was to me. My own identification with my Jewishness had very little to do with religion ever since I was thirteen and went out for a slice of sausage pizza in the middle of a Yom Kippur service and wasn't struck down by lightning. Still, I knew I would always be seen as Jewish by others, no matter what my beliefs.

Can you say more about that? You've said that doing *Maus* made you overtly Jewish to the world.

Yes, though it wasn't a big secret to anyone who could read my last name.

Doing *Maus* meant probing at the specific texture of the oppression directed at my own family—no more cozy liberal displacement of the discomfiting aspects of my own past onto a strip about black mice and Ku Klux Kats (though that idea keeps rattling around in my head even thirty years later).

It has become sort of a given that one of the badges of Jewish identity is pride in one's lox and bagels, and the other given is the fact that they tried to wipe us out and, by God, it'll never happen again! The problem for me is that I have an uncomfortable relationship with all this, because the only parts of Jewishness that I can embrace easily are the parts that are un-embraceable. In other words, I am happy being a rootless cosmopolitan, alienated in most environments that I fall into. And I'm proud of being somebody who synthesized different kinds of culture—it is a fundamental aspect of the Diaspora Jew. I'm uneasy with the notion of the Jew as fighting machine, the two-fisted Israeli. I'm a wimp. But I must insist, as Woody Allen once put it, "I'm not a self-hating Jew. I just hate myself!"

One of the most striking things about the animal metaphor is how it breaks down...

I guess it's all an inquiry into what it means to be human in a dehumanizing world. When my father told me about his long death march out of Auschwitz near the end of the war, he describes hearing gunshots and then, at some point, he sees far ahead of him, "somebody jumping, turning, rolling 25 or 35 times around and stops." He tells me, "Oh, I said, they may-be killed there a dog," because my father

FACING PAGE, TOP LEFT: Fips on interspecies racial defilement, *Der Stürmer*, 1934. "The Spider.
Many victims get stuck in the web, lured by flattery. Rip up the hypocrite's web so German youth will be free."
LEFT: Fragment of A.S. storyboard for sequence in HBO's cancelled film project, Paul Auster's *I Thought My Father Was God*, 2004.
ABOVE: Draft for page 242 with crayon marks to indicate page composition.

hadn't had that many experiences of seeing people shot close up, if any (although of course he did shoot someone from a distance when he was a Polish soldier). And he goes on to say, "When I was a boy, our neighbor had a dog what got mad and was biting; the neighbor came out with a rifle and shot. The dog was rolling so, around and around, kicking, before he lay quiet, and now I thought, 'How amazing it is that a human being reacts the same like this neighbor's dog.'"

When he told me that anecdote, he certainly wasn't thinking about me telling his story with animal surrogates—but I instantly knew this would become a key page in the story. I worked hard to make the transition between human/mouse and animal/dog as clear as I could. My father describes how "the dog rolled around and around, kicking before he lay quiet," and that is worked out visually as a roll across the page. I didn't try to present it cinematically, which would have been a bit corny,

but I took advantage of the way the eye assimilates a page; it was analogous to showing a human rolling around, fading into a dog rolling around, and fading back into a human as it dies.

Another page where the human/animal dichotomy gets called into question is the page with the rat in the basement...

Yeah, that one started as a real stumbling block. I thought, "There goes the whole ballgame." Vladek and Anja are hiding in a basement, and they're temporarily safe. They're lucky to have that storage space to hide in but my mother is terrified because there are rats in the basement, and my father comforts her by telling her, "Oh, they're not rats, they're just mice."

My father told me this anecdote two or three times. And one of the things I kept trying to figure out was how not to queer my representational system and deal with what he was telling me. At first I assumed

BELOW: Sketchbook strip, Sept. 1977. FACING PAGE, TOP LEFT: Goofy Gander's pet dog chases Peter Pig's sausages. *Goofy Comics* no. 38, 1950. TOP RIGHT: Bottom half of page 149. RIGHT: Study for page 149.

I should just show him talking in the present so it wouldn't bring "the rat thing" too much to the foreground. The fact that Vladek and Art are mice—you just don't notice that anymore—and they're just conversing. For a moment I figured, "Maybe I can turn the rat into cockroaches or spiders or something else lower on the evolutionary scale!" but that just was totally dumb, even if it did feel like the only way to keep my conceit from collapsing.

What came to the rescue was my comic book reading as a kid, especially Carl Barks' Donald Duck. In that whole universe of Mickey Mouse and Donald Duck comics, one is expected to embrace the ducks and Mickey Mouse as human, but accept that Mickey has a pet dog, Pluto, as well as a pal named Goofy. They're both dogs. And it really was almost like a Zen koan for me as a kid: does a dog have a Goofy nature? And Donald Duck with his nephews, Huey, Dewey, and Louie, would go off to Grandma Duck's farm for turkey dinner on

Thanksgiving and Christmas—it was kind of horrifying to me, but a useful literary reference point when I had to solve that particular piece of my father's story. So the whole page was built around showing as "rodentized" a rat as possible, showing Vladek and Anja on a page anchored by as unpleasant a rat as I could draw.

I should also point out that once I chose mice, I was sure that some Nazi somewhere would mutter, "Yeah, Spiegelman is just trying to whitewash the Jewish people. They're not mice—they're rats!" I think it's implicit in the choices I made—like that page where Anja's tail is so jarringly ratlike. Here's one place where the rodent is made very clearly ratlike to call their disguise masks into question, even if you'd managed to fall into the dream state that all narrative provides.

You kept lots of pictures of mice and other animals around while you were working. Which ones were especially significant?

135

I hunted up as many images as I could find of mice and cats drawn through the ages, especially anthropomorphic images. The New York Public Library's picture collection was invaluable. I found a photo there, from a Beatrix Potter ballet, that had humans wearing very furry, large-sized animal heads. I kept a copy of it around for a long time. It was evocative: the outsized and rather convincing heads on the biped dancers.

A series of postcards made in Europe—I think in Belgium—were very popular in the '30s and again in the '50s. They were very sweetly painted watercolor scenes of daily life that had cats, mice—some were with pigs—as anthropomorphized characters. It seems to have been a popular postcard genre. I never found out the artists' names, but there was one whose style was especially solemn and sober—paintings that had an almost Magritte-like solemnity to deny their unreality—and I kept these around me one way or another throughout the project.

Then there's that crazy cat artist in England around the turn of the last century, Louis Wain, known for his popular cuddly cat paintings, who went mad and painted schizophrenic, psychedelic cat pictures that I discovered in some Time-Life book on the mind and its aberrations. I loved his work, before he lost his marbles and after.

I also looked at lots of stray kidbooks from various countries and decades. I knew that I wasn't going for Disneyfied animals or animated cartoons. I looked first to my European roots, you know? One book I became aware of only after I was already well-launched on *Maus* was Calvo's *La bête est morte!*—a picture book about World War II drawn during the Occupation and published months after the Liberation. He was a masterful French cartoonist who drew his animals in a very

THE SATURDAY EVENING POST April 6, 1940

"WHAT... MATCHES AGAIN!"

Mice start fires by chewing matches

TRUE? . . . FALSE? . . .

you vote? To test this popular belief, ce were half-starved and turned loose it of matches. No action. The hungry

of fires throughout the country are received daily and studied. Progressive measures of fire prevention resulting from these studies have

Your local insurance Agent or a distinctive feature of rapit company fire insurance servic- for your financial safety . . .

FACING PAGE, TOP: J. J. Grandville, *Public and Private Lives of Animals*, 1866.
ABOVE LEFT: Louis Wain's '20s and '30s late Schizo cat paintings (in J. R. Wison's *The Mind*, Time-Life, 1969).
ABOVE RIGHT: Insurance ad, *Saturday Evening Post*, April 6, 1940. BELOW: Misc. mid-20th-century anthropomorphic postcards from A.S. collection.

convincing Disney style—so convincing that Disney threatened to sue for drawing the Big Bad Wolf as Hitler; in the second volume of his book he had to change the round nose to a square nose to avoid further problems with Disney. I don't know the history of it fully, but it was a children's book about World War II presented as a sort of barnyard fable, representing the French as rabbits, the British as bulldogs, and the Americans as buffalo.

By the time I discussed how to draw Françoise in my second volume, I was well aware of Calvo, but in the beginnings of the project, I just wasn't. I showed my work in progress to Etienne Robial and Florence Cestac, friends in Paris who ran a bookstore and publishing house called Futuropolis, and they said, "Oh, you've got to see Calvo!" They found me a copy of his then very rare book. Unlike him, I don't have the ability to render and draw the really convincing bird's-eye views with thousands of characters all in clear focus and the jaw-droppingly well-cartooned figures. The text was lugubrious and naive, but it was exquisitely illustrated. It didn't have a direct influence on me, but was, if anything, a kind of validation—just like when, years after *Maus*, I discovered there was a cartoon booklet drawn in 1942 by a prisoner in a French internment camp (he died in Auschwitz later that year), called *Mickey in Gurs*—another validation that I'd stumbled onto a way of telling that had deep roots.

At some point during those years I saw a book of artifacts that had been found in Auschwitz, and there was a walking stick

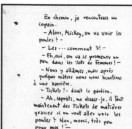

TOP: Edmond-François Calvo's *La bête est morte!*, © 1944-1945. ABOVE: Horst Rosenthal's *Mickey in Gurs*, 1942.

that had a Mickey Mouse head carved on it. That juxtaposition of the grimmest of real reality and media reality—the same thing that struck me most when I was in the Anne Frank House in Amsterdam, and saw the photos of American movie stars taped above her bed—gave me the corroboration I needed to continue. So much of what I know and experience is shaped by mass media…but so were the psyches of those victims of genocide.

that said something like, "Spiegelman was right!" It has people sending in photos of cats that look exactly like Adolf Hitler. This was especially interesting to me: though I didn't paint those spots on those particular cats, once the nexus of ideas has been created, that imagery reverberates. If I had decided to draw the Jews as rhinos, I don't think there would have been as many cultural correlations.

A photograph of your *Maus*-era workspace shows that you had a postcard of a cat in a police uniform above your desk. Can you talk a little bit about this image?

I don't remember where I found that postcard, but as I worked on *Maus* through the years I found more and more visuals that "rhymed" with what I was working on. I probably found the uniformed authority figure with a cat mask on sometime in the '80s. These visual rhymes kept coming up over and over again, and still do—most recently on some website that was called to my attention

TOP: Lots of "Kitlers" on the Web. RIGHT: Working in the *Maus*-hole, 1983. INSET: "Cop Cat" postcard, © 1982, Alfred Gescheidt.

139

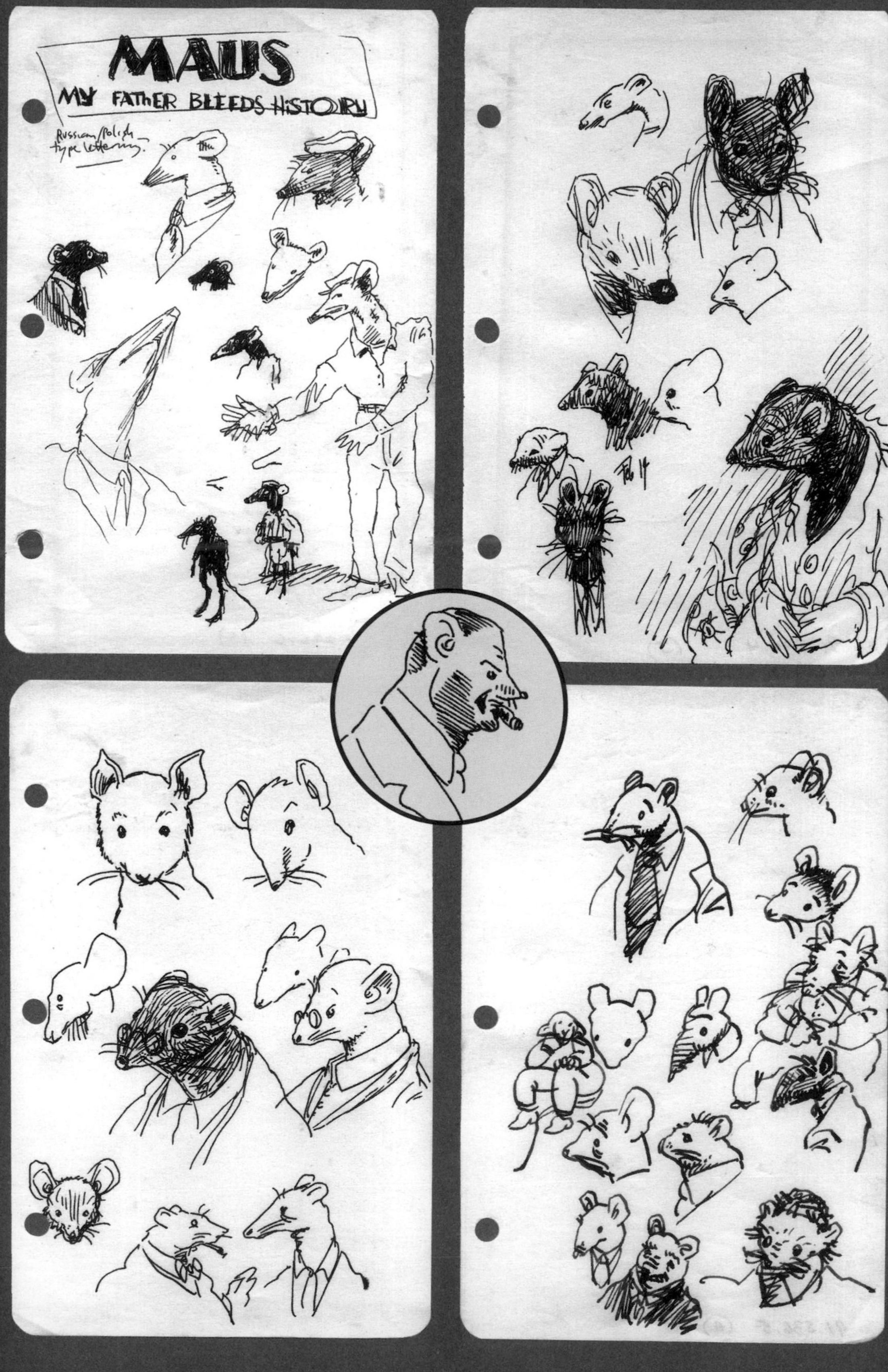
MAUS
MY FATHER BLEEDS HISTORY
Russian/Polish type lettering?

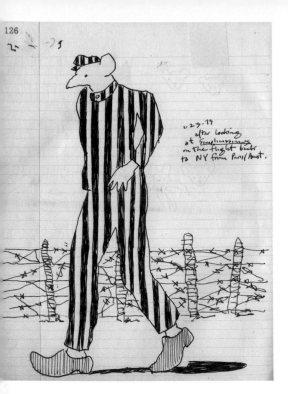

The easy and iconic example for me is Roy Lichtenstein, who—as soon as he discovered the uninflected, machine-like mark of big comic book dots and the templated thick-and-thin soulless line—made it his signature. And whether he was painting his version of a Matisse painting, or of a Greek statue, or of a comic strip, he presented it through that extremely limited ironic filter so one always knew one was in the presence of a Lichtenstein.

Most cartoonists and illustrators—ultimately, we're also operating in a marketplace, just like Lichtenstein—are

Why were you studying these anthropomorphic images?

It was all part of my search for a graphic style to use in *Maus*. All my strips, long or short, seem to demand that I go through that particular process—searching for a surface as well as searching for essence.

The best description of style I ever read was in a book of interviews with Picasso. He says style is the difference between drawing a perfect circle and a circle the way he draws it freehand. It's a wonderful statement, even though it's totally disingenuous in his case, because he sure was able to consciously shift styles more than most artists. It's more common now, when every postmodernist uses a palette of styles that quotes every way of making a mark that ever came before. Still, there's a kind of impulse—the capitalist impulse—to turn a mark into a trademark.

LEFT, ABOVE, and RIGHT: *Maus* studies in style, 1978 and 1979.

rewarded for finding one way of making a set of marks. One of the most reassuring things about *Peanuts* is that it's always *Peanuts*. Charles Schulz found a distilled style and used that distillation over and over again to play variations on his theme.

For whatever reason, it wasn't my natural disposition. I was just lucky if I could get the damn nose to look like a nose and I didn't care which way I did it. But I got fascinated by, "Oh, this cartoonist does it by making a sausage"—like in *Mutt and Jeff*. And this one just makes a little V-shape. If you make an S it looks like the inside of an ear, but there are lots of other ways to make insides of ears, and it in fact is a way to try to identify the anonymous artists in old comic books working in the house styles. Eventually it turns into a

LEFT: *Maus* studies in style, 1979.

vocabulary of marks that one can lean on when trying to make different things felt.

How did you decide on the visual surface for *Maus*?

While doing my interviews and breaking down sequences, I ran through a number of options, ranging from old Mickey Mouse to Beatrix Potter to George Grosz. One thing I tried out was scratchboard illustration that reminded me of Eastern European children's book illustration. It was interesting, but really stopped the flow of storytelling dead in its tracks. First, it insisted on my superiority to the reader, in the sense of, "I have a certain expertise at making this thing that looks like wood engravings that you don't have, so shut up and listen." It had the authority of looking

labor intensive (although the way I finally distilled the drawing style of *Maus* took almost as much labor to achieve), but each box in that approach led to one slowing down to look at that box as a drawing—it interfered with the process of actually reading comics where one would glean the visual information necessary and march forward toward another picture.

There was one rendering of a cat in full Nazi drag that looked sort of like Marlon Brando in *The Young Lions*. It was the most noble and savage version of the Nazis, tying into the stereotypes that presented Nazis as somehow sexy. It reminded me of the whole *Night Porter* genre of pornography that involved SS uniforms and scared me away from drawing *Maus* with really large-scale cats.

TOP LEFT: Page 53, final art, 1983. TOP RIGHT: Scratchboard experiment, 1979.

ABOVE: Early draft, color experiment, c. 1980. FACING PAGE, TOP: Study, page 124. RIGHT: Undated sketch, late '70s?

During that period of groping for a style, I also thought about cutting between the present and the past by having black and white line drawings intercut with gray wash drawings, or using full-color, which would have been way too decorative (and, besides, from years of looking at documentary photos I unconsciously believed the war took place in black and white). But I did seriously toy with using a two-color system, like orange and black for the sequences in the present, to help pull those away from the sequences in the past.

One thing that's striking about the way you finally rendered and drew the mice in the book is the simplicity of their faces.

In the breakdown sketches of my pages I wasn't self-consciously thinking about style, just making sure you could tell a mouse from a cat in the thumbnails, using simple, anthropomorphized Spiegel-mice. I was hanging out with underground independent filmmaker friends back then, whose modernist and painterly sensibility disposed them toward preferring the gesture more than rendering. I'd find it maddening that every time I showed them my stylistic research drawing they'd unanimously suggest, "Oh, just use your draft sketches, complete with cross-outs and mistakes. They're great. They're vital. They're alive." It confused me, though it did make me somewhat more accepting of my innate lack of real drawing chops. I just knew I needed something with more precision than those first-draft sketches and it eventually led me to the codification I used, com-

plete with mouse heads that are basically triangles without mouths: just a nose and eyes—very different from Mickey Mouse with his smiling have-a-nice-day face.

You show mice with their mouths open so few times in the book. Was that deliberate?

When I show the mouths, they're almost always there as cries and screams. It's not usually used to show characters yukking it up and laughing really loud. It's that triangle inverted as you look at it from underneath with a kind of scream face. It allows for a kind of vulnerability, coming in toward the underbelly of the mouse. The screaming mouth completes the face; it's a way of making that face human.

I was really struck when I was reading through some of your notes about Anja feeling awkward about being bald in the camps. Because none of the mice have that hair.

Yes. Although the characters don't have their heads shaved, the effect of the almost identical mouse heads is analogous to dehumanizing prisoners by shaving their heads and rendering them anonymous, harder to recognize as individuals.

Can you talk about your decision to draw yourself with a mask in the beginning episodes of the second book?

It came as a result of how the book came into the world. Which is to say, I never intended it to take thirteen years to make this thing, and because *Maus I* came out before *Maus II* was finished, the success of the first book took me by surprise and led me toward a kind of breakdown. I didn't know how to proceed through the gates of Auschwitz—I felt unable to proceed with the second volume, even though I'd already drawn the first chapter, "Mauschwitz," before *Maus I* came out—which led me to seeing Pavel. I think that the shock of becoming celebrated, rewarded for depicting so much death, gave me the bends…it left me trying to burrow into a mouse hole and disappear. It's a very natural desire: to look away. It's what keeps people from wanting to read about Africa, it's what has people looking at the cover of *Maus* and saying: "Ew! It has a swastika on it! I don't wanna read it!" It's what Pavel brings up, in a whole other context, of life taking the side of life. One averts one's eyes when walking past a graveyard.

It was only after my long sessions with Pavel that I was able to distill the sessions down to a few pages and basically

start again—and starting again implied a new present tense. I was acknowledging that Vladek had died; when I first thought about doing the book, I had no idea he'd just leave while I was still working on it. Since Pavel was a survivor of Terezín and Birkenau, his acceptance and tacit approval of what I was working on helped me get over my paralyzing issues. And talk about transference! On the one

BELOW and RIGHT: *Maus* notebook, Feb. 1987. Photo inset 1991, © Basso Cannarsa.

March 17 86
Talking to Pavel:
Pavel- PRIMO LEVI WAS RIGHT. The only thing a survivor can do is kill himself
Art - What?
Pavel- Everything is Auschwitz. Auschwitz is everywhere. People eat meat. Life feeds off life
After the optimism of liberation all the optimisms failed. Socialism, Zionism,
love, sex, friendship dont offer any succor as you get older
The impossibility of communicating what happened so it could make a difference
The only thing for a thinking person to do is say no.
All the anger - Who can you get angry at 40 years later? All you can do is
protest - but to who? All you can do is say I won't drink your stinking soup anymore

hand, Pavel offered me an opportunity to continue the conversations that I'd had with my father in a richer way, since he was more articulate and reflective about his own somewhat analogous experiences; and on the other hand, our talks helped me find my way back into the story from a new vantage point. And so, all of a sudden, there's a new layer of time the reader enters into. Before there was a nominal present that consisted of Artie going back to visit Vladek and then Vladek telling his story, and those two things were interweaving. But now, in the second book, I

needed a more up-to-date present. I found it had been implied already by my upper- and lowercase lettering at the very beginning of the first book: "I went back to see my father" was written from a temporal vantage point different than the rest.

It's only when I was introducing chapters in the so-called present with Vladek that the lowercase appears, so I realized I could indicate my new present tense with balloons in that lowercase, but I also needed to find some more visual marker that might indicate this different time frame—

147

art spiegelman, 1989

and for me it was one that portrayed me as the human that had donned the mouse mask to make this book. So to show Pavel as a human wearing a perfunctory mask and myself as a human wearing a perfunctory mask—with Pavel very specifically wearing a mask that had those little Uncle Scrooge glasses to indicate that this was like a continued conversation with my father who was represented with the same glasses—offered a solution.

What do you mean about you being the human who donned the mask in order to make the book?

It's really implied in the first panel of the first chapter of the first volume. I had to put on a mouse head to enter into my father's story. It was only over time that I discovered the implications of that. And I elaborated the image further as the author's "photo" at the back of many editions of the book. It was my intensive rethinking of how to get back into volume two, into a story that I was trying to evade—that is, how to inhabit the oxymoron of presenting life in a death camp—that made me understand I had to fully acknowledge myself as the author wrestling with making a book. It became useful to indicate that, hey, you know what, there are human faces under these mouse heads, on the analyst's couch, grappling with my father's legacy.

You've described the animals in the book as a "cipher," and in the beginning of the first book, you even say to your father when you're visiting him that the personal material about his life before the war makes everything more real—more human.

It was only in the course of really immersing myself in the work till it became my life that teasing out the implications became possible. This human versus mouse cipher also became an issue when dealing with my mother's suicide. The comic I include within *Maus*, "Prisoner on the Hell Planet," was drawn years before, in 1972, but I knew I'd have to present the facts of my mother's death in *Maus* again. I didn't see how to enter that bit of deposition into the new bigger deposition—redraw it with mouse masks? Just offhandedly refer to the fact that Anja committed suicide and not probe what a deep scar that had made on me and on my father? Literally including the earlier piece made several things possible: having the mouse cartoonist draw this comic inside a comic with humans once again allows the central

conceit to dissolve while also contrasting the emotionally-charged expressionist rendering of my own trauma with the more notational style of the larger book.

One thing that I found fascinating about the way the book was received is this whole problem of taxonomy that has to do with drawing animals. Do the animal features disturb a kind of realist interpretation, and how have people responded to the idea of the book as nonfiction?

I very briefly considered dropping the animal thing when I started thinking about the long book, but it was so embedded in my thinking that I just couldn't quite picture it that way, even while pursuing my parents' story in great detail and striving for accuracy. Paradoxically, while the mice allowed for a distancing from the horrors described, they simultaneously allowed me and others to get further inside the material in a way that would have been difficult with more realistic representation, where one could constantly question my choices: "Is that what that guy looked like?" and you know, I actually have no idea. It gave me a certain degree of wiggle room, a certain kind of slack, about getting a detail wrong despite all my research. And I didn't need to make up the very specific physiognomy of a specific person that I could never have known. I was doing as much research as I could, but having that mask as a prophylactic, I was able to protect myself from inaccuracies. By going back to Little Orphan Annie's eyes—letting the reader discover the expression reading into that face, as one always does with

TOP LEFT: Original art for "author's photo" in *Maus*, volume 2, 1989. LOWER LEFT: Sketchbook drawing, 1987. LOWER RIGHT: Panel from "Portrait of the Artist as a Young %@&*!" in *Breakdowns*, 2008.

A Problem of Taxonomy

Were you surprised when the *New York Times Book Review* put the book on the fiction side of the bestseller ledger?

It was unsettling, after having gone to such lengths to get the facts and details right. I ended up writing a letter to the *Times* saying, "Well, if you had a Literature and a Nonliterature section, I'd be happy with this, but fiction means made up, and that would be a whole other book than the one I'm making." To have this testimony presented as fiction could only delight some Holocaust denier somewhere. Because I have friends who worked at the *Times*, I was told of a remarkable exchange that happened after the editors got my letter and were debating about whether to move my book over to the nonfiction list or not. Eventually, the powers that be decided they would; after all, Pantheon had published the book as nonfiction, and in those days that sufficed. But one editor was furious at the idea, saying, "Well look, let's go out to Spiegelman's house and if a giant mouse answers the door, we'll move it to the nonfiction side of the list!"

comics—it all actually becomes a lot more open to one's inner sets of associations. In other words, you've got to do the work the same way you do when you're reading prose, and *Maus* retains that attribute of prose. We're wandering away from the issue of mice and cats here, but we are getting very close to the heart of the *Maus* project specifically, which had to do with a comic so heavily based on language. It's probably part of why *Maus* became a crossover hit with readers uncomfortable with comics.

I still puzzle over what fiction and nonfiction really are. Reality is too complex to be threaded out into the narrow channels and confines of narrative and *Maus*, like all other narrative work including memoir, biography, and history presented in narrative form, is streamlined and, at least on that level, a fiction. There are fictions that usefully steer you back directly to reality and fictions that beckon you off into the author's dream life and only reflect back onto events obliquely. I figured that *Maus* belonged on the nonfiction side of the *Times*' system of divvying up books. Still, when *Maus* was offered an award by the *L.A. Times* for best work of fiction in 1992, my editor convinced me to shut up and accept it gratefully.

me a "face," though, at the same time, I continue to try to avoid, duck, and evade that Maus mask, as in the sequence I drew in "Portrait of the Artist" showing myself trying to flee the shadow of my father's enormous mouse monument. It's all just proof of my ambivalence on parade.

Aside from *Maus*, you've employed, and identified with, your image of yourself as a mouse. Why has it become prominent in your life?

Well, as a cartoonist who never developed a fictional persona, I never knew what to draw when autographing books . . . it offered me an ongoing signifier. I don't even think about it as being a mouse anymore. It's just the character I'd draw—like Zippy might be for Bill Griffith or Popeye might have been for Elzie Segar. *Maus* gave

FACING PAGE, TOP LEFT: Letter, *New York Times Book Review*, Dec. 29, 1991. CENTER, ABOVE: Stationery, c. 1973. BELOW: Change of address card, 1975.

TOP RIGHT: Panel from "Portrait of the Artist as a Young %@&*!" in *Breakdowns*, 2008. LEFT: Birthday card in back-lit frame (light reveals little lizard), 1986. ABOVE: Event poster, *In the Shadow of No Towers*, NYC, 2004.

How many foreign editions have there been of the book?

I've never kept good track of this stuff, in terms of knowing how many copies were sold. It is well over a million copies of each book in America. But I don't even have a full list of languages it has been translated into . . . I think it's around thirty, including Chinese, Korean, Catalan, Serb, Croat, and Pashto. It never did get translated into Arabic.

Why, do you think?

To the degree that this is a narrative about Jews as sympathetic characters, it doesn't seem to be what the Arab market is looking for.

Did you try to oversee the foreign editions of the book?

To a small degree: I'd look over the lettering and insisted on keeping the covers and format the same as the U.S. edition. The Japanese edition is the only one that had permission to publish in a larger format than anyone else, close to magazine size. My translator and friend, Kosei Ono, explained that my pages were so dense with information

compared to manga, that Japanese readers would need a crowbar to pry it open.

I did pay special attention to the translation of some of the editions; specifically, the Israeli, the German, the Polish, and the French. I have a strong cultural connection to France through Françoise, and it's the comics capital of the western world in terms of its sophisticated understanding of comics. So that edition required special thought and, thanks to Françoise, the translation was thoroughly vetted. The editions where the history brushes up against the languages involved were the ones that really were central for me.

The Israeli edition published by Zmora Bitan back in 1990 was a strange experience. I think Hebrew might be the only language in the world that's more efficient and shorter than English, so there

LEFT: The work of art in the age of mechanical reproduction. Some foreign editions: Swedish, Polish, Dutch, Korean, Danish, Italian, Greek, Israeli, Serb, Finnish, Spanish, German, French, Hungarian, Portuguese, Argentine, Brazilian, and Czech. BOTTOM LEFT: Japanese edition. BELOW: Draft, page 202.

publisher insisted and I caved in. I don't think it sold very well and they didn't put out the second volume. Another Israeli publisher has put out *Maus* now, complete with Vladek's broken syntax. It's the first time the second volume has been published in Hebrew.

It's surprising that there was no *Maus II* in Hebrew until now.

A lot of Israelis did read *Maus* in English. But some of the antipathy may have had something to do with the fact that the book doesn't posit Israel as the happy ending to the Holocaust, like, say, *Schindler's List*. If anything, this is a diasporist's account of the Holocaust. But that wasn't an ideological decision on my part—it simply had to do with the fact that my parents came to America. Had they gone to Tel Aviv instead of New York after Stockholm, it would be a very different book…probably one without pictures. I don't know that I would have become a cartoonist there. But Israel doesn't really figure as a factor in this story.

were often these big swimming balloons with just a few poorly placed words in them. But the most vexing translation issue that came up was when that publisher became adamant about not translating Vladek's language into a broken version of Hebrew. I took great umbrage, but finally—try to argue with an Israeli…just ask a Palestinian. It was just impossible to get them to do it right. They kept telling me that there is no such thing as broken Hebrew, that everybody learns it within a few months, and if they still speak in a broken Hebrew they would be like greenhorns, and that's a whole different thing. I knew that it wasn't true. Other Israelis confirmed it wasn't true, but my

IF your book was about ISRAELI Jews, what kind of animal would you draw?

I have no idea. …porcupines?

EXCUSE ME…

153

I'm talking a little bit past my pay grade here, but it seems to me that the ways the Holocaust has been mythologized and used in Israel are different than the ways it gets mythologized and used in America. Perhaps it's because I don't show Vladek as a more heroic character, perhaps it's because of the implied insult in using rodents for humans, perhaps it's because Israel doesn't figure in the work, or maybe it's just because they have a surfeit of their own Holocaust narratives and comics have been alien to them till the day before yesterday.

One change I had to make in the first Israeli volume is worth noting. I had to agree to redraw Pesach Spiegelman's hat as a fedora and not refer to him, as Vladek had, as a Jewish policeman on pages 121 and 126 of Maus. Though under Haskel's protection in the ghetto, he evidently wasn't a member of the Nazi-installed Jewish police like Haskel. Menachem, Pesach's son (who was adopted by Haskel after they both survived the war), lives in Israel and threatened to sue the publisher for libel. Being called a Jewish policeman collaborating with the Nazis is no small

charge. Pesach died during the war, but only in Germany and Israel, interestingly, do libel laws extend past the grave.

So I begrudgingly changed Pesach's hat, indicated that Pesach was Haskel's older brother (not, as Vladek misremembered, his younger one), corrected Pesach's wife's name to Bluma (I had arbitrarily called her Rifka, needing a first name in one balloon), and appended an author's note at the end of the volume summarizing Menachem's understanding of the past, including the fact that Haskel was cleared of war crimes charges in a postwar trial in Poland. I wrote that I had made minor revisions in my art and text but found them

an intrusion into the process of trying to visualize and inhabit my father's specific memory and understanding of what happened. That process is indeed the story inside the story of Maus... What is being portrayed is, specifically, his [Vladek's] story, based on his memories. This kind of reconstruction is fraught with dangers. My father could only remember/understand a part of what he lived through. He could only tell a part of that. I, in turn, could only understand a part of what he was able to tell, and could only communicate a part of that. What remains are ghosts of ghosts, standing on the fragile foundations of memory. The issue of memory is central to the sequel to *Maus* that I'm currently working on: *From Mauschwitz to the Catskills and Beyond...*

I did consider incorporating my cousin's competing memories of Haskel and Pesach into what became the second volume of *Maus* but just couldn't find a way to do it.

What about in Germany?

The initial response to the book in Germany in 1987 was intense. I was at the Frankfurt Book Fair when it came out, and was aggressively barked at by a reporter: "Don't you think that a comic book about Auschwitz is in bad taste?" I liked my response. I said, "No, I thought Auschwitz was in bad taste."

Germany hasn't had much of a comics culture till recently, though they seem to appreciate Carl Barks' *Donald Duck* and, I guess, *Asterix*. Around 1978 I developed a relationship with Zweitausendeins, the German publisher of deluxe facsimiles of R. Crumb's sketchbooks, who commissioned me to do as I pleased with the covers of their translations of Boris Vian novels. And as soon as they heard I was starting on the long *Maus* book they optioned the rights—way before there was an American publisher. We had discussed how it would be translated and of course it was essential to keep Vladek's broken language intact. It's not decoration; it's at the heart of the work. My publisher said, "Well, we'll just have to do some kind of Germanized ver-

sion of Yiddish." But when getting ready for publication years later, Zweitausendeins got a very well-respected translator who came back with Vladek talking like some kind of hip Berliner. My publisher then insisted that if they did Vladek's language in a kind of Yiddishized German, no German would understand it, and it would also be seen as anti-Semitic. I found that difficult to wrap my brain around, figuring either it was anti-Semitic, or nobody would understand it—but if they didn't understand it why would it come off anti-Semitic? They tried a second time, and I checked it out with the help of a German cartoonist friend by retranslating it back into English inch by inch. It clearly wasn't anywhere near what I needed, and I ended up buying my rights back, not knowing if I could find another German publisher. My agent eventually found a perfect home for it, Rowohlt, and it was translated by a husband and wife team: one a professional translator, and the other a German journalist whose parents were Eastern European Jews. They did a good job, I'm told, of catching the specifics of the linguistic oddities rather than ignoring the issue or resorting to some kind of Borscht Belt Yiddish shtick.

Wasn't there also an issue about the swastika on the cover?

Yes! As I mentioned, I insisted that foreign editions use the same cover as the Pantheon book, but my German editor, Michael Naumann, explained that they had a problem since it's against German law to show a swastika, except in works of serious historical research. He got

FACING PAGE: Sequence, page 121, and altered in Israeli edition, 1990. ABOVE: Draft, page 202.

IT WAS WEIRD BEING A JEW IN ROSTOCK ON YOM KIPPUR...

I VISITED THE BUILDING OF GYPSY ASYLUM-SEEKERS FIREBOMBED BY SKINHEADS IN AUGUST.

THOUSANDS OF LOCALS FROM THE NEIGHBORING BUILDINGS CHEERED.

THEY GAVE THE HITLER SALUTE: "FOREIGNERS OUT! GERMANY FOR GERMANS!"

AFTER WWII MAYBE TH JEWS SHOULD HAVE IN HERITED GERMANY..

THE GERMANS COULD'V RESETTLED IN PALESTIN

TWO YEARS OF WEST GERMAN MARKS HAVE MADE DOWNTOWN ROSTOCK QUAINT, PRETTY, AND PLUSH.

BUT THE WORKERS' LIVING UNITS ARE STORAGE LOCKERS WHICH STRETCH FOR MILES, DULL AND DEHUMANIZING.

UP TILL NOW GERMANY HAS BEEN A GENEROUS HOST TO ATONE FOR ITS GENOCIDAL PAST. IT HAS LET IN ANYONE SEEKING ASYLUM.

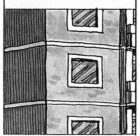

BUT EAST GERMANS DON' IDENTIFY WITH THE NEV BEGGARS FROM THE RE OF THE CRUMBLED EMPIR

A SLIGHTLY DRUNK OUT-OF-WORK WORKER SAW US...

IT'S SAD. ROSTOCK IS NOW WORLD-FAMOUS...

GYPSIES WERE LIVING NOT ONLY INSIDE THE BUILDING BUT IN THE BUSHES, WITH NO SANITATION. IT WAS A PIGSTY!

WE COMPLAINED, BUT THE MAYOR DID NOTHING. HE'D JUST GET **MORE** GYPSIES. NO ONE LIKED WALKING IN SHIT TO GET TO THE MARKET.

HEY, I LIVE IN SOHO AND I MEMBER HOW ANGRY WE G ABOUT PLANS TO DOCK A PRISON BARGE NEARBY

I READ IN THE "TIMES" THAT GERMANY IS DEPORTING GYPSIES BACK TO ROMANIA. THAT'S NOT THE WHOLE STORY.

THEY ARE PAYING OFF ROMANIA TO TAKE BACK REJECTED ASYLUM-SEEKERS AND IMPROVE GYPSY LIVING CONDITIONS INSIDE ROMANIA, BUT GYPSIES SEEKING ASYLUM STILL GET FOOD, SHELTER, MONEY, AND THE RIGHT TO APPEAL. HARDLY CATTLE CARS EAST.

OF COURSE, THE NAZIS DI MURDER ABOUT 500,000 G SIES... IT MAKES FOR AN E BARRASSING P.R. PROBLEN

ABOVE: Visiting the former East Germany in 1992: "A Jew in Rostock" (*The New Yorker*, 12/07/92).

T'S NOT JUST ROSTOCK, OR NLY IN THE EAST... THERE'S EO-NAZI VIOLENCE IN GER-MANY EVERY SINGLE DAY.
KOHL DIDN'T SEEM ALL THAT WORRIED TILL THE JAPANESE SAID THEY WERE AFRAID TO COME OVER OR INVEST.
WHILE I WAS IN MUNICH I HAD DINNER AT A RESTAURANT WITH A FRIEND. HE WARNED ME AGAINST OVERREACTING.
HE QUOTED WILHELM BUSCH:
W. Busch
"ONCE YOUR REPU-TATION'S SHOT, YOU CAN GET AWAY WITH QUITE A LOT."
OVERHEARD SOME CCENTED ENGLISH T THE NEXT TABLE.
VE SHOULD ASK HIM VOT'S GOING ON THERE IN NEW YORK.
I FIGURED THEY WANT-ED TO COMPARE THEIR RACISM WITH OURS...
WHAT ABOUT NEW YORK?!
VE'LL BE THERE FOR A VISIT IN DECEMBER.
TO "CATSKILLS ON BROADVAY," YOU TINK IT'S HARD TO GET TICKETS?
N REUNIFICATION DAY, IN RANKFURT, I MARCHED GAINST RACISM WITH VER 10,000 GERMANS...
WE WERE ALMOST ALL OVER 30 AND UNDER 50, EXCEPT FOR OUR BABIES, IN STROLL-ERS AND SNUGLIS.
ON THE SAME DAY, IN STUTTGART, NEO-NAZI THUGS VANDALIZED A JEWISH CEMETERY.
THE KIDS TODAY, THEY DON'T KNOW FROM GUILT.
E YOU **REALLY** GOING ROSTOCK ON YOM PPUR?
UH-HUH.
WELL, I KNOW YOU'RE NOT RELIGIOUS...
BUT IF YOU DON'T INTEND TO FAST AT LEAST EAT LIGHT.
ANOTHER FRIEND SAID, "THE SITUATION HERE IS DRAMATIC BUT NOT REALLY SERIOUS."
I GUESS THAT'S TRUE... BUT IT ALWAYS RAINS WHERE IT'S WET.
© art spiegelman '92

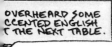

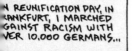

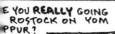

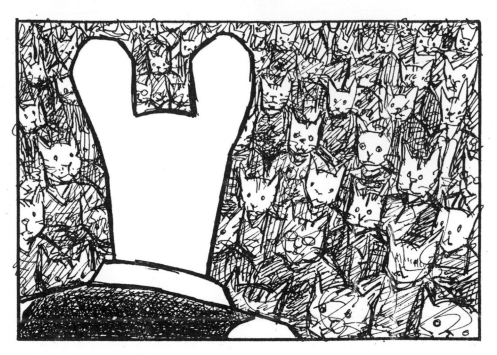

BETTER A SONDERPREIS THAN A SONDERKOMMANDO

Published as "Playing Cat and Mouse in Germany," *Newsday*, July 29, 1990

(In mid-June I was invited to the Fourth Biannual Comics Salon in Erlangen, Germany, to receive an award for the German edition of Maus...*The "Sonderpreis," the "special prize," consisted of a medallion, a certificate, and two yard-long loaves of regional bread baked into the shape of Max and Moritz, Wilhem Busch's 19th-century cartoon characters which inspired the creation of* The Katzenjammer Kids. *What follows is my acceptance speech.)*

It's a strange thing for a mouse to receive an award from a gathering of cats, for telling a story of how cats killed mice. It's a strange thing for me as a Jew to be here in Germany, getting an award for describing how your parents and grandparents were accomplices in killing my grandparents and family. It's strange for you also, giving me this award—it might indicate a lack of sensitivity on your part, considering our history. But giving me this award could be seen as the result of a guilty conscience, a kind of War Reparations to a child of a survivor.

Ach! Here come the Jews again, inflicting guilt, and on such a pleasant evening. We have a long tradition of inflicting guilt, it goes all the way back to those damn Ten Commandments ("Don't have dirty thoughts about your neighbor's spouse," "Be nice to your papa and mama..."). It's more polite to talk about Remorse or Responsibility rather than Guilt. It's an unpleasant concept, guilt. But, actually, I think that guilt has an undeservedly bad reputation. I feel guilty about lots of things: the homeless, the underclass of Blacks all over New York, my impure thoughts, not using recyclable products... and perhaps guilt is a useful civilizing agent that keeps people from behaving worse than they otherwise might. Guilt can be an explosive thing to live with, but it may be the price we humans must pay for civilization while trying to learn true Empathy. And, frankly, I would feel safer with a guilty Germany than with one that could get caught up in a nationalist euphoria now that it looks like, in some ways, Germany has won World War II 45 years after it ended.

You see, my father never wanted to set foot in Germany after the war. He never got bread shaped like Max and Moritz from your parents or grandparents. His bread was shaped like a coffin, and most of the time he didn't even get that. My father was very upset whenever I bought a product made in Germany. He was very upset that I drew cartoons with a German-made rapidograph pen. When I was a kid I thought his attitude was kind of stupid, but now I think he was right...

Rapidograph pens give a very insensitive mechanical line. I now draw exclusively with a Pelikan fountain pen; it's German also, but far more flexible and lively.

Dankeschön for this prize.

permission from the German government to use my cover! But in the wacky world of unintended consequences, a few years later I saw a documentary about skinheads in Germany and one of them had a *Maus* bookstore poster in his bedroom—it was the only swastika he could get, poor fella!

After Michael left Rowohlt and became Schroeder's Minister of Culture, my relationship with Rowohlt soured, but I found an incredibly sympathetic editor, Hans Balmes, at Fischer Verlag, who has kept my work very visible in Germany.

In general have you had any bad experiences in Europe or elsewhere doing promotion for the book? Has anti-Semitism ever surfaced?

Not overtly, but under the surface I'd say Philip Roth got the British version of anti-Semitism down cold in *The Counterlife*. When I was first being interviewed and written about in London, in the '80s, I'd sometimes encounter a subtext, a hostile attitude I couldn't get a handle on. At first I thought it was just a general English chilliness or maybe simple disdain for comic books. It was probably just my paranoia, but it did seem connected to my Jewishness. I'd never come up against anything like it in America. Maybe it's because, as I've heard, Jews control all media here in the USA. I wasn't aware of anything that palpable in Italy or France or even in Germany, but maybe the language barrier protected me.

When I was interviewed in Sweden, I sometimes did feel like The Other, but it was all very affable. One journalist, a very big, apple-cheeked and blond fellow, politely listened to me deliver a long and convoluted answer to some question, then after a long pause he just said, "Did

anybody ever tell you—you remind me so much of Woody Allen." It seemed to come out of nowhere. I giggled and said, "And, y'know, you remind me exactly of Ingemar Johansson!!" Johansson was a famous Swedish prizefighter in the '50s, and the only famous Swede I could think of besides Ingmar Bergman, who this fellow really did not resemble.

The nuances of differences in the cultural reception to *Maus* fascinated me. In France there was no problem dealing with *Maus* as a comic—even provincial newspaper reviews talked about panel breakdown and drawing style when it first came out. In Italy, they seemed really interested in the psychology of father and son, not at all in World War II. And I rarely ever understood their questions. It was the opposite of the German response. In the 1980s, there really was a serious German response to *Maus*, but interviews focused almost entirely on the story in the past, not at all on the intergenerational conflict.

Did you feel beleaguered doing publicity for *Maus*?

I tend to identify with journalists, and, to a point, I like the interview process as a way to sift through my thoughts about what I've done. It's just that after a while it started seeming like *Groundhog Day*. I suppose it led to the image of me perched on a pile of corpses with a lot of microphones aimed at me in the "Time Flies" section of *Maus*.

RIGHT: Study, page 202.

ABOVE and OVERLEAF: Progressive drafts of page 201, the first page of "Time Flies."

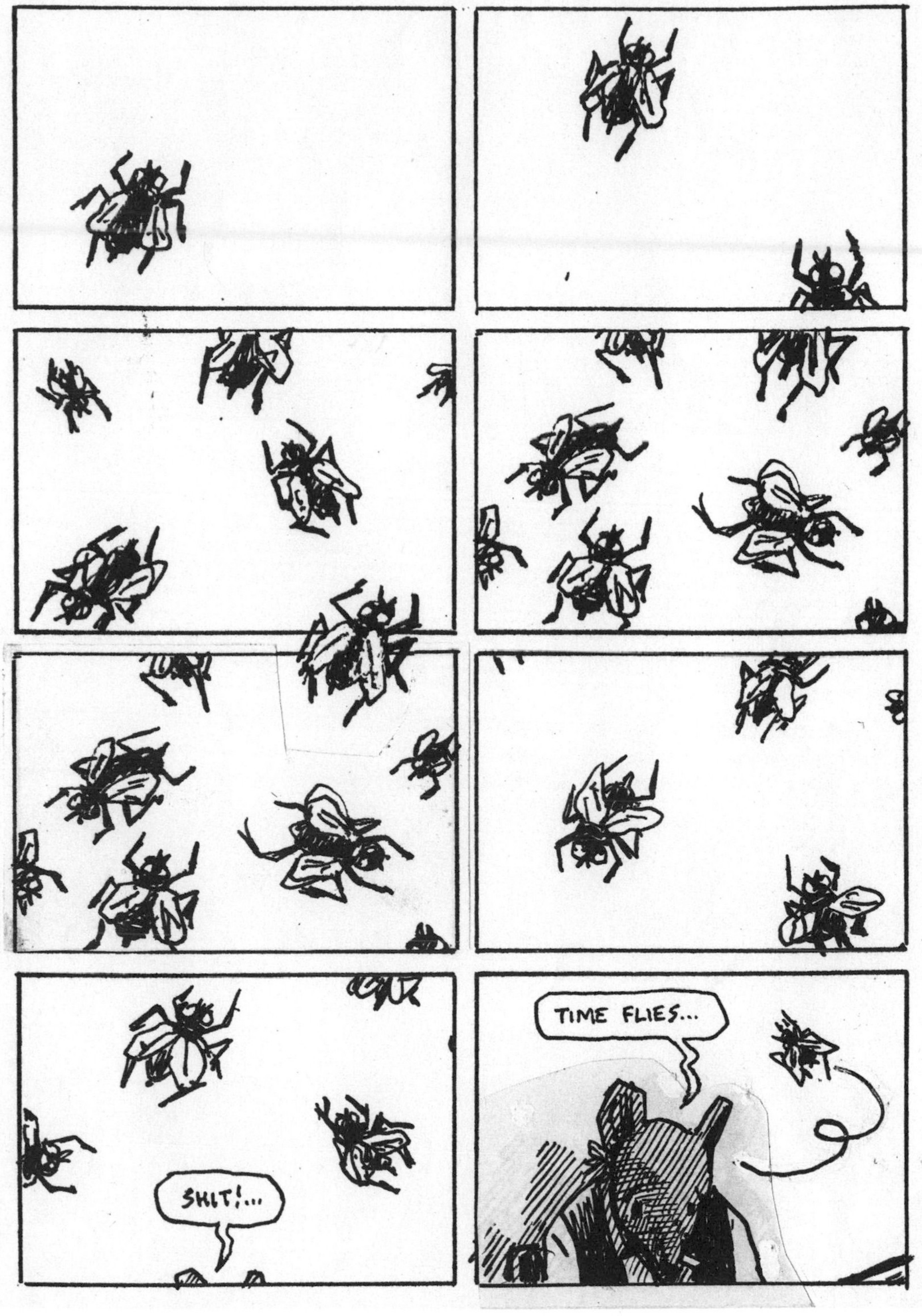
SHIT!...
TIME FLIES...

Time flies...

Vladek died of congestive heart failure on August 18, 1982...

Françoise and I stayed with him in the Catskills back in August 1979.

Vladek started working as a tinman in Auschwitz in the spring of 1944...

I started working on this page at the very end of February 1987.

In May 1987 Françoise and I are expecting a baby...

Between May 16, 1944, and May 24, 1944, over 100,000 Hungarian Jews were gassed in Auschwitz...

In September 1986, after 8 years of work, the first part of MAUS was published. It was a critical and commercial success.

At least fifteen foreign editions are coming out. I've gotten 4 serious offers to turn my book into a T.V. special or movie. (I don't wanna.)

In May 1968 my mother killed herself. (She left no note.)

Lately I've been feeling depressed.

Alright Mr. Spiegelman... We're ready to shoot !...

ABOVE: Final art (actual size), page 201.

WHY C

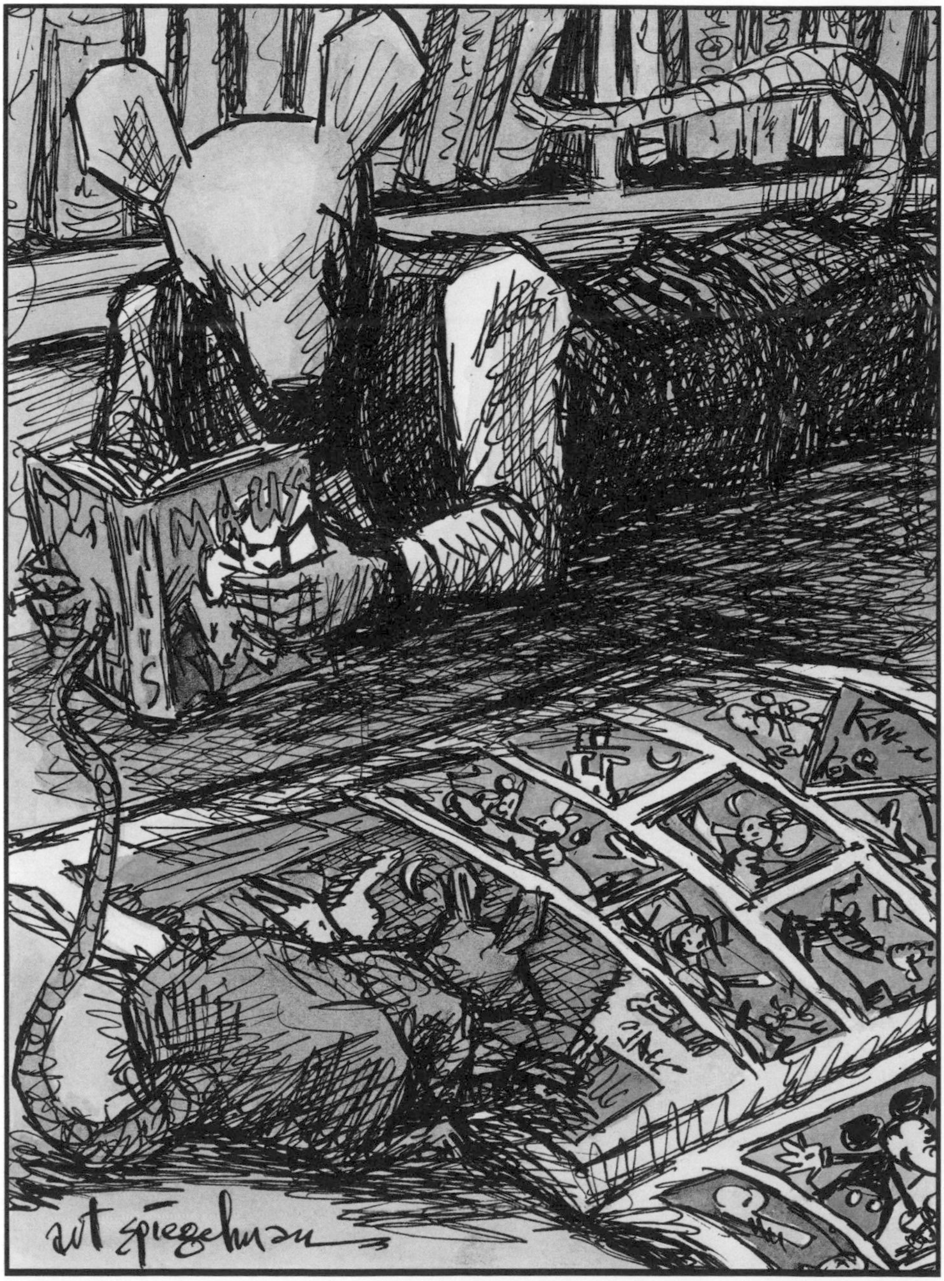
MAUS
MAUS
art spiegelman

OMICS?

The first page of the "Time Flies" section in *Maus II* is to me one of the key pages in the book.

I think of "Time Flies" as a *MetaMaus*-like commentary on the whole project. It sits on top of *Maus* the way my character in a mask sits on top of all those bodies. In its earliest iterations it was longer and more abstract, starting with a page of flies buzzing around in blank panels. I was really moving back into my "experimental comics" land. It certainly focused one on how time moves through panels by just having this page that could either be flies in space or flies in time. But it would have tipped things way too overtly toward my interest in comics structure and the whole section already risked unbalancing the book. Mostly I kept my structural interests sublimated and below most readers' consciousness, like the hidden swastika on the first "Time Flies" page. It's difficult to see, but it's there: made out of the angled black shadows that define the spotlight on the drawing table. The blacks travel through the page and make a broken swastika that holds the page together on top of the pyramid of bodies.

Every time I re-read *Maus*, I find things I hadn't seen before.

My obsessions with comics form do inform the whole book, but it's not exactly a matter of trying to embed—what do they call those extras hidden inside a video game that you might stumble into

LEFT: Self-portrait, 1999.

on your twentieth play? Oh yeah. Easter eggs! Perfect for a Jewish book! I didn't even have a concept like that in my head, let alone a phrase for it. All these things are part of what it meant to make the drawings around a restructuring of my father's narrative.

You once told NPR, "I think anybody who liked what I did in *Maus* had to acknowledge that it couldn't have happened in any other idiom." Why tell *Maus* in comics form?

It never could have occurred to me to tell it in any other form. Comics are just the idiom that naturally came with trying to fulfill a mandate I wasn't conscious of fulfilling when I went back to *Maus* in '78—my mother's desire that I somehow tell her story. What consciously motivated me was the impulse of wanting to do a long comic that needed a bookmark.

What is most interesting about comics for me has to do with the abstraction and structurings that come with the comics page, the fact that moments in time are juxtaposed. In a story that is trying to make chronological and coherent the incomprehensible, the juxtaposing of past and present insists that past and present are always present—one doesn't displace the other the way it happens in film.

Is it useful to talk about other forms—like cinema, or theater, or music—to describe what comics does?

I guess every medium has its strengths and limitations. Despite the commonly held belief that comics are some sort of storyboard waiting to become a movie, maybe a certain kind of comics has more to do with theater. It offers encapsulated sets of abstractions that trigger a response. But theater, like cinema, straps the audience to a chair and hurtles you through time. Whatever's dramatic in a comic can be stopped with the blink of an eye.

Most dramatic films have a hard time with the Holocaust as a subject because of the medium's tendency toward verisimilitude and reproduction of reality through moving photographic images. Holocaust movies usually look like they're populated by fairly well-fed inmates, for example. Movie makers can get involved in some kind of crazy trying-to-rebuild the camps, as opposed to creating it as a mental zone, which *Maus* does.

Do you have a functional description of comics?

I just stuck with the dictionary definition I found years ago: comics are "a narrative series of cartoons." That's what my old

American Heritage Dictionary said, and it'll do. No definition can be all embracing and inclusive; definitions are more like indications rather than recipes. One can always keep refining and say, "No, no, a narrative series of juxtaposed cartoons. And why 'cartoons,' maybe we should use the word 'diagrams,' or just 'drawings'!"

But what was very useful for me is that when I looked up the word "narrative" right after reading the definition of comics, I found that a narrative is a "story," and that a "story" comes from medieval Latin historia. It refers to those very early comic strips made before the invention of newsprint: the stained-glass windows that told a superhero story about that guy who could walk on water and turn it into wine. This is how in English, the word "story" has come to mean both story as in stories of a building and story as a narrative. And at that point one is steered toward an architectural model for what a comic is, something very basic about comics narrative. Comics pages are structures made up of panels, sort of the way the windows in a church articulate a story. Thinking of these pages as units that have to be joined together, as if each page was some kind of building with windows in it, was something that often happens overtly in *Maus*, and sometimes is just implicit in the DNA of the medium. I also used to talk about the page by comparing it to a paragraph with each panel or tier of panels like a "sentence." But all these comparisons are attempts to get at what the architectonics and grammar of a narrative

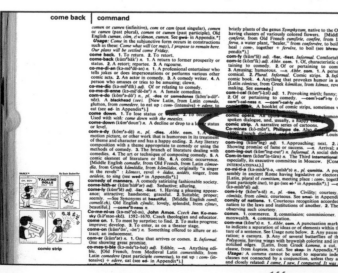

LEFT: *The American Heritage Dictionary*, 1973. Definition of "comic strip," with Ernie Bushmiller's diagrammatic *Nancy* as the definitive example.

ABOVE: Draft, page 76. RIGHT: Pages 76 and 77.

pane of glass has become a panel in the bottom half that repeats what you saw in the top half in terms of the family groupings. One pane shows Anja, Vladek, and Richieu. And you get to see that again on the bottom half of the page as the characters are identified in the caption below. And naming is what helps give people their individuality in a visual sign-system where everybody tends to look alike. Something is told about each of these characters in each temporal panel that repeats a fragment of the large top panel. It allows me the space to give necessary information. At the end of the page, that system is interrupted by an inset of Vladek on his Exercycle, as at the top, but there's no frame around this drawing—which allows re-entry for a moment into the present that holds that page together as a unit.

might be in the case of comics. I end up having all of these top-pieces and foot-notes and end-spots, because a page is a visual paragraph.

One of the most literal iterations of the architectural approach to a page appears when Vladek re-enters into Anja's family's household before they're moved to the ghetto, on page 76. There's kind of an inset window at the top, of Vladek in the "present," on his Exercycle, saying that the house looked exactly as it did before he'd been taken off to prisoner of war camp. Your eye enters into the household through a window—in that sense a classic "cinematic" panel. The panes of that window into the household are then repeated as the bottom half of that page, so that now, literally, each

Then, no longer mediated by the window panes, the next page shows the members of the household interacting at their dinner table. It demonstrates the sort of thing that

comics are made to do, allowing a visual narrative to not be a simple reiteration of the text. Richieu spilling soup is a sub-narrative that happens while Vladek is being caught up on what life in Sosnowiec has become under the Nazis. It's completely visual and offers different information than that in the speech balloons. It's what comics do. I always had to be cautious in *Maus* about how to remain in service to my father's deposition—his voice—while not reducing the images to mere illustration.

You've emphasized that, as a form, comics doesn't have to be about good drawing per se. Instead you talk about what you call picture writing.

If anything, the comics that I have the most difficulty looking at are the ones that are more illustrative, because they're the ones that break the spell rather than create it. There's a sub-genre of comics known as *fumetti*—the photo-comics that have been very popular in Mexico and Italy—that tend to really not work well formally. Photos tend to have too much information; it's very hard to suppress the unnecessary. The work that actually works best deploys information visually to give you the necessary signs and not too much more. I love doodle-writing and prefer signs made with verve that express the personality of the sign-maker.

The cartoon is a drawing that gets to essences. And narratively, comics are an essentialized form of diagramming a narrative movement through time. For me, it's an art of compression that breaks narrative events down to their most necessary moments. If you show the same panel three times, that is a lot of time passing. If

you want to indicate that kind of duration in film it takes quite a few attenuated beats to make it register. These sorts of things really preoccupied me when I was working on the strips in *Breakdowns*.

Can you talk more about your formal interests previous to *Maus*?

I'd become interested in the avant-garde cinema of the '60s—nonnarrative films by Ken Jacobs, Ernie Gehr, and Stan Brakhage became important to me. They led me to ask: at what point do juxtaposed pictures become comics? And that led me to do a page in 1973 called "Don't Get Around Much Anymore." It mostly shows a man sitting in his living room, and details of that room. The captions are just flat, alienated sentences, like "The refrigerator is empty." It was based on something I'd written while depressed and I decided to use it as a scenario for a comic even though—or, rather, because—almost nothing happens. I wanted to find out what could happen when nothing's happening. Everything's "out of sync" between the words and the illustrations—they're not functioning as illustrations so much as visual tugs that keep your eye moving around the page but trapped on it, which I guess is why the strip is titled, after the Duke Ellington song, "Don't Get Around Much Anymore." There's only one moment of continuous movement on the page: out the window, your eyes skitter back and forth between two panels to see a kid bouncing a ball. It's the only escape into life and physical movement. It was a hard-won page, one I remain inordinately proud of, trying to find a new way of using these words and pictures together to indi-

cate the languor and timeless depression I still remain prone to: the feeling that "Oh, here I am again, trapped, and I ain't never gonna be anywhere else."

With *Maus* I had the advantage of having, once I untangled it, about as compelling a story as one ever needs to find, about surviving in extremis. I spent an incredible

LEFT: *Breakdowns* cover, 1978. ABOVE: Original art for "Don't Get Around Much Anymore," 1973.

amount of time figuring out what I absolutely needed to draw and couldn't get away with not drawing. It's not exactly the same as minimalism, but it is about getting it down to what can't be not there. If something could be presented in one page rather than three, I would aim for that. I kept trying to figure out what could be left unsaid but still be clear. A corollary of Beckett's "every word is a stain on silence and nothingness," I guess.

People often confuse comics for a genre, instead of a medium—why?

In America comics got very wrapped up with the superhero in the '30s and '40s. The superhero craze went into remission after World War II in favor of other genres like horror and crime comics—maybe readers realized that Captain America couldn't KO Hitler without a lot of Russian soldiers at his back. The heroes came back with a vengeance by the early 1960s after the Comics Code shut down a lot of the more lurid paths comics were taking toward older readers. And superheroes of course are the genre most American readers think of first when they think about comic books at all. The medium of comics simply deploys a bunch of pictures, usually with text, to get you your story. This delivery system, even when superheroes were flying high, also delivered westerns, romance stories, funny animal stories, war stories, adventure stories, science fiction stories, horror stories—lots of genres. If I was disposed toward any genre, it was humor comics. So *Maus* was an attempt

to see what one could do as a structured thing that had the beats and rhythms of a novel. After finding that my first book, *Breakdowns,* had an audience of maybe 3,000 readers or so at best, with most of them kind of uncomprehending or uninterested in the concerns that filled that work, I had to think about another part of my private definition of comics, which is "intended for reproduction." Comics are different than working on a suite of paintings, say, that use comics terminology. At least for me, the printed object is the final goal, not the original drawing that might be printed. Woody Gelman, my mentor at the Topps Bubble Gum company, put it perfectly: "You can make one and sell it for a million dollars, or make a million and sell them for a dollar each." I had a class bias toward the latter and *Breakdowns* sure wasn't going to get me there.

Would you talk about the tension between avant-gardism and the mass-market audience that informs your work?

I guess it's no different than the tensions in any other medium, though until my generation I don't think there was such a thing as avant-garde comics—pleasing the audience was the name of the game. Although catering to a mass-market isn't at the core of my work—except, I guess, for my decades-long day job with the Topps bubble-gum company—I do like to communicate clearly. It's a pleasure. And as soon as one is involved with communication, one's already suspect in the High Arts. A lot of

ABOVE: Splash panel from a comics-format review of Michael Chabon's novel *The Amazing Adventures of Kavalier & Clay* in *The New Yorker,* 10/30/00. RIGHT: "Comics as a medium for self-expression?" *Print* magazine cover, May–June 1981.

170

what happens in the more rarefied precincts of art is that the word "communication" gets replaced by "communion," and one is involved in a kind of religious experience with the artist as shaman. And that's really different than, "Hey, I'll tell you a yarn." Or even "I'll tell you a parable," if you want to be didactic. And it's always been either a skill or a deficiency that I try to make contact with other people. From my own solipsistic place, I still try. Comics lend themselves to direct communication and clarity. Their show-and-tell attributes are well suited to the task by inviting both halves of the brain to grapple with the information. I like the idea of telling you how a magic trick is done and still making it seem like magic when you see it. It's actually at the heart of what interests me...

What was your working process like and what materials did you use to make *Maus*?

MAUS [working process]

Starting with a transcript of interviews with Vladek (A) I search for a page breakdown in my notebook (B), looking for a logical narrative unit of information to form a drawn page out of key scenes. Tracing through a transparent grid (C), I write and rewrite possible text (D) to "spec" them to fit in my boxes, trying out various page schemes (E, F, and G) until arriving at a workable page draft (H).

A.

was healed, they let me out, they – back, back to this place where I was before. And then I met you see the French man. And uh, I – and he helped me a little, and I helped him a little with English, and this way it was.

So it was going on another few weeks; I don't remember exactly the time, but all the time what I was in Dachau, it was – from the end of January – (coughs) Oh, I made a mistake; I told you, I t – now I remind myself, the date when we went out from Auschwitz. We didn't go out in October-November. We went out from Auschwitz January twenty-fourth, 1945. This I know exactly now the date. And I was in Dachau from February till the – till the middle of April. This time I was in Dachau.

I came back, then I – it was may[be] a little bit easier because I met the Frenchman, and I got us the soup every day, because I had for some – I had something to exchange for another shirt, to have an extra shirt. Not to have it on, but only to clean it. And to – only for showing, that it is clean.

But after a few weeks, I got sick. I couldn't eat, couldn't sleep. And I got typhus fever. Of course every day it was a lot of people dying there from typhus, who didn't come even to the infirmary. At night time, when I went down, when I went down to the, to the W.C., it was full full on the place, on the whole corridor it was full with dead people; you ha – couldn't go, you couldn't go through; you had to go on the heads and this. And this was so terrible, because you stepped on the head it was so slippery. The head, it, the, the skin was slippery, and you were, you always thought that you are falling down. And this was every night.

Now – that time I said, "Now it is my line. I will be laying here so like this one, and somebody will step on me. But the next day I was still alive, and when the guy came from the infirmary, and checked how the people [are] looking here, so I approached, I told him, "I am feeling very bad, I didn't sleep at night," and he took the fever and he has seen that I have very high fever. And he took me right away to the infirmary.

ART: How come the other people weren't taken to the infirmary also?

VLADEK: Because he couldn't do it. It happened so fast, they couldn't survive. He – he got this –

[Off mike: "Everybody straighten up!" Voice continues shouting some kind of instructions.]

VLADEK: He got this sickness, and he died after a couple of hours, after three-four hours. And – secondly, they didn't come every day to check; they came every second day, every third day. They didn't worry if, if another hundred

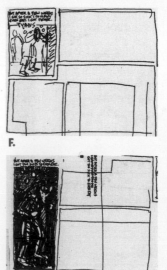

B.

C.

D.

E.

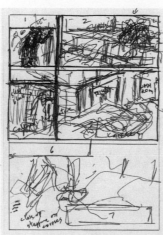

F.

G.

I.

J.

Studies are then made for each panel, usually in progressively darker colored felt-tip pens, to bring the drawing into focus (I, J, K, L and M). The finished art is then traced and further tweaked directly in ink through a light table. (All pages were drawn at the same size as published in *Maus*.)

L.

M.

H.

K.

N.

I decided to work same size as publication: the drawings that you see in the book are in exactly a one-to-one ratio to the size they're drawn. It affords a degree of intimacy, an "I-thou" kind of moment, that doesn't allow me to take refuge in the minimizing of one's hand tremor and possible lack of skill that comes with the common practice of drawing upsize. Drawing large and reducing the art for publication tightens it up, makes the art look more crisp and "professional." Reproducing one's own mark—offering up a facsimile of one's own handwriting—makes it more like looking into an actual journal, like Anne Frank's or maybe Alfred Kantor's notebook drawings of Auschwitz. This approach led me to abandon most of my art supplies for *Maus*, to work on typing paper. Using stationery store supplies, bond paper, typewriter correction fluid and a fountain pen made it more like writing, like offering up a manuscript, something made by hand.

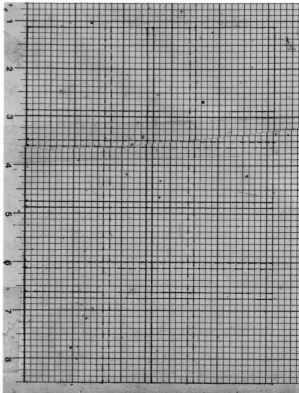

I worked with a fountain pen—actually two. One was a standard gold-tipped Pelikan fountain pen, and the other one was a specially retooled Pelikan made by an old penmaker, Kenneth Planck, who modified the pen-point to make it as flexible as a dip-pen and hollowed out the chamber so it could withstand waterproof India ink. I went through a few of those Planck pens and mourn him and that old pen.

I used cleanstick address labels available at the stationery store (which I now regret terribly as I watch the glue-stains appear) and Liquid Paper for my corrections, and a lot of tracing paper and layout paper for my studies.

So the process for doing *Maus* started with a thumbnail breakdown of my visual "paragraph," then a direct sketch draft of the page—just a first stab at making the page. Then I'd refine each of the panels, trying to find a zone somewhere between the casualness of handwriting and the precision of a typeface. I could only arrive at that by doing study after study, building up layers of tracing paper with colored felt-tips.

All these pages were drawn over a grid that could use either three tiers or four tiers—or a combination of the two—and panels were initially divided in halves, thirds, or various increments in a relatively flexible but important-to-me set of possible layouts for each page.

ABOVE: 30-year-old plastic *Maus* grid. RIGHT: Same size study with Planck pen for one of the largest panels in *Maus*, page 34.

Can you explain the importance of the grid to making the book?

I'm kind of a structuralist who keeps losing his moorings. I give myself an absolutely mathematical set of rules, and then find that I'm not quite able to make my things work within the set of rules, so I poke at the edges of the rules and then violate them until I come up with something that does the job. I tried to keep to my grid because it made the beats and rhythms easier for me to find when planning the story. I worked with the metaphor that each panel was analogous to a word, and each row of panels was a sentence, and each page was a paragraph. It's an imperfect metaphor, but OK, so is *Maus*. And the grid allowed those sentences and those paragraphs to be visible to me. It was

very important that I not be constructing run-on sentences that could just go until a sequence was finished. And the size of a panel was of utmost importance, whether a picture takes up a half a page, a third of a page, or is part of a row of narrow boxes has meaning.

Why in some places do you have these very large panels that seem to take over the page?

A large panel allows you to enter, pause, and understand the importance of a moment. These weren't just used decoratively; though they do fight "eyeball fatigue," they had to be used sparingly. The goal was to make a Very Long Comic Book, but I believe comics are an act of intense condensation. The phrases have to be

condensed a lot to fit into those little balloons. Without wanting to do a caption-
box kind of storytelling, I did want it to
have the kind of urgency that would come
from a story told as efficiently as it could
be. Of course sometimes that efficiency
needs to make room for "inefficiency"
and digression, when that's called for in a
given sequence. Still, everything had to be
rewritten until it took up as little physical space as it could. Maybe it was very
mouselike that way.

Panel sizes were very consciously thought-
through, so that in the first volume the
largest image in *Maus*, up until the end,
is when my parents first see a swastika,
on page 34. It's a half-page-sized picture.
The only panel that's bigger in that volume
is at the very end when they come to the
gates of Auschwitz, and the image bleeds,
literally—this is the phrase that printers
use—off the edges of the page; and that's
the largest panel.

That page, when my parents first see a
swastika on the train to a sanatorium in
Czechoslovakia after my mother's breakdown, is an exact visual rhyme of that
last page of the book's flashback to the
gates of Auschwitz. I didn't expect this
to consciously register on most readers,
but assumed it would somehow reverberate anyway. At the top of the page there's
a half-height horizontal of a train, then
a conversation in a tier of panels seen

through the window of the train, and then
the half-page of the passengers looking
out at that swastika through the window.
At the end of the book, there's the truck
across the top half-height horizontal panel
with Vladek and Anja being herded into it;
then a conversation in a tier of panels seen
inside the enclosed truck, and then the
large last panel. (That panel on page 159
also has, although somewhat off-center
and smaller, the same swastika
on the side of the truck that
was the flag in the center of the
panel on page 34.) The scale
and size of panels is just one of
the most basic aspects of structuring and making a comics
story happen.

**Can you say more about the
quality that you were trying
to capture in condensation?**

It was a matter of finding
how much drawn information
each box could contain and
imply in a flowing and easy-
to-unpack way so that things
remain prioritized. The story
should unfold in the reader's
head. It involved a lot of
rejiggering each composition
to make it work, and since I
was drawing so small, it was
sometimes difficult to make
sure that the essentials stayed
clear. Working in that scale
kept me honest, because there
just wasn't room for flourish
and decoration. Somewhere
between composition, eye-flow,
and information content, the
panels had their own demands,
and had to be worked out
individually and then with each
other on the page.

How long did it take you on average to work through each page?

I have no idea. None. There were pages that came together relatively fluidly, and other ones that didn't, and not always the ones you'd predict: something that seemed relatively straightforward could take me forever to get right . . . and in some cases I never did, dammit. I struggled for days on one nothing panel of Vladek's father hovering over him in bed, trying to get him prepared to evade the draft—and for some reason I just couldn't get the scale of those figures to match. It was the first time Vladek's father appeared in the story, and I hadn't figured out how to draw him, but worst of all, I just couldn't accomplish the most basic cartoonist journeyman work of situating one character in space standing next to a bed, and another character lying in it. It's just one example among many, but once I got hung up, I kept spinning my wheels despite dozens of stabs at it. That panel first appeared in *RAW* in 1982, and I even tried to redraw it, along with

TOP LEFT: Page 34 and page 159. BELOW: Study for page 159, including bleed area.

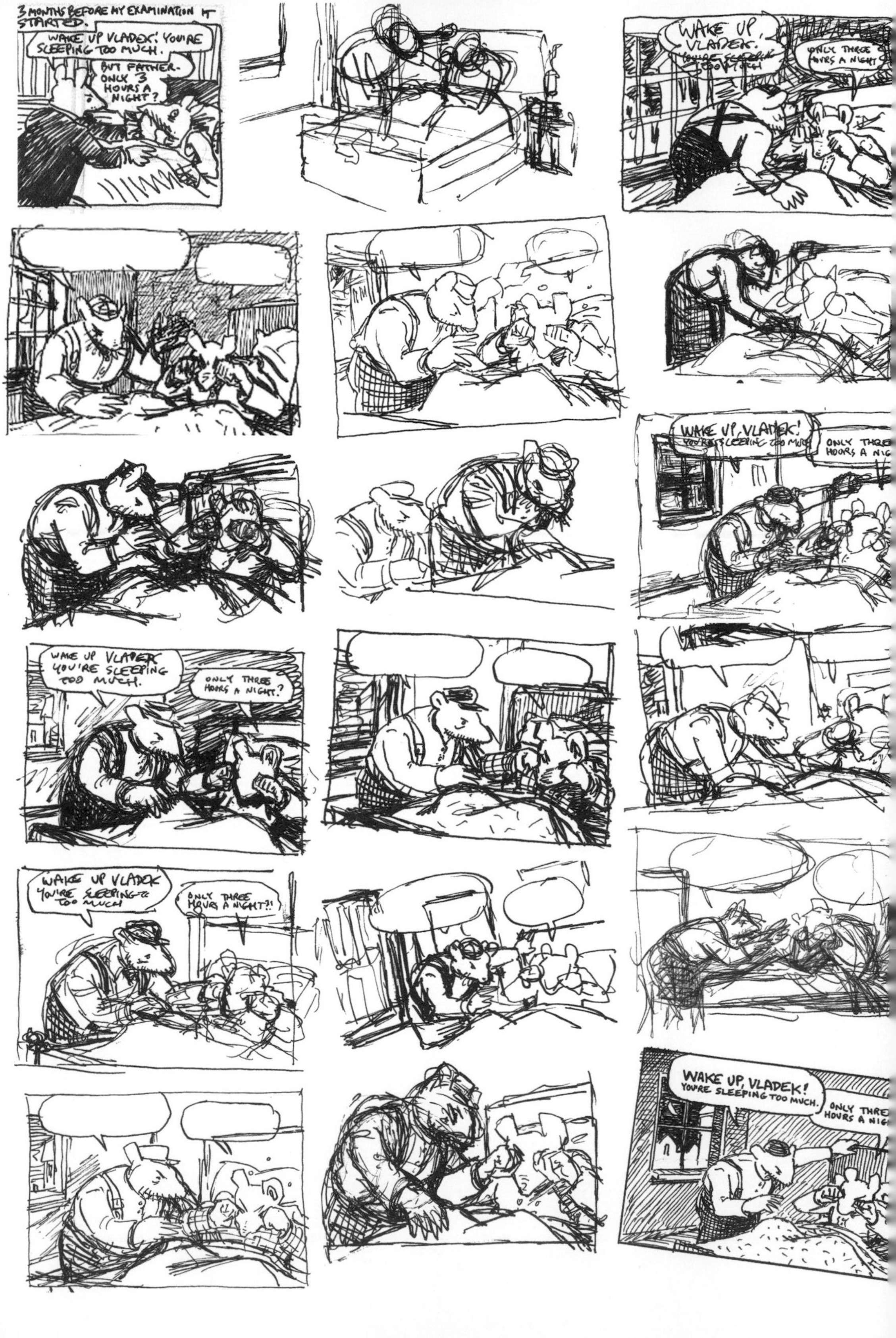
3 MONTHS BEFORE MY EXAMINATION IT STARTED.
WAKE UP VLADEK! YOU'RE SLEEPING TOO MUCH.
BUT FATHER- ONLY 3 HOURS A NIGHT?
WAKE UP, VLADEK.
ONLY THREE HOURS A NIGHT
WAKE UP, VLADEK!
ONLY THREE HOURS A NIG
WAKE UP VLADEK YOU'RE SLEEPING TOO MUCH.
ONLY THREE HOURS A NIGHT?
WAKE UP VLADEK YOU'RE SLEEPING TOO MUCH
ONLY THREE HOURS A NIGHT?!
WAKE UP, VLADEK! YOU'RE SLEEPING TOO MUCH.
ONLY THREE HOURS A NIG

a number of other panels in the early chapters when I was putting together the first Pantheon volume in 1986, but I just never could nail it. Far more complex panels came together with no problem, but I froze up on that one. When I refer to my relatively limited drawing skills, I am not just being modest. Of course, neurosis and obsessive behavior also do play their part.

In the world before computers I found myself rewriting each phrase maybe twenty times. Whatever appeared in a balloon would sometimes look like concrete poetry after I finished distilling the language on a sheet of paper. Since every eighth of an inch was significant, I couldn't use Vladek's language verbatim. I'd find myself trying to rephrase something that still kept the cadences of his broken language, but would reduce it down. So, for example, I might use "go" instead of "walk," since it only took up two characters rather than four. I feel sorry for all the poor foreign translators of *Maus*, since often my decisions can't be replicated in another language.

The bottom half of page 124 is a relatively rare case of staying as close to my father's verbatim language as I could. I'd listen to the tape and choke up while I was listening, so I had to step back and allow it to retain whatever emotional resonances it has. Still,

FACING PAGE: Page 48, a few panel studies for panel 2, 1982. TOP RIGHT: Studies for revised panel, 1986. ABOVE LEFT: 1982 and RIGHT: 1986 published panels.

I was always trying to capture the essence of a cadence, the essence of a phrasing, and obviously the essence of the information.

Were there any instances where you changed Vladek's meaning in editing his language?

Well, on page 193, there's a spotlight that functions differently than spotlights on Vladek and Anja elsewhere in the book. It creates a kind of a sun, a radiant center on the page. I tweaked the phrasing, but only a hair. He was proud of how he looked in his brand-new uniform, and I'm pretty sure that what he said was, "With this uniform, I looked like a million dollars." By cutting the word "dollars" off the phrase, it took on an added meaning: I looked like a million. I looked like six million.

You said that an "architectonic rigor" was required in this book. In certain pages one can really recognize the architectonics, like when Vladek and Art are talking about Auschwitz in the Catskills on page 211...

I should point out a basic principle of the structure in *Maus*: there are two basic time schemes (well, actually three, with "Time Flies"). There's the story in the past that's based on Vladek's deposition and there's the other story of Art and Vladek together. The strands are dealt with very differently in their rhythms and the narrative strategies. The stuff in the present I lived

through, and therefore, whether I was thinking about it or not, I could conjure up every second of it. Though clearly condensed from reality, I could reconstruct those experiences fairly fully and it led me toward what one could crudely compare to theater, since theater also uses condensed dialogue and compressed time, but "feels" like real time as you experience it in its moment-to-moment movements. And those parts of the book are presented as continuous scenes. Beyond the actual use of the mouse masks, there are only rare overt metaphors that break into that present, and the movement from box to box is just that. So I used a dual approach; for the present, I mostly used simple, same-

TOP: Draft, bottom half of page 124. ABOVE: Top of page 193.

sized boxes. The boxes become invisible, so one can enter into them and see, for example, Vladek and Art walking around a Rego Park street.

The sequences in the past required very different visual strategies, and often had to have a graphic notion. The more I strived to create the same kind of verisimilitude for the past, the more hollow and made-up the story would feel. I hadn't inhabited it and I needed to keep Vladek's voice in the foreground. Yet I couldn't not show, in this show-and-tell medium, so I had to find representations that would allow much shorter bursts of interaction between characters in the past story. I built, whenever I could, sequences of people talking, but knew that they couldn't go on that long, and I couldn't move them easily as they talked from space to space because I'd start moving through outer space, through a vast invented space.

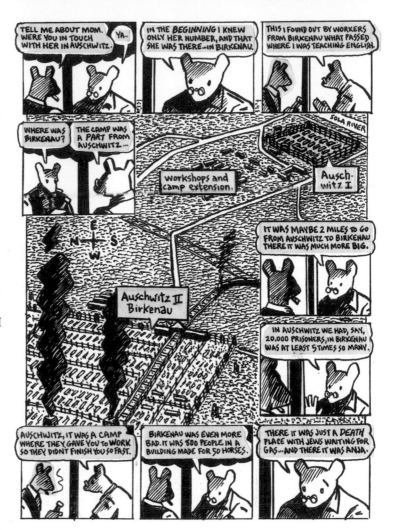

The page when Vladek and Art are talking about Auschwitz in the Catskills is an example of butting those two systems up against each other: Vladek and Art are talking in a series of same-sized boxes—relatively even beats for the conversation. But on this particular page, what would have been a grid of fifteen small boxes, some have fallen away to reveal what's underneath. Since the dialogue is about me trying to get a sense of where Vladek was in Auschwitz, and where Anja was, I'm basically asking for a map. By peeling away what would have been six of the panels on that fifteen-grid page, the map of

TOP RIGHT: Original art, page 211. LEFT: Page 211 grid notes.

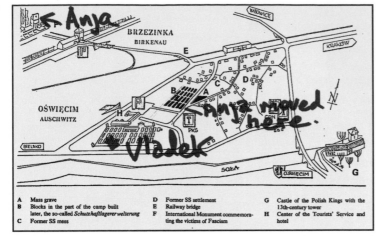

A   Mass grave
B   Blocks in the part of the camp built
    later, the so-called *Schutzhaftlagerer welterung*
C   Former SS mess

D   Former SS settlement
E   Railway bridge
F   International Monument commemora-
    ting the victims of Fascism

G   Castle of the Polish Kings with the
    13th-century tower
H   Center of the Tourists' Service and
    hotel

chapter, on page 24, when Anja gets the letter from Lucia, and says she got a letter that says that "you have a very bad reputation . . . that you have a lot of girlfriends, and that you're marrying me for my money." She's isolated from the man she wants to marry, and the tilted panel shows her literally destabilized; it indicates the emotional jolt that otherwise would have been submerged within the grid of the panels surrounding it. The letter itself is fluttering to the ground in an echoing tilt, so that the panel itself becomes analogous to the letter. And the next tilted panel, on page 33, is a kind of re-referencing of the one on page 24, where Anja begins to have her nervous breakdown. It's an extreme close-up: the lines actually get much more expressionistic; the word count gets smaller inside the balloon, and the lettering gets larger: "But I don't care, I just don't want to live." The panel again shows her nervous, frail, alone, out of step.

Auschwitz that underlies our present is revealed, and the reader can see the leap that has to be made by me from one small box to the next—to climb over the mapped terrain of Auschwitz and understand what my father is telling me.

How did you decide to mess with the griddedness of the page and tilt certain panels out of the tiers?

Well, it animates the page. At the risk of over-explaining, the first time I used a tilted panel it was to represent a photo of Anja that Vladek is inspecting and placing on his mantel, on page 19. It makes sense to place that photo on a separate plane from the other pen-and-ink drawings around it, and that visual device lets it happen. It's on a tilt, a portrait of Anja alone. The next tilted panel is at the end of that very

Spotlights and circles seem to have a special meaning in *Maus* as well...

Circular motifs do have a privileged role in the book, if nothing else, because it's inte-

TOP: Tourist map of Auschwitz and Birkenau. ABOVE: Draft, page 19. Final, part of page 24. Study, page 33.

182

gral to the swastika logo-design. Near the beginning of the first volume, on page 35 [see *MetaMaus,* page 54], it's used rather clearly. Right after the page that has the Jews in the train talking about what's happening in Germany, the swastika is used as kind of a moon hanging over these various visual events, in a chapter called "The Honeymoon." And just two pages after the swastika-moon, on page 37, Vladek and Anja are seen bonding—they're an item, a real couple. They're dancing in a spotlight, and their movements in a sense reference the swastikas that you just saw.

And, of course, circles are always useful for focusing meaning. Vladek is captured and taken to a prisoner of war camp and, in the upper right panel on page 53 of

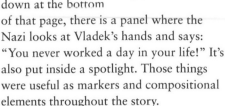

Maus [see *MetaMaus,* page 142], a Nazi says, "We should hang you right here on this spot." It is given emphasis through that circular panel. Diagonally down at the bottom of that page, there is a panel where the Nazi looks at Vladek's hands and says: "You never worked a day in your life!" It's also put inside a spotlight. Those things were useful as markers and compositional elements throughout the story.

On page 68, that honeymoon that we saw earlier is reflected again when Vladek and Anja are allowed to knot, to come together, after Vladek returns from the front. Did we talk about the concept of knottings and branchings? Klaus Wyborny, a German avant-garde filmmaker, did some experiments that involved re-filming classic films like *Citizen Kane,* some D. W. Griffith films, and others. He'd shoot a certain number of frames every time there was a cut in the original film, so that you would see the whole film synopsized down to be, instead of an hour-long film, a minute-long film. A John Ford film would be a lot shorter than a film like *Citizen Kane,* because it had fewer cuts. In the course of doing this, of reducing work down through this mechanistic re-filming, he discovered a new way of talking about narrative. It was a real eye-opener for me—he

TOP RIGHT: Study for pre-title of part 2, page 163. BOTTOM LEFT: Study for part 1 contents, page 9.

183

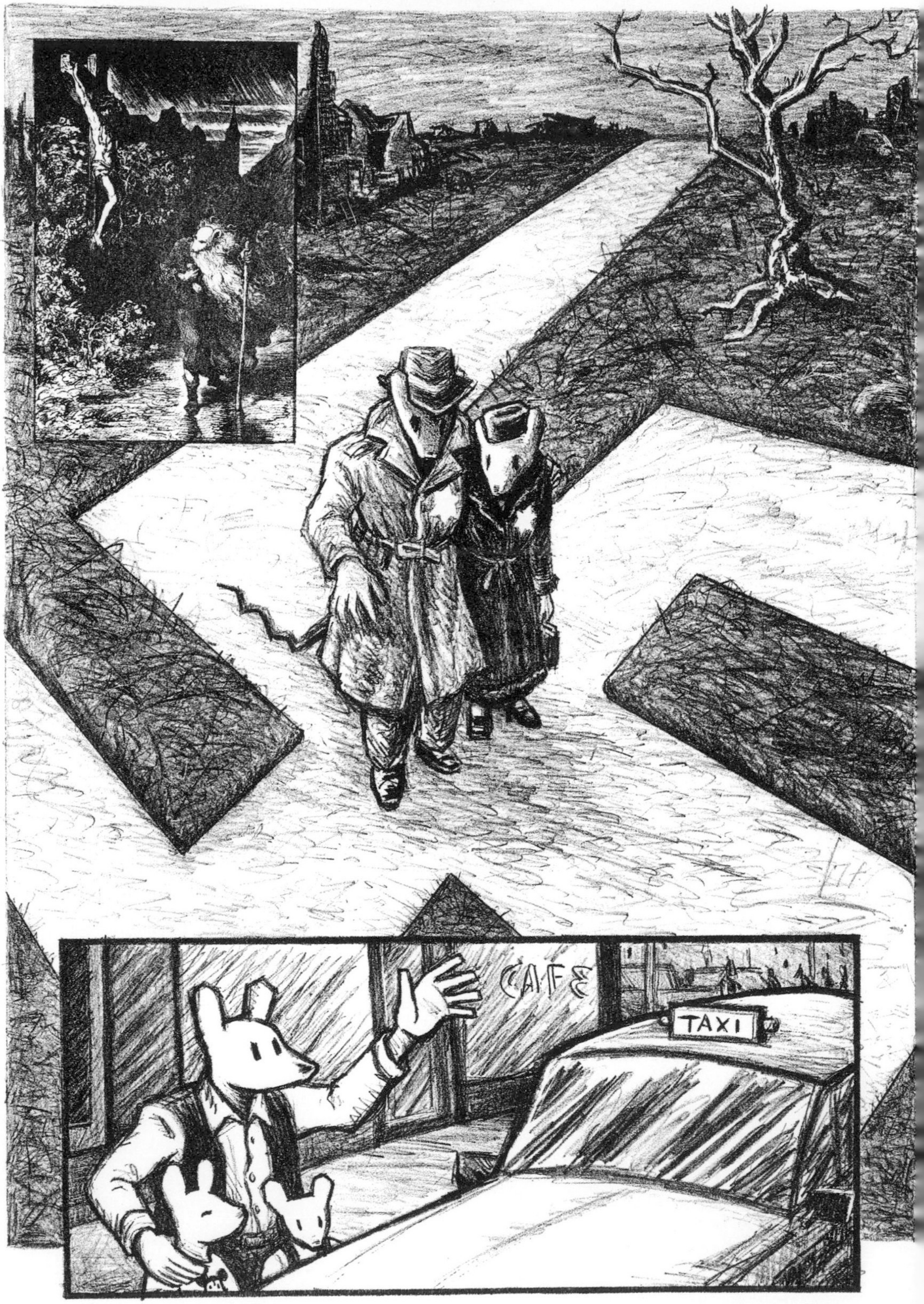
CAFE
TAXI

pointed out that all narratives have central characters who are shown within a few cuts as being in the same physical space. The villain, the hero, the beautiful girl, whatever. That's the setup. Then there are "branchings" wherein the characters move away from that space into different spaces. Two of the three characters might come together, until finally all of them come together; so there are these branchings and then knottings together. Turning narrative into geography is a much more sophisticated way of talking about boy meets, loses, and gets girl. It's a vocabulary that I ended up internalizing.

When Vladek and Anja are brought together on page 68, it's a kind of knotting and that moonlike motif behind them makes it more emphatic. And on the very last page of *Maus*, page 296, after all they'd been through, they finally come together inside that same circle.

Could you talk about the few instances in the book where you decided to use overtly symbolic panels?

It would've been crazy to not use all the elements of visual language at my disposal,

starting of course with using the animal heads, but if *Maus* was overloaded with visual stunts and ideas it would become something else. I had to use such things sparingly. In one panel, on page 127, when Vladek and Anja are in hiding, they walk along a road, not knowing where to go for safety, and the branches of the road form a swastika. It's quite visually dramatic, but that kind of metaphoric use of space couldn't be allowed to overwhelm the literal use of space, because then you wouldn't believe in the space anymore. These metaphoric panels are much closer to the cartoon project, rather than the comics project. The nature of cartooning is to emblematize: the political cartoon, the gag cartoon, is always about finding a representation for many moments in one image. But it's not exactly the same as the more nuts-and-bolts comics-making project of creating individual moments that add up to having some overarching meaning beyond the individual moments.

Walking along the swastika and having choices, all of which left you stuck inside the swastika, was the kind of image-making that's often effective in posters and led to the Op-Ed style illustrations that the *New York Times* used to rely on.

You talk about comics as a form of diagramming, and there are pages in *Maus* that show comics to be diagramming in a very literal way . . .

Yes, like on pages 112–113, where it becomes part of the subject matter of the page. In order to explain where he was

LEFT: "Crossroads." Lithograph. Tandem Press, 1996. TOP: Detail, page 82. ABOVE: Panel study, page 68.

hiding, Vladek actually had to draw a diagram of the very complex bunker that was built under a coal bin. On page 112, a grid of what would otherwise be twelve little boxes in the present is interrupted by a close-up of what Vladek is drawing in my notebook. To explain that bunker to Art, he made a rather clear set of diagrams that I approximated.

The next page moves from the diagram to a cut-away—a dimensional reiteration of the diagram—to bring you back into the story in the past. In that cutaway, which takes up the top two-thirds of page 113, the small box in the lower left shows their bunker, the little corner that they're squeezed into. In the tier right below that, you have pretty much the same panel, the same scene, but now with balloons. It's no longer part of a diagram, but part of the ongoing exposition in boxes that lets the story get told.

Right after that sequence Vladek talks about his next bunker—up in an attic, the entrance concealed by a chandelier. In the three-page version of "Maus" I'd already

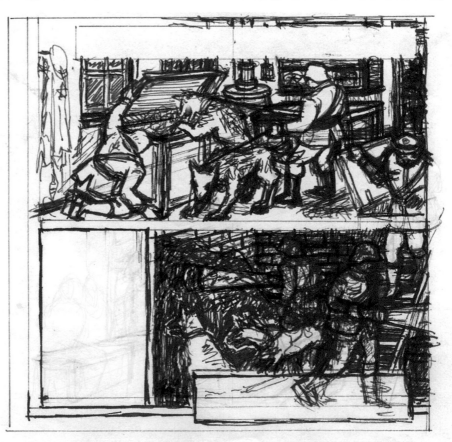

depicted that sequence [*MetaMaus*, page 106] and already had a penchant for diagrammatic panels, but my degree of sophistication about these things had increased a lot in the intervening years.

Page 115 directly reiterates the scene in that three-page ur-*Maus* where the family looks down at the informer sitting below. They then bring him into the bunker and have to decide whether or not to kill him. They take pity on him, let him go, and the next day he does indeed return with the Gestapo. To set that up visually presented a problem in panel progression for me. If I hoped to retain the cut-away of the family huddled in the attic, it had to be on the right-hand side of the page. I just couldn't put it on the left and still keep the horizontal at the bottom of the page showing the Gestapo marching the family off without either losing crucial panels that came before or adding a lot of unnecessary ones. Since we read from left to right, I was stuck with the problem of stacking two panels to the left of the vertical panel and arranging them so the reader would read them in the right order.

Most hastily constructed comic book pages used to ignore this or use awkward arrows to steer you through. I invented a device, the balloon—"He's lying!"—that liter-

ally bridges to a further close-up of Lolek talking. You're yanked down before you're allowed to go to the right, and then see that the division between the two boxes is no longer a division into two separate panels—but the cut-away view with another balloon now traversing the two floors and literally holding it together.

This visual vocabulary reminds me of your *Breakdowns*-era page "Day at the Circuits."

Yup! All of the things I had been exploring in the 1970s in *Breakdowns* to obstruct and slow down narrative comprehension now had to be spun in reverse, since *Maus*'s primary obligation was to its story. "Day at the Circuits" was a page brimming with arrows, so you could read the sequences in five or six different ways as various expansions, contractions, or variants of each other. It was inspired by my early *Mad* lessons in comics semiotics

FACING PAGE, TOP LEFT: Pages 112 and 113. BELOW: Study, page 113. LEFT: Detail, page 115. ABOVE: Study, page 115.

the time I was really entering into it: how does one immerse oneself in the death camps and show that oxymoronic notion of life in a death camp? It was so hard to visualize, but obviously, I had no choice. So I set up a key sequence in which, after wandering around the bungalow colony with my father, page 184 ends with a very small panel, a close-up of a snarling Nazi, that interrupts the fairly fluid stroll through the country. It's very abrupt and perfunctory in that it doesn't allow for the momentousness of the moment. And on page 185, you have no choice but to read down the vertical panels in the present, separated by a wider-than-usual gutter from the panels to the right. Vladek is pulling me back into a discussion of Mala again: if he can avoid talking about Auschwitz, he will. I rather unpleasantly say, "Auschwitz, tell me about Auschwitz." He explains, "Auschwitz was in a town called Oswiecim. Before the war I came often here to sell my textiles. And now, I came again." Now you must read down again and re-enter the past for a second time, literally descending into Auschwitz.

combined with contemplating a circuit diagram and deciding it could make a dandy page layout. But even though it was presented as a "funny page" of some kind, it was very much engaged in the process of trying to understand how eye movement works on a page.

In the second volume of *Maus* there's one sequence along these lines that made effective use of the same principles. Vladek is just beginning to tell me about life in Auschwitz. This is the one section of the book that I most dreaded doing before I started and had me almost paralyzed by

ABOVE: "Day at the Circuits," 1975. RIGHT: Study, page 184.
FACING PAGE: Draft and study, page 185.

You're being dropped down...

You're being dropped down into the hell-pit, into the beast's maw in the lower right, screaming, "Shut up, Yids! To the bath-house. Quick!" With whatever little you might know about Auschwitz, you'd be as scared as Vladek, who explains, "We knew everything by the time we were brought to Auschwitz." That descent is accomplished through strictly formal means, where the top panel has these people in civilian clothes; the second has them now either naked or in striped uniforms being struck by guards; and the third one has them naked, huddled, and being told to shut up and get to the bath-house. The panel structure is how the narrative is delivered.

Which cartoonists contributed to your understanding of comics generally, or to a specific visual vocabulary?

My most central influence was Harvey Kurtzman's *Mad*. It's what doomed me to cartooning. His *Mad* (different from the *Mad* that came after) was a thoroughly radical invention. He left after the first twenty-four issues. It was postmodernism avant la lettre in that it fed off other media, and fed it back to itself through a cracked lens, and was very self-referentially engaged in its own form. One story was just about the sound effects in comic books, told through sound effects. One was an essay on humor's connection to pain and to comics style in the form of a parody/analysis of George McManus's classic *Bringing Up Father* strip. Kurtzman was the editor and formative sensibility of what became *Mad* and has since become American culture: *Mad* really entered deep to inform the second half of the century.

189

He was not only a great artist who was very methodical in his drawing—and taught me ultimately how to build a drawing in layers and take way too long on each panel—but he was also a codifier of important aspects of the grammar of comics storytelling. He was very aware of the beats of a page, for example, using equal-sized panels. He'd use a three-tiered grid, that could consist of one panel across, or two, three or four panels across, but all rigorously the same size to emphasize those beats. His scrupulous parsing of the page is what pulled me into the structure of comics. His content tended to be about culture, in the form of satire mostly. When he was parodying movies he would echo the look of the movie; his parody ads looked like the real advertisement...only more so. It has all become so basic to what we now think of as humor in America that it's almost invisible—everything from Jon Stewart to the latest *Dumb and Dumber* movie has roots in Kurtzman's work. My Topps Bubblegum job consisted of feeding back my *Mad* lessons to another generation in the form of *Wacky Packages, Garbage Pail Kids,* and lots of other less successful cards and stickers, sometimes illustrated by the same artists— my childhood idols!—that Kurtzman collaborated with at *Mad.*

Kurtzman's non-*Mad* work—the war comics that he wrote, edited and sometimes drew in the early '50s, *Frontline Combat* and *Two-Fisted Tales*—were well-researched stories of war that came from, if not an antiwar position exactly, perhaps a humanistic tradition. They were in sharp contrast to the propaganda pin-ups of the other war comics that were coming out during the Korean War, like Stan Lee's *Combat Kelly,* where we'd get a grizzled GI tossing a grenade while snarling, "Here, ya yellow-skinned Commie monkey! This one's from my Aunt Tillie!" Kurtzman's GIs were scared children in uniform who are about to get killed in something too big for them to understand. The stories were somehow profound, historically accurate and they undoubtedly informed the making of *Maus.*

Even in terms of the so-called graphic novel, it makes sense to me that Kurtzman kept trying to sell one before the term existed. One important work that he did after his *Mad* career blew up in his face was a mass-market paperback called *Harvey Kurtzman's Jungle Book.* It was hardly a big commercial success, but it was a collection of new stories that each parodied a different aspect of the mass media, in what now can only be understood as a graphic novel. As a cartoonist and an editor, Harvey was a visionary.

Since I thirsted for approval on some level as a kid, *Krazy Kat* shaped my artistic aspirations. It was the one comic strip that found an escape clause in the general disdain for comics. I liked it well enough, but didn't really understand why it had gotten the cultural high sign withheld from

ABOVE: Anja and Art, 1960. RIGHT and OVERLEAF: "A Furshlugginer Genius," *The New Yorker,* 3/29/93.

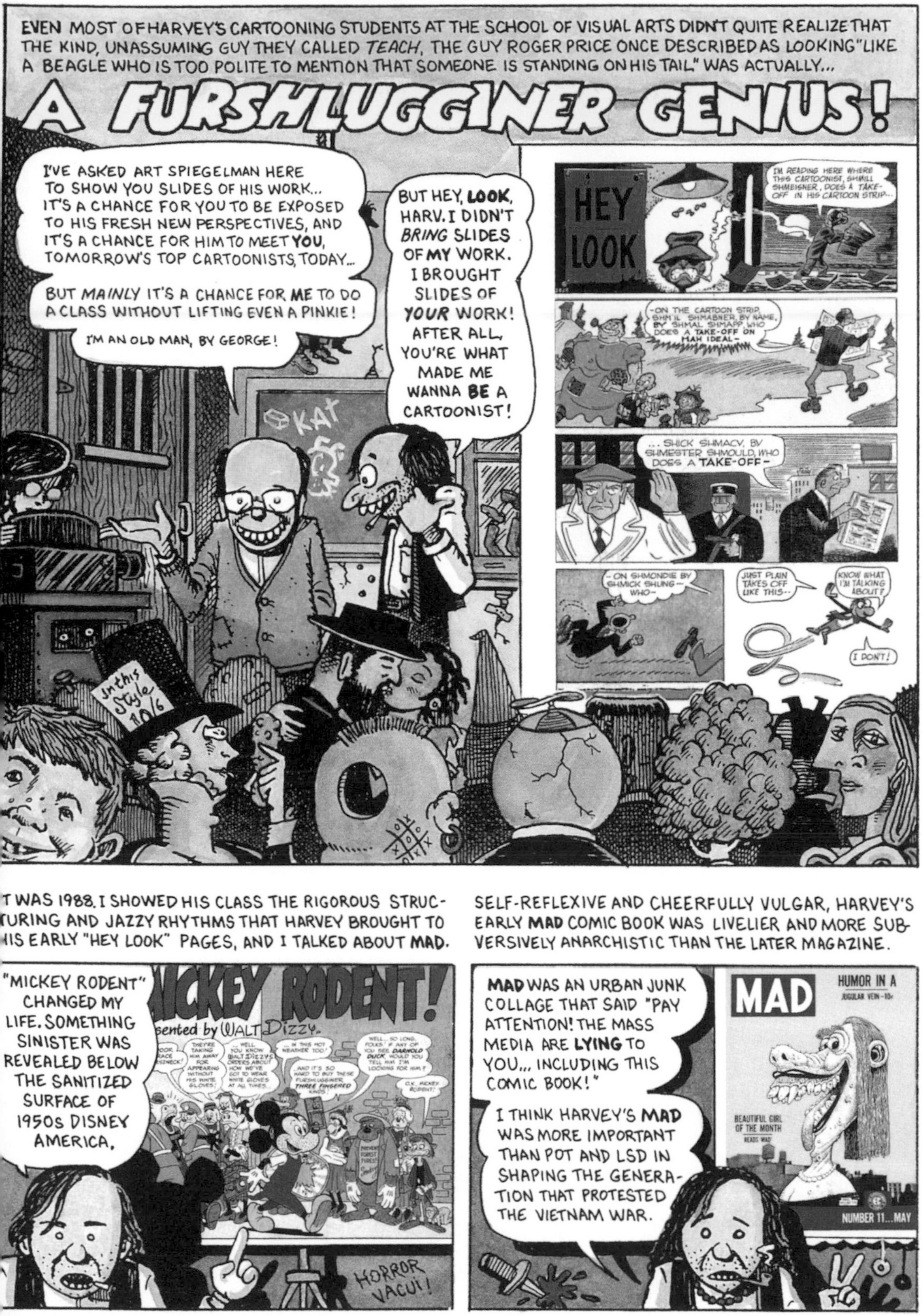
EVEN MOST OF HARVEY'S CARTOONING STUDENTS AT THE SCHOOL OF VISUAL ARTS DIDN'T QUITE REALIZE THAT THE KIND, UNASSUMING GUY THEY CALLED TEACH, THE GUY ROGER PRICE ONCE DESCRIBED AS LOOKING "LIKE A BEAGLE WHO IS TOO POLITE TO MENTION THAT SOMEONE IS STANDING ON HIS TAIL," WAS ACTUALLY...
A FURSHLUGGINER GENIUS!
I'VE ASKED ART SPIEGELMAN HERE TO SHOW YOU SLIDES OF HIS WORK... IT'S A CHANCE FOR YOU TO BE EXPOSED TO HIS FRESH NEW PERSPECTIVES, AND IT'S A CHANCE FOR HIM TO MEET YOU, TOMORROW'S TOP CARTOONISTS, TODAY...
BUT MAINLY IT'S A CHANCE FOR ME TO DO A CLASS WITHOUT LIFTING EVEN A PINKIE!
I'M AN OLD MAN, BY GEORGE!
BUT HEY, LOOK, HARV. I DIDN'T BRING SLIDES OF MY WORK. I BROUGHT SLIDES OF YOUR WORK! AFTER ALL, YOU'RE WHAT MADE ME WANNA BE A CARTOONIST!
HEY LOOK
I'M READING HERE WHERE THIS CARTOONIST, SHMILL SHMEISNER, DOES A TAKE-OFF IN HIS CARTOON STRIP...
-ON THE CARTOON STRIP SHM'IL SHMABNER, BY NAME, BY SHMAL SHMAPP, WHO DOES A TAKE-OFF ON MAH IDEAL-
... SHICK SHMACY, BY SHMESTER SHMOULD, WHO DOES A TAKE-OFF-
-ON SHMONDIE BY SHMICK SHUNG--- WHO-
JUST PLAIN TAKES OFF LIKE THIS--
KNOW WHAT I'M TALKING ABOUT?
I DON'T!
KAT
In this Style 10/6
T WAS 1988. I SHOWED HIS CLASS THE RIGOROUS STRUCTURING AND JAZZY RHYTHMS THAT HARVEY BROUGHT TO IS EARLY "HEY LOOK" PAGES, AND I TALKED ABOUT MAD.
SELF-REFLEXIVE AND CHEERFULLY VULGAR, HARVEY'S EARLY MAD COMIC BOOK WAS LIVELIER AND MORE SUBVERSIVELY ANARCHISTIC THAN THE LATER MAGAZINE.
"MICKEY RODENT" CHANGED MY LIFE. SOMETHING SINISTER WAS REVEALED BELOW THE SANITIZED SURFACE OF 1950s DISNEY AMERICA.
ICKEY RODENT!
sented by WALT DIZZY.
THEY'RE TAKING HIM AWAY FOR APPEARING WITHOUT HIS WHITE GLOVES!
... WELL YOU KNOW WALT DIZZY'S ORDERS ABOUT HOW WE'VE GOT TO WEAR WHITE GLOVES AT ALL TIMES..
... IN THIS HOT WEATHER TOO!
..AND IT'S SO HARD TO BUY THESE FURSHLUGGINER THREE FINGERED KINDS!
WELL... SO LONG, FOLKS! IF ANY OF YOU SEE DARNOLD DUCK, WOULD YOU TELL HIM I'M LOOKING FOR HIM?
O.K., MICKEY RODENT!
HORROR VACUI!
MAD WAS AN URBAN JUNK COLLAGE THAT SAID "PAY ATTENTION! THE MASS MEDIA ARE LYING TO YOU... INCLUDING THIS COMIC BOOK!"
I THINK HARVEY'S MAD WAS MORE IMPORTANT THAN POT AND LSD IN SHAPING THE GENERATION THAT PROTESTED THE VIETNAM WAR.
MAD
HUMOR IN A JUGULAR VEIN
BEAUTIFUL GIRL OF THE MONTH
NUMBER 11...MAY

HARV DIDN'T CHANGE THE CULTURE ONLY BY CREATING A NEW MODE OF SATIRE. AT THE HEIGHT OF THE KOREAN WAR HE EDITED, WROTE, AND DREW WAR COMICS—NOT JINGOISTIC TRASH BUT THOROUGHLY RESEARCHED NARRATIVES WITH GREAT MORAL PURPOSE.

NEXT SLIDE, PLEASE.

NO SMOK

VA-VA VOOM! WOO WOO! HOTCHA!

HEH, HEH— WRONG SLIDE. "LITTLE ANNIE FANNY" WAS FROM A LATER POINT IN HARV'S CHECKERED CAREER.

HIS DRAMAS REFLECTED HIS HUMANISM. THEY WERE ABOUT THE PAIN AND SUFFERING OF WAR.

NO MACHO HE-MEN, ONLY SCARED KIDS. THE ENEMIES WEREN'T DEMONS, ONLY OTHER PEOPLE.

TWO-FISTED TALES

I ANALYZED HARVEY'S VISUAL STORYTELLING STRUCTURE TO SHOW HOW HE CREATED A PRECISE FORMAL "GRAMMAR" OF COMICS.

I MENTIONED HIS IMPORTANCE AS AN INNOVATOR OF EDITORIAL FORMATS, AND CONCLUDED BY TALKING ABOUT HIS SKILLS AS AN EDITOR WHO NURTURED THE TALENTS OF OTHERS.

EACH PANEL ON THIS PAGE IS BUILT ON VERTICALS. SO, NOW TAKE A LOOK AT THESE PANEL RHYTHMS...

THE CLASS SAT IN AWE. SARAH DOWNS, HARVEY'S ASSISTANT, WAS WEEPING SOFTLY. ONLY HARVEY'S SWEET, FRAIL VOICE, TREMBLING WITH THE PARKINSON'S DISEASE THAT RAVAGED HIM, BROKE THE SILENCE.

GEE, ARTIE. THAT WAS TERRIFIC! COULDJA COME BACK NEXT WEEK AND GIVE US THE SAME LECTURE AGAIN?

AFTERWARDS HARVEY GLOWED WITH PLEASURE. HE WARMLY CLASPED MY HAND.

GOSH, IT WAS INSPIRING! YOU EVEN MADE ME WANNA DRAW COMICS. THANK YOU, ARTIE!

NO, HARVEY. THANK YOU. FOR EVERYTHING!

I LOOKED LOVINGLY AT MY ROLE MODEL, AND FOR A LONG MOMENT WE EMBRACED...

ARTIE!... ARTIE!...

OH, HARVEY!

MY MENTOR WAS WHISPERING SOMETHING TO ME. HE WAS BARELY AUDIBLE:

ARTIE... PLEASE... LET GO... YOU'RE CRUSHING MY DAMN GLASSES!

WHAT—ME W
1924 - 1993

other strips I cared for. Still, I used to keep finding ways to write papers about *Krazy Kat* when I was in junior high and high school in the early '60s. If the assignment was to compare a poem to another work of literature, I'd write about the poem and then compare it to *Krazy Kat*. Y'know the joke about the British kid, the French kid, and the Jewish kid in school, where they're asked to deliver a paper about the elephant? The British kid gives a talk about the elephant and India and the Empire, the French kid delivers a paper called "The Sex Life of the Elephant," and the Jewish kid's paper is "The Elephant and the Jewish Question." Similarly, whatever the essay question was, my answer was *Krazy Kat*, since *Krazy Kat* lends itself to interpretation, and I felt I might be able to sneak that past my teacher's radar in a way I couldn't have if I had written about "Big Daddy" Roth's Rat Fink

Panel from *In the Shadow of No Towers*, 2004.

cartoons or even *Mad*. I only came to love the strip fully as I ripened into adulthood. And after the traumas of September 11—when old comics were the only culture I could bear—*Krazy Kat* sustained me.

The comics I saw as a really young kid imprinted themselves on me deeply—like Little Lulu, the first comic character I copied assiduously, and Donald Duck. Carl Barks' Donald Duck had a lot more depth for me than Clark Kent. Whatever the funny animal surface was, I could climb way further behind that surface

than I could when trying to identify with, say, Peter Parker's problems. And Uncle Scrooge's pince-nez seem to come from the same optician as the ones that Vladek wears in *Maus*.

I discovered *Little Nemo* thanks to Woody Gelman at Topps. He was an inveterate collector of old paper when nobody else seemed interested in such things. He rescued most of McCay's originals from destruction and had runs of all the old Sunday pages. McCay's work was sublimely aware of the structural implications of his beautifully built pages, and studying them was very important to my development. Chester Gould's *Dick Tracy* is another of my core influences. We were talking before about comics as diagrams, as picture writing, and Gould was the consummate diagrammer, a stunning artist who was often dismissed by comics fans as a lame draftsman. His drawing was really made for comics, reducing things down to not just diagrams, but diagrams within the diagrams, so the panels are filled with labels and arrows pointing at things, like the "two-way wrist radio." His art had the vehemence and delirious violence of George Grosz or Otto Dix, and few of the illustrative values of, say, *Prince Valiant,* or *Flash Gordon.* Dick Tracy's two-dimensionality and its strong graphic use of black and white made me respond very deeply. I was pulled into Gould's approach as a kind of ultimate cartooning, making what I called Blueprint Expressionism.

IT'S AMAZING TO ME!... SO MANY OTHERWISE EDU-CATED PEOPLE NEVER EVE HEARD OF WINSOR McCA

BUT McCAY CONVINCING MAPPED OUT THE MIND' INNER DREAM-SCAPE DECADES BEFORE ANY "SURREALIST" DRAPED P MELTED CLOCK ON A TRE

AND HE UNDERSTO COMICS... LOOK AT TH NEMO PAGE FROM 19 AND IMAGINE IT AS FIRST APPEARED, AS LARGE AS THIS WHO NEWSPAPER PAGE.

HE LOVED HIS NEW ARTFORM PASSION-ATELY, AND IDEALISTICALLY REFUSED TO PATENT HIS TECHNIQUES. SADLY, THEY WERE PIRATED AND PATENTED BY AN UNSCRUPULOUS BUSINESSMAN, JOHN BRAY, MORE INTERESTED IN ANIMATION AS COMMERCE THAN ART.

EVEN MORE SADLY, HIS EMPLOYER, WILLIAM RANDOLPH HEARST, DIDN'T SHARE HIS PASSION FOR ANIMATION. JEALOUS OF THE ENERGY McCAY EX-PENDED IN THIS AREA, HE USED HIS MONEY AND HIS POWER TO SQUELCH McCAY'S ANIMATION CAREER.

FOR THE LAST TWO DECADES OF H LIFE McCAY WAS USED BY HEAR MOSTLY AS AN ILLUSTRATOR OF THUR BRISBANE'S BOMBASTIC D LY EDITORIALS. TECHNICALLY IMP SIVE, BUT RELATIVELY SOULLES THESE DRAWINGS SEEM ULTIMAT TO BE A WASTE OF McCAY'S GIFT

ABOVE: Review of *Winsor McCay, His Life and Art*, by John Canemaker. *USA Today*, 6/23/87.

Harold Gray's *Little Orphan Annie* influenced *Maus* fairly directly. Like Gould, Gray had found a cartoon-based—rather than illustration-based—vocabulary for moodily representing melodrama. Amazingly, his stories, corny as they were and as reprehensible as I found their underlying politics, could make me cry, something I never felt from superhero comics. *Little Orphan Annie* offered me a more direct validation that comics could actually carry emotional resonance despite (or probably because of) the abstraction of the language and visuals.

Some people have noted the influence of Will Eisner on your work. You once mentioned that there's only one moment in Maus where you really felt you were drawing inspiration from Eisner.

Eisner's *Spirit* had been an influence on me from the time I was fourteen or fifteen. I really liked its voraciousness, the pulling everything from movie posters to postage stamps to any old thing that might represent a panel, to thinking about windows as panels; all of those things were useful to me. But very often it would move, even in the older work, let alone in his graphic novels, toward a kind of heavy-handedness. He was a more overt influence on some of my pre-*Breakdowns* underground comics work, but in the first chapter of *Maus*, on page 17, there's a caption, something about Vladek taking a trip to Sosnowiec, that is designed to look like a train ticket—it's a Will Eisner trope. I remember debating whether to leave it in or not since it really called attention to itself in ways that don't operate with the same level of humility that the other kinds of invention that move through the work do. It was a moment of, "See, I'm clever! I can do this! I can do that!" Ultimately, it just activated the page better, so I let it happen.

Your early Viper stories seem to be influenced by Eisner's page layouts. Do you see those stories as related at all to your later work?

AIEEE! The horrors of leaving a paper trail. Well, the Viper stories were a cluster of formative and misguided pieces that I

LEFT: "Dead Dick," *Lead Pipe Sunday*. Two-sided lithograph, 1990.
RIGHT: Obverse side (detail) of *Lead Pipe Sunday*. "The Bastard Offspring Art and Commerce murder their parents and go off on a Sunday Outing."

did right around the same time as the first three-page "Maus," but still part of my apprenticeship as an underground cartoonist. It's as if I got the memo that said "Okay, now we're gonna do transgressive comics!" and I tried to do stuff that would make S. Clay Wilson's twisted pages for *Zap* look downright wholesome.

At the same time, I was also trying to assimilate the "cinematic" things that Will Eisner and Jack Cole had done in the 1940s. Those Viper stories were a regrettable but necessary part of my learning curve, and all I can say in my defense is: "At least I didn't go into advertising."

I was drawing the most perverse and violent atrocities I could, but not even consciously connecting them at all to the atrocities in my own life and background. The first Viper story I did was about a little kid named Eddie Putz who, with the Viper, rapes his mother and then murders his father. Oddly, it didn't register on me as having much to do with me, except for me trying to stretch toward the forbidden zone.

After I'd done several Viper stories, Justin Green provided the example of going into the real forbidden zone of one's own guilts, doubts, and nightmares directly, as expressed in what became *Binky Brown Meets the Holy Virgin Mary.* That concept of approaching things by looking directly at what had happened in one's own life made it possible for me to get in touch with a different kind of cartoonist than I was able to be before.

Isn't there a Viper character named Willie?

Yes. I did one story with some immigrant kid, Willie Wetback, a deracinated immigrant who said things like, "Gracias, Monsieur!"—speaking in a different dialect in every panel. He gets off a bus and eventually finds himself decapitated and fucked in the neck by the Viper, since that was the most depraved thing that I could come up with. I'm not even sure

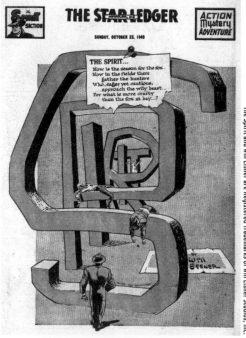

TOP LEFT: Study, page 17. ABOVE: *Spirit* splash page, © 1949, Will Eisner Studios, Inc.

I connected the character's name to my father's; I thought of Villie as me. It was all somehow connected to the Oedipal crucible, but not knowing how to grapple with it. What is one going to do with the sewage of one's own brain?

When I look back and say the Viper strips were Oedipal, maybe part of that is: "So, how did you get born when you weren't supposed to?" In a way, taking on my parents' Holocaust story was a way of getting to the primal moment of my birth, because there was no way that they were both supposed to be alive and coupling after World War II. It is a specific journey that has nothing to do with history and everything to do with history: one or both of these people is supposed to be dead, which means that I'm not supposed to be here. It involved the very primal quest to find your parents before they are your parents. Maybe the Viper was a way to fantasize

my parents' death in a world permeated by evil, and trying to express that in a form that echoed 1940s American comic books made before I was born.

Speaking of American comic books, you've written about Bernard Krigstein several times.

Krigstein was a painter who became involved in comics mainly to earn a living. He was slumming in comics at first and then started taking it seriously, discovering it as an untapped medium. He worked for the same comic book publishing house that Kurtzman worked for, EC Comics. Unlike Harvey, he was an illustrator. He never wrote his own material but was really invested in what could happen from box to box, and how the pages worked. He's an example of an artist who adapted his vocabulary to reflect the story he was presenting: a Chinese scroll–inflected look for a Ray Bradbury adaptation that took place in ancient China, a very Expressionist set of marks for a horror story he signed "Doctor Caligari Krigstein." It became a clue for me that one could use different surfaces to represent different emotional states.

TOP RIGHT: T-shirt design, 1973. ABOVE: Viper splash page, "Pop Goes the Poppa," in *Real Pulp Comics* no. 1, 1971.

Krigstein was quite intellectual and analytic about the process, but was rarely given scripts up to his ambitions. When he found one in 1955 called "Master Race," he had something that was virtually singular in postwar popular culture: a comic about the death camps. It was planned as a six-page story with the kind of mysterioso O. Henry–like twist ending that EC specialized in. Krigstein saw its potential and pleaded for more pages. I came to think that all the EC horror comics were a secular American Jewish response to Auschwitz but this was the only time it became overt.

When I discovered "Master Race" at the age of about seventeen, almost ten years after it was published, I couldn't find anything else in my medium that acknowledged what my parents had gone through. Even had it been a far dopier thing, it would have held my attention for that reason alone. But because of the intelligence with which Krigstein developed a new comics grammar, this story transcended the comic book as I knew it. (It was a different comics grammar than Kurtzman's, one that actually put them at odds with each other when they tried to collaborate.) He distended and foreshortened time from page to page and did it quite consciously; he used references to painters' vocabularies, like Duchamp's, rather than the more standardized cartoon glyphs. One of the sadnesses in my life was that, the one time we met—I was showing him a college paper I wrote analyzing "Master Race" that was being expanded for publication in an EC fanzine—Krigstein and I argued.

What happened?

He started out very disinterested, saying he was glad to be out of the field. He was

actually a teacher of illustration at my old high school, the High School of Art and Design in Manhattan...I'd steered clear of him, having heard of his antipathy for comics. He thought of himself as a painter now, but as I read my paper to him, he became more engaged because somebody was finally acknowledging what he had done. And we were doing great until I said something about writing and drawing being extensions of each other and that, as a result, the Platonic ideal form of comics to me was something that was written and drawn by one person. Krigstein clearly did not subscribe to that notion. He used the analogy of opera, the collaboration between librettist and the composer, set designer and musicians. It's a decent enough argument, but the comics I'm most compelled to try to understand fully are the ones that are made by an individual. It seems to me that, unlike film, unlike theater, unlike opera, a comic can be made by one person and as a result maybe that's the Platonic form of what a comic can be.

ABOVE and RIGHT: B. Krigstein's "Master Race," in *Impact* no. 1, March 1955. Splash page and sequence from page 7. © William Gaines, Agent, Inc. reprinted with permission.

When one's trying to get what Sven Birkerts in *The Gutenberg Elegies* posits as the great pleasure of literary fiction—which has to do with entering into another's brain and seeing the world through that set of eyes—I think it is more likely to happen when there's only one brain one has to enter into. An artist's limitations—whether those be on the narrative side of comics, or the graphic representation side—are actually an asset: you enter into a person's brain and world, and every brain has its deformations and its limitations. That's part of what it is to see through somebody else's eyes.

Krigstein's role as he saw it was as a new kind of illustrator, one who could fully inhabit a narrative. But illustrating can

be very different than comics-making, and that's where he and I were at genuine odds. He didn't think about it as picture writing at all, but rather as picture making in the service of storytelling. He didn't, for example, think about panels in terms of left to right movement, the way one reads. And as a result, late in "Master Race," there's one sequence in the story where the person who's slipping off the subway platform is hit by the subway. One way I could read it was: the train is about to hit the man, or the train has somehow passed him, but he's not squished. I would have to flop the image to understand it clearly as the picture of someone being hit. And to me this was a grammatical, syntactical "error" in what I understood as picture

201

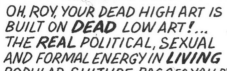

ABOVE: Review of the High/Low show, a project for *Artforum*, Dec. 1990.

writing. But Krigstein's whole point was, one doesn't look at pictures from left to right—each picture is a totality. I believe each *page* is a totality.

I'm some kind of graphic designer, but not an illustrator able to represent the subtle gesture of a body the way Krigstein could—he actually drew "real" figures with tangible weight, slumped over the way people actually might slump. For me the drawing has to have the word "slump" built into the drawing, the essential sign of slumping to communicate the gesture efficiently.

How do you feel about your work being exhibited in galleries or museums?

It was all part of my "Faustian Deal" with the culture: if comics are to survive for another century, once they're no longer a part of the most-mass part of mass culture, they've got to redefine themselves as Art or die. I was, of course, very flattered when the prestigious Galerie St. Etienne wanted to show my work in the beginning of the '90s. They were a 57th Street gallery that showed George Grosz, Otto Dix, and Käthe Kollwitz! Their only contemporary artist at the time was Sue Coe, who introduced me to them. I hadn't thought through my relationship with a gallery,

though: galleries exist to sell things. I was just interested in displaying my things. And I was flummoxed that they wanted to sell pages of *Maus*, while they were baffled that I wouldn't want to. I certainly couldn't break up the artwork that makes up the final drawings for *Maus*. It's all one work, even though it takes place over about three hundred pieces of paper. But it did seem possible for me to cut loose my sketches and studies when the gallery put pressure on having something to sell.

I didn't originally intend to hold on to that stuff. But at some point I started saving them rather than tossing them out at the end of a day's work, specifically with the idea that, when I eventually self-published *Maus* through *RAW*, I could put one little original sketch in each copy.

Tell me about what you called your own Low/Low show, a response to the High/Low show at the MoMA.

The Museum of Modern Art's 1990 "High and Low: Modern Art and Popular Culture" show tried to grapple with the then-starting-to-be-fashionable issue of how the popular arts interacted with the more rarefied ones. Unfortunately, the show squandered the opportunity, merely ratifying the museum's long-held tastes and hierarchical predispositions. It displayed paintings by Lichtenstein and then, in a small display case, had the lowly comic panels that he swiped from to compose his oversized paintings, without even crediting the comic book artists by name—which simply confirmed what's implicit in the Lichtenstein paintings: that the original artifacts were beneath contempt. There were paintings by Miró on the wall next to *Krazy Kats* because, as far as I could figure out, they both had crescent moons and surreal landscapes. I liked both works but they sat very uncomfortably next to each other. Frankly, the Herriman, as beautiful as it is on its own, doesn't adhere to a wall the same way that something made to be put on that wall does. The way I understood it at the time was, "I guess the paintings win the wall and the comics win the catalogue." The comics looked better because they were made for reproduction. For the most part the show seemed to condescend to the low-art artifacts.

In 1997 I got a call from a curator in the drawing department at the MoMA wanting to buy some originals of mine, noting they only owned one lithograph. Much to her surprise—and even to mine—I found myself saying, "The last thing I'll ever do is sell you guys any of my original art." "What? Why?" And I said, "Well, you know, when you did a show of *Maus* drawings at the MoMA in 1991, I spent some time in your vaults and I got to see the stuff that never comes out, and if you actually bought my artwork it might come out every ten years if you do a human torment show or something, but mostly it would just molder in your vaults. The museum doesn't know anything about comics." She said, "But we're interested in knowing more." And I responded by inviting some curators from the MoMA to my studio for a lecture on comics, a crash-course distilled from the lectures I'd given as an instructor at the School of Visual Arts. I ended up inviting people from the Met, the Whitney, the Guggenheim, the Brooklyn Museum, the Smithsonian, the Library of Congress, and some downtown galleries—thirty or more curators all agreed to come to my studio for a summit conference! Amazing!

Basically I wanted to plead for redress for the MoMA's High/Low show by asking for a Low/Low show, the point being that if one looks at the work on its own terms rather than next to paintings on a wall, one could begin to understand that comics weren't trying to be painting and failing at it; it's drawing, with a different purpose. The same way that the MoMA could show architectural drawings, let's say, but one would have to understand what an architectural drawing is and why it exists. Similarly, comics usually follow different rules of drawing than drawings by Picasso (who my perverse friend, the painter Alex Melamid, insists is a great cartoonist but a rotten painter).

The talk went rather well, but not much seemed to come from it right away. It all fizzled into having been one more odd day in the life.... except for Annie Philbin, the director of the Drawing Center around the corner from my studio. Several years later she called and said, "Good news! We're finally going to put on your show! I'm now the director of the Hammer Museum, and I think we can do it here." A few more years passed and eventually

Price $3.00 THE NEW YORKER April

art spiegelman

Brian Walker was brought in as a co-curator. So I got to have a say, even got included as one of the "masters" exhibited but didn't have to bear the responsibility for what eventually became a fairly extensive mini-retrospective of fifteen comics artists, past and present. I'd wanted many more artists represented, with fewer works by each artist, but that show did help move the conversation well past the polemics of the MoMA's High/ Low low point.

Aside from Expressionism, what aspects of visual—or literary—modernism have you found productive?

I was interested in the fact that us low artists were the keepers of the flame—the only artists still interested in drawing the

a show began to come together at the Hammer Museum and at the Museum of Contemporary Art in L.A. called "Masters of American Comics." I was delighted by everything except when Annie called it my show. I didn't want to be a curator per se, to decide who should live and who should die in that context, especially after having had so much anger directed at me in my experiences as a magazine editor in the past. But I did agree to be sort of an éminence grise. John Carlin, who I came to know when he was a grad student curating a beautiful small show of comics and paintings at the Downtown Whitney (eight years before and far more sophisticated than the High/Low show), was designated curator and I became—what's the high-class word for kibitzer? A consultant!

human figure when all of modernism was moving away from that. I certainly found the modernists who were still involved in the figure at the earlier parts of the century more directly useful to me than the ones who had moved into Josef Albers–like concern with retinal information rather than drawing per se. That aspect of modernism that distilled drawing down past its representational point, but was still representing, had the most impact on me. To me, it's the place where it's easiest for cartoonists and artistes to overlap. And certainly the ways in which modern artists, both verbal and visual, allowed one to see the construction and seams of their work led me toward things that were fruitful. Although *Maus* is called postmodernist, I'm not sure where modernism stops and postmodernism

LEFT: Installation photo, Art Spiegelman: Making Maus. Museum of Modern Art, NYC, 1991. ABOVE: *The New Yorker*, 4/19/99.

205

begins. There's a continuum that has people referring back to stylistic quirks, collage, and self-conscious representation that runs all through modernism.

Did an awareness of modernism inform how you structured the book?

Narratively, one of the real temptations in *Maus*, because of the way the story was delivered to me by Vladek, was to try to deal with his own dissociated time—the fact that he could easily slide between 1955 and 1945 and 1935. Being true to his story in some ways would have moved me into a kind of Joycean time field. But I now believe I made the right choice in trying to cobble together an insistence on chronology, including insisting on chronology within the book so one could see that the artist was insisting on chronology even if the teller of the tale, Vladek, wasn't.

Had I gone that route, of moving really in a fragmented way through time—the way that maybe *Slaughterhouse-Five* does—it could have been thrilling to work on but it would have been getting in the way of something else. And if the story was worth telling, it was also worth not creating "artificial" obstacles to understanding that story. The story's actually so hard to understand even when clarified, because it's so far away from one's daily experience. Making the story as clear as possible without pushing that clarity over the edge into simplification presented enough of a challenge. The alternative would actually be: "Well, it's a story like any other, but the way I'm telling it is going to give you that frisson of the new." And I suppose one could argue that just by doing something serious in comics I was already doing that. Yet for me, it was natural to work in comics with personal subject matter—but it was much easier to maneuver a story of a guy sitting at a window looking at a ball being bounced than to be in total service to a chronological narrative. But of course, nothing ultimately is chronological. As soon as you're asked to tell any story you will break it—either in your mind, thinking of something else that happened later or earlier—or something will interrupt the telling and you're in the present of what's being told rather than in the past that's being recounted. So inevitably I had all of these breaks present, and certainly was aware of how much further I could have gone in that direction.

In terms of organizing Vladek's testimony into a chronological narrative, how did you deal with the discrepancies?

There's one page where I'm quarreling with Vladek about how long he actually spent in Auschwitz, and what he was doing there at various periods. I kept a literal chart—a graph of time—and as I'd find things out from him, I'd place them on the chart to understand what had happened. One specific time-bar had me trying to find out where he was from 1944 to 1945. It led to a conversation with Vladek in which I ask him how much time he spent in a shoe shop in Auschwitz, as opposed to just being sent out to so-called black work of just lifting and hauling—the thing that would have ordinarily been a death sentence. And there are some discrepancies that have me finally jogging his memory, and he recalls that he got back to the tin shop after they had closed it down, to help dismantle the crematoria in Auschwitz before the retreat from the Russians. That information was significant but so was Vladek snapping at me that there were no watches in Auschwitz, that my attempt to rationalize his story by putting it on what's literally the grid of time was not the way it was experienced by him at all.

And this way of mapping out time, which is what comics do, is the kind of thing that gave me pleasure while working on *Maus*. I did that page (page 228) in such a way that a version of my time-chart is shown as a vertical bar superimposed and traversing several panels, but Françoise enters and interrupts our conversation waving, "Yoo hoo, I was looking for you" with a speech balloon superimposed on top of that bar at exactly the December/January/February moment that was in contention. How much time did you spend here or there? Well, now I didn't have to nail it because that interruption let it remain as unresolved as it actually had to be. That's a good example of deeply layered information: although

1944

JAN

FEB

MAR — VLADEK + ANJA TO AUSCHWITZ. MARCH 16
role in Hungary to Nazis

APR

MAY — V. BECOMES KLEMPNER
5·16 – Sept. Hungarian Jews

JUN

JULY

AUG — SHOEMAKER?

SEP

OCT — ANJA TRANSFERED TO CAMP EXTENSION Oct (AUS HANDBK P. 24)
Oct 7 Sonderkommando revolt

NOV — last gassings dismantling cremo 2+3 (Himmler's order 11/26.

DEC

1945

JAN — Jan 5. Union Werke women hanged
Jan 18. March from Aus
Jan 27. Sosn liberated. [P.24]
JAN 26. VLADEK IN GROSSROSEN

FEB — FEB 4. ARRIVE IN DACHAU
liberation MAY 1945.

ENGLISH LESSONS
KLEMPNER
SHOEMAKER
BLACK WORK
SHOEMAKER KLEMPNER
KLEMPNER (OVENS)

initial specialising:
maybe V. worked longer as a klempner. It was getting cold when V. worked shoe job. During Sept. 44 6000 Polish Russians sent to camps in the Reich. This may be when the Polish shoemaker was removed. (see V.'s transcript page 33)

V. sez he was on black work when Anja came to Aus. BUT if Bima and Renya are right about the 4 women being hanged, and Vladek witnessed the hanging; he probably was in the shoe shop thru part of October.

Vladek and I are shown in the present while bickering about the past in those first six panels, we're then genuinely yanked back into the present by Françoise—all literally layered around a timeline.

How you did you decide to make *Maus* a narrative framed by its own process, and how is comics form a part of that?

Visibly juxtaposing pasts and presents allowed there to be a continual kind of flashing back and forth that wouldn't feel like a total flashback to an ersatz reconstruction of the past. Telling a story as if I was the invisible hand that allowed Vladek to make a comic about Auschwitz would have been so fraudulent. It's the fraudulence that informs a lot of the Holocaust comics that have come since. One doesn't want to give a counterfeit experience; better to give the problematics of reconstruct-

ing that experience. It was never really a question for me, that I would have to include the telling as well as what's told. Even in that three-page "Maus" the narrative is bracketed by a father telling a son a bedtime story. Everything drawn in the so-called past in the story that Vladek is telling is very clearly an attempt by the son to show what the father is telling. And that offered a margin within which to operate authentically. The fact that you're told that I'm trying to show you what I understand of what Vladek is telling me is built into the fabric of the narrative itself, and allows that narrative to get told.

Could you talk about the page in *Maus*, after the prologue, in which the narrative first dips into the past?

The prologue itself is a form of dipping into the past, though not visually represented, but I figured those first two pages would function, thematically, as a fractal of the whole book. It seemed that positing this sort of normal childhood moment with a chilling shadow cast over it was an appropriate lead-in.

In the very beginning of the first chapter, after the introduction of Vladek and Art coming together, on page 14, we go into my old room and Vladek pedals away on his Ex-ercycle as we begin to talk about the project. An important page—it

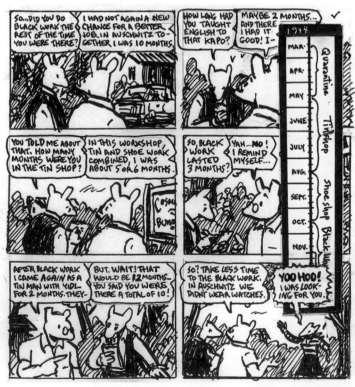

LEFT: Draft, part of page 228.

ematic language, fade or dissolve—from the spin to him as a young man in the past. It allowed me to use an unusual angle to call attention to certain things; Art is shown seated in his childhood room, framed between the handlebars, with Vladek's tattooed number visible on his left arm. The wheel at the bottom of the page is the first use of the circle as a meaningful shape. On the next page, the poster of Rudolph Valentino as the Sheik appears in a spotlight that echoes the circle in which Vladek appears as a young man. I remember when I first began working on the book, I showed this page to a Spanish publisher of fantasy comics who asked to see what I was working on. I showed him the first pages and talked him through it like I did just now and although I did say that I didn't expect any reader to pick up on this stuff consciously, it was how I thought about my pages. And he looked at me cross-eyed—he was publishing a magazine with big-busted barbarian babes on every page—and fled as soon as he politely could.

begins to churn up the past. Vladek on the Exercycle dominates the page by traveling from the second tier down to the fourth: there's a kind of fractured but nevertheless visible version of him sitting on the Exercycle that travels down the whole page. It's a little Cubist, but basically you can see his head on one tier, his arms on the other, and his legs pedaling on the bottom.

That allowed me to bring us into the story in a way that has a cinematic analogue, although this is hardly a cinematic representation of a cinematic idea. It might even be corny in a movie, but what happens is: Vladek gets on the Exercycle to pedal, we look at the wheels turning, and as he begins to spin his yarn there's a kind of whirling—I don't know the exact cin-

Were there times when you felt that perhaps comics wasn't the best medium for your father's story?

TOP: Study, page 14 and (inset) final panel as published in *RAW*, vol. 1, no. 2, 1980. ABOVE: Page 14.

((Everybody in the camp got cigarettes?)) Yes. Three cigarettes a week. ((Really?)) And I took them together, the cigarettes, and then if I was very hungry and I didn't have any bread, I exchanged them for bread. ((Everybody in the camp got cigarettes?)) Everybody got cigarettes. As we got our portion of bread, once weekly it came, I think it was on a Sunday, everybody got three cigarettes. ((Every once in a while I just hear something that I can't understand like how could they be killing everybody and giving them cigarettes?)) Because these people they needed for work. They took us every day to hard work. And we got meat. What kind of meat? Horse meat. Sausage from horse meat, either once or twice weekly, such a piece like two fingers. ((How many times did you get to eat in a day, once in the morning and once at night?)) Once in the morning, once when we came from work. That was the whole food. ((We can stop. I think this is very good. I got some very important things that I didn't have before. It's not insulting when I interrupt you. It's because I have a lot of the story from the last time you told me, so I don't want to tire you out, to tell me again.))

2/7/66

☐ MUSSELMEN
☐ "ORGANIZING."
☐ TINSHOP IN CAMP EXTENSIO
☐ FOREMAN A COMMUNIST.
☐ A "FRIENDLY GUARD SAW BIRKENAU.
☐ SELECTION.
☐ Friend selected.
☐ 3rd selection: HID IN BATHROOM.
☐ BUNKMATES SHARING FOOD. TALKING ABOUT FOOD
☒ VISITING MANDLER IN INFANTRY.
☐ GOT CIGARETTES ONCE A WEEK
☐ Meet MANDLE
☐ Looking for MANDLE after the WAR.
☐ Mandle helps Anja
☐ Vlad goes to BIRK
☐ Vlad sees Anja.
☐ beaten up
☐ ▬▬▬▬▬▬
☐ Vlad sleeps on wet clothes laundry.
☐ Vlad taken out of LINE for smuggling. NOT caught.
☐ Punishment between the wires in DAC
☒ Vlad's BOX stolen
☐ Vlad switches to SHOE SHOP

PRISONER'S DAY

4:00 reveille gong
      beaten + cursed out of bed
      Build bed or else.
      Washing
      "Coffee" (bread from night before.
ROLL CALL
Marching out past orchestra w. work commando.

6 AM – 5 PM   WORK DAY.
½ hour lunch
Return - march thru gates. search. turnip = sabotage.
Roll Call
9 pm lights out

Well, I came up against things in *Maus* that involved imparting general information, and those were the moments when I would despair and think: Well, maybe I should just do something that's a combination of prose and comics, use comics when it's appropriate, and just typeset pages of prose when that seemed appropriate. But that would have been a real cop-out on the bet I had placed on myself, so I kept trying to find solutions. Page 209 offers one of the most severe cases of this dilemma:

ABOVE LEFT: Transcript of conversation with Vladek labeled "Fishing Expedition, 6-2-79." LOWER LEFT: Undated notes.

I was trying to find out from my father, and from my research, what people got to eat in Auschwitz. Not at 7:30 a.m. on July 7, 1944, but what they were given to eat daily. It's the kind of information that could most easily be presented as a menu, if that is an appropriate word to use about Auschwitz food. A list! In a novel or in any kind of nonfiction prose, it would be an easy paragraph to write. But here, I had to have some visual component to hold a place for the information, and it took a long time to figure it out. At some point in the interviews Vladek explained what it meant to stand on line to get food. This line allowed for something visual to literally move through the page. Two panels, silhouettes of Vladek and Art under a sun umbrella in the Catskills, bracket the main visual on the page. (I suppose I could have done the whole thing as just talking heads at that table, but talk about cop-outs!) In that first balloon Vladek begins to talk to the question, saying, "In the morning for breakfast we got only a bitter drink made from roots." He gets to give that slice of generalized information. In the right-hand flashback panel there's the beginning of a food line to stand on, a line that moves diagonally down through the second tier and continues to the first panel in the third row. Vladek talks about the optimal place to stand on that line, and the picture of a line gave me space to drape captions that told about the other kinds of food that they got on an ongoing basis. It was a visual placeholder to keep one's eyes occupied while the information was served up.

There's a kind of footnote across the bottom of this page as well, where I was able to enter the last bits of the information I needed to place somewhere: "In the evening we got a spoiled cheese or jam." After having stood on the line, there's now a line of prisoners sitting against a wall, eating

ABOVE: Facts and narrative points for the Auschwitz chapters (prioritized by color), Feb. 7, 1986. LOWER RIGHT: Study, page 209.

their soup at the bottom of the page, with a small inset caption on the right side of that horizontal, about the same size as the two small text boxes that begin and end the soup line. It's placed right below the dead bodies piled on each other, almost as if it was a separate panel placed there, as an afterthought—"If you ate how they gave you, it was just enough to die more slowly." It's a tightly packed page.

I came to think of that "menu" of food at Auschwitz, that list of things, as vertical information. Horizontal information, on the other hand, is exactly what movies transmit easily: the Hulk lifts up a car, he throws it across a room, it smashes through a wall. That's active, and can be shown easily in comics panels. Vladek throws a parcel of food to Anja, who's on the other side of a barbed-wire fence,

ABOVE: Draft, page 209. TOP RIGHT: Final art, page 209. RIGHT: Page 225 and two panel studies.

on page 225. It's seen by a kapo who chases her. There's a chase. Anja runs, ducks into a barrack, and is hidden there thanks to another prisoner. One action moves to the next—it's a good example of comics functioning in their comfort zone. A chase scene and hiding is much more straightforward to depict than some of what came in the previous couple of pages, like the chart that shows what the trade value of cigarettes was as barter and exchange.

One of the things I find so striking in *Maus* is your way of crushing together the past and the present, the continuousness of the past and the present, continuous even within frames. One example is page 229— can you talk about that?

Right after the page with the timeline that we were talking about earlier, we begin to move back toward a section of pages that are very architectural and diagrammatic, that show you the crematoria, because Vladek actually saw them; he was one of the workers pulling them apart. So what leads into

showing the death camp killing apparatus, on the last panel on the page, is the caption: "For this I was an eyewitness." It appears under a small panel showing a crematorium chimney. It follows—or interrupts—two panels of progressive

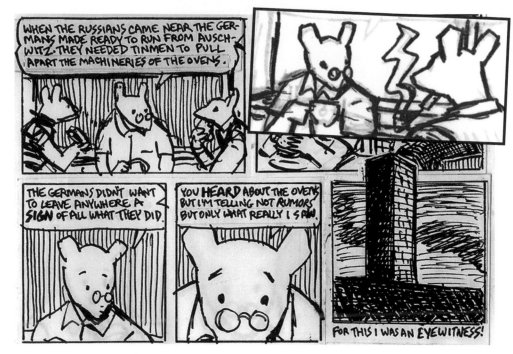

close-ups on Vladek's face. Had I shown three panels of progressive close-ups across a tier—as I did, say, on page 111, where Tosha says, "No! I won't go to their gas chambers! And my children won't go to their gas chambers"—it would've been a classic Harvey Kurtzman trope. He used those progressive close-up beats for dramatic effect in lots of his EC comic book work.

Here, on page 229, it's almost set up as a rhythm: there's the progressive two-panel close-up. But instead of the third panel of the close-up on that last row, what you have is what he's witnessing as an interruption of what would have been a more glib zoom into his glasses. At that point you're entered into the chimney that lets you know what's being shown and dismantled on the pages after.

TOP: Draft and inset study, page 229. ABOVE: Rejected panel draft, page 229. LEFT: *Maus* notebook, 1988.

Because panels do juxtapose past and present, that lower right-hand panel sits immediately below Art and Vladek talking at a table where Art's cigarette smoke is coming out of the chimney—I was very impressed with you when you noticed that! I didn't mean to hammer that home, but on the other hand I do believe that the self-destructiveness of my smoking is not totally unrelated to the secondhand memories of secondhand smoke, so I entered it into the visuals there for what it's worth. I expected it to be read as smoke coming out of the crematorium chimney, but it wasn't, sigh, lost on me that it had another implication.

Maus is very attentive to what Vladek actually was an eyewitness to, and what he heard from others.

I tried to stick fairly closely to what was actually seen and told by Vladek. For example, on page 110, Vladek says something like, "They were taking people to Auschwitz, over a thousand people, some kids were screaming, and they couldn't stop, the Germans swung them by their legs against a wall," and this is why it was important to Vladek to send his son away. Now, he explains that he didn't see it with his own eyes; someone told him the next

day while they were in hiding and Vladek says, "Thank God with Persis *our* children are safe." I tried showing exactly what Vladek was describing that he hadn't seen, which is swinging a small child by the legs against a wall to just, literally, bash that kid's brains out. And I felt like not showing it would be to not acknowledge what actually was done and done routinely; but to show, on the other hand, was to move in the direction of something drawn by, say, Graham Ingels in an old EC horror comic book. Grand Guignol was not what I was after, so instead I drew the *action* of swinging, rather than the result.

There's a panel in which a near-silhouette of the Nazi is swinging some kid by the leg, but you just see the leg, the swinging—as represented by a swooping action line—and the spattering, but there is no focus on what that spatter actually is. And then, where one might see the gore in the next panel on the wall, you see a bit of the spatter, but it's covered by a balloon of Vladek and Art in the present, where Vladek very specifically says, "This I didn't see with my own eyes, but somebody the next day told me..." And that balloon actually covers up the gore that one would otherwise be looking at. I was trying to not be coy, and not be gory.

TOP RIGHT: Page 110, study for penultimate panel, and last panel final art. BOTTOM: Study, page 111.

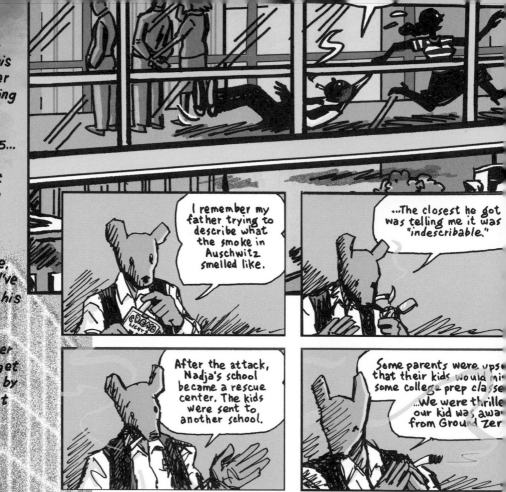

This self-consciousness is so key for a book that deals with the issue of brute suffering.

Dealing with suffering—or anything else—there's a dialogue going on in my head that consists of at least two voices: one voice trying to get something said, and another interrupting to talk about how it's getting said. I can't turn that off even when I'm working. To have suppressed it would have cut me off from too much of how I apprehend the world.

TOP: Fragment of *In the Shadow of No Towers*, July 2002.
BOTTOM LEFT and RIGHT: Page 110, study for penultimate panel, and last panel final art.

IN THIS WAY THE GERMANS TREATED THE LITTLE ONES WHAT STILL HAD SURVIVED A LITTLE.

THIS I DIDN'T SEE WITH MY OWN EYES, BUT SOMEBODY THE NEXT DAY TOLD ME. AND I SAID, "THANK GOD WITH PERSIS OUR CHILDREN ARE SAFE!"

You have some notebook entries on your doubts about the book that say things like, "I feel like I never earned a right to the material..."

I like the word "material," because it both brings us back to the garment district, from which us Eastern European Jews sprang, but also because, on the one hand, it allows me to objectify my process; it says: "Oh, it's material," it's not blood and sinew, it's material. And on the other hand, it's also material, in the sense that it has tactility, weight, and texture and has to be made into something.

An important part of the self-awareness of the book as a comics text comes from its inclusion of just a very few photographs. Tell me about your decision to draw some photographs in *Maus,* **but to actually include others.**

The first photo that appears in the book is in "Prisoner on the Hell Planet," the strip that I had done in 1972. It's a photo of Anja and Art—I'm a ten-year-old kid. And it seems friendly and benign, and seems to have some subtext to it, and offered the verisimilitude and authority that identified the strip as a true story. At a time when autobiographical comics weren't quite as common, it seemed important to find a way to show "this really happened," as a phrase. And that visual phrasing could be done by holding that photo up in front of the Hell Planet. Having it in juxtaposition with that expressionist drawing style allows the photograph to carry the kind of "authenticity" snapshots carry, and incidentally allows one to see a couple of the protagonists, Mom and me, in a summer between tragedies.

You know, spreading out whatever snapshots I had, I thought that this image both had the innocence of childhood with my five-foot-tall mother as a large figure with me kneeling next to her, but showed her hand on my head with a certain kind of body language that said: "Stay small, my boy. Don't grow up." If I try to understand what happened, part of her suicide had to do with feeling unmoored as I was breaking away from the nuclear family. Keeping a hand on a head is both a maternal gesture, but also a pushing down when somebody's trying to get up. It evokes my childhood in an economical way that has something in common with the two-page prologue to *Maus.*

It's very different than a photo of Anja evoked on page 19, where Vladek has a photo of her on his mantelpiece. I could have put some prewar photo of Anja there, but it would have been premature to have insisted on the objective correlative that a photo would invoke, when one's still

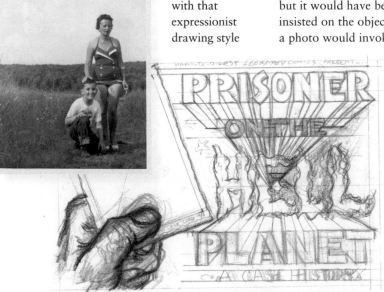

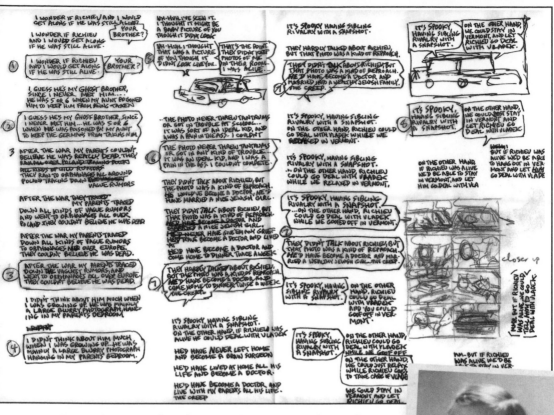

getting used to my cockeyed notion of drawing mice for people, anyway. Instead I had this kind of vulnerable-looking mouse shown with the scritchiness of line that indicates a drawing of or from a photo.

The next actual photo in the book is the one that starts volume two, the photograph of Richieu as a young boy that hung in my parents' bedroom.

How did you choose this photo?

Oh, it's the photo—it chose me! It's the one that's referred to in the drive to the Catskills; the photo that was hanging up over the bed as a large blow-up from a small picture, so it's a little ghostly.

And at the front of the second book, it forms a kind of grounding, of this real person who was lost. It's useful to see that photo, to have the little simple glyph of the photo that appears elsewhere in the book as a drawing... It does a lot of work by being up front over there.

Did you always know that you wanted to use this photo in the book?

No. The photos came out a bit more organically than that. The photo of Richieu hovered as a presence over my childhood, as said in the book, but I hadn't thought about it one way or another for *Maus*. But we had just had a kid, and by then I knew

FACING PAGE, LEFT: 1958 photo and splash panel study, *"Prisoner on the Hell Planet,"* 1972. RIGHT: Panel studies for page 19. ABOVE: Scripting/text formatting ("type spec-ing") for page 175, and photo of Richieu, 1940.

that the book was sort of going to be for my child, or eventual children to come. And then somehow the shape of the story came together, which included realizing that my phantom brother was a presence through not just my childhood, but now somehow still hovering even in the interview moments with Vladek. And instead of a photo of my own kid, I realized: well, no, no, this other picture is far more locked into the narrative, and it allowed for each member of my childhood family to have a photographic representation.

The photo that I needed to have most specifically—in the book I even talk about "I need to have that photo, you've gotta find that photo"—was the one that Vladek had as a "souvenir" of his time in the camps. I knew how important this was to the entire project, and I knew that placing it was important. It had to come some-where after other things had happened in the book. By the time one nears that point in the narrative, one already has a very clear picture of who Vladek is, even though one hasn't a clue as to what he looks like. And what became so interesting

to me was the photo—the thing that gives you that "objective correlative"—tells you so insanely little. The fact that it's a posed photo, after the fact, where he's donning a costume version of his uniform…

It's almost literally unbelievable, it's so strange . . .

It's so off. I mean, you do get real information from it. You get to find out that, well, he was a fairly good-looking guy. You can verify that, this Rudolph Valentino stuff wasn't only self-aggrandizement; he was perceived as attractive by women. But there's also the jauntiness of the angle at which he carries the cap, and his full, full face, fuller than it was when I knew him and probably fuller than it was before the war. This fullness was a kind of fleshing out after the years of starvation, but doesn't tell you about those years of starvation. And the relative high-spiritedness of the facial expression and the hat just seemed so at odds with the person that I'd come to know through an entire lifetime as well as through the conversations about what he had gone through. So to be left with a photo that tells you something, but only in

ABOVE: The original copy of Vladek's photo on page 294 inset onto detail of page draft.
RIGHT: Original art, page 275, surrounded by "Family Album" drafts and studies.

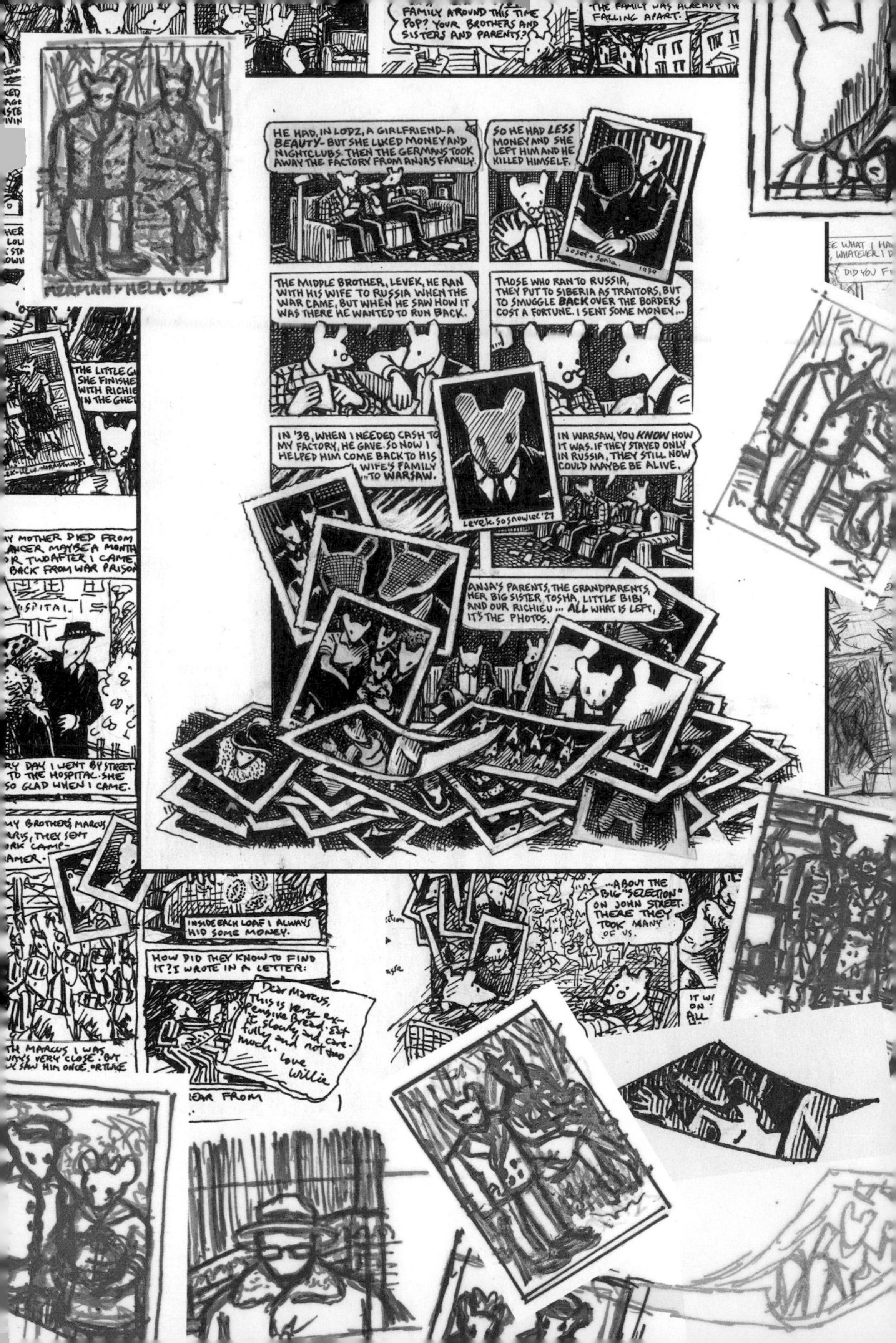

HE HAD, IN LODZ, A GIRLFRIEND-A BEAUTY- BUT SHE LIKED MONEY AND NIGHTCLUBS. THEN THE GERMANS TOOK AWAY THE FACTORY FROM ANJA'S FAMILY.
SO HE HAD LESS MONEY AND SHE LEFT HIM AND HE KILLED HIMSELF.
Josef + Sonia. 1939
THE MIDDLE BROTHER, LEVEK, HE RAN WITH HIS WIFE TO RUSSIA WHEN THE WAR CAME, BUT WHEN HE SAW HOW IT WAS THERE HE WANTED TO RUN BACK.
THOSE WHO RAN TO RUSSIA, THEY PUT TO SIBERIA AS TRAITORS, BUT TO SMUGGLE BACK OVER THE BORDERS COST A FORTUNE. I SENT SOME MONEY...
IN '38, WHEN I NEEDED CASH TO MY FACTORY, HE GAVE. SO NOW I HELPED HIM COME BACK TO HIS WIFE'S FAMILY ...TO WARSAW.
Levek. Sosnowiec '27
IN WARSAW, YOU KNOW HOW IT WAS. IF THEY STAYED ONLY IN RUSSIA, THEY STILL NOW COULD MAYBE BE ALIVE.
ANJA'S PARENTS, THE GRANDPARENTS, HER BIG SISTER TOSHA, LITTLE BIBI AND OUR RICHIEU... ALL WHAT IS LEFT, IT'S THE PHOTOS.
1939
FAMILY AROUND THIS TIME POP? YOUR BROTHERS AND SISTERS AND PARENTS?
THE FAMILY WAS ALREADY
FALLING APART.
HERMAN + HELA. LODZ
INSIDE EACH LOAF I ALWAYS HID SOME MONEY.
HOW DID THEY KNOW TO FIND IT? I WROTE IN A LETTER:
Dear Marcus, This is very expensive Bread. Eat it slowly and carefully and not too much. Love Willie
...ABOUT THE BIG "SELECTION" ON JOHN STREET. THERE THEY TOOK MANY OF US.
HOSPITAL

WHAT ABOUT YOUR SIDE OF THE FAMILY?

MY SIDE?... MY FATHER AND FELA AND HER 4 KIDS I TOLD YOU GOT TAKEN FROM THIS STADIUM IN '42

ZOSHA AND YADJA, MY YOUNGER SISTERS, HAD ONLY 1 KID EACH, AND CAME WITH ME INTO THE GHETTO BEFORE THEY ALL DIED LATER TO AUSCHWITZ.

MARCUS, MY CLOSEST BROTHER, AND MOSES WENT TO A CAMP, TO BLECHAMER, SOON AFTER I CAME OUT FROM THE ARMY.

I SENT THEM MONEY BY THE RED CROSS... I HID IT INTO BREAD.

I WROTE THEM: "THIS BREAD, IT'S EXPENSIVE. EAT IT VERY SLOW AND CAREFUL." I MET AFTER THE WAR A GUY, HE SAW THEM DIE, BUT WOULDN'T TELL ME HOW.

MY OTHER BROTHERS, LEON AND PINEK THEY DESERTED OUT FROM THE POLISH ARMY TO LEMBOURG, IN RUSSIA.

A FAMILY OF PEASANT JEWS KEPT THEM SAFE. PINEK HE MARRIED ONE OF THEM. BUT LEON GOT SICK. DOCTORS SAID IT'S TYPHUS, AND HE DIED OF A BAD APPENDIX.

SARAH+PINEK TEL AVIV 1962

SO ONLY MY LITTLE BROTHER, PINEK, CAME OUT FROM THE WAR ALIVE... FROM THE REST OF MY FAMILY, IT'S NOTHING LEFT, NOT EVEN A SNAPSHOT

in my immediate family in an encapsulated manner. Going over these photos laid out over the page allows for rather telegraphic, but efficient information about brothers, uncles, whatever. And, very specifically, these photos allow one to see things about Anja's family—not Vladek's family—because those are the photos that survived. What's left are only early postwar photos of Vladek's brother who managed to hide in Russia, and was living in Israel.

But the photos of the Zylberberg family survived because they were part of the possessions put in safe-keeping with the Polish governess. She kept their furniture and stuff and wouldn't give that back, but since the photos had no meaning for her, they were passed back to Anja and made it to Queens, where I was able to see them. In most of them, I just have no idea who the people were, and never will know.

relation to the drawn and written telling around it, informs what you thought you knew by making you re-examine it.

What about the pages that come before with the drawings of many, many family photos?

But the accumulation of photos becomes something. On page 275 there is a pile-up of photos at the bottom of the page that somehow refers back to the pile of bodies as it bleeds off the page. The pile of anonymous pictures.

After Vladek finally has unearthed this box of photos, it's a way to at least begin to understand the destinies of other people

Here it's Vladek who's commenting on the pictures that did survive. Some of those photos had the kinds of damage that include faces cut out of a photo . . .

ABOVE: Draft, page 276. LEFT: Study, page 275.
RIGHT: Pinek, Sarah, Zev, and Zipora, 1948.
FACING PAGE: Prewar photos from Anja's album.

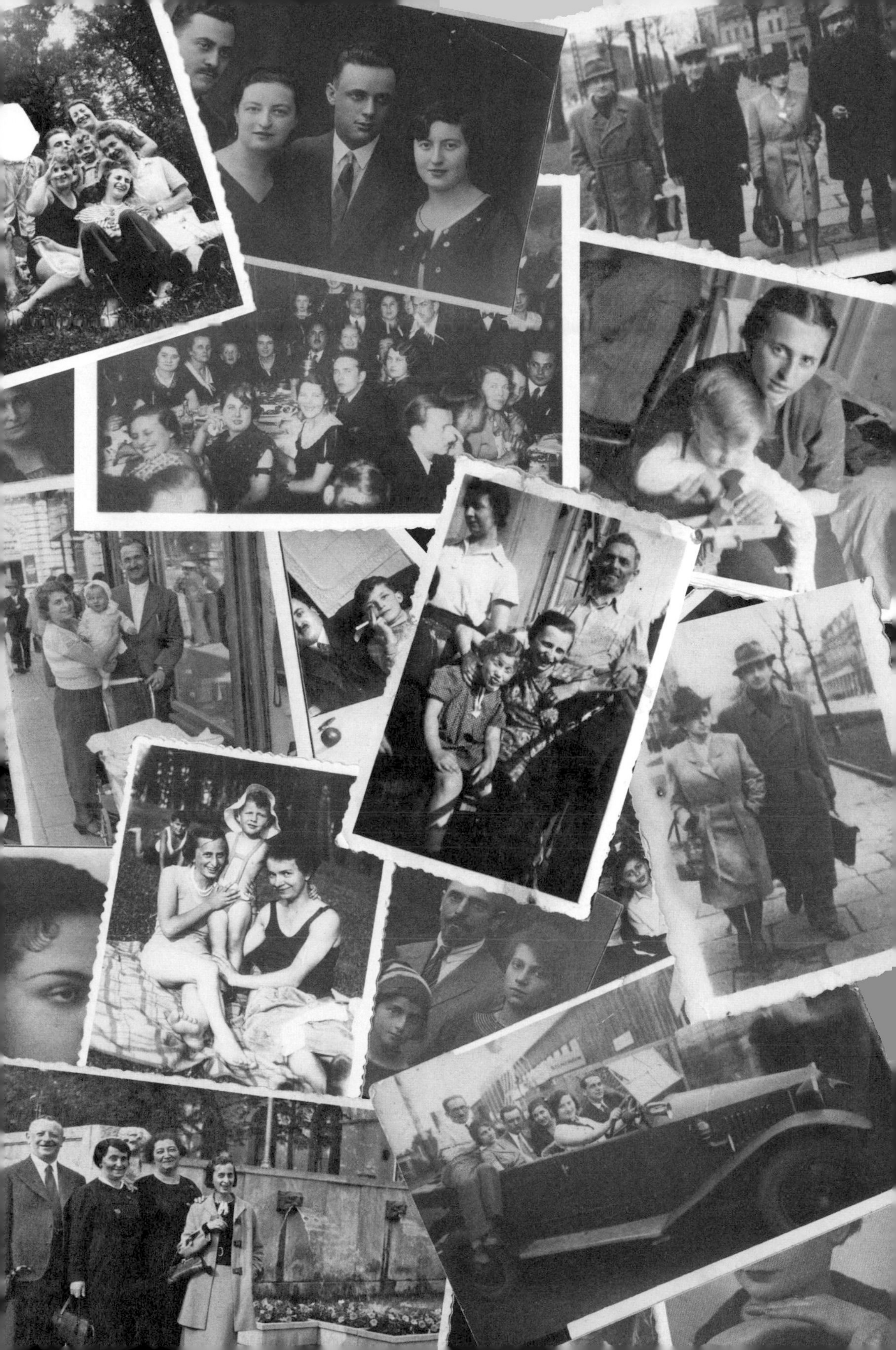

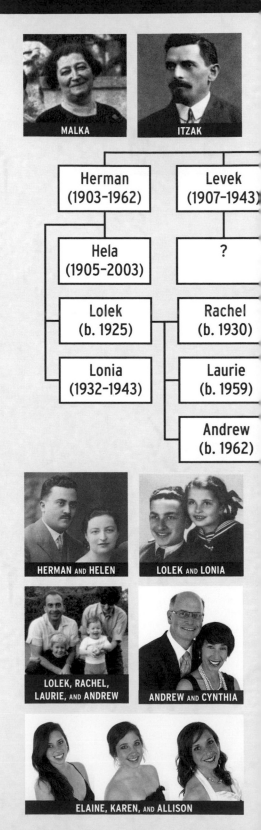

Right. The dialogue here is, "So he had less money, and she left him, and he killed himself." So it seems like she's absented in a very deliberate way . . .

More likely she's absent because she was used for a locket. But these things have multiple meanings. Vladek is seen right behind that cut-up photograph as if he was going to put his head through it, filling the hole by telling. His face replaces the missing face.

After addressing the destiny of Anja's family I had to find a way of talking about Vladek's side of the family without even photos to hold that place. So Vladek's body has to hold that place on page 276. It's another one of those cases where there is that superimposed grid on a figure that travels through several panels, similar to the one of Vladek on the Exercycle at the beginning of the book. Vladek's body has to stand in for all of the bodies that didn't make it into the then-present. Trying to make sequences that are moving but not manipulative is a tricky business.

Interview continues on page 232.

ABOVE: Study, page 276. OVERLEAF: Study, page 239.

BERBERG FAMILY TREE

Ruchla Karmiol
(?–1941)

Heschl Karmiol
(?–1941)

...srael Itzak Zylberberg
(ca. 1883–1943)

Malka Karmiol
(?–1943)

JOSEF

Tosha
(1910–1943)

Josef
(1915–1942)

ANJA
(1912–1968)

TOSHA, BIBI, AND WOLF

**Wolf
Steinkeller**
(1906–1943)

Mina

**VLADEK
SPIEGELMAN**
(1906–1982)

LEVEK

Bibi
(1930–1943)

MALA
(1917–2007)

Cynthia
(b. 1960)

RICHIEU
(1937–1943)

MALA

...laine (b. 1987)

**ART
SPIEGELMAN**
(b. 1948)

**FRANÇOISE
MOULY**
(b. 1955)

...aren (b. 1990)

...lison (b. 1993)

ANJA AND VLADEK

NADJA
(b. 1987)

DASHIELL
(b. 1991)

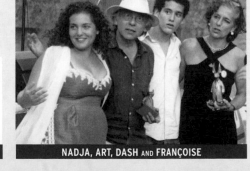

RICHIEU

NADJA, ART, DASH AND FRANÇOISE

I recently became aware of the scope of my second cousin Simon Spiegelman's forty years of genealogical research into our shared family. His extensive and ongoing work of scholarship, retrieval and memory can be found on the DVD that accompanies this book. (No equivalent work has been done on the Zylberberg family.) Part of his narrative history appears below along with two key charts that offer a fractal snapshot of the fate of Eastern Europe's Jews.   —a.s.

THE SZPIGELMAN FAMILY IN POLAND

For many generations, the large Szpigelman clan had homes within the Zaglebie district of Upper Silesia, covering a hub of adjoining towns that spanned Dabrowa Górnicza, Sosnowiec, Będzin, Wolbron, Sławków, and Zawiercie. The region is rich in coal deposits, and so it has been an area contested by Germans and Poles over the last two hundred years. It is today part of Poland bordering Czechoslovakia in the south and Germany to the north and west. Our earliest family recollections go back to my great-great grandfather, Majer Szpigelman, who was born around 1820. He spent his days observing the "mitzvoth" or good deeds, engaging in prayer and Talmudic study. His spouse, Zysla, sustained the family by running a small grocery store in Wolbron. Their oldest son, Chaim Leib, born in 1838, was the progenitor of my branch in the line of descent.

Chaim Leib amassed a fortune from very modest beginnings. When he reached adolescence, his mother came up with the idea of producing candles in her kitchen using simple hand molds. She sold the candles in her store and the surplus to other merchants. It generated immediate income and their store grew into a shop producing Sabbath and general-purpose candles. In his late teens, Chaim Leib started selling the product in adjoining localities and eventually larger cities such as Katowice, Sosnowiec, and Kraków. The factory did well and the family prospered. Chaim Leib married Feigla Szpringer in 1858; they had six sons and two daughters. Chaim Leib's sons and sons-in-law were either engaged in one of his businesses or in ones he helped finance. Chaim Leib's son Wolf was my grandfather.

Wolf Szpigelman's flight from Poland in 1922 was told to me by my aunt Lorre and a bit by my mother, Rose. Another version was told by my father's first cousin Vladek Spiegelman; the narratives are, in all likelihood, fragments of the same story.

According to my mother, the months following the annexation to Poland in October 1921 were uncertain for the German population in the region, but particularly perilous for the Jews who had sympathized with the German cause during the 1914–1918 war. They were now labeled "German collaborators." According to Rose, Abram Szpigelman, Wolf's brother and Vladek Spiegelman's father, was singled out by Polish nationalists and arrested. Abram was jailed in the local prison that faced one of Chaim Leib's buildings. At the appointed time, when the prisoners were allowed to exercise in the central courtyard of the prison, members of the Szpigelman clan would stand on the rooftop of an adjoining building accompanied by their children waving to Abram and signaling messages. Because of what had happened to his brother Abram, Wolf decided it was time for his family to leave Poland. According to my aunt Lorre, Wolf received threatening messages and one night was fired upon as he walked home. He dodged his assailant's bullets and escaped in the dark of the night. Wolf and his wife, Sura Rywka, gathered their six children and headed for Schopenitz (Szopienice) across the German border.

Abram's son Vladek provides another facet of the story. As he tells it, the family's assets had been liquidated during the hard times following the First World War, and they were desperately looking for a source of income. A seltzer factory was still in the family's hands even though the brewery was idle; it was capable of distilling and bottling spirits. Abram and Wolf saw an opportunity in producing vodka. The demand was high and sales very profitable. They did, however, lack a license or "government seal" from the new Polish authorities, who had taken over the local administration in October 1921. The brothers and a cousin, Rafnietz, decided to manufacture vodka using the idle fermentation and distillation equipment. The process would provide carbon dioxide for carbonation in the soda water plant. Rafnietz put up the money for the conversion, Wolf sold the spirits, and Abram ran the inside operation with Rafnietz's sons. It was a very lucrative business, but short-lived. Difficulties arose when they refused to bribe a Polish worker to gain his silence; he subsequently denounced them to the Polish authorities. Abram and Rafnietz's sons were arrested when the factory was raided by the police and Wolf, upon learning the bad news in the streets, hopped a trolley and crossed over to Schopenitz, a German town across the nearby Brynica river. Abram and Rafnietz's sons were defended by a prominent Warsaw lawyer hired by Rafnietz and were released after spending several months in prison. Abram eventually returned to Sosnowiec and reopened the seltzer factory; Wolf and Abram were never business partners again. Their respective sons, Max and Vladek, would become partners as diamond dealers in New York, thirty years later.

The Zaglebie district was home to most of the large Szpigelman family, and its towns were the first to be occupied by the Germans. The German army invaded Poland on September 1, 1939. Within days, the Germans set fire to synagogues in Sosnowiec, Dabrowa Górnicza, and Będzin. Almost immediately, the Nazi authorities enacted repressive anti-Jewish regulations. By the end of 1941 all Jews were compelled to move to distinct sections; this was followed by deportations to forced labor camps.

By mid-1942 transports from the Zaglebie towns were systematically carrying human cargo to Auschwitz, only thirty miles away, for annihilation. The largest round-up in Zaglebie took place on August 12, 1942, when 50,000 Jews in Sosnowiec, Będzin, and Dabrowa Górnicza were assembled in their localities for selection and deportation. That day, almost all of the Jews of Sosnowiec—21,000 people—showed up at the town soccer field that had been designated as the assembly area for "revalidating" required documents. German guards interspersed with unarmed members of the Jewish Order Service surrounded the crowd as they entered the soccer field. The exits were blocked by German guards in machine gun emplacements. Over ten thousand people were thus "selected" and sent to their death in Auschwitz several days later.

In the spring of 1943, the remaining Jews were ordered to move into two neighborhoods: Kamionka, near Będzin, and Srodula, near Sosnowiec. The two sites bordered each other and constituted a single ghetto. However, Aktionen—systematic round-ups—continued, with a majority selected for deportation to Auschwitz each week. On August 1, 1943, the final liquidation of the ghetto began and lasted eight days, during which 45,000 people were deported.

Of the vast Szpigelman family that populated Poland, very few survived the Nazi juggernaut. Out of the 100,000 prewar Jewish residents of Zaglebie, perhaps 5,000 lived through the Holocaust.

—SIMON SPIEGELMAN

Chaim Lajb Szpigelman (1838–1911)

Fajgla Szpringer (1840–1896)

Moszek Moshe Szpigelman (1858–1919)
— Chana Zysla Rajsfeld (1858–1933)
- Icek Wolf (1881–1943)
- Hendla (1882–1943)
- Maria Laja (1889–1943)

Menachem Mendl Szpigelman (1860–1932)
— Chaja Majerczik (first wife) (?–1905)
— Chaja Sura Lauber (?–1942)
- Majer Jozef (1885–1943)
- Andzua Hendla (1886–1943)
- Berek (1888–1919)

Majer Szpigelman (1865–1941)
— Ruchla Altman (1870–1943)
- Ziser (1890–1892)
- Mordka Hillel (1893–1943)
- Abram Wolf (1899–1943)

Jozef Henoch Szpigelman (1873–1943)
— Zysla Zylbersztajn (1873–1943)
- Jakob Szlama (1895–1943)
- Fajgla Rywka (1896–1944)
- Abram Szaja (1897–1944)

Sara Szpigelman (1876–1941)
— Fajwel Kronenberg (1875–1941)
- Fela (Fajgla) (1900–1982)
- Majer (Max) (1907–1942)
- Burech Mordka (1909–1909)

Chana Ruchla Szpigelman (1877–1943)
— Mendel Zygrajch (1861–1943)
- Fajgla (1895–1943)
- Ajzik (1896–1943)
- Fiszel (1898–1943)

Abram Szpigelman (1880–1943)
— Pesla Zylberszzac (first wife) (?–1902)
— Chaja Goldberg (1883–1943)
- Izrael Szymon (1901–1943)
- Fela (Fajgla) (1915–1942)
- Marcus (Mordka) (1905–1943)

Wolf Szpigelman (1883–1942)
— Sura Rywka Kolin (1889–1942)
- Max (Majer) (1905–1991)
- Lorre (Zysla Laja) (1908–1995)
- Frieda (Fajgla) (1910–1990)

GELMAN FAMILY TREE

AT THE START OF WORLD WAR II

Lotte (Liba) (1914–1965)

Toni (Tauba Chana) (1916–1976)

Helene (Chaja) (1918–1991)

ANJA ZYLBERBERG (1912–1968)

RICHIEU (1937–1943)

Moses (Mojzesz) (1910–1913)

Mendel (1911–1911)

Leon (Chaim Lajb) (1912–1943)

Zosha (Zysla) (1917–1943)

Yadja (Jacheta) (1920–1943)

Pinek (Pejsach) (1914–1991)

VLADEK (1906–1982)

Majer (1903–1909)

Pejsach (1907–1943)

Dwojra Ita (1909–1943)

Chaim Lajb (1914–1943)

Abram Jakob (1916–1990)

Jacheta (1910–1943)

Chaim Lajb (1911–1942)

Jakob Josef (1914–1943)

Dawid Moszek (1915–1943)

Pinkus Lib (1907–1926)

Frajda Rachela (1908–1943)

Chaja Sura (1910–1943?)

Hendla (1912–1939)

Jacheta (1914–1935)

Mariem (1916–1943)

Frajda Rywka (1899–1943?)

Arie (1906–1915)

Zysla (1904–1943?)

Szlama Becalel (1900–1906)

Rywka Zysla (1894–1943)

Lola (1904–1943)

Regina (1899–1943)

Eliash (1900–1943)

Miloch (1908–1976)

Pesach (1910–1943)

Haskel (1912–1979)

Rojza (1891–1943)

Majer Jozef (1892–1944)

Jakob Szymon (1904–1943)

Anja, Richieu, and Vladek, c. 1940.

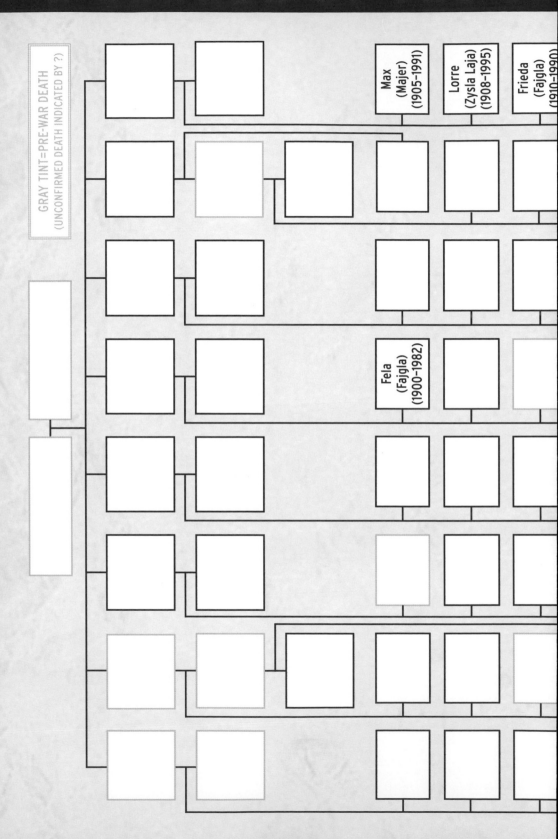

GRAY TINT=PRE-WAR DEATH
(UNCONFIRMED DEATH INDICATED BY ?)

Max
(Majer)
(1905–1991)

Lorre
(Zysla Laja)
(1908–1995)

Frieda
(Fajgla)
(1910–1990)

Fela
(Fajgla)
(1900–1982)

GELMAN FAMILY TREE

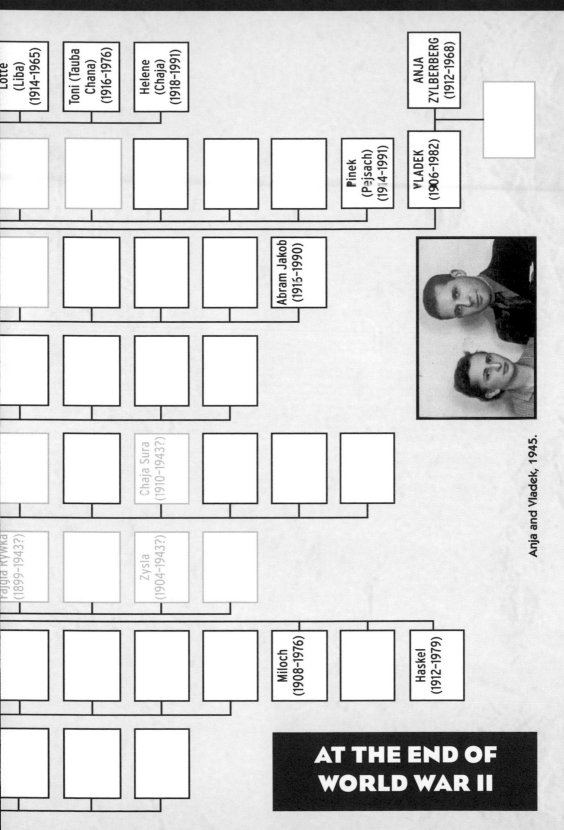

Lotte (Liba) (1914–1965)

Toni (Tauba Chana) (1916–1976)

Helene (Chaja) (1918–1991)

ANJA ZYLBERBERG (1912–1968)

Pinek (Pejsach) (1914–1991)

VLADEK (1906–1982)

Abram Jakob (1915–1990)

Chaja Sura (1910–1943?)

Fajgla Rywka (1899–1943?)

Zysla (1904–1943?)

Miloch (1908–1976)

Haskel (1912–1979)

Anja and Vladek, 1945.

AT THE END OF WORLD WAR II

And that page is as good an example as any of what comics can do that no other medium can: Vladek is in conversation with Art in the surrounding panels, but he also looks terribly isolated and alone with the photographs. It is immediately understood visually, but difficult to describe. I think even though he's presumably still on the couch next to Art, like he is in the two small panels at the top…he's not there, Art's not there. The big picture of Vladek, his isolation while holding the photo of his brother Pinek in Tel Aviv, and the scattering of photos below, carries some of the same idea of the bursting page that came right before. It carries the same weight but is now emptied out.

Part of what is so moving is that the emptied-outness is not something that you necessarily verbally underscore. You just let him and his body show it.

It was borne out of the formal problem, again: what can I show? I mean, I couldn't make up photos that didn't exist, though I did try that in some early drafts, and I didn't want to just talk about Anja's side of the family because there happen to be photos. The other people died just as surely.

You had many, many different possible endings for the book over the years. So I was wondering if you could talk about some of them, and how you decided to construct the last page the way you ultimately did.

Well, as I mentioned, one issue that came up was that I naïvely thought I would get the whole thing done in two years. The notion of a present and past could have stayed relatively stable if I could have been that efficient. But everything changed, including my father's death and the interruption and division that came from publishing the book in two parts. It meant

that my original notions of how to end the story, which were a little bit vague anyway, kept changing.

There's one sketch of you looking at yourself in the mirror and calling yourself a murderer.

I don't remember that, but you've gone over my notebooks far more recently than I have. There were many possible things I was aiming for. By the time I was really getting to the serious business of ending *Maus*, all I knew was that I didn't know what I was going to do. I did have to deal with the fact that Vladek died somewhere in the making. I got some of that told in the "Time flies…" section, but it was important to the story to allow weight to whatever closure death brings, and not just make it an aside. I think I gave myself permission to have kids because I no longer was one, after my parents were both dead. I began to try to find endings that would have to do with having, at that point, baby Nadja. (Baby Dash wasn't yet even a gleam in our eye at that moment.) There's a natural kind of—again—life siding with life that would make it a reasonable place to go.

I just kept trying things out, and part of the ongoing creative block of *Maus* was trying to figure out how on earth to bring this thing in for a landing. At some point during the period that I was seeing Pavel, I remember reading a lot of interviews in the *Paris Review*—writers talking about whether they type on 20 pound bond or 16 pound bond and so on, but in the course of this also talking about the craft of writing. And in one of these interviews—I have no idea which one anymore because I read volume after volume of those things—there's somebody describing how important endings are. I ended up reading that several times over.

Draft, page 296 (mistaken death date for Anja, August 21, appeared in final art and was corrected to May 21 only in the second printing).

of the story moving toward a present. It gets to the point in Vladek's narrative where he literally suggests the Happy Ending: Boy meets, Boy loses, Boy finds Girl. There's the story, you know? It's just that "loses" happens to move you through the railroad tracks to Auschwitz. But he meets Anja, he loses Anja, he gets Anja; on some level, that's his story, as he tells it. So it moves up to that point where they finally, after everything, are in the same physical space again. They're knotted together.

That in some ways is the end of the story, and it's kept there with this moon of the honeymoon, of them embracing again, as a very satisfying end. "I don't need to tell you, we were both very happy, we lived happy, happy ever after." Three times "happy." Which is hardly something that holds up, after having lived through seeing what Vladek is like now (that's sometime after "ever after" I suppose), and seeing Anja's postwar life—she ended it herself. Still, all of that didn't let the book end in a way that would be anything other than partial and probably ersatz, but it allows one the illusions and satisfactions of closure that Hollywood traffics in.

The writer was using the metaphor of weight, saying the last chapter weighs as much as all the chapters that came before, and basically each paragraph in that chapter has to double in weight until one gets to the last paragraph, where each sentence has to double in weight. And the idea of that weight, of that anchor that holds everything else that came before in place, allowed me to finally find what satisfied the book's requirements.

It involved several things. The whole last chapter is a rather encapsulated version

But it's the few panels after closure that double in weight again. Vladek is dying—he's beginning to lose it. I collapsed a lot of progressive "losing it" that was part of the life I experienced with Vladek. But to have that all take place and anchor itself to the phantom brother in Richieu allowed a lot of my problems, and my problems with Vladek, to be brought back into that last exhale, that last phrase. And it doesn't call the narrative into question exactly, but it does make one have to reconsider

Panel study, page 296.

what Vladek's aware of and not aware of at different points in his telling. Vladek had a sentence that he did say and that I used, although it was certainly not one of the very last sentences I heard from him: "I'm tired from talking, Richieu, it's enough stories for now." Even after he had said in the beginning of the first book, "people have had enough of these stories, they don't want to hear any more stories," there is that thing of having been pulled on some level into telling a story; we've just gone through what ultimately has been shaped into being a story.

To have all of that rest on a tombstone allows this to be, for me, like my version of a *yahrzeit* candle, a memorial. So to have the whole book poised on the tombstone of Vladek and Anja together at last allows for the flipside of what's shown when I showed them embracing two panels earlier. Putting their dates in and then following it with

my dates, as part of the signature, was not gratuitous. It's part of knotting up, tying everything and leaving it as neat a bundle as one can without simplifying and distorting and lying. A place to stop.

You've also said that doing this makes the narrative snake back in on itself. You're ending here by reminding us of the process.

I guess that's true. It's certainly a reminder that the book is made by someone. That it's not an actual false window into what takes place as "a story," but is a made thing. And that made thing is a three-hundred-page *yahrzeit* candle. An unconventional way of remembering, from what I'm told, but it was, for me, a way to commemorate. More meaningful to me, actually, than a tombstone that I don't think I've ever gone to visit in the last twenty years. Here the tombstone serves as a block that all these other blocks rest on.

—ART SPIEGELMAN,
with Hillary Chute. NYC,
2006–2010

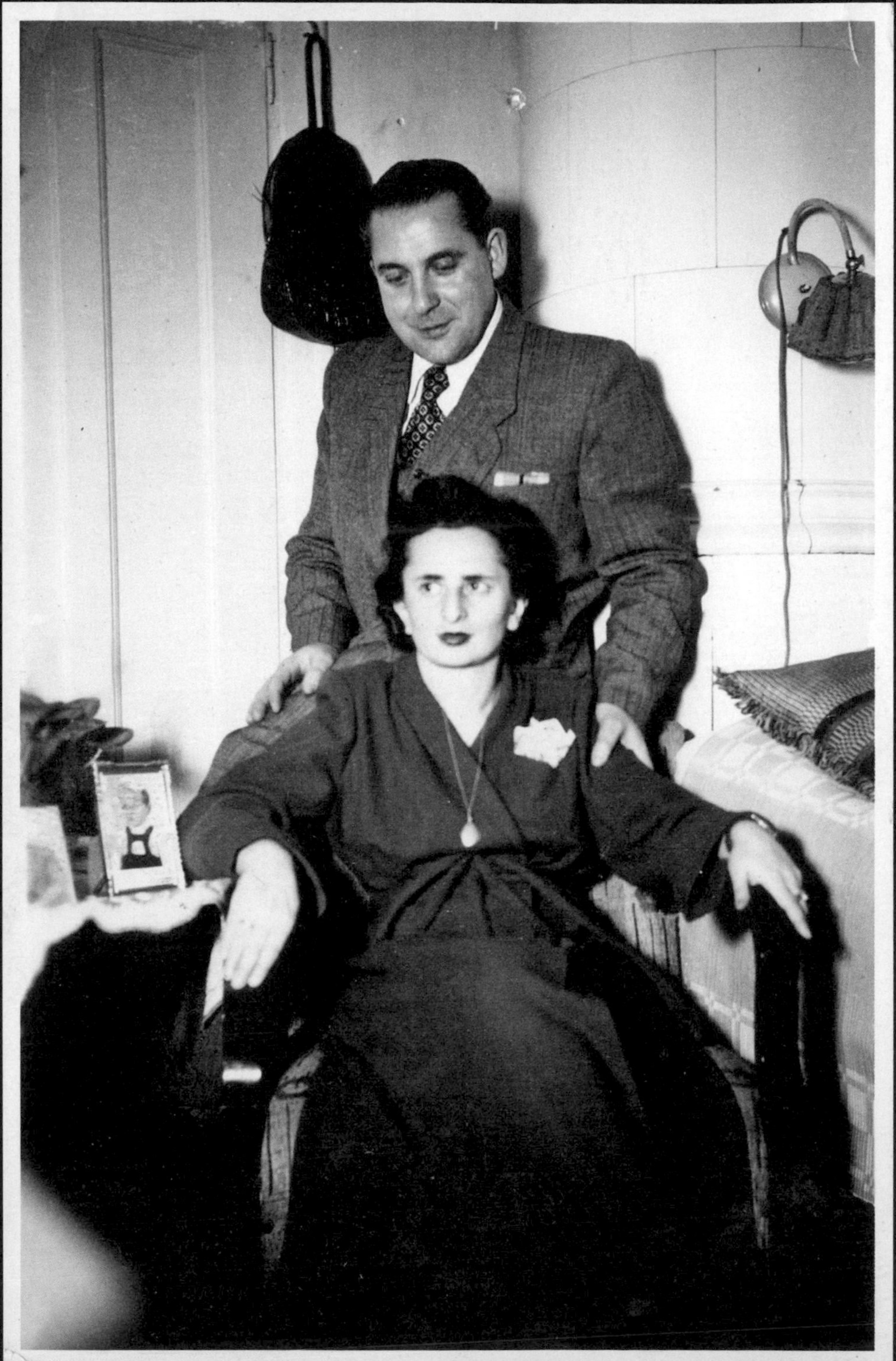

VLADEK, 1972

THE TRANSCRIPT

OVER A PERIOD OF SEVERAL DAYS IN JUNE, 1972, I first began interviewing Vladek on a borrowed reel-to-reel tape recorder. Those tapes became the cornerstone of *Maus*. Starting in 1978, when I decided to adapt his story into a long comic book, the original tapes were supplemented by many others, sifting through his narrative over and over to glean more details and to prolong my connection with my father, until shortly before his death in 1982. A longer version of the following text, as well as other tapes and transcripts, can be found on the DVD that accompanies this volume.

Vladek's discursive chronological shifts and repetitions may occasionally become confusing—and are exacerbated by gaps made when I forgot to turn the tape recorder on or accidentally taped over some of the previous material, or, later, when transferrring the reels onto cassettes may have garbled chronology further—but what follows is a lightly edited verbatim transcript of my record of those first sessions. It offers direct access into my father's story as he originally told it to me...

VLADEK: Well, now I want to tell you from the very beginning, that you will know how it was in the very beginning, and how my married life started. In 1936, I met Mother. And—in February 1937, uh, February 14th, we got married. My mother's [*sic*] parents were very well off, they lived in Sosnowiec, but they had a factory in another town. They had a factory from stockings, one of the biggest in Lodz, and he was a millionaire.

We had a nice wedding and we're happy and after a few months we had a son. My father-in-law had a big house, so we lived there in the very beginning a year. Till the end of '37. And then, my father-in-law wanted to arrange me. To make me a, a nice home, and to have everything what we need.

I had a little money, but I didn't have, uh, such, uh, big expirations [*sic*], for such big stories, like factories. I was in—in textile line. I wanted to open a shop, as I had it before, as a bachelor. My father-in-law said, "I want that you will have

a—a textile factory." And this was in another textile city, Bielsko. I told him, "Well, but you know how much a factory like this—how much money it will get involved?" "Don't worry about it." The money was about a hundred thousand *zloty*—it is like a hundred thousand dollars now—to, to get started. He told me so, "Listen, don't worry. You have fifty thousand *zloty*. Start. Start, only, and I will give you credit."

The yarn, what we had to get for the factory, it was from a convention, and we had to pay in advance, so I gave them—notes. And my father-in-law endorsed them. And so it was going on, and in a very short time, I was very well off—very well off. And we moved over to Bielsko, we had a nice apartment, a son, and we had two maids, one was in the

photo: Ken Jacobs, circa 1970

house, one was a special maid for the child, and we are very, very happy.

This was—until August 24th, 1939—when the war broke out. I got a draft card. Cause I was in the army two years before, the parents of my wife, were very afraid that we lived there, because it was nearer to the frontier. So he called me up, "Take a taxi and come over here, with everything." We couldn't get a taxi, because there was a big panic right away.

But—my father-in-law managed, sent him over with the taxi to—to Bielsko, and my wife and the child and the maids, they were in in the taxi, whatever could take along, they took along. And I locked up my textile factory, and took a little valise—we went in different direction. My wife went home to parents, and I went to the army, because I had to be the next day at the frontier.

From there, we—we got trainings and preparations, till September 1st, 1939. September 1st, 1939 we were on the line—at the frontier. They explained that on the other side is the German...

Of course, everybody got—made, uh, such uh, uh, places to, to lay down in the ground and to dig it out, and for the machineries and the cartons and everything. And we got ammunition. And we are laying. And waiting. It was very quiet. In the right side, it was a big bridge, what went over to the other side, because there was a little river between us. I was laying in my trench, around—digged out around safely. And all the line were laying soldiers. And it was very quiet, we didn't hear any shooting.

After a couple hours, they started shooting, in both sides. The side from the German and this, and this from the other side. And—then—they—I knew that the German are on the other side. I have heard—shots, but I didn't know, I didn't see anything, so I didn't know, where and ever it is. So I didn't shoot.

Then, an officer came to my place, and he said, "Make the trench a little deeper, around. Otherwise they can kill you." I figured that he is right. "Why are you not shooting? I see that you have all the ammunition, you are not—didn't shoot." So—I made the trench deeper, and I started shooting, and he went away. And when I started shooting, I—I heard shoots in my direction. And all of a sudden, I felt that there are bullets going

"...a tree was walking. If I see something alive, I have to shoot."

on my helm—through my helm. And one bullet hit my helm. So—then I have seen that the officer was right, that I have to be digged in more, so I started whatever I could, and I digged in more, myself, and the trench was well made.

I didn't shoot anymore, because what will I shoot, I didn't know where, what. And why have I to kill people. But I said to myself, "But you see that they are killing—they want to kill you." And all of a sudden I looked straight ahead, I have seen a tree, started running. "How is it possible a tree running? I have vision here." It was at nighttime. But really walking—a tree was walking. But in spite of it, if I see something alive I have to shoot. And then I started shooting, shooting to this tree, and this tree fell down. And then he showed a hand, out. It means that he is wounded, that I will not shoot anymore. But I was shooting still, because I didn't know—maybe he puts out the hand and he may shoot me, because he knew where from the bullets are coming. So I gave still a few shots in this place, and that's it.

Laying there a little longer, I heard an explosion, from my right side. I look there, I have seen a bicycle flying in the air. "Whoa—how is it? How is it possible, a motorbike?" I have seen pieces from uh, from the bridge, so the bridge exploded, and maybe somebody was still on the bridge, and uh, he's gone also together, and the bicycle is flying still. It was a terrible shock. Well, then I waited not long, maybe a couple hours.

Then I have heard steps in the back—and the German were already there. I look back, a German patrol is coming. And they started talking to me. "Get up!" In German. I answered them in German. Then one soldier took right away my gun. And the gun was hot, still. "Why did you shoot? Why did you shoot? Why were you shooting all the time, you see how the gun is—" "I didn't shoot all the time." So he took the gun, and turned it upside down, and wanted to hit me on the head.

So the other stopped him. "Wait! He must be from ours. Where from are you?" "Here, from Oberschlesien." Oh, so he heard that I know—I am speaking German. And this was near the frontier, so he was sure that I am a German also. I am a Pole, but uh, I am from the—from the place where it belonged to German, where it was occupied by the Poles once, in 1918. So he stopped him from shooting.

So I told him, "I didn't shoot all the time, but I started shooting half an hour ago. The officer came, and he took out a revolver, and wanted to kill me, because I was not shooting. And he told me, 'Why are you not shooting? You have all bullets, and then—' Then I started—then I started shooting, in—into the sky. In the air. Therefore is the gun so hot."

"Where is the officer? When was he?" "He was here maybe half an hour ago." "In which direction he went?" "In this." I showed him. So he sent out two men: "Go in this direction. Maybe we'll still catch him." And he did so. They took me with them. And then they took some more from the line, and they—we went around there, where the bridge exploded. Oh, where the bridge exploded I have seen there more people from our battalion. One was very wounded. He had a bullet in the chest. And he was laying separate, and all other ones were laying separate, and we have to put away everything what we had and they took us along. To help them. And we helped—lying big uh, wood, on the water, so that they will be able to go out on the other side. It was maybe twenty, twenty-five people, together with me. And we came over in the other side. Oh, I have seen a few cars, the Red Cross cars, and they took people who were wounded in, and there came other cars, and there was a big commotion there.

And then—he took us to go back to left, to the left side. And he said, we have to pick up here all German who are wounded, and to bring them over here. I knew where I was laying on the other side. And I knew where I was shooting, to the—to the tree, and the tree fell down, so I—I told them, "Oh, I think that here, I have noticed somebody laying" (I didn't notice yet). But when we were going there, closer, we have seen somebody is laying. So one approached him: "He is not alive anymore." And everybody had you see such a chain with his name, his name was Jan. And he said, "Ausgeblütet," it means, he ran—his blood ran out, that he is dead. So we took him also, on the car. And still other ones, and—and I knew that I killed him. But I said, "At least, I did something."

So we went back to where the Red Cross cars are, and we loaded them and so on. This went on maybe a whole day. From there, they took us to another place, where—there, it was a lot war prisoners already. And when we were standing, then it came a captain, and a major, and a colonel, and he looked at us around. The first words he started: "All Jews—out! Step out! Three feet out."

Of course, I did it too. And he started screaming at us. He said, "You! You Jews—that's your fault that, that the war started. You all are going to be hanged—here—on this lot, on this place. Everybody of you."

Of course we didn't answer a word. And from there they took us to another place. The Poles, they put in, in such little houses. And us they put in there in a basement. They started treating us—bad right away. First, when we came there they looked over all our things, our belongings, and they took us—they took away everything. They took away the money—I had you see a watch, and I had a little money. More than, uh, anybody else. Maybe on our money it is about three hundred dollars. It was quite a lot. And some other ones, the Poles they had five dollars, six. Five *zlotys*, six *zlotys*—about five, six dollars.

So—they started screaming: "You—came over here, why you took so much money? You thought that you will do here some business? Show me your hands." I showed them the hands, and my hands are very delicate and thin skin, around. "You never in your life worked. We'll find work for you here—don't worry."

> **"You! You Jews—that's your fault that the war started..."**

Of course, they found much work for us. First, they took us the—to the stable where the horses are. We were only four or five people. It was a big stable, and he said to us, "In one hour, this stable has to be cleaned. Everything has to be thrown out. And cleaned out completely. Then you will get your soup."

It was impossible to do in an hour. But we did it one and a half hour, and he came after an hour and screaming: "It will cost you from your soup—you will have less soup for it, because you are playing around." And we worked very hard to do it, but we couldn't do it in one hour. And then so on, so on, they gave such job for us. And from there—from this place, they sent us to Nuremberg.

Of course, they separated the Jews and Poles. The Jews were in a special place, and the Poles—Jews were in worse condition than the Poles, the Poles were in little, wooden houses, and we were in tents. The Jews got only one time daily, uh, soup, they got two—twice daily soups—plus an oven—and they had it warm there, it was a very severe winter, it was 1939, in whole Europe, was a very severe winter, once when I was still in the army there, we were looking up, we have seen, like birds are getting frozen and falling down. Such a winter it was in '39.

And we were laying in tents. We didn't have enough food. And we didn't have—anything to put on. Because when we went out, it was still warm—when we went to the front. And later on it got so cold, but nobody had any clothes, to get warm. What we had only our clothes, it was only a blanket, what we got from the German. But they the Poles, they had warm houses, and living like human being.

"If I will die, I want to die like a human being in some place."

With us, it was terrible. Because people were frozen and they—and they—and they got frozen wounds from the freeze, and these wounds it was filled with pus, with the wounds, it was lice. In such conditions they were laying there, and some people they took away from there they were very sick.

I had there a friend, we were together laying on one place, with straw. I got up early in the morning, and there was water, cold water. And I washed with cold water all my body. Everybody looked like I am crazy. I thought, this will keep me alive. Because I am frozen, I didn't feel in the cold water when I washed myself completely. But later on, I, I felt warm all day—because the body was very cold and this temperature what was there in the tent, it was very warm for me, and I have seen that this does good for me, I did everything—every day the same—washing with cold water and doing a little gymnastic and going in. And we didn't do any work, they didn't take us to any place.

From there everybody was allowed to write through the Red Cross, home. But we had to write in German and to be very careful in writing. Of course, I s—I wrote a letter home. And the letter came to the right hand—to my wife. After a few weeks, I got a package from the Red Cross. It was a two pieces of chocolate, it was little cigarette, oh it was so treasuring for me this package. First at all, that it I had you see a sign that they are alive, where they are. And later on, I had something to help myself in the food. And I exchanged cigarettes for bread and so and so, because—I was not smoking.

We were laying there maybe, so—six weeks, in these conditions. And, all of a sudden, in the morning, I have seen the announcements on the walls that "Everybody who wants to work, a company is coming and will take over all the people, and they will live—they will live in very good conditions. They will have food how much they want, and they will live in houses, and they will get warm clothes," and so on and so on.

Of course, all my comrades, they didn't believe, they said, "It's another trick. We want to die here." I told them, "Oh no, my friends. I am not going to die. If I will die, I want to die like a human being in some place. I will—register myself for this trip." And I found out by registering that a big company, who lost all the workers—the workers had to go to the front—they are looking for other people to replace them. And they came to take all the young people who are strong enough to work. And they prepared the—places for them, and they will work, and they will have living conditions.

We were a bunch together. I was at that time very religious, and the whole bunch, we were praying every day. We didn't have else to do. We played a little cards what we made, I made a chess board—we played chess. The chess was made from stones, from little pieces of bread, figures, and so—we were spending there the time. And—if they have seen, that I am registering myself, so they said, "If Willy is going, we are also going." And they also registered themselves.

All the people who were registered they took to these trucks. We went a few hours in the trucks until we came—we went through cities. But then we came where it's no houses, there was only very small, nice building, nice houses—wooden houses, put on for us. We came in there—went out, "Woo!"—We have seen beds—with linen—a pillow, with linen—what we didn't have there for a long time. And it was a—an oven in the middle, and very hot. And they gave us a hot soup, and they gave us coffee, and they gave us bread.

And the first day we didn't do anything, only re-recuperating. And we were very happy. But somebody started complaining, "We don't know what it will be. We don't know to what kind of work." So they said, "If somebody's unhappy, you can go back. You can go back to Nuremberg, to this, to this, uh, uh, pens. And to lay there. And to starve. And to freeze."

ART: What do you mean?

VLADEK: There were a few people who registered to go back. I don't know what happened with them; they went back. But 80 percent, they stood.

They said I am right; we have to work here, and to do everything. And so it was going on; some people, elderly people, they couldn't do the job, so one helped the other one. Because around they—there were standing the Wehrmacht, with, uh, weapons, and they watched us. And they also chased us doing faster the work. And they didn't allow to stand.

But we got good food, enough food, a warm place, a house. And clean clothes. Every third day we went for showers. I was satisfied with it.

Once, in the morning, when we went praying—we had a rabbi from Warsaw. It was a clique maybe eighteen or twenty people, who came every day in the morning, very early in the morning, before going out to work, and we were praying. I had a dream at night, but the dream was that somebody's talking to me but I didn't see anybody. Somebody's talking, a voice is talking to me. "Don't worry. Don't worry, my child. Don't worry. You will get it over. That's good that you are here. You will come home, but not so—but not now. I will tell you when." And he told me a date; the date was mentioned in the Bible, with a, a Sedra, it was Parshas Truma. He told me, "You know that Parshas Truma, you will be free, and you will go home."

And then I woke up, right away. Parshas Truma, Parshas Truma—I don't know even when it is; I don't know what it is. And then I was so tired from work I fell asleep. And the dream was again. The same dream with other words. And again and again "Parshas Truma, Parshas Truma." And then it was a, a ring to get up; it was five o'clock. I jumped out from bed. And we went to pray first, and then I went to the rabbi, and I told him about the dream. "Could," I asked him, "could you tell me, when comes the date when it is Parshas Truma?"

"I don't know, because I lost track of everything." He told me, "Parshas Truma, it will be—oh, my child, my child, very long, very long. It is still a very long time." This was maybe the end of November, and every day was for us a year. And Parshas Truma comes out in the middle February. So he figured out so many, so many weeks. "But what is the Parshas Truma; why are you asking me about this date?"

Parshas means, every week on Saturday, they are reading at the Torah, in the Bible, the parsha, and each week we have another parsha, and so it goes on all year around. And then it comes again and again, the parshas. And this was Parshas Truma, it was on one Saturday when they are reading it.

Well—"But," he said, oooh, if he heard my story, my dream, he said, "Ooooh, let me—in spite of it it's still nice few weeks, but let's hope that your dream will be accomplished from God. And we will be free so as you are telling me. Because I think that we'll not overcome here, that it will never end, that we'll not come out anymore from the Germans and from here."

"Now, let's hope," I told him, "it must be something," I told him. "I think that my father talked to me, I know that he's not alive anymore. Because he looked so like my father, but I didn't, I didn't see him well." All right, and then we didn't talk anymore about it, and went to work, and so it was day after day, and we were very busy with our jobs and work; everybody struggled. We were also allowed from there to write once a week a letter home. I wrote also a letter home, that I am well off; I don't need any packages now. Because I have enough food, cause I was thinking of it maybe they don't have enough—maybe for them it is

"... and every day was for us a year."

also hard to get chocolate and the other things. I don't eat chocolate now; I need only bread, and I have bread here and soup. I am working hard; this they can't help me.

Week by week, every day the same, every day the same work, and it was really very hard to do, because we were not used to such work. But—we survived. We were together and we survived. Until once—we were working maybe a couple hours in the morning, and, all of a sudden, we looked out on the road, we have seen that so many cars are coming, and on horses—horses are coming, on the horses were the Wehrmacht, and Gestapo, and they stopped right in front of the place where we were working.

Oh. We were not at ease, because we are always afraid that maybe something will happen, they will take us away—we got used a little to this work, and we had everything what we need. We have enough food, and sleep, and a home. And then—it was a Kommando [command]: "Everybody has to leave the tools and to go out in the street and to stay in two lines!" Of course, we did so. I stood always in the second line, I don't—I didn't want that they—that they will see me much.

And—I looked at the right side, I have seen that somebody is changing—changing, uh, places, in order to come closer to me. The changing places was so: if he was standing in the second line, so he gave a sign to the third or the fourth man, that he will move out, that he will change with him the place that he wants to be closer. If nobody saw it, he moved it. So far, so long, until he approached to me. And I look at him, this was the rabbi. The rabbi what we are praying every day together. And I told him my stories, always.

He told me, "Do you know what is today?" I told him, "Yes, it's Saturday." Of course, I always knew when it is Saturday. "Do you know what a Saturday it is?" "No." "You know this is Saturday Parshas Truma what you told me?" "Oh, boy—yes." But he was very frightened, "I don't know what's going to happen to us, where they are going to take us. But your dream, what you told me so many weeks ago, calmed me down. Let's hope for the best. God took care of us all the time; he will do it now too."

"God took care of us all the time; he will do it now too."

And it went very fast—we were marching back—to the places where we lived. When we came there it was a big yard. In the yard, there were standing tables, such, bridge tables. At every bridge tab-table was sitting a, a German, from the Wehrmacht, with books and pencils. And on every table, it was a letter, starting from A to Z. And the commander came. "Everybody, not to go in the houses! Everybody has to stand at this table where his letter begins! His name begins. His second name, surname." Well, everybody was running, running, running, and a few minutes, course the German, they had a big order. And they did something, they did it very good—this I have to uh—to, uh—add, that they did right. And so they did also of course with the finishing so many millions of Jews, so systematically, that it went a very long time, that people didn't know even that they are going to be burned in the gas chamber, until the last minute. A lot of people didn't know this.

I stood at S, and ah, and he started asking me: "When are you born? Where from are you coming? Where are you living? Where is your family living? The closest family? Do you have a wife, are you married?" "Yes." "Where—where is your wife now?" I told her [sic], "She is with her parents, in Sosnowiec, but I lived in another town." "No, but where is she now?" "She was—" "Where do you want to go?" "I want to go to the place where my wife and child is." So he made the note. And so it was with everybody. After this, we went into the houses. We came in there, everybody started talking differently, and [the rabbi] approached to me, "As I see, it is something good going to happen. I start to believe more and more this what you told me." And it didn't take 'em a day, but only the night over, and in the morning. They took us out from there, and they loaded us in passenger trains, everybody got from the Red Cross a package. And everybody went into the train, and we were going to, in the direction to Poland.

By filling out application there in the yard, when they were writing down everything, so they gave me something to sign—and this was a paper that they are releasing me as a war prisoner, that I am not, as soon as I signed it—I had also, my uh, uniform on, the Polish uniform, but I was released as a war prisoner, and I signed for it.

We were loaded in the trains, and the train went in the direction to Poland. But when we stopped at the town, they let out some people, and then we went farther, I didn't understand exactly how it is.

But they told us they divided all—all the Polish cities, to—on two parts. It was so named: Protectorate and the Reich. To Protectorate the people were belonged where the middle part of Poland is, and the Reich belonged the frontiers what belonged before 1918 to Germany. So—these people were divided from the other people, and there was a frontier also there, that people who lived in the Protectorate, they couldn't come over to the Reich—it was Poland everything, because after '18 it was Poland—after 1918. But the people from the Reich couldn't come over there to Poland.

Of course people who lived in the Reich, they were a little better off than the people were lived in Poland. My hometown was Sosnowiec—Sosnowiec, it is close to Katowice. It was Oberschlesien, and this belonged to the Reich. So I passed already Sosnowiec, and they didn't let me out. Therefore I was very—very, very worried, but they explained to me later that people who lived in Kraków—my friend lived in Kraków, and they let him out in Kraków—people who lived in Warsaw, they let them out in Warsaw.

But when I came to Warsaw, Close and the rabbi went out, so he said, "Now I see that your dream accomplish—that you are," he told me in Hebrew, "that you are a *roh-eh es hanoled*. It means that you see what the future will give us. But if I will be my hometown," he took the address, "I will write to you." Of course I never heard anymore from—from him. Because they went through such a misery later that nobody was alive, from these people.

They didn't let me out in my hometown, but they took me up—up, up, very far maybe it was three hundred miles from my hometown, and I was very worried, why, if I was so close, they didn't let me out? And they took me to Lublin, in Lublin they let us out, and there were prepared such big tents. And they let us in the tents, and I have seen that people, the Jews, are very sad. And they told me, "Listen: before you came here, it was a company—it was a party who came about six hundred people, Jews, also, war prisoners who were released. And they took them from Lublin to Biala Podlaska. This is a place like—uh, uh, a hundred miles, maybe, seventy-five till eighty miles, maybe a hundred, I don't know exactly the measurement.

"And all Gestapo took them out from there, from these tents. And they were on horses, guiding them around and watching them, and, with, uh, uh, with weapons, they kept—the weapons close to them, and they were on the horses, and the Jews, were marching, marching. They were drinking, they were drinking vodka, all the time, and at nighttime, they killed all of them—they came to a forest, and they killed all of them. They killed six hundred people in one time. And you are now the next party." So I was very frightened.

But somebody told me that the—that the Jewish—the Jewish Gemeinde, Gemeinde it means the Jewish authorities what they had there, they—they bribed the Gestapo, they bribed all the people, after this what happened, they gathered some money, and they paid for everything, and they said, that "Every party who will come, we will take them over, we will take them over to our houses, if they are families or not family, we will take them over." So somebody told me, "You have to tell, right away, that you have somebody here, if they will ask me you have a cousin so and so, you have a—don't, don't matter, whatever you will say, but then, then they will come and they will take you out, and you will be safe."

Of course, I knew somebody. The family was under the name Orbach. When I went for trainings before the war, they sent me to Lublin, and I know this family very well. We sent them later on

packages, because they didn't have so much food as we had, and I gave them the name, I remembered, I gave them the name and "Here they are living," and it took maybe an hour, he came over there, and he told me, "Don't worry, don't worry, I'll take you over to my home, as a cousin of mine." And so it happened, he took me over there, and I came out from this hell.

In this horrible place I stood only one night. At night I needed to go out, to urinate. When I went out, to the side, then I have heard that somebody is repeating a gun. And I looked back, I have seen the guard, and he shoot at me. But I ran fast back, and he didn't hit me. I came in. I waited so and thinking of different things till the morning what's going to happen with us.

And as soon as it was light, as soon as we didn't have even yet breakfast, this Orbach man, he came right away to me, and he called, "Spiegelman! Spiegelman!" I came out. Oh, he is happy that I am alive, and so. And then he told me, "Don't worry," he calmed me down. "Don't worry, I'll take you out from here." He took only ten minutes, he signed different papers, and we are on the outside.

Oh, I really was so happy, so happy. I came to his house. I remind myself that before the war, I was in this house and they had two beautiful daughters. And I had, I had two, two blocks of chocolate, from before with me, and I didn't want to eat it, I always saved, I always saved different things, in order to have maybe it will come a moment that I will not have any food. And when I gave them, each one a block of chocolate, American chocolate what I got from the Americans before. So they were so happy, and they didn't eat all the time. And they didn't know what to do for me.

Well, I was there a few days, and I looked around; what to do now? Hey, what my, my aim is to come to Sosnowiec, where my wife and child is. I found a way, that I must have different, formalities, to go through, in order to get the allowance, one that they will allow me to go back, in this place, because there was the Reich and here is the Protectorate, and it will go for—through different hands, it will go over, and maybe they will not let me go back, from here. So I decided I will do it by myself.

> "'Spiegelman! ... Don't worry,' he calmed me down. 'Don't worry, I'll take you out from here.' "

243

I had also the uniform as a war prisoner. For the German it was not anymore a war prisoner because I signed before that I am not—that I am re-signing from a war prisoner and I am going home. I understood the whole situation.

I went to the railroad station. And there were still such trains, whose loads was coal, or uh, wood and other things, in the direction to the Reich, to, to the other side of Poland. So I came back, I told them that I am going back, to my hometown, maybe I'll found a place, and I will go through the frontier. There, close to Sosnowiec, where the Reich is, it was a little frontier, that the German looked over whether somebody from Protectorate is not coming over there.

So I said good-bye to them, and I started. From the passenger train I went to another train, and—and the trainman, when he came to me, he has seen my uniform, that I am a, that I am a Polish prisoner. He started a conversation with me, they were sure that I am a Pole, that I'm not a Jew. And I told him, oh, that I ran away from, from the German camp, because here I was on the Polish side. "I ran away from the German camp as a prisoner, but now, now my aim is to come to Sosnowiec. Could you help me?" "Yes," he said, "I will tell you how you have to go, and you will go straight there. Don't worry, and don't be afraid. That's good that you have still the uniform; everybody will give a hand."

That time it was the beginning of the war, it was only half a year, but the Poles, they were very bittered on the German. And I found out right away, that if I will talk only something bad on the German they can help me, if they will find out that I am a Pole, and I was, and I was in the war prison they can help me, and so it was. And they really helped me. From one train I went to another train, until I came close, close to the train, where it has to go through the frontier. I went to the train-man, and I told him, "Listen, I am going into this train. How is it here, to go through the Kontroll there? Will, will they ask me questions, will they do, 'What ah, what happened to you? Where were you?'" I told him, "Listen, you are a Pole, so I can tell you: I am also Pole. I ran away from the German war camp, and I came over here, and I found out that I have still some family in Sosnowiec, and

> "...I have seen my three-year-old boy... And I grabbed him. He started screaming when I approached to him."

my wife and child is also there, and I want to go this direction."

"Don't worry, come in in the train." And I was there, in the train sitting, but when we were close to the frontier, he called me, and put me in in such a, in such a, a little, a little room in the train. It was not a room, but it was a, it was a, a . . .

ART: —baggage compartment?

VLADEK: Like a baggage compartment, and he said, "You sit here, don't move, don't go out, until we come through." I was there—and the German came up, and they looked at everybody's passport, and they didn't see me. And when the train went over on the other side, they let me out.

And I didn't have any difficulties anymore. I went through straight, even the German didn't ask me anything. And in this way I came to Sosnowiec. I went out, I came, I went—first at all, I went to my parents' hometown, because I didn't want to come all at a sudden there. Maybe they didn't get my message that I am coming. I only wrote them about my dream, that I will be, that I will be, on the day of our wedding anniversary I will be home. This I wrote to them three or four months before: "I know that you will laugh at me if I write so, but I had a dream that I will be on the day of the wedding home, and this I want that you will remember."

But I went ten, ten kilometers from Sosnowiec lived my parents, and there, there I showed up first. Of course they were happy when they saw me, and Mother with me went to Sosnowiec, because she went from time to time there, to my wife and to my wife's parents, to find out whether they didn't hear from me anything. Or they know any-thing where I am alive and so on and so on.

So she told me this. So when we came to Sosnowiec, I told her, "Listen, Mother, you go in first, and ask whether they heard something of me, because you got a letter from me that I am com-ing and I supposed to be any day here." So they started screaming, "What? He has to be any day here?" And I was outside standing, so I have heard the screams, they [said] "Oh, it's good, he's coming home."

And so as they were talking there and argu-ing with them that he said, that my mother said that he is coming, and they said, "No, we didn't hear from him, so he is not coming. First he would write to us that he is coming." So, I opened the door and ran in. So I don't need to tell you, you can imagine how the joy was, and I have seen my three-year-old boy, one minute, yes, he was three and a half year, three and a half year, no, yes, three-and-a-half-year-old. And I grabbed him. He started screaming when I approached to him. So later on I asked him, "I am your father, why are you screaming, why are you afraid for me?" "Oh, I was afraid for the buttons, what you have on the, on the jacket. I was afraid for this uniform with such buttons." And then he calmed down, and we were together. And what more, then they screamed, "You know what day it is? February 14, what you wrote to us!" And this was the day when I came into my house: February 14.

I came into my father-in-law's home, and he lived in a luxurious place. They had maybe ten rooms, two bathrooms, and everything was so like before the war. I was afraid, I thought that I will not have a home there; that nobody is there anymore. But in the beginning the German, they couldn't destroy everything. They started systematically.

We were happy what it is. It was very hard to find any work to do, but I found out that they are catching young people and taking them to labor camp, to Germany, to replace there their people who went on the front. Of course, I arranged myself, my father-in-law arranged something, that, that I had a paper that I am working, for the Wehrmacht. And I had such a, such a, Besierschein, such a receipt, and this was from a tin shop. He had a friend who lived there in his, in his house, and he had a tin shop what the German took it over. And he registered me that I am working, from time to time I went in only, you see, to have, to be covered; that, in case if they catch me that they will not send me out. And this worked, of course. So if I have seen that it is something bad in the, in town, they are catching people and, and checking their Besierscheins, their, their cards, so I ran in into this shop and I worked a few hours.

So we lived a little happily there, maybe a full year, or maybe over a year, and we were in this, in this house. It was not a house, it was a rented apartment, but in this beautiful apartment with beautiful furniture. But later on, the German came out to such houses, and they looked over. If they have seen nice furniture, they confiscate it and they took it out. Of course, in my father-in-law's house, it was everything new furniture, because they, they took this apartment half a year before the war broke out, and they arranged themself

beautifully. But most of the furniture they took out, little by little. And at the end it was no furniture at all. Bedroom, living room, dining room, so and so.

Later on, it came out something new; that all Jews, from all, from all part of Sosnowiec, have to come to an old part of Sosnowiec. And there is maybe two long streets, or three long streets, that everybody has to go there to live. And from there the Poles have to go over to this apartments, what, what the Jews

> **"German they always thinked of it in their head: What to do? How to have all the Jews together? So now they had all the Jews from the whole town only in two streets. But this was not a ghetto."**

had. That it was very, very bad. We had to, to leave everything what we lived, still in a little luxury, and we took over a very old, old place, in an old house, only two rooms, and a kitchen. We were a bigger family that time; two rooms and a kitchen got our family only, from fourteen or fifteen people, we were not fourteen-fifteen people, but my father-in-law got influences, a little in, from the Jewish authority. So they gave him a little larger room, a little larger place to live. So we moved over there.

The German they always, you see, they thinked of it in their head: What to do? How to have all the Jewish, all the Jews together? So now they had all the Jews from the whole town only in two streets.

But this was not a ghetto. We could still go out from this place to another place. We could still move. We could go by streetcars to other places. But we didn't think of going, because it was better to, to turn around only in these places where we are allowed. Being there, it was also very hard with food, because on the other side where the Poles lived it was easier to get the bread, where on this side, for money, where on this side where we lived.

A little later on, it came an order from the Germany, that "all older people, they are going together, they have to come on one point, and we'll send them to Theresienstadt, to a city where there is a big camp, a working camp, and people who cannot work, they will, they are resting there." It looks like a convalescence; it looks like, uh, uh, [convalescence?]

ART: Oh, convalescent, convalescent home.

VLADEK: In our place was still a grandfather and a grandmother. We kept them together always, and we watched them. Of course, we were hiding them, but they could, they didn't find them, this time. I took care of them, I made such bunkers there, and they were sitting in the bunker.

When it was over, we took them to the house, but we didn't let them out. Then it calmed down a little in the city. Later on, it came all young people have to stand or be sent out, boys and girls, they will be sent out to working camps. That time they sent out quite a lot of youngsters. I survived because I had such a card that I belonged to the tin, tin shop. And I was working there. So they didn't send me out, I was still.

It went over another year. It was up till 1943, in the beginning of '43. It came another order. On the whole Reich, it means it were, it was the three cities together, close one to the other; Sosnowiec, Będzin, and Dabrowa, that all people—young and old, kids and no kids, old people—whether they can go they had, whether then they can't go they have to take carriages and this—to come on the one lot. And everybody has to get on his passport, a stamp. Then, if somebody will be checked, will be in the street, will be checked by Gestapo, and he has the stamp, then he will be free. We knew that it is some trick from the Germany. But we didn't know what to do. Some people they were afraid to come on such a point. But then they said, "How? We'll not come on this point and will not have the stamp on the passport, they can anytime check our passports and they'll send it out. Everybody who will not have this stamp on the passport will be sent out to Auschwitz."

This was such a point that everybody has to come. People were hiding before, they didn't want to come. They were afraid that it was not the stamp. Of course this was a trick from the Germany to have them, all the people together, all the Jews from this, from this gathering there in this place Sosnowiec.

And there were different gates, alphabetical gates, we had to go through. If somebody went through there, and he was young, and, without, without kids, without small kids, and he was young to work, and he had, and he had, a receipt from the German authorities, that he is working in this and this place, there were also you see a few places, like, uh, uh—there were a lot of youngsters, and middle-aged people, who worked, who worked for the Germany there, in this town. They went out every day to work and came back. It was a lumberyard, it was, it was a textile place, where they made you see different shirts and dresses and everything, everything for the Wehrmacht, for, to send to the front. And if somebody had this card to show, they let him on the, on one place. It was divided as certain place. If somebody didn't have this card, they put him in another place. And everything was guarded by Gestapo and by soldiers around.

If they sent it to the other place, where they didn't have the cards, they sent there children, they sent there older people, very old people, and people who were not working for the cards, such people they sent. And on this side, on the better side, they sent over such—let's say if a family, that the husband and the wife they worked on a very important place, for the Wehrmacht, and they had one child, they let, they let them through, also with one child. If he had more children, two or three, they, in spite of if he had the card, they sent him to the wrong camp, to the bad camp, together with the old people. But we have seen the segregation, so we understood that this must be very bad—that if they are sending young people all over there, so these people they will not be let out home. And really these people who had, you see, the cards, and they went to the good; they went segregated to the good side. They got the stamp on the, on the passport, this one was through, was true, but the other people they didn't get. These people who got, you see this stamp, they went, they went out of it. They went back home. And the other people didn't go anymore home.

They, they were gathered on different places, and from there, they were sent over to Auschwitz. To finish them. Straight, straight to the, to the chamber, to the gas chamber. I had a sister with her husband. And they had four children: two twins, and two children. With four children they didn't let them go, and they went on the other side.

My father, he was also working on a place. He was working on, in the wood shop. And they let him through together, together with me. But then, he found out, that my older sister with the four children, she's sent to the wrong camp. He said, "How is she going to manage alone with the four children? She will be lost in the camp. She will go to work and the children will remain home." They were very small children; from two till five till four years, till five years. So he jumped from the good

246

camp to the bad camp. I didn't see it, but I have heard later. So he went together, with the daughter and the grandchildren, to finish them out.

And, and the action, what it was before with the older people, when we survived our, our grandfather and grandmother; they said to Theresienstadt, but it was not Theresienstadt, they sent them to Auschwitz-Birkenau, there, to the gas chamber. But now we took them along. Because we took them along, we are afraid that he will not have, they will not have, you see, the stamp on the passport. We didn't know what was going on behind. So of course they took him now. So they found everybody. So it was left only very little people from the hometown, what it was forty thousand Jews in Sosnowiec, maybe we had only five thousand left.

And then it was again quiet, for a certain time. A few months. Then it came another order, that all Jews who are here on this, gathered on this place, they have to go out of town, to a very small village, and this will be the ghetto. They will live there ever after, but they have to be in the ghetto. So we are arranged here a little bit, and the Poles from this little village have to go over and to come to this place, and to take over our apartments. People didn't know what was going to happen now, and of course they realize, they arranged it so, that, the Jewish authorities they helped also arranging it, they worked together with the Gestapo, they don't, didn't need you see so many people. But they were, they had to do it to keep in order everything.

And there it was the leader was Moniek Merin. And he was the leader who brought over all the Jews from here what are still alive, to this ghetto, and the Poles to bring over here, and he exchanged, a bigger family gave a bigger apartment. It was not apartments, it was not, it was only small, small little cottages. You see, if it was a family of seven, eight, nine people, he gave the whole cottage. And they took over the whole apartments from them. And this was done very fast, but there where we came in there, we are looked around, we have seen all around this village, where every fifty feet is standing a soldier, or Wehrmacht, with a gun; that nobody could come out from there.

And close to this place was also a police station, and they watched also, the German police. And being there, arranged with everything, and we lived there, from time to time, they came, and they, and they caught people. They caught people, they wanted—they wanted that this will be less

and less. But every day in the morning we went out to work, by guards, but the guards, they were from, from the Jewish authorities. The Jewish authorities have, had also police. And they took them out to work, and they brought them in. They had always to sign how many people they are taking out from ghetto and so many people they had to bring into the ghetto.

Well, I went out to work, and that time I worked in a—I worked together with Lolek, who's a niece [sic (nephew)] of mine. We worked in the wood shop. And we came back in the evening. But later on we have seen that this is going on, they are also catching people, all of a sudden. So everybody started preparing his bunkers. It means, under the place where he had, he was thinking of different things: under the

> "The Jewish authorities worked together with the Gestapo. They had to do it to keep in order everything."

ground, on the ground, over the ground; different things. So, I was together a little with my family. Of course, my son was not anymore there. But he was sent over, by a cousin of ours, what he took him over to Zawiercie, to another town, and there were, we had two nieces, and my son, and he was a relative of ours, so he took them over there to Zawiercie. Because we were thinking of it that there he will be safe. He was one, like, like here Moniek Merin, one of the oldest. He was the head of this small little town, there was also a ghetto, and he was the head. He had a father, in the age of ninety years. When they caught people there, in the town and he knew what's was going to happen. His father was sitting in his room, on the third floor, and downstairs, was standing a guy, a Gestapo, and didn't let in anybody to this house, such big influences he had.

So we were so happy that we sent over our child there. And the same was, when they caught children, nobody could touch them, because they were in his house. We always said, "That's good that our son will be saved, because he's there in such hands."

Going back here to our ghetto in Srodula: I was thinking of making a bunker, and I found a very good place. We had you see a small house, such a cottage house, built—built with bricks. I shortened the basement with a wall. And the wall what I made from stones and bricks, I covered the wall full with coal, that will not be recognized, that,

that the basement is shortened. And if you came into the basement, it was a little bit smaller, but it was coal, and the coal covered the new wall, so it didn't show anything like the other walls. And this little part in the basement, upon the basement, this little part, was the kitchen. Now, how to make an entrance, to the kitchen, to the basement?

In Europe there were such little cabinets, it was a stove and coal, and—close to the stove was a cabinet. And in this cabinet it was coal. When we made fire, we took out the coal from the cabinet, to the oven. When it was no coal, we went down to the basement and brought coal to this cabinet. So I figured out, that the entrance must only be from this cabinet. I will make an entrance from this cabinet, it will be safe, that we'll be safe there inside, in the basement. But how to do it?

"The dogs smelled out wherever somebody is."

It was a deep cabinet, maybe one and a half yard deep. So, on top I took out the bottom from the cabinet, and I made the cabinet on the top, not on the top, but half a yard from the top, maybe not half a yard, maybe ten or twelve inches, one foot from the top. And I fixed the cabinet, with the bottom what was down, completely down in the cabinet. I fixed it up, twelve inches below the top. And there it was a cover. And this twelve inches I put full with coal, till the top. And, if you wanted to take out coal, you lift up the—the part—the upper part, and it was to open, on hinges, and you took out coal. But always I tried, took, that this part will be full with coal. The cabinet I screwed to the, to the floor, that will be impossible to move, that it will look that the cabinet is full with coal, and then you cannot move the cabinet, because it is very heavy.

And it was such a design, in the front of the cabinet, with two plywood, a design like two windows. I made one plywood window removable. We opened this plywood, and there—and there I made a hole already to the basement. How, how big was the cabinet, I cut out a hole, and I knocked through the stones, to come to the cabinet, and there I put a little leather. We took out the plywood, we went in with the head, with the legs first, then we came to the, to the—then we came to this, to the ladder, and we went down from the ladder to the basement. And this was a very good bunker.

We survived a few actions what they did, and they looked for people, and they looked on the bunkers, but our bunker they didn't, they didn't find. They came with dogs, what the dogs smelled out wherever somebody is. The dog was running like mad. We heard it. He was in the kitchen, and he was in the basement. And barking, barking in the kitchen, barking in the basement, running back and forth. So they understood that here must be somebody. So they came to the oven, the oven is an oven. They came to the cabinet with the coal, they started moving the cabinet, but it was so heavy, they didn't want to bother and they went away.

And there we were, sometimes, two-three days, two-three nights, there we had prepared some food also. And when it was quiet, peaceful, we have seen that people are coming out, going to work, we went out. In this way you survived. Until, we were moved from this place to another one. And it was very little people there.

They took out also from bunkers, they took out little children, two or three years old, they started crying. It was a big truck, so they throw them on the truck. If some of the children cried, so they took it the legs and they hit the head in the wall, and then they throw it out on the—on the—on the truck, that will not be able to cry anymore. And we have seen it from the bunkers. I personally didn't see it, but somebody saw it, who tell it, in which way the children went away, who were still saved a little.

I told you before that our three children, my son, and two nieces, our friend who was such a big shot, in Zawiercie, nearby ghetto. He took them over, and he, he saved his family, he even saved the father, was ninety years old, that nobody approached to his house. All of a sudden in the same time, the same time when it was finishing up the ghetto, in, in Srodula, where I was, when I were in the last bunker already, we have heard later on we found out, that it came a Gestapo from Opole, another Gestapo, and first at all, they took big shots what they were involved in something, like, like my cousin, in Zawiercie who took over our children, and they shot them. Later on they cleaned out everything, our children, and the whole ghetto from Zawiercie. They cleaned out, to Auschwitz-Birkenau. And so it was finished up there.

Now, it came also the last moment here. When I was in the last bunker, what I said previously, with the chandelier to go there. That time, in the morning, when I went into the bunker, to this bunker what I had prepared the last one, I have heard that at night time, Gestapo came in, and they took Moniek Merin, he was the, the chief manager there all the years, from the Jews. And his whole staff. He had you see people who were working with him, girls who were working with him, maybe it was the, twenty or twenty-five people, all of them they took to Auschwitz, and they finished them out in the gas chamber.

Then, it came an order, that everybody who was still here alive, to come on this lot, where the Jewish organization is. There was a big Platz, a big place. And all came there. Of course, I didn't come there. I didn't want to go there. I had prepared a new bunker what I figured that I will survive here. So I didn't go, and they liquidating people from there. Some, some they took right away to, to Birkenau, where the gas chamber was. And some people they picked out, who took them still to Auschwitz, on different jobs, and different work.

And I was in the bunker until they discovered my bunker. And I was on the point where they are going to send us out to Auschwitz. Then I found out, there is still maybe two hundred fifty or three hundred Jews, who survived, and they have a shop, a shoe shop, what are working for the Gestapo. And I succeeded also through a cousin of mine who was a policeman, and he took us over to this shop. So he took over me, my wife, and my nephew. And there we were in this shop, until they liquidated this shop, and from there, when they liquidated the shop, I went to, to the bunker to, to the city, on papers. I had, I had papers as a—my passports as a Pole, in order to show if something happens very bad. And from there I came to different hiding places what I said previously. And this was the whole story till the end. From, from there where I went. I, I wanted to be smuggled over to, to Hungarian, and instead I came to Auschwitz. And that's it: my life story.

VLADEK: See I was afraid to—to believe the people, what they want to take us to Auschwitz, but they said—to, to take us to Hungarian. But I—but they said they took already a few, huge people over to Hungarian. How—and I can also go with them, and there I will be safe. There I met a friend from my hometown, and I told him, "Why are you—why are you here?" Now here I had a connection to go to Auschwitz—to go—here I have to Hungarian. And you will know you see what I mean. And, but I am afraid, I don't know the people. And there it was his nephew also there, he said, "Un-

cle, I will go first, and I will write you a letter, that everything is good and safe, then you will come." And I said, "If you will go, I will go also. So we go together." And we were talking Jewish. And this two guys—this two guys, they were confident—they, they understood Jewish.

ART: The two guys that were ...

VLADEK: Two guys what they were the smugglers. They understood Jewish, and, and they over listened the story. So the guy, the nephew of the uncle, he said, "All right, I am going first." And we were waiting still a few days there, until it would come the letter.

After a few days, maybe three days, they came back, and they brought the letter. We waited for them. And he gave him the letter. And the letter he wrote so—in Jewish: "Uncle: Don't lose time. It is very dangerous that you will be here. Come as soon as possible. I am free and happy." And signed Abraham—his name was Abraham—and signed Abraham. And he showed us the letter; we decided to go. Of course, Mother didn't want to go; she didn't believe. I telled—told her, "Listen—I don't know a way that we'll survive here. We don't have any other alternative; we have to go."

All right. Next day we made the appointment, that we meet together. So he and his family —he had a wife, and uh, and uh, a daughter, and a niece also. And I and Mother, we went together to Katowice. It was not far from Sosnowiec.

In Katowice—in Katowice there on the station, they bought tickets for us. They got the money before, in advance, the—I had a golden watch—a gold chain

> "I wanted to be smuggled over to Hungary, and instead I came to Auschwitz. And that's it: my life story."

and other things, a few dollars; I gave them everything. Only to bring us to freedom there on the other side. And when we were waiting, you see for the train, one moved away—there were two guys, one moved away. Oh—we were very afraid: who knows where he's going? And in this time he went to the telephone and called up Bielsko.

ART: And you're on the road at this time?

VLADEK: No, no, but he was also going with us—the two guys who were going with us.

ART: Were you on the way?

VLADEK: No—we were waiting for the train, I told you.

ART: Uh-huh.

VLADEK: And one moved away from us and went to the telephone to call. And he notified the Gestapo in Bielsko, it is um, from Katowice to Bielsko maybe it is about a hundred miles.

ART: And what—when was—how was he going to smuggle you? Was he going to give you—did you have false papers, or—?

VLADEK: No, listen, he said, "We have to go this way, and uh—till the frontier, and there, at the frontier, we have still other guys, what you—I am taking you to this two other guys, and the two other guys will take you over there farther—over the frontier. And this was the way to go."

But we came only till Bielsko. In Bielsko, when we came, the train stopped; Gestapo came in from both sides: "Here are Juden!" It means, here are Jews. "Out!" And the two guys, the smugglers, they disappeared; I didn't see them anymore. And they took us to prison, all of us.

ART: To prison?

VLADEK: To prison. In—in Bielsko to prison. In prison we had to wait until—until the wagon will come to take us to Auschwitz.

ART: Uh-huh. Did they leave—keep you all together in prison?

"We were sure that we are going to be—finished."

VLADEK: No—men extra . . .

ART: So you and Mother were separated.

VLADEK: I was together with this friend, and Mother—Mother and the other women were also separate. In that time they met there Marisha—Schubert; she was there also in prison.

ART: Is this Mancie?

VLADEK: And then we waited three days. They came, and they said, "Out."

ART: Did they treat you badly, those three days, or—?

VLADEK: They didn't treat us badly, but they gave us only very little food, once a day or something like this.

ART: They didn't make you work, though, those three days?

VLADEK: No, we didn't work; they didn't want, you see, that we'll work, that we'll go out, because if we are going out we can run away.

ART: So they just left you alone?

VLADEK: Yes, and this, and in there we were with other prisoners—with Polish prisoners, other prisoners. But after three days they took us out from prison.

ART: Everybody.

VLADEK: Everybody who had to go to Auschwitz. And outside was standing such a—a bus, a closed bus, without windows.

ART: A truck, or a—?

VLADEK: It was like a truck, no—a closed—it was with a—with a roof. With a roof and a very small, two tiny small windows. It was trucks, uh, like uh, horses—there, would uh, take over horses or cows, it such a truck.

ART: I see.

VLADEK: Not you see cars. And they put us—pushed us, in there, in this truck, and they closed the door. Until we came to Auschwitz.

ART: With wood, right? Wood or metal, the—

VLADEK: No, wood, wood. When we came to—but we didn't know. We were sure. In the truck, we were all together; I, I was—Mother, and they, and a woman, then, everybody together.

ART: You were sure what?

VLADEK: We were sure that we are going to—to be—finished.

ART: Executed.

VLADEK: Executed. To me, it means, yes—

ART: You didn't know that you were going to Auschwitz.

VLADEK: We knew that we are going to Auschwitz.

ART: Oh. And you knew that Auschwitz was the death camp?

VLADEK: But—yes, but we knew that we—that we'll go there and will not come out anymore, this we knew. That they will gas us and burn us in the oven.

ART: You knew and—did you know about the showers before, or—?

VLADEK: Yes, sure, we knew everything. Late. It was very late in—very late in season, I [inaudible] to say, you see. The war started in 1939, and this was 1943 already. And we knew everything what was going on. This was not right away. Through '43 I was in ghettos and hiding. I did—from '43 when they finished everything, then I came to Auschwitz. I was still two years.

ART: Two years—in Auschwitz?

VLADEK: Not in Auschwitz, but I was in Gross-Rosen and Dachau too.

ART: Oh, okay, so—

VLADEK: Other camps. Yes, then I came. But I was in this camp, Auschwitz, until they liquidated when the Russian came close, to Auschwitz, they liquidated Auschwitz.

ART: Auschwitz was in Poland?

VLADEK: Auschwitz was in Poland.

ART: The others were in Germany?

VLADEK: The oth—in Germany, yes. So they—they wanted to run away with the, with all the people what they had, closer to German, right away.

ART: Why didn't—why didn't they just kill the people, when they liquidated the camp?

VLADEK: They couldn't kill so—everybody so fast; they couldn't—they, they couldn't—they were together, they were different people—

ART: They would have if they could have?

VLADEK: If they cou— they killed every day—this I will tell you how it, later, how it was you see, how the procedure was working there, with the gas chambers. I will tell you it—how they were. And they could kill only you see a certain amount a day. It was burning twenty-four hours, and during the twenty-four hours they could—they, they could kill this and this much, but they were coming in more and more, people, you see; they couldn't kill everybody in one time. At the end they did. You know, what the end—but later on, I will tell you later on about it what was—so, now we came to Auschwitz, oh—

ART: You were in the truck?

VLADEK: We were in the truck, but the truck came to Auschwitz.

ART: Auschwitz. OK, so then—

VLADEK: Auschwitz. Then they separated us, the women, men, extra, and we were sure that we are going to be finished. But somebody approached to us: "Don't be afraid. You are going—you are going still to the—to camp, to Auschwitz camp, to work. You are not going to be burned—to be gassed and burned."

Yes. He was also there, working. Because he had seen that we are so frightened. He said, "If you are coming this way, so it is different. You are not going straight there; you will go first to work. We don't know what it will be tomorrow with us, but you are not going to be exterminated right away." So—he told us so: "Listen. If they will give you anything, to—to put up, remember: whatever they will give you, pick it first and run, and go!" Because we had to undress everything.

ART: But they gave you clothes?

VLADEK: And they give clothes, other clothes. If they will give, don't look at the clothes—because if some people, they came there, they looked at the clothes, they have seen, they, they—he was such a big fellow, they gave him such a, such a small pair of shoes. So he said that he will not be able to put them on. So they hit him over the head and with the shoe and he had to go.

So th—first you have to take—whatever they give you. You have to—they will see, what to do. So I knew it already, because—so they put the number, this number on—there in Auschwitz.

ART: Oh, I wanted to know what's the number; maybe we can read the number into the tape also: One seven—

VLADEK: Hundred seventy-one—

ART: One seven oh, one one three. Right? Or one seven five?

VLADEK: Seventeen fifty-one, thirteen. Yes. So—

> "I was in this camp, Auschwitz, until they liquidated when the Russian came close. And they could kill only you see a certain amount a day."

I—we went through, and they gave, whatever they gave me I took, and I go off. And I put it on. So my friend, who was with me, he got—he got two shoes, they were, Holländerkei [inaudible], you know what Hollä—they, the—

ART: Wooden shoes?

VLADEK: Wooden shoes. So they gave him one shoe, such a big one, and one shoe, such a small one. So he said, "What am I going to do?"

"Listen: Take it; put on one shoe, and one shoe keep in hand. Later on, if you will meet somebody who has one big shoe, and needs a smaller shoe, you can exchange, if you come to camp." So he understood, because they told—somebody told me how to do it. But it was very cold and so high snow. He had to step with one shoe and one barefoot, in the snow, and so we are going out.

Once we are going out, from there to c—to, to the working camp, so somebody's running from far. Who is running? This Abraham. Abraham is the nephew, his nephew. He is coming: "Uncle! You are also here?"

"You wrote me that I have to come!"

So he said, "I went till Bielsko."

"So we went too also till Bielsko!"—till Bielitz, Bielsko.

"And there in Bielsko, the Gestapo took me up, and this two guys, the smugglers, they told him everything what we were talking, in Jewish. So one Gestapo stood with one weapon in this side, and the other one this side, and the third one here, had the weapon." And he said, "They dictated me what I had to write. They also knew Jewish. And they dictated me, and I have to write the letter, so, as I wrote you."

Because the uncle was surprised—"You wrote me to come, and now you are asking me 'Are you also here?'" So then we understood the whole story, what happened, how it—that everybody who went through this smugglers came to this place.

But after let's say, we were there maybe—even not a year maybe, nine or ten months—we have seen, the same two guys, the smugglers, in Auschwitz too. Because they didn't need them anymore.

"VLADEK: **We worked very hard.**

ART: **What kind of work did you do?**

VLADEK: **But I was very happy.**

ART: **You were happy?"**

ART: But they weren't Jewish.

VLADEK: They were not Jewish. But they knew too much. They—they brought them there, and they finished them also. So they were working; the German worked in this way.

Well—and there, in this camp it was very, very hard, to stay alive. We worked very hard.

ART: What—what kind of work did you do?

VLADEK: But I was very happy.

ART: You were happy?

VLADEK: Happy, there. According to all other guys, I was happy.

ART: You were fortunate.

VLADEK: Fortunately happy. Why? When—when we came in, it—we went into one big hall, like a, a supermarket, such a meat [inaudible] or an empty one. And there it were, maybe two thousand people. And in every—in every place, it was also somebody from, from the people, a, a Pole or a Jew, one representative working. And there it was a Pole, a Pole from Oberschlesien—it means from, from this part what belonged once to Germany and they—and they, when they took it over, so they took it, them as German, Reich German, so—and they made him for such representative of all these guys.

So he said so: "Quiet, quiet! Who knows English?" [pause] "Oh—who knows English has to pick up a hand." There were hundreds of hands—hundreds. Because there was a big group also from France. France—from France, Jews. Jews—Jews from France. And everybody picked up the hand, that he knows English. So I didn't—I didn't lift. I knew English also [at] that time, so I didn't lift up the hand. And all of a sudden, I see that all th—"Everybody has to come front, to me!" They went. After—five minutes—everybody's back.

ART: They took one person.

VLADEK: No. He starts again. "Who knows English and Polish?" He was a Pole. English and Polish? So I, I lift up my hand. And maybe it was three, or four other hands. In front of me. We went there. Stand in the line, and he approached to everybody, and said, "No—do you know English?" "Yes." "Polish?" "Yes." So he talked to him a few words Polish, and a couple of [inaudible] English, but uh, he didn't understand much, and the guy who talked to him didn't understand much. He knew a few words English. To the other one the same, the third one the same, but when he started talking to me, "Ask me something," I talked to him so much in English, and asked him so many questions, that he couldn't answer me. Because he couldn't, he answered me in Polish. He couldn't answer in English, because he didn't know this much. And I, I was a teacher in English. Here I couldn't be, of course. But there I gave lessons.

ART: Where?

VLADEK: In—before the war. Before the war. I took lessons a few years, and there I gave lessons. From Berlitz school, from Berlitz book, because I took [garble] So I knew—then he brings me the Berlitz book, the first Berlitz book and second Berl—so, "Did you finish the first?"

"No, but I have also the second Berlitz book, because I figured, if I will finish the first Berlitz book and here I will not get, so I will have the second Berlitz book." So he talked to me.

"Tomorrow morning, if everybody will stand—" Yes, every day in the morning, they took out the people from this hall, and they stand in a line, and the Gestapo was picking out to work, everybody—till the end. I didn't know. "You have to stand in the left side, the last one. Don't go in the middle, don't go in—in the right side, only the last one." So—and I was with my friend, and I took him also, there on the left side. When— we—I see.

ART: Why?

VLADEK: In the left end, you see, it was . . .

ART: Why did he tell you to do that?

VLADEK: He—I don't know—I didn't know— listen, I will tell you. So: I was standing in the left . Then they came, and they, and they started counting—counting, counting, counting, counting, counting, counting, counting, count. And the left ten or fifteen people they cut off: "Back— inside." And then—they took away, someplace.

ART: To—to what: to kill, or to work?

VLADEK: No, no, not to kill—to work. They sent them away to work. And this they sent back. So I was back in. It was good, because I didn't—

ART: Where?

VLADEK: Back—back to the same hall, where I was.

ART: With a courtyard, or—

VLADEK: No, no. From th—it was a courtyard, but we came in, I told you, like a supermarket, such a big hall, a close—there we were sleeping—

ART: A hall!

VLADEK: A hall, yes. They were sleeping in this hall, and the next day in the morning, we stood there in the line.

ART: Now, what kind of—other people did what kind of work?

VLADEK: Of work? Most work was the, you see, with a, a shovel, and a, and, and a rake, and other thing—the plantation. It means so: they took us to such places—

ART: The farm.

VLADEK: It was not a farm. It was a long long [inaudible], and here was a—here was a hill, in one side, in one side there was a, a valley. And we—they, we had you see to straighten out the [inaudible], to make, to make a straight level. So, we had you see, to—we put in this, this soil, on such—little wagons, and carried them over, and covered this. So to make a ground—a straight ground, yes.

ART: [says something, obscured by noise in background]

> "Every day in the morning, they took out the people from this hall, and they stand in a line, and the Gestapo was picking out to work, everybody—until the end."

VLADEK: What? Yes, that they will be able to build, to farm—different things. And they—this was most of [inaudible]. And they—and specialists they took to, to factories.

ART: Also in Auschwitz.

VLADEK: Yes. Yes, from Auschwitz, they—there were in Auschwitz there were shoemakers, there were, there were, uh, tin—tin men, tin, uh, what?

ART: Tinsmiths.

VLADEK: Tins—?

ART: Smiths.

VLADEK: Tinsmiths.

ART: Okay, so anyway—uh, you were telling—I interrupted, and now?

VLADEK: And, well, so I was again in. And then he, he had written in my name, because he asked me the name, so he called me: "Spiegelman! Come here!"

ART: They called you by name, not by the number.

VLADEK: No.

ART: By the name or by the number?

VLADEK: No, no. He c—by number. They called by number.

ART: The Germans.

VLADEK: The Germans. They all—they all called the number. But he called me the name, because he was friendly with me already, you see, from yesterday. [clears throat] I came to him, and he said, "Come with me." I went into a room. In the room, I have seen the first time a table—a long time what I didn't see it—a table, a chair, and on the table I have seen a plate. I have seen two rolls. I have seen eggs. I didn't know for whom he ma—he, surely that he didn't eat still breakfast, and he is going to eat. I was sure that he is going to eat—"No, you sit down, you eat." To me.

Of course, I was very hungry, and I have never seen you see such, such food, a very long time—since the—in the ghetto we didn't have even this kind of food. So I ate, very, uh, very fast, and it was some coffee or some tea, I don't remember. And when I finished eating, he said, "Come with me." I went to another room. And in the other room, it was clothes, underwear. "Everything take off. Put on good underwear, that you will fit; put on other shoes, that will fit; and put on your uniform, but it will fit." It was the stripe uniform—he, he didn't show me, you see, anything civilian, civilian clothes. But the stripe, but this—but I had you see a torn one, and I had you see a, the slacks were too tight here, and the jacket was so big. So I put on everything, it was—"Now you are set?" I said yes. "Come in, with me." We went back to this room where—

"I brought him shoes, and I brought him a belt. I am telling you that he was so happy that he started crying."

ART: —the second day that you were in Auschwitz.

VLADEK: Yes, the third day, till then. [inaudible] When I was set, I approached to him: "Would you allow me to take a belt?" I got, I took also a belt for me, but everything wa—"I would like that you allow me to take a belt, and a pair of wooden shoes." He told me, "What for you need it? You came here already to do business?"

"No," I told him, "I came with a friend over here, and he got a pair—a pair of uh, of slacks, they were so big, and he has not a piece of coat, to hold them. So he has to hold, with one hand, the, the slacks. With the other hand, he has to hold the sh—the wooden shoe, because one wooden shoe he wears, it is good, and the other is small. He has to hold the wooden shoe, and with the third hand, what he has not more than two, he has to—to hold his, uh, his dish, to get a little soup. And always if he comes to the place to get you see the, the spoon—the few spoons soup, either he spills a little, or he cannot manage, and they chase him away. Because he cannot do it, with the two hands to hold everything. And he said, 'God, help me that I will have a piece of coat, a piece of coat for my slacks. And that to find a shoe on my other foot, that not to go, to walk in the, in the snow.' This he said always to me: 'God help me.' So I remembered, that I am lucky now, to take it."

"No, I understand. But remember that you have to bring me the other shoe. The other wooden shoe. You have—you have a pair of shoes, but you have to bring me the other pair of shoes."

ART: To prove that it was true.

VLADEK: Yes, to exchange. "Pick out which one he needs." I took my number, but he was a little shorter than I—I took my number, and I brought him shoes, and I brought him a belt. I am telling you that he was so happy that he started crying. This man was much older than I. He had a few houses in Sosnowiec; he was very rich. They had a co—they had a, a [inaudible], a Konditorei, um, a bakery, a bakery, with very fine cakes and so on. And he had a few houses in Sosnowiec, was very rich, the guy. And he—

ART: You knew him before the war.

VLADEK: Yes, I knew him before the war, therefore. Now I brought it to him, and he was really lucky, I have seen that he was lucky with this, that I brought him a—

ART: Where were you working?

VLADEK: No, he was still with me, it was the or the third day.

ART: The hall.

VLADEK: I kept him always in the left side. And so it was—here it was good, because we didn't, we didn't work, we didn't go out to work, because we were there a few days, we only cleaned up the place around—outside, inside. And so it was going on maybe one week.

ART: What were you doing with the guy, who—that you knew English, you helped him—?

VLADEK: No, no—listen, yes, then I went out, to the other room, where I had the breakfast, I had my breakfast, and—[Art sneezes.] Bless you. So he took out his books and paper and a pencil. I listened to him, what he said, and I started with him from the beginning. Because he didn't know the spelling; he didn't know the writing—I told him, "This is very important," that you have to know the spelling and the writing, because this is a complete other language than Polish.

ART: Now, I want to ask you, why—

VLADEK: And I—I taught him a little. I was teaching—

ART: Why did he have to know English, why did the Germans want to know English, do you know?

VLADEK: He was not a German; he was a Pole.

ART: But how come he had so much interest, then?

VLADEK: He had interest in it because he knew English a little, a little bit he knew, what he took lessons before.

ART [says something that gets drowned out.]: He was a prisoner in the camp also, right?

VLADEK: Yes, he was a—

ART: Why did he have such influence? [Something gets drowned out.]

VLADEK: You see—to make such a representative, they picked out such guys like he, who belonged, who the place belonged sometimes to German. It was Oberschlesien called.

ART: He was responsible. He was one of the people in charge of the whole camp.

VLADEK: No, he was in charge only on this hall, on this people, on this place. The people who are coming, you see, the newcomers, and he was watching, then he was watching that they will go out, you see, to stand in the line, and to keep the place clean, and if somebody needed you see some workers, he sent out—only in this place. He was not safe, he was the same thing what I.

ART: Oh, he wasn't—

VLADEK: He was the same, he was—

ART: But he had food.

VLADEK: He was a camp—he was like, like me, he was also a prisoner. He was a prisoner like me, but he was [inaudible] in better condition, because first at all, he was from Oberschlesien, he was not a Jew, and later on, he got you see, he was a representative. So he got other food, he was better food, and he was well off.

But he didn't have the freedom; he was also in concentration camp, like all other ones. Once he told me, "Listen: It is—you ca—" And I told [inaudible] him always on my friend, that I am keeping him; he knew it, and he let it go—this is the friend what I took from him shoes, and a, and a belt. He told him, "I don't know, because you see maybe that they will take him tomorrow or the day after." But he, he couldn't tell him, "Don't take him," if the Gestapo came—he was nothing there.

ART: Right.

VLADEK: Well, how long I could keep him, I kept him. But later on, they took him away.

ART: But—like, they knew not to take the last ten people or something?

VLADEK: Not they knew. He knew before how many people they will need.

ART: Oh—so he just told you where to stand so you wouldn't get picked.

VLADEK: Yes. So they took him. And later on, for instance, they needed two hundred people. And he had hundred eighty. He told me, "Don't go

"I told always on my friend, that I am keeping him...Well, how long I could keep him, I kept him. But later on, they took him away."

out. Sit here; hide here." Because he wanted to keep me.

ART: Right.

VLADEK: You understand? Once he locked me up in his room, and everybody went out, so I was again saved for another couple days.

ART: Something about your friend was?

VLADEK: And he was [inaudible]. Because they took him. With him he didn't have any business, and me he wanted, uh, that I will be as strong as possible.

> "They needed two hundred people. And [the kapo] had hundred eighty. He told me, 'Don't go out. Sit here; hide here.' Because he wanted to keep me."

And so it was every day in the morning when I came, I got such a breakfast. And I was teaching him. It was going on for maybe three months there. And I was dressed that everybody who came in a newcomer, he thought that I am a big shot. They, they approached to me and they were afraid to talk to me, because they, they, I looked like a big shot; I was b—a little better dressed, and I was standing always around there behind him, on the other side. And they, he didn't send me to any work, and didn't give me you see the broom, to clean the, to clean the place, but all other ones. [clears throat] Therefore I was—

ART: And you got along with this guy? You liked this guy. Or—

VLADEK: I—I didn't like them, but—

ART: But he—[inaudible]

VLADEK: I liked him because he helped me, and I—and, and I was teaching him. Well—once in the time, he said, "Listen: Vladek." He told me, my name is in Polish, was Vladek—William. William in Polish is Vladek. And he called on the name, "Vladek—listen, Vladek: I think that I will not be able to keep you any longer. But I would not like you to go to such work what they are sending; I would like to send you here to a professional work. But you have to tell me what a profession you are." I was not. But I told him, "Klempner." Klempner is in German a tin man—a tin man.

Because I—when I was in the beginning to war, the beginning when I was in Sosnowiec the war, everybody has to be registered, and they could catch everybody always you see, and to send away

to work, to a working camp. But there were some working places in Sosnowiec who worked for the Gestapo. And these people who were working, they had you see a certificate. And I got a certificate for the tin factory. And in case if they—sometimes they, they were catching young men in the street—I, it was very close there, I ran to this tin factory and I started working. But—

ART: How did you get such a certificate?

VLADEK: From—because this guy, who had—who had the place—you see, if somebody had a place, you see it—I have to tell you a lot of things to it that you will understand. [cough] You see, let's say a Jew had a big tins factory. They send—they put in a Gestapo.

ART: Oh, I know, I know about that; I was reading about that.

VLADEK: And he—yes, and he was watching everything what to do, and he took over.

ART: So somebody you knew has a factory—

VLADEK: And all the business he take, and this guy, he was a tenant, in my—in my father's house, not in my father but in—in Mama's father's. And I, I had half of this house that time, before the war. And he was a tenant there. So he knew, he knew my stepfather—not, uh, my father-in-law, knew my father-in-law. So my father-in-law asked him, that you have—

ART: But you had never been a tinsmith?

VLADEK: No! "You have to try a certificate for me that they will not take him away. Because he works—we, we don't have, we don't make any money now, and he is making a little money, doing some business, and he helps out the whole family."

ART: What type of—[inaudible]

VLADEK: I was sometimes buying something and selling. [clears throat] And if it, if they were running around and catching people, so I ran there into this place, but if I came there, I had to do something. So I was standing together with the other, with the other really specialists, the tin men, and I was knocking, and I have seen what he did, and I have seen how he makes a, how he makes a, a pipe, and I did it, and I have learned a little.

ART: So you picked up a little.

VLADEK: So I understood a little and I—so,

therefore I told him I am a tin man. "So all right, if you are a tin man, you, you will be well off here. Because maybe they will send me away also from here. And before they will send me, I will try that you will come into the tin men, so—shop." It was a tin men shop in Auschwitz. So he sent me over to the tin men shop as a tin man. I was working there, of course it was a little better, it was not in camp; they took us out from camp.

ART: Did you get [inaudible] a little bit better also?

VLADEK: They took us out from camp, outside, and we were working with Poles. And from the Poles we could exchange sometimes, if we had an extra shirt, I gave him an extra shirt; he gave me half a bread, and so.

ART: Where could you get things to exchange, though, [inaudible] inside the camp?

VLADEK: [cough] It was possible. I had—I had another friend who worked in, who worked in the, uh, in the cleaning store, to clean, to wash, and, and he has stolen a shirt from there, and gave it to me. When I wo—went out to work, I put on two shirts. If I came out there to work together with the Poles, on a, on a place they are building or something, I took off one shirt and I gave it to him, and he gave me half a bread and half a, and half a piece of butter, so.

ART: And you would bring back some for the other guy, who gave you the shirt?

VLADEK: No. And I b—and I brought it to the, to camp, and I gave it to him half.

ART: The guy who—

VLADEK: Yes, who gave me the shirt. You understand?

ART: —[inaudible] just curious, what happened to the guy who you were protecting a little in the beginning—was he alive?

VLADEK: What?

ART: Remember, in the beginning, you—the guy—

VLADEK: Yes, he's not alive. The wife, Lipsie [inaudible—in the book he is called Mandelbaum], and two sons live here in New York.

ART: But he, uh—you never saw him again after that?

VLADEK: No.

ART: You never saw him again.

VLADEK: Very little people came back. You see, it was—this, this work, what they send there, it was such, to finish them out. You know what they did? He had, he had on here a cap. The guy who, who was uh, watching them, took his cap and threw it far. "Run, and take the cap!" He was running, to take his cap. And he shoot him.

ART: Oh, so that they were just, like—toying with them at that point.

"This work, what they send there, it was to finish them out."

VLADEK: Yes, and this—no, and then he reported, "He wanted to run away." He shoot him. They must have you see—it was the German—they—

ART: Just for s—for fun.

VLADEK: Yes. No! He wrote down that this, "This number wanted to run away from work. I shoot him." He didn't like him; he wanted to shoot him.

ART: I see. And do you know, that that's what happened to your—

VLADEK: Yeah. Now, it—no, I don't know—I don't know whether this happened to him. Maybe it happened that they, that they hit him in the head that they killed him. I don't know, but I am telling you only how, how it was doing—done there. And there it was very hard work, and very little food, and they couldn't keep out long. If somebody was sick, and they took it, they took him to the Repier [inaudible], it was such a place, like a, a hospital, such a room. And from this hospital every week they took, to Birkenau; Birkenau was the place where, where the ovens were.

ART: Next to Auschwitz, or—

VLADEK: Yes, close to Auschwitz, and there they gassed and they burned them.

ART: Auschwitz didn't have ovens itself?

VLADEK: It was called everything Auschwitz, but it was maybe two miles—it was a section. There it was also a camp, but there were the, the ovens also.

ART: And what happened—at this time were you in touch with Mother at all?

VLADEK: Listen. I didn't know—I knew only that Mother is in Birkenau. Mother was in Birkenau. Yes, to—no, it, it was a working camp like this. But there in the other camp they were the ovens. Direct in Auschwitz the ovens—there were not the ovens. The ovens were the other camp. It was two miles or three miles maybe to the other place. And—and I have heard that she's alive and she's working there, because—

ART: Where did—where did you hear that?

VLADEK: Because people from there came—came ov—came ov—also from o-other specialists came over to this place, and one—if I met somebody, I asked, I asked this somebody. And—and once I came to a place where I was working, it were a few women working, and there were one Hungarian girl, and I looked at her, and she looked so very good to me, so I asked her whether she can do me a favor: "I know that my wife is alive, and she is in Birkenau. Her name is so and so; her number is this and this. Maybe you could find her."

> "'I know that my wife is alive, and she is in Birkenau. Maybe you could find her.' I have only her number and the name what I know, but I don't where she is."

ART: How did you know Mom's number? Wasn't that after they went into the camp they gave you numbers; weren't you separated?

VLADEK: No, I found out the number because I knew already that she is alive, and she has a number—I knew that she is alive, and she has a number. But I do—I—more I didn't hear from her; I have only her number and the name what I know, but I don't know where she is. "If you will find her, tell her that I am all right and I am alive. But I will give you a few words, a little letter."

And I wrote a—but this was very dangerous; for this you could get killed, if you gave off the letter to send a message. I gave, I wrote a few words, and I gave it to her.

ART: What did you write? Do you remember?

VLADEK: Yes, uh, exactly I don't remember, but uh, "Keep out; keep strong; if we kept so long, maybe—maybe we will come, we will come it over, we will keep it. And try to keep it out. I am alive; I am all right. Next time I will send you two pieces of bread."

Well—it was after few days, she was again working, and she brought me a letter back.

ART: That was very—uh, that was very kind of her.

VLADEK: Yes. Yes, was very, very good of her. And—and I had an extra piece of bread; I gave it to her that she will give it to her. And o—and so it was—

ART: Did you also give some to the girl who was doing the messaging?

VLADEK: No; she didn't need; I asked her whether she needs message—whether she needs bread; she has enough food. She wasn't in—she was lucky because she was in this, in—it was some places where, where they were lucky. Not lucky—so lucky that they had a piece of bread more. In some places it was terrible. [cough]

So I was as a tin man working, and there I was much better. But the representative from the tin men was a Jew, a Russian Jew. And he found out right away about me, that I am not a tin man, because he looked at the work as I am working; he said, "Oh no, you are not a tin man—how are, can you come in here?" In that time, they—they liquidated also the—it—I worked there a little bit, a few weeks, and they liquidated the place; they took out tin mans from there. Specialists. I don't know where they sent them and so on. And it belonged everything from him. Whom he wanted, he gave out. The better workers he kept. So I was afraid, that, that he will give me also t—out from there, and I wanted to stay here.

Well, when I organized, I, I—"organized," it means that I made, I made a little bread, a little butter, by exchanging something. I came in once I gave him a package of butter. And then he was quite different to me.

And in this shop it was one Polish guy, what he was a shoemaker. Only one shoemaker. And I looked how he is working. And there, it was also one, uh, representative such like this what I told you in Auschwitz, I had in the very beginning. He was also from Oberschlesien. He was there around. And all of a sudden, they took the old, the old Polish guys from there, from this part around, and they sent them away—I don't know. So it was no shoemaker there. And I was afraid that finally he will give me out, because o—if he will not give me out, it will be liquidated here, because I see so little people here.

So I approached to this, uh—his name was uh, uh, Vlakowie [inaudible]. He was on the block the, on the block and a, a representative; he was a leader. So I, I ap—if I have seen that the shoe-maker is not in there, he approach—I approach to him, I told him, "Of course, you need another shoemaker."

"Sure I need here, because all the people from here around and the Gestapo, they bring in here the shoes to fix."

"I am a shoemaker."

ART: But you weren't.

VLADEK: I—I understood a little. Because in the same story was there in the shoe shop, when they liquidated the ghetto, and I was still in the shoe shop working. Sometimes it came Gestapo and they looked around what we are doing, so I had to run there and to sit down; I was sitting at the shoemaker, and he was fixing the shoe and, and he showed me how you have to do, because "they will look at you, they will see that you are not a shoemaker." So—in the ghe—there, when they liquidated the ghetto, I told you this in the beginning. It was still a little place of workers. In this way I have learned a little. Therefore I know so many things. [cough] Because I was everything. And this helped me; this saved my life.

So he had two shoes, uh, ski shoes, such big, heavy shoes, very high one, and one shoe was open—ripped open. He throw me this shoe: "Fix me the shoe; I will see whether you are a shoe-maker." So he gave me the shoe, and—and I took a, a thread, a double thread, and I saw it was a double thread. Because this I have learned there, I have seen—I have seen the shoe shop, how they are doing it. And I have—I, I did it very fast, and I thread it. And it was very good made. If I gave him this shoe, "Oooh—you are I see a good shoe-maker. You made the shoe better than my—than the other one," than the other shoemaker. "So you are accepted."

Then I was sitting there in the little room; it was warm, and I was working. I put on sole—soles. I put on uh, uh, rubbers and—

ART: So this sort of stuff was easier for you to do than the other. [inaudible]

VLADEK: It was easier, it was in a place. And I—

ART: The other work was harder than that, right?

VLADEK: No, it was not harder, but I was always, always out. Out on the, on the place where, where they are working. It was—it was a building, on the building.

ART: You were always—

VLADEK: I was always on the b—the b—on the building, working there, outside, and it was very cold; it was a very heavy winter, that time. And here I am sitting warm. This number one. And number two, I was afraid that this, this will be liq-uidated. And then I will be out of it.

And—I—my, uh, Mother want—and there, where we were working in Auschwitz, it was also a few blocks, new blocks, separated, with chains, separated with such wire, wires, it was a women's sh—a women's shop, where women were working. And these women who were work-ing in Auschwitz, they were much better off than in Birke-nau. So Mother wanted to come over here. And I wanted to have her closer here, to see her. Because there we could see because—one yard was together with the other yard, only separated with the chain, with the—[cough] with the wires.

> **"Mother wanted to come over here from Birkenau. It cost me a lot of work. I didn't eat: I starved a little, in order to save cigarettes. And there were such people for a hundred cigarettes, they could arrange."**

So it cost me a lot of work. I started—I didn't eat; I starved a little, in order to save cigarettes. How can you save cigarettes? Because if you gave a piece of bread, you got three cigarettes. And I had no bread, because I traded bread for cigarettes, and I put together let's say a hundred cigarettes. And there were such people for a hundred ciga-rettes, they could arrange. A hundred cigarettes and a bottle of whiskey—vodka. And I had, I had a hundred cigarettes and a bottle of vodka. For myself in time, what I worked.

ART: [inaudible] that this was all from, like, made the shirts?

VLADEK: Yes.

ART: What other kinds of things did you do, other than, like, getting the shirts?

VLADEK: Not only shirts—it was you see bed-ding, pillows.

ART: But the guys in the laundry would [inaudible]

VLADEK: Yes—not pillows, but uh, but pillow-cases. Pillowcases, you see, uh, the covers—and he gave it to me, and I had to put in, under the shirt, and we smuggled it out from the camp. And when I came there, and I sold it. I was in touch with the Po—the Poles, they didn't have anything, because it was no stores, it was a, a very poor country. If somebody got only a piece of bread, they were happy. And to eat something. And the Poles, they had more. Broad [inaudible] they had farms; they had from dirt [inaudible] farms, they had—they had hens, and they had, they ma—they had a cow, they made butter, and [inaudible] this way, they had milk a little. So they had a little more, but they couldn't [inaudible]—they couldn't go out and buy something. Because there were coupons, and they didn't have enough coupons to buy, to have it.

In this way I had—and from this, I exchanged for bread and the—so. I made, I made a bottle of vodka, and I made a hundred cigarettes. And—I brought her over. She was very happy. I brought her over from Birkenau, and she was working here. And here we had such a connection, that through the wire sometimes, if I have seen no-body sees, I c—I could put a piece of bread, a letter, there, and then she go—

"A German was chasing [Anja]. And she started screaming, 'I know that you are here! Out! I will kill you!'"

Once she had you see, she was very frightened, be-cause a German representa-tive, a woman German representative has seen it, and she was chasing her, and she was running and hiding, but—she came out of it.

ART: Wait—what—I don't—

VLADEK: She—

ART: She hid from her?

VLADEK: No. She saw that she is grabbing some-thing there, where the line is it. They were not a—allowed to approach to the wires.

ART: But she saw that—

VLADEK: That she saw that approach and, and took something. And to—

ART: And so [inaudible] Mama disposed of it?

VLADEK: No—no, she ran away and she went to a block, and there, and there she had a friend that she knew, that they are chasing her. And she

put her in, in a bed, and she covered the bed. And there were hundreds of beds. And she started screaming, "I know that you are here! Out! I will kill you!" And s—

ART: This was the German?

VLADEK: The German, yes.

And she was laying there—she didn't find her. She was running around; she threw out—she turned around beds upside down—and to this bed she didn't come.

ART: But after that, how come the woman didn't wait for her to come back to the courtyard again? For this—Mother still worked there, right?

VLADEK: Yes, but, but she couldn't stay there and wait a long—or all day.

ART: But the next day?

VLADEK: The next day she came back, she didn't recognize her. Everybody looked the same. And she didn't know her name; she didn't know the number. And they looked about the same. There was one everybody the same uniform.

She was, when she was in the line, in the eve-ning Appel—you know what Appel means? Appel means every evening, before bedtime, everybody had to stand in the line in the courtyard, and they counted, whether there is not missing anybody. So she came and asked, "The woman who ran away from the, from the borderline, and I was chasing her, has to come out." And she told a few times, and Mother didn't go out.

ART: Of course. But it's crazy that they'd expect her to come out.

VLADEK: No—but she frightened there, so that she will do, she will kill, she will—everybody will suffer, they have to give her—nobody gave her out. They knew and so on.

ART: And everybody had to suffer for her?

VLADEK: Yes. They made the, they made special trainings there, and so on; they let them go.

ART: Drills, or what?

VLADEK: What? Running, running, stopping, bringing [inaudible], bending, so. And then they went over.

ART: But nobody gave her out. How many people were there?

VLADEK: No. But the—not everybody knew her. It knew her only two-three girls, what they were together, they were their fr—her friends, because the bread what I gave her, she shared with them. She gave them too. You understand?

ART: Well—we have to interrupt. Uh-huh.

[Musical interlude—Art accidentally taped over part of the interview.]

ART: Hello, hello, testing, testing. Is this in functioning order? Testing. Okay, this is two days later, June 3rd, 1972.

VLADEK: While Mother was in Bi—while Mother was in Birkenau, the—she had you see a representative, a woman what was [obscured by noise]. And she was very severe, very bad woman, and she was hitting everyone around, what came only to—close to her. And she had—this representative was not, was not a German representative, but she was also from the, from the people who were in camp, from the, uh—so sh—she was, it, it was so named, she had the, she was the representative on the block, but she was also a prisoner. But she was, had more privileges as a prisoner, because they came from, from the German part. And they were choosen [sic] out as—that they will, that they will watch the other prisoners.

So she had a pair of boots, and they came to—they were torn. And she couldn't—and she liked them very much, and she couldn't get them repaired there, because there it was not a place to go to a shop and to br—and to repair it. So Mother approached to her, because she knew that I am already you see there as a, as a shoemaker, she approached to her and told her, "Send over this, uh, this boots to my husband; he is working as a shoemaker in Auschwitz, and he will make you—he will fix them."

Of course, when I got the, the boots, I put new soles, and I sew and patch it up, and the—and the boots looked really very nice, and I send it through a messenger back. When she got this boots, and so she called in Mother, and she gave her some more food, and she was on specially privileges. Before she came to Auschwitz, she was very happy that I, that I arrange this boots.

Well, so it was going on; she was there in Auschwitz. But being in Auschwitz there one day—it was three girls from our hometown, what they caught them, that they are, they are—they were working, they were working at—uh, in the

factory, where they make the ammunition. That they gave out secrets, out, out of Auschwitz, to some people. And they caught them. And these three girls, they hanged them in the yard in Auschwitz. They were girls in the age about twenty, twenty-two. And they were very good friends of Mother.

And even [inaudible] we stood there an—and looked at it, even the men, they took—they made an Appel, on all men, and they went there to the yard, and they were standing there. They had to stand there as they were hanging them. And they were hanging about two days and two nights, in the yard, until they cut them off. This was very—a very bad, uh, picture, a very bad view for everybody.

> "These three girls, they hanged them in the yard in Auschwitz. They were girls in the age about twenty, twenty-two. And they were very good friends of Mother."

Well, this happened, this is gone. Shortly after this, we have heard that is coming, that the Russian are coming close to Auschwitz, and they are going to liquidate, they are going to liquidate Auschwitz. It means that they have everything to wind up here in Auschwitz, and they are going to take us deep to Germany.

ART: How—how did you hear about it? They—they made an announcement about the Russians, it was a rumor—

VLADEK: No. They didn't make any announcement, but we heard, we d—We had you see secret, secret, uh, news from some people, what they were hiding, and they were had you see radios and so on, it was if so—if they caught somebody they killed them on the place. So that we had some news of it.

And we heard also about that they are going this and this date, they are going to liquidate. Well, as you know, that in Birkenau, were the ovens. It means, the ovens were where they burned—they burned the people. This was burning day and night. When we went to work at night, at daytime, the flame was from the chimney, maybe hundred yards high, big flame. Because they, they burned, they burned half of [inaudible] the people.

And they looked for some, for some, uh, uh, tin men, that they will come over there, to disassemble them. To disassemble the old machineries.

And, and—there it was not many left in the tin shop, so I was registered there as a tin man, so they took me too also, from—they took me away from the, from the shoe, from the shoe shop, and to the tin men, and they sent us, they sent maybe a dozen tin men, to Birkenau, that they will take assemble [inaudible].

I cannot even describe what I have seen there. I had—everything what I had heard, I didn't believe this much what I have seen there. It was a building like a big, big, big [brick?] bakery. With a lot of chimneys around—tall chimneys and high chimneys and, and small and short chimneys. And it was also stairs to go down. And it was also beside the stairs, in the one side, it was such a slide, if they brought in people who cannot—who cannot walk, they put them on the slide, and they came down.

> "I am telling you only this what I have seen, what I went through. Not this what people were talking, rumors and other things."

You see, the procedure was there in this way, in Birkenau: when they—when it came a transport from Europe, transport of Jews or other people, what they had you see to finish them out, they told them that they are going, that they are going to—

[tape interruption]

ART: They are going to—

VLADEK: They are going to a shower room, first at all. Everybody has to get undressed. Everybody has to take the soap, and not to forget the soap and a towel. And here it looked exactly like if you are coming to a, to a house, a, to a—

ART: Showers.

VLADEK: —to a house of showers, to a—there were such, uh, such closets, everybody got his closet and a number, and got undressed, and put in the, the ever—the old belongings, they told to take all, all belongings what you have to this box, and here you have a s—a towel, and a piece of soap, and go this direction, to the shower.

Of course, everybody did so. Some people who came, they had a little savings. A, say, a little money, or some gold. They put it in, in the showe—in, in the box there, where they put the clothes, they put in the top, under the, under the floor and this, because they were sure that they will come back here to—that then they will have it, after the shower.

ART: But hadn't they heard about the showers before?

VLADEK: They had—but this I have seen when I came over there—how it, how it worked. I have heard much about it, but now I have seen everything. I am telling you only this what I have seen, what I went through. Not this what people were talking, rumors and other things. From there it was a little corridor; you went in to a shower room. It was a big, big shower room, full with—on the ceiling, it was a lot of showers, maybe hundred, maybe hundred fifty, maybe ninety showers there. From the ceiling down, it looked like the showers that are coming out water. And the door was hermetic closed. It was a very heavy door, and—and it was covered with some insulation, but when the people went in there, they closed the door, and the door had also a little window in the middle, to look in there, to the shower room.

So people went in there with the soap, and the to—and the towel, and they waited for water that it will come up from the showers. But—no water came. Instead of the water, came gas—poison gas. What it poisoned them from half an hour till three quarters. And, and the German, they looked in there, through the window, until everybody is dead already. Later on, they put on an exhaust of the gas—it was another machine, what the exhaust worked [walked?] out, that, that took out, through the s—through a chimney, out on the roof, the old gas from this room, and then they opened the door. This didn't do the German, but this do the, the prisoners. But they, they showed them what to do. And then, there were such, uh—such little wagons, what they put them on, and all the people were dead that time, they put them on, on the wagons, and they carried them to the oven. And the oven, it was a wall, with ovens, let's say, um, maybe a hundred, eighty, from eighty till a hundred yard. And it was—it looked like an oven as you are going to put in a goose, or a, or a capon. But they were very deep, very long. And each side, each side had maybe twenty-four or twenty-eight ovens like this. In each oven they put in two people. And so all these people

[tape interruption]

So they stuffed all drawers, with dead people. Maybe in one time they could stuff, uh, let's say a hundred people—more than a hundred also in one time, because there in the, in the showers it

262

went in more than a hundred, from a hundred till a hundred fifty people. So they could stuff a hundred people in one time, and they put—pushed in the drawers, and then they started burning. And so it was going on all the years—day and night, day and night, without stopping. Until it came—until it—yes, when this was finished, when they have heard about, that the Russian are close, and they want, and they want to liquidate it, that there will not be any sign; they didn't want to leave all this mess; they wanted to destroy it. It was even a rumor that they are going to bomb everything when, when they will leave Auschwitz.

So they took the Klempners—the, the, the tin men—Klempner is on German. They took all the tin men there, that they will take apart. It was standing there big boxes, wooden boxes, and they gave us tools, to take apart all machineries, what it was necessary to it—to the ovens. And the mach—the, the machinery, the exhaust machinery, and the other one. Everything we took apart and put in in the boxes, and then it came you see big cars, trucks, and we have loaded it on the trucks.

That time I had you see—I was an eyewitness how it—this was built, how it was arranged. It was arranged in this way, that people came in there; they really were sure that they are going to a shower and they will come back. But they never came back. And—and people told, told me there, who worked there, when they took them out, the—they took out the people from the gas chamber, they were this—this or—this. No, they the, the, that if somebody was short, he could be very long. If somebody—you see they were—

ART: Distorted?

VLADEK: They were distorted, they were, the, the, the dead people, they were different, you see they were not, they were not like a people who is dying. Somebody had the, could have you see a longer hand. Because they were—when the gas came in, they wanted to save themself, they didn't know what to do. And they started climbing on the, on the straight wall, but they couldn't come; they had you see broken fingers, broken nails. And they fell down. They climbed up till the ceiling and they fell down. And, and in this way, there were a few million people, they perished there.

Now I am coming back to this what it was in Auschwitz. Before they liquidated Auschwitz. When the Hungarian people came to Auschwitz—

that time, the Hungarian Jews, when the German came into Hungaria, and the—they liquidated Hungarian Jews, they brought them over to Auschwitz. That time it was no room to burn them in Birkenau, because everything was filled. And they were waiting in line to be burned.

So they digged—they digged very, very big holes in the middle of the yard. And when the holes were very deep, they said to jump in in the holes, and they threw in a little gas in the holes, and they threw in gasoline, and they made a fire. So people were burned alive; they were not yet gassed. But they want to burn them all, but they couldn't burn them in the oven—they were gassed before and then burned. And here the people, they threw in, uh, a let's say five hundred or thousand people to such a dig, and with gas, it couldn't be that all were gassed. It could be gassed maybe 50 or 60 percent, and the rest were alive. Till they poured in gasoline and they made a fire, and so they perished.

ART: Didn't the people, when they knew that this was going to happen, didn't they at least try to kill a German at the same time?

VLADEK: It happened in some spots they, the people tried to do it. But there were machinery all around—hidden machinery in the woods. If s—if they tried, they, they got killed right away. They couldn't do—they could kill somebody. They killed one German. But they couldn't do more. Because they had you see machine weapons around standing. If only it was an uprising, if they started shooting around that everybody got killed. Nobody was alive. And so there were also no—nobody alive, they were also killed.

But uh, the work in Birkenau, at the gas chambers, and at the ovens, they were working prisoners, Jewish prisoners. But they didn't let them longer than thirty days. Every thirty days, they burned this people; they pushed them in in the gas chamber and they burned them, and they took another section of thirty people to do the work. Not longer, because they have seen too much, and they didn't want that something will come out. In spite of it, it came out everything, because, because everything what I have seen, I was an eyewitness and everything, I knew before, but I didn't see it, but I knew also talking about it.

"When the gas came in they started climbing on the straight wall. They climbed up till the ceiling and they fell down."

Of course, it was, it was terrible. So it went on, a certain time, you came—I came back to Auschwitz. And we have heard that in, at the end, at the end of, or I don't remember exactly the time, but I think it was in summertime, at the end of July—no, at the end of May, at the end of May, of all—at the end of May in 1944—no, no, it was not in May, it was the winter, ach, what do I say? It was in November, in October or November, either. No—the end of October or the end of November, 1944.

Then we have heard this was legal, to everybody they said, that next day, or next two days, later, we are going to march out from Auschwitz, everybody. Nobody will be left here. We are going—we are going to Germany.

ART: People from Birkenau also?

VLADEK: No, no, this—Birkenau also, but they, I was in Auschwitz, I didn't know, I didn't hear this what was in Birkenau.

Of course, we knew, we heard, one side we heard the good news, that the Russian are close—maybe we'll survive. But the other side we heard also that we are going to, to German. What we are not so happy. I knew some people, very close, they were working in the office. And they brought me news from the office, different news, and they decided that the day what, when it will come, that everybody is going out, I have a hiding place, and we will hide, in Auschwitz— because there were, there were such houses, blocks—a block, like this, a house you see, from, uh, the house was, uh, two flights up, and was in a hundred square f—hundred yards, square yard. Such a few blocks, it was a number on each house, like this, in this block.

And here is on this block, there, up on the, on the attic, he has there a place, what we could hide. We will not, we will not stand on the Appel, we are not going to stand there in the yard, by marching out. We will go there, and we'll hide, and after a few days, we'll come out, and the German will not be. And this was a very good idea, but we were—it has to be strict confidential. And, and we started saving bread from our portion, everybody had to

> "When it will come, that everybody is going out, I have a hiding place, and we will hide, in Auschwitz...We have seen screamings going on, the Gestapos running and chasing everybody in the march."

put away half a portion, and we carried, we carried it over there, to this attic—we were together maybe seven or eight people—to this attic, and there we have hidden the bread, that if the German with all the prisoners will come out, we'll be still there, and we'll wait a few days, until it will be quiet, and then we'll run away. And this was a very good idea.

So I and some friends of mine, we came together there, and we have seen through the windows from there, from uh, from the top, top attic, we looked down, we have seen—eh, screamings going on, the Gestapos running back and forth, and chasing everybody in the march, and putting the people together. And everybody got a bread, and a piece—a full, a whole bread, and a piece of uh, a piece of uh, sausage. And they are going out, out, out the gate, out the gate, out the gate. It was thousand, thousands of people there. It took the march, took out from five o'clock it was six in the evening, and still people were going out and we were laying.

ART: Mother wasn't with you.

VLADEK: No, this was Auschwitz, and this—and this was in another part, because they connected, the women they took before, back to Birkenau, and from Birkenau they marched. In Birkenau they did also the same. Marching to deep, to deep, uh, uh, Germany. And all at a sudden it was maybe seven o'clock, it was very little people in the yard around. This guy, who worked there in the office, he came back, and he said [inaudible] "I have bad news. That they are preparing everything here to bomb all the blocks. They don't want to leave the blocks even here." The blocks it means the houses. "They are—they will put everything in fire. They'll throw bombs, and they put everything in fire."

We have heard this. [cough] And we were prepared already there with civilian clothes. Everybody had civilian clothes under it, and on the civilian clothes he had, he had a—

ART: Uniforms.

VLADEK: He had the uniform, the, the Auschwitz uniform, the stripe uniform. And everybody had civilian clothes, because—

ART: What col—what color were the stripes?

VLADEK: I will show you. [clears throat] I have a picture. I will show you, the stripes, uh, were blue stripes and gray, blue and gray, very heavy stripes, like a pajama look—look. So we figured that if everybody will go out, we'll throw down you see this, uh, this uniform, and we'll be in clothes—in civilian clothes, and then we'll be able to move and to run out.

The civilian clothes took us a long time until we got it. We had to buy for bread, for soup. From, uh, uh, from the place where they gave to wash this, the German people, it was there, it was there such a, a *pleigne* [inaudible], what do you say?

ART: Laundry.

VLADEK: A laundry. And in the laundry, to the laundry you see they gave you see some, uh, clothes to wash, and it was lost; they couldn't find. And then it was lost, somebody stole it, and he sold it for bread. So like I sold [inaudible] you about the linen, about shirts, and I bought it, I had you see a pair of clothes, a pair of shirts, and a blouse, and a shirt.

Well—but if he came with the bad news, we left everything there. We left even the civilian clothes, because we were afraid. And we put on only see this, the, the striped, the striped uniform. And we were running, running, and we were maybe— maybe the last one. We got our bread and sausage, and we joined. We were marching out.

So the march started. We marched all night, because we marched out about seven or eight o'clock in the evening; we marched all night. And we have heard from time to time shooting. And we didn't know what the shooting was. But they were shooting to prisoners. Later on we found out. Because when we were walking, we have seen some prisoners laying on the—laying on the, on the highway, dead.

So we found out that they, that the prisoners, who c—who were tired, who couldn't walk anymore—they were worn out because some were starved; they were, they looked like uh, it was a word so called *musselman*. *Musselman* means that they, he was thin, thin like a, like a tree, like a thin tree. And pale. And looked a, like a dead man, like a—like he wouldn't be alive.

Such people they couldn't, they couldn't walk, and they were behind. If somebody was behind, at the end, and from the side, the German people with the, with the weapons they were going around and hea—and, and, uh, watching us from all sides. Who was only behind, they killed him. Who was behind, they killed him.

I didn't see until in the next day, or in—during

the night I didn't see anybody killing, because where we were together, everybody was marching well. Until we came to a stop. And then I heard a shot, and I looked; I have seen that somebody is wiggling [sound of Vladek wiggling something against a hard surface] around, so, so, so, so turning around around around around maybe, maybe twenty-five or thirty times, and then he stop.

Oh, I thought that they shot a dog. Because when I lived in my hometown, I was a kid. There was uh, in, in the same house, it lived a barber, and he was a hunter. And he had a big—a big dog, like Lassie. And once the g—the dog got mad, and the dog went out and started biting the kids. I had that time maybe eleven or twelve years. He came out with a rifle, and shot the dog. And the dog was turning around on the back [sound of Vladek rattling something again], maybe—maybe thirty or forty times, and then— quiet. He was dead.

So I was sure that they had, that they killed a dog, because this is the second time as I have seen, on my own eyes, and I went closer, oh, I have seen that they—that they shot a prisoner, and I said how amazing it is, that a human being is like a dog. And I remind myself this story what was twenty years ago, or eighteen years ago, as the, the barber, the hunter who shot his dog, how he was reacting, and so are reacting the people too.

[tape interruption]

There it was a rest, maybe half an hour. We rested, we were sitting; if somebody had still a little piece of bread, he didn't finish his bread— because some people, they were so hungry, whatever they had they finished in one time. And I always divided my bread you see, on portions, to have it for a longer time, because I didn't know when I am going to get another piece of bread. So I ate only one piece, and wa—a little water I was drinking, and then it was, uh, announced to get up and to march, and was marching.

And around me there were some prisoners, what I knew them still from the tin shop, from the shoe shop, from Auschwitz there in the place whe—from the block there where we s-slept to-gether. And they told me—you see, every, every ten

"We were maybe— maybe the last one. We were marching out of Auschwitz...Oh, I have seen that they shot a prisoner, and I said how amazing it is, that a human being is like a dog."

feet it was, every ten feet it was a watching, a, a, a watching German with a gun. In this side—in the right side and in the left side. And we are marching in six. Or in five. And so it was the march. And they watched us.

And one who was in the side, at the German, he started talking to him. And he told him so, "Listen: we want to escape from the march. But we have here a little money and a few dollars. We w—" and somebody, I don't know, somebody saved pieces, it was, it was still possible to save. "And we will g—we are here, eight people, and we will give you this, and you will tell also your fellow in front, and your fellow in the back, and you will share it, and we'll make a sign when, we'll run away—it will be at nighttime when we'll come to a forest—we'll run away, and you will not kill us."

So he said, "We'll have to shoot, but we'll shoot in the air. You can run away." They came to me also: "Maybe you have some money. You can join us." Of course, I had still something. But I didn't want to give them; I didn't believe the German, that they will not shoot. And this—this transaction was gone on during the day, all day, and at nighttime, I have seen a commotion, close me, and a few people maybe eight or ten people were running to the forest, on the right side. Then the Gestapo—it was not Gestapo, but it was you see the, the, the watch—the, the watchdogs. So they started shooting. Of course, they didn't shoot in the air, but they shoot at the people, and they killed all of them.

Then the march was going on until we came to Gross-Rosen. It was a camp also—a camp similar to Auschwitz, but there it were not ovens with gas chambers. There it was very, very bad. We came there; we have seen the commotion what's going then on. It was thousand, thousands of people, from all other small camps, already there. Because everything what was close to Poland what they have heard that the Russian are coming. So they, they marched to, in the direction to German. They wanted to take out everybody, not to leave behind you see the prisoners.

So they starting—they started to give out you see a little soup, to everybody. This was terrible, terrible. They called me also to carry, to carry, uh, such, uh, *kotch*—[inaudible] such a, a, a pail of

> "So I looked for someone who's strong, not looking so like a dead man, and I took him as a partner."

soup, a big pail, the pails were, were like a big garbage can. And it was very heavy, and two had to carry it. But it—this was so heavy, but you couldn't carry, two people couldn't carry it, but you had to be very strong to carry it. And if you didn't run with it, go fast, there were standing in the back one Gestapo, he started—he started hitting you in the head so, until you fell down, and then he shoot you.

But I—and I have seen this, so all my strength—and then I looked around: "Listen! Listen! You will—you will take with—you will catch with me the, the, the pail with food." Because they took out maybe twenty people that they will carry, and I was also among them. To carry it to one spot. Because from there, they were—they started sharing the portions. And I looked for s—and I was stronger a little than the other one, because I was lucky that I had a little more food than some other people—than some other prisoners. So I looked for someone who's, who's strong also, who looks like me, he's not looking so like a dead man, and I took him as a partner. "You will take in one side and I, but remember, you see what's going on—we have to go, and to go fast with it there."

"All right, so k—stand, stand in my side." And of course we grabbed—it was when it was our line, we grabbed the pail, and we are going, not going but running, so, till the place. And the other were behind. So he started screaming a German: "You see how these two people are carrying this, this pail fast that they are carrying—and you cannot even—even lift it!" So they hit them, I do—I didn't look back even, what had happened to them.

Of course, not everybody was—could still do something. And there, and therefore that we carried this, we were lucky with this that we came over with the pail, so we got you see our dish, and we got a li—a bigger portion. There it was somebody, "This they brought over here the, the pail, they are getting a bigger portion." We got a bigger portion, and went away, and we ate.

There we were standing overnight, until the morning. But in the morning they said that we are not going to stay here. From here, they are going to transport us farther, but who knows where? Maybe—maybe they are going to finish us up; maybe they are going to kill us in some place. Well, whatever it will be, it will be.

We were waiting next day, and everybody was chased out. And we were chased out till the street, and from the street to another place, they are going, going there it was empty, no, no people, no priva—no private people going around there; we didn't see anybody. And there it was a, it was a, a train, a train line. A train, uh—

ART: Depot?

VLADEK: No, it was a—

ART: Tracks?

VLADEK: It was a t—it looked like a train—tracks. Train tracks. And we are approaching there, and they chased us there, and there from far away have seen, we have seen a, a long train, but it was a train like, like, the, uh, like for, for horses, for cows—such a train.

And they startened [sic]—they opened it, they opened the door, and everybody they pushed, they pushed in, they pushed in so fast, so fast. And everybody they pushed on one side of the train. Half [cough] that half a train. And then, when it was pushed in, like herrings, they closed it, this part. And the other part, is, was empty. So I thought, "Oh, this they have you see, they don't want to count. If they push like herrings in one side, so they—they open this side, and they let them go, so we'll be able to move." Because on this side, it was like one after the other, like you see, like you have a package of matches, one is laying on the other, so we were laying there one on the other.

But no—when this was finished, they started pushing in in the other side, other people—in the same way. And then they closed the doors. And they locked it, with, with latches, with chains and so. I have seen what's going on, so my only think was, they started pushing and going, that I push to a corner. I think, a corner, a corner I will have a little room, protecting what, what the, what the car is protecting me. And here it will be people around. So I was lucky that I came to the corner, and on top, on the corner, it was a very little window—the window it was maybe five inches by ten inches. And also you see, with iron, iron—

ART: Bars.

VLADEK: Iron bars. But this was very high.

But I noticed also that on the ceiling are such hooks. The hooks maybe they were to chain the horses, to chain the cows. So I had with me a, a blanket. So I have seen that's impossible to stay because they were so pressing, it was no room to stay. I—I went on the shoulders, on another pris-oner, and I hooked up, I hooked up my blanket in one side, strong, and in the other corner pooked [sic] up another, the other corner. And I was sitting on the blanket. So I came up. So I could—I could breathe, and rest. And beside this, I had a little air, from the little window.

I was very happy and lucky. That I came on the idea in there, and beside this that I was there. I was so lucky that I could survive. Because from this, from this car, it wa—it didn't go, came out maybe more than twenty-five people.

ART: And you watched them die.

VLADEK: And this was—so—the car was moving a little, and then it stopped. It stopped for days, for nights; they didn't do anything.

ART: No food.

VLADEK: No food. No—no noise, no voice, no nicht. Only screaming from the inside [clears throat] in the car.

ART: You didn't have any food or anything to drink.

VLADEK: Every—only this what somebody had still left, in, in his, uh, kn-knapsack.

ART: You had something.

VLADEK: I had still something in the knapsack, but not much.

But there were also some people, who had, some prisoners, who had sugar—I don't know; they organized in some places sugar. So they lived on the sugar. But—the sugar started burning them, because they didn't have any water. And I could push out my hand through the bar from the little window, and I lived mostly on the snow, because it was a lot of snow on the roof, and I grabbed the snow, and I lived on the snow, and I had a small pieces of bread.

But later on, I manage that I got sugar. How did I get the sugar? Because the people who were down, standing, they begged me for a little, little bits of snow. But I told them I cannot reach. I reach only a little bit for myself. So they gave me a spoon of sugar, and for a spoon of sugar, I gave him a handful of snow. To save his life.

ART: People didn't even have room to sit, right?

VLADEK: It was not room to stand.

> "It was a train like for horses, for cows. And when it was pushed in, like herrings, they closed it."

ART: Uh-huh.

VLADEK: And this standing, what they said that they are, that they are, how do you say, jagging with the knives, it was so that people who fainted, they fell down. And they couldn't—if somebody fell down, if somebody was leaning on the other one, he ha—he was so weak that he couldn't hold him. He moved away. So the other one moved away, so, until he fell down.

But when he fell down in the car, somebody stepped on him. Not o—somebody, but everybody stepped on him. If we stepped on him, he had a knife in the pocket. He managed to take out the knife, and to cut the le—in the legs, to push—

> "We have seen from far, on the line are we see a lot of trains; some are standing there for weeks, for months. They put in people, and they left them on the side... All the people died there, because they wanted to finish them up in this way."

ART: One person, or a lot of people?

VLADEK: One person. So he did, and, and this, this was not only with one, this was with many—in different places around. Because he was dying, and he wanted to save himself, he wanted to get up, and it was so many people were standing on him. But he could still reach to the pocket and to take out the little knife, and to, to touch [inaudible] him in the kni—in the legs.

Of course, it didn't help him much; it—he died anyway.

ART: You spent the whole time on this one blanket, seven days sitting on a blanket?

VLADEK: Yes, yes, seven days.

ART: The whole time?

VLADEK: The whole week, the first week I was in the blanket.

ART: You couldn't even move.

VLADEK: I—I couldn't stand; I couldn't move. And during the seven days, if somebody needed to—to do something, to pish or to this, they did it, there, inside.

Later on, they opened the door, they told us to throw out the dead people. I don't remember how much, but I remember only, that it was move to stand. That was move that somebody who could stand, or could, or could make two steps. They

said to, to clean up. We cleaned up, and we threw out this.

And we have seen from far, we have seen that on the, on the line are we see a lot, a lot of trains; some are standing there for weeks, for months. They put in people, and they left them on the side. Such—it was, it was a dead—how do you call this? Some trains stood on the tracks for weeks, and they didn't even open them. All the people died there, because they wanted to finish them up in this way. But ours was lucky; after a week, six days or a week, they opened it, we threw out the dead. But when we threw out the dead we were lucky too, because at least we could stand. I could [inaudible] down also from the blanket, and could stand myself, on the feet.

And from that time, after this week, it was—we were still going, and going, and this—

ART: I want to ask, what did you do during the day? In—in the, in the car, were people talking, or something?

VLADEK: Nothing more than talking one to the other: "I am dying"; somebody got crazy and they said, "Come together; go out and to—and [cough] and they are giving coffee now, they are giving coffee—why do we are standing here?" They were screaming so; they were—they got crazy.

ART: You didn't make any—you didn't make any acquaintances, nothing like that.

VLADEK: We couldn't do, we couldn't do anything; everybody was like, like dying.

ART: Everybody was dying.

VLADEK: [cough] And next—and this was—and then they closed, they closed the cars. And we were—we had a little bit of relief, because we could stand. And—and no more, and we went again till next day. Next day they opened, they opened the cars again, and asked how many dead, this.

But the deaths what we've—then we could move. We took all the dead people close to the door [cough], because we knew that it will happen again, that they will open the door, and we pushed them, we pushed them, so four in one line, and four in the other line. So we made such a pile, that we will have more room to, to move there inside. And we made a pile till the ceiling; if one pile was finished, we made another pile. Then when they opened the doors, we threw them out. Of course, we—we looked over the packets, if somebody has still a cigarette; if somebody has a piece of bread we took it away; he doesn't need it anymore. And we—and we could use this. If somebody had a belt and we needed a belt; if somebody had a knife and we don't have a knife, we took it away. Until—until we threw them out. But the next day, when we threw out all dead men, they to—told us to go out from the car, and we have seen that the Red Cross is standing there with coffee.

After a few days maybe, it was eight or ten days, and everybody got a portion with coffee and a piece of bread. We were very lucky with it and happy, and when—and then they chased us back—

ART: The German Red Cross?

VLADEK: German Red—we don't know; I don't remember; I didn't even look at when it was a Swiss German, a Swiss Red Cross or a German Red Cross; I know only a Red Cross it was, because—because the girls had, you see, red bands—they had white bands with red cross. And they were standing, big kettles with uh, coffee, and portions of bread everybody.

ART: Can I ask—how come they even bothered—

VLADEK: This trip was from—this trip was from Gross-Rosen, but we found out that we are going to Dachau. In the, in the middle of the road, we didn't know before.

ART: Now you were walking again?

VLADEK: Not marching—we are, we are on the trains. And finally we came to Dachau. But . . . aaahhhyy, my God. It was only maybe, maybe a, forty or maybe fifty people alive. From the whole car where I was, what it was a three hundred fifty.

And finally we came to Dachau. And this was a camp—terrible. Then it started my misery, in Dachau. I went through this much, that I cannot even tell anybody what I went through in Dachau. We were closed in barracks, and they didn't let us out, they didn't take us out to any work, and the—we waited only to die there in this place. They gave us one time a portion of food, and every day there were dying people from typhus. They were taking them out from this place where I was to the Rivier [inaudible], and there they were dying. And some of them were dying during the night, and we, we, we put them on one spot there in the washroom.

But—it was very misery, that when we came, when we came to the, to, to get the food, what we got once a daily a portion of soup and a thin slice of bread—

ART: In the morning?

VLADEK: During the day it was about twelve o'clock. There was a sanitation standing. And he told us to show the shirt. And everybody took out the shirt, before coming to this, and they looked over the shirt; if they found a lice, a louse in the shirt, they find lice, so they throw him away from the kettle and he didn't g—get his portion.

And how was it possible? Everybody got lice. We are laying on straw. And from the lice they got—they got typhus fever. And this was impossible to get, to get a portion of soup. But there, I—I had a little, a light, a light, a light few hours, I met a—I met a Frenchman. He was, he was not a Jew. But the French people were also there together with the Jews.

And he got, through the Red Cross, he got packages, with food. Not packages—got [inaudible] a little package from, uh, let's say from five pounds, four, five pounds, and there it was chocolate and other thing. And I liked him; I started talking to him, and he talked to me but he talked French. I didn't understand. So I started talking English. He was so happy. "Oooh, you know English!" "Yes."

And our conversation was very good. And he di—he was not so much advanced in English as I, but then we were happy both, because every day in the morning we met each other, and we were talking stories, and I told him in English, and he—he has learned a lot from my English. And every day he could talk a little more and better. And he brought me once half—half of a chocolate what he got. And once he brought me from the package something else, a piece of zwie [inaudible], a piece of bread, and I was very happy, but for a very short time.

But I wanted also the soup, and the coffee to get. So [clears throat] I exchange with one guy, I gave him a piece of chocolate that he will give me his shirt. Of course he gave me the shirt. And I washed and wash this shirt. And I looked over thoroughly [inaudible]—every thing that [there] will not be even one louse, the shirt. And I managed, and the shirt was clean. I dried it in outside. And I looked it over again and again and again, and I was happy to find a piece of paper, and I rolled the shirt in the paper.

> **"Then it started my misery, in Dachau. I cannot even tell anybody what I went through in Dachau."**

And the next day, when it was an Appel for soup, and everybody had to stand with his shirt, I put away my shirt to the packet, and I was without a shirt, and I had only th—the clean shirt I kept in my hand. And when I approached with the clean shirt, he looked it over and he gave me right away the soup and the bread. And so I did for a long time.

[Tape interruption; new recording session starts.]

Before—before I met the Frenchman, it was, it was much worse for me there. And I got an infection on my hand. I don't know how it happened, or I—but I made the infection each time bigger, by myself, in order that they will take me to the Rivier. It came there—

ART: What Rivier?

VLADEK: Rivier—it is a hospital, such—it was not a hospital; it was a room—

ART: An infirmary.

VLADEK: An—yeah?

ART: An infirmary.

VLADEK: Infirmary. Yes. They, they took me to infirmary. Because I have heard that in the infirmary, you are sleeping in a clean bed, and you are getting three times daily something to eat, so I wanted to go there. Well when—it was also once daily coming in somebody from the infirmary and looked over the people. If he has seen that somebody has an infection, or somebody is half dead, they took him out, to the infirmary. But the guy who looked at my hand every day, and he has seen. "Well, that's getting worse." I made it worse for myself. Because I wanted to get out from here, to the infirmary.

So finally they took me to the infirmary. And there it was like a paradise, in difference there where I was. I was sleeping on a bed; next day they gave me coffee, and a piece of bread.

ART: The workers in the infirmary were also Jews? Not German. Or German?

VLADEK: Was only one German on the whole infirmary. And all people who were working—they were Jewish doctors, prisoners. If somebody was

> **"I washed and wash this shirt, that [there] will not be even one louse. I was happy to find a piece of paper, and I rolled the shirt in the paper."**

a doctor, if I could be a doctor, so I could come into the infirmary and work there, then I would be happy, but I was not; what could I do?

So they took these sick people who can go down and do something, so I had to work with one hand. Whatever I could I did only, that they will like me there, that they will leave me as long as possible.

Of course, they put on ointment, and they put a—they cleaned it, a bandage, another bandage; it got better. But next day I irritated it again. And then, they have seen that something fisheye [sic] here, because it's supposed to be over already, he said. The doctor, I remember, said, "It's supposed to be over."

So then he made a big cut, what it hurt me very much, and I was afraid for my hand; I have still now a sign on this place. And I let it heal. When it was healed, they let me out, they—back, back to this place where I was before.

And then I met you see the Frenchman. And uh, I—and he helped me a little, and I helped him a little with English, and this way it was.

So it was going on another few weeks; I don't remember exactly the time, but all the time what I was in Dachau, it was—from the end of January—[coughs] Oh, I made a mistake; I told you, now I remind myself, the date when we went out from Auschwitz. We didn't go out in October-November. We went out from Auschwitz January 24th, 1945. This I know exactly now the date. And I was in Dachau from February till the—till the middle of April. This time I was in Dachau.

I came back, then I—it was may[be] a little bit easier because I met the Frenchman, and I got us the soup every day, because I had for some—I had something to exchange for another shirt, to have an extra shirt. Not to have it on, but only to clean it. And to—only for showing, that it is clean.

But after a few weeks, I got sick. I couldn't eat, couldn't sleep. And I got typhus fever. Of course every day it was a lot of people dying there from typhus, who didn't come even to the infirmary. At nighttime, when I went down, when I went down to the W.C., it was full, full on the place, on the whole corridor it was full with dead people; you couldn't go, you couldn't go through; you had to go on the heads. And this, and this was so terrible, because you stepped on the head it was so slippery. The head, it, the skin was slippery, and you were, you always thought that you are falling down. And this was every night.

Now—that time I said, "Now it is my time. I will be laying here so like this one, and somebody will step on me." But the next day I was still alive, and when the guy came from the infirmary, and checked how the people [are] looking here, so I approached, I told him, "I am feeling very bad, I didn't sleep at night," and he took the fever and he has seen that I have very high fever. And he took me right away to the infirmary.

ART: How come the other people weren't taken to the infirmary also?

VLADEK: Because he couldn't do it. It happened so fast, they couldn't survive. He—he got this—

[Off mike: "Everybody straighten up!" Vladek continues shouting some kind of instructions.]

He got this sickness, and he died after a couple of hours, after three-four hours. And—secondly, they didn't come every day to check; they came every second day, every third day. They didn't worry if, if another hundred people will die.

[tape interruption]

—were—not many people were lucky to come to, to the infirmary. When—when they got sick, on typhus. Because they died before the, before somebody came with help. So finally I came in to [the in]firmary, I was laying on a bed, as I remember. And . . . they gave me a portion of bread, because they gave every day, everybody a portion of bread.

They got—in the morning, everybody got in the morning a portion of bread. I took my bread and I couldn't eat, but I took it. I hold it under the pillow. The next, the next two days [Art coughs] the next second or third day, they have seen that I have the—piled up the b—the bread, so they, I didn't get any food at all.

So I ask for a little tea, for a little soup, for this they gave me. But they took away all the bread from me. I wanted to keep the bread; maybe I'll be able to exchange for something, for a cigarette. But it was—there it was not anybody to exchange, because everybody, if I had a, if I had a fellow, what I talked to him a little, after a couple hours he was dead and they took him out.

The crisis went through and I was still alive. And then, it came a new order, that they will take all the people from the infirmary, and they are going to send them to the Swiss frontier, and to exchange for, for German prisoners. I was very

happy. Of course, they didn't take, they didn't take the people, they didn't take the prisoners from camp, but they took everybody from the infirmary. To get rid of the infirmary, first at all.

And finally, next day, I got up—of course I couldn't stand on the legs, but there was a fellow what I made friends with him; I gave him my portion of bread what I couldn't eat. He helped me by going out from the infirmary. But by walking I fell down a few times on the knees, because I couldn't stand. And then, until we came out, a č—until we came to the gate, at, at the gate, I have seen a train, and tracks. But not a train like I have seen when I came here to Dachau, but a train w—for passengers, for people. [Dog yips in background.] Not for uh, for dogs or for uh, horses.

But this, this can't be for us, maybe Gestapo came also. No—the train was for us! And there, before going into train, everybody got a box. A box from Swiss Red Cross, and I grabbed the box, and I went into the train. I opened the box; there was many things, a few cigarettes, a piece of bread, a piece of chocolate. Marmalade. Oh, it was a big, a big treasure for me.

And this, and the train started moving. A train— the first time I came into a train where people are. For living people. And the train took us; we went a few days, I don't remember how long. I was feeling very bad, and sometime a little better, but this helped me, what I had. But I—we had to be very careful; at night I could sleep, but I didn't sleep on account of my treasure what I have. Because they were stealing. Other people finished it up in one night, or one day, so they didn't have; they have stolen from other ones. I was laying on it and holding. And a few times at night I grabbed somebody who wanted to steal my, my treasure.

Of course, if I would have more sleep, I would feel much better. But I couldn't sleep, because this was more for me than sleeping. I knew with this I can survive.

"When I went down to the W.C., the whole corridor it was full with dead people. You had to go on the heads."

[tape interruption]

So finally, the train, the train from Dachau, where we were stopped. It was close to Switzerland. They unloaded everybody and we are standing in line, and we started marching. Marching and stopping, marching and stopping. We went in this direction, where the, where the frontier from Switzerland is. There was supposed, supposed to be the exchange from the war, the German war prisoners to us. They wanted to throw us over to Switzerland, and to take from there the war prisoners, their, the German war prisoners. On the way, it was much commotion, standing, going, going and standing, and later on, we have heard: the war was over. "The war is over!" They said, they, they screamed.

So, we marched back. We marched till the trucks, where they were. At the trucks, there were again the, the, the trains, what had the, not passengers train, but [voice off microphone—"freight"] What? freight trains. And they, it was maybe three cars, and they put out, in the, they started loading us in the three cars, open cars, and in another direction they sent us back. We went, maybe, twenty minutes, twenty-five minutes. Somebody stopped the train there, and there were standing Gestapo. And we had to go down. The train went back. And so it was back and forth, until all, until all of us were over there on the other side. It was about, let's say, ten miles.

And there they took us over again. And we couldn't understand what's going on. They took us on one big place. It was a river there, and around it was a forest. And there they located us all. But we were first at all, first we were happy, and now we are very sad, because there were rumors that they are going to kill us here, that somebody noticed that around the forest, machine weapons. And they have to kill all of us here.

I remember that one guy jumped in in the water and started swimming, on the other side. The river was quite wide. And they started shooting him, but they didn't hit him, and he came over on the other side. We were, I and a friend of mine were together, his name was Shivek, and we said, "No, we are, we will not jump in the water. We'll have time when they will start shooting. Then we'll, we'll jump in in the water." We were sure that all they will finish us out here.

And so it was all night, we were very frightened, and expecting that they will start shooting to us.

And early in the morning, it was very quiet, and the people who were together, they started moving, and talking. "What happened?" we asked. "There is not even one German here with us." Everybody ran away, and they left, and they left the machine weapons and I really saw the machine weapons they were prepared. And they told me, somebody who was very close to the machine weapons laying there, he said that there was one woman, who asked the, the chief one, there, he was a colonel, "Leave them, don't, please, I beg you, don't shoot them! Don't kill them all. You see that the war is over. Leave everything; let's run away." And this woman, she saved our life. She was a lover maybe of the guy, the colonel, so, everybody, everybody was very happy, and we started going.

And we packed ourself, and we went out from this spot. When we came to the street, we are standing again, again Wehrmacht, it means, with, with weapons and around and they kept us again, and they took us to such barns. And they kept us in these barns, they didn't let out anybody. Because, they, they waited, they waited until, they waited until it will, for a message, they didn't know what to do with us. So we were, we are in prison again. And there we were all night. In the morning, again nobody's there. They ran away.

So we went on, everybody went on his, on his own. I and my friend went on his own, this was such a little town and from far away have seen a gasoline station. We went to the gasoline station and begged him, that he will leave us here a place that we want to hide. He didn't want. But later on he said, "There, go there, under the bench there, deep, you will see there a hole, go there in and lay there." And we went there, and we are hiding there for a few hours. And then came a few German on bicycles, on motorbicycles, and that he will repair something and do something. Later if he did everything, they wanted to leave, one of these guys told him, you know that here are two Jews, from, from the camp, from concentration camp, hiding. They didn't want him, to listen to him, but they ran away very fast. It looked so that everybody was running, running, running. And they wanted to save themself. They didn't, they didn't care for us anymore.

So we went farther, a place and I have seen a little house, a barn, and, and it looked like, somebody's living here. So I thought that if we will come there, maybe the German are living here, German, German people, private people. No, but we have seen them, their military people. So we were afraid to go in, but we went into the barn, from the barn we went up there. It was and I made our hiding place, and we were sitting there listening. They were going back and forth and talking German, and I understood what they, what they are going to do, I understood that they are going to run away, to leave. And all of a sudden we have heard an explosion, a big explosion, and this was a bridge nearby what exploded. So it means, oh, I told to my friend, "Now it means that the German are really running away, and they are exploding the bridge that they will not be able to chase them."

Later, it was very quiet. I listened, no German, no talking, nothing. It was so peaceful and quiet, that we didn't hear any voice. I said, "Let's go down." My friend he didn't. I jumped down, and little by little I moved out. I have seen that nobody is here. I went in, to the, to the house there, what I have seen it was only a big dish with milk. I put in my head, and I drank out, maybe half of this dish. And then I took a jar, with, of milk, and brought it up to my friend. I told him, "Here, you have milk," because we were there laying a few days, and we didn't have anything to drink.

He was drinking and then he came down. Oh, it was a place deserted. Nobody was there. Only chickens, duck, ducklings, and they were going around, back and forth. My friend took a chicken and, and killed it, made a fire, and made something to eat. And so we were there, maybe two days, and we didn't see, we didn't hear anybody, but we ate chicken, duckling, and we made fire and we ate. And we went in in the houses, and we put on other, we changed other clothing, we threw away the, the, the uniform, the uniform from concentration camp and we put on civil clothes. And we're there around, later on, we have heard talking English. The Americans are here.

And the American came in. So we are so happy we have seen them. I talked to them. My friend didn't understand. And, and they came here, to this place to live. So they ask me different questions, "How are you survived, how you are coming here?" I told them exactly how it was, and he said, "You have not to be afraid of anything. You are safe, we are over." But then I heard again shooting. And we started shivering. But they took they, they caught the weapons, nothing. They went back. They said, "Oh no, now they will not come

back anymore. If there is anybody, either he's alive or he's laying someplace, hiding."

And then they, they gave me cigarettes, chocolates, and, and conserves, I had everything, but we couldn't eat because we got diarrhea. We, we were starving for so long and we started to, very fast to eat, such things what, what were not allowed to us. So they wanted that, they said, "You can stay how long we are here, you can also live here. One room, you have both. But to clean our rooms every day, in the morning, to clean everything, to make the beds, and so." We did. And we have everything.

Later on, one, we had a few, a few suits, later on came one woman, with, uh, uh, with a Gestapo. No, no, he was not a Gestapo, excuse me, came two women came, and they had two American, American soldiers. And they showed on us, that we took the clothes from their husbands. So they asked us to give it back. We gave it back. But we had clothes enough in other places. Later on, the German went away from there and it came other, it came other people from the concentration camp around. And it—

[tape interruption]

Later on, we were there a short time, in this camp, and and once I got an itching, I got an itching in all the body. It itched me in the throat, in the ears, inside, outside, and I couldn't sleep. It was those such a little place where there were some doctors, infantary? [inaudible]

ART: Infirmary.

VLADEK: Infirmary. And they took me to the infirmary. And they gave me injections and they calmed me down. And they said the next day, that you are going to get an illness. But we cannot tell you what kind of an illness because we don't have the machinery here. We don't have to make the, the tests. We don't have any equipments. So when I went out, I felt well and I started going moving there. And I knowing English, so I had it very well. Because there was an American there and I started talking to him and I told him what he wanted to know. He was very happy and he gave me right away cigarettes and chocolate and conserves. We had quite a load, it took a little, a little carriage and we put in everything and we were moving it. Then, little by little, if we had already our cards,

"We were going. Sometime I didn't know where I'm going."

273

identification cards, we were free to go anyplace somebody wants. But then my friend said, "Oh, I had a brother in Hannover. Let's go, he is alive, because he married a Gentile girl before the war. And I know that he is alive, he has kids and he is alive." So we started going, but this was quite a hard. He wanted to climb over there, it was no trains, you couldn't go in to buy a ticket, and to go by train. It was only the trains ... the trains ... the ...

"There was two girls who came from Sosnowiec. From my wife's hometown. They told me, 'It's very bad in Poland. People who are coming back to Sosnowiec, a lot of people got killed.'"

ART: Freight.

VLADEK: The freight trains. And if you came on a freight train you had to watch where you are going, whether you are not going in a bad direction. So we asked always and we came on a freight train. Until the train stopped but we didn't have water. So I went down from the train to look for water.

I came to, I came to a place so named Würzburg. But Würzburg was, it was no, it was not it was a house, a straight house. It was a part of the house, or a heap of stones. But I looked, I was going around looking for water.

And I asked the people, "Maybe I can find here some water."

"We don't have any water for three days already!"

So we went, we slept over there in some place. Right in the morning, we went back to the tracks and we tried to go in the direction until we came to Hannover.

[tape interruption]

—ain and we were going. Sometime I didn't know where I'm going. And we had food enough with us. [tape interruption] These trains stopped very often, and it stopped, we looked for food, and we looked for water, and once I remember we stopped on one place, it—the name was Würzburg, it was only ruins and ruins and ruins, and we didn't have a—even a place to go in to sleep. And we didn't have water. And we met there people who lived there. They say that three days they don't have a, water, they cannot find any water, everything is destroyed. But, of course, we were very happy to see it. The American bombed them and they—and they destroyed so much.

And then we passed by Nuremberg. I remind myself, when I was a war prisoner from Poland they took me to Nuremberg, and I had—I had to clean the streets, the—I went to this place, I wanted to see whether I recognize, I didn't recognize anything, because all—everything was ruined, and only a big o—a big heap of stones was laying, no houses.

So we went back to the tracks and now we to go to Hannover. Until finally we came to Hannover, and he met his brother. Of course they were very happy, and they—and they gave us a room and we both were sleeping in the room.

From there, was very close, a liberation camp. There were a lot, a lot of people. And there, in this camp, I was there a few days, I met there two cousins of mine, they were uh, uh, Poldek, Poldek 's sisters, from Chicago. And they were, there were all from different camps, and there were surv—they were alive, and they came into this camp. I was there a few days. And once—once I have, uh, seen a big crowd, in the morning. I ran to this crowd, and there was two girls who came from this hometown, from Sosnowiec. [cough] From my wife's hometown. And I asked them a few questions about what's going on, and they told me, "It's very bad in Poland. People who are coming back to Sosnowiec, a lot of people got killed."

And they told me also from a friend of mine—

ART: By the other Poles, right?

VLADEK: They were killed by the Poles, because they are coming back. They, they didn't want to see them anymore, and they, and they took over their possessions, the houses, and everything what the Jews had, the business. And now, if the—some Jews got saved and they came back to Sosnowiec, they wanted it back from them. And at night they killed them, they told me also from one—from one friend of mine his name is Gelber—his name was Gelber—that he came and they, the parents had a big bakery, and they were very—very well off, they were rich. And when he came back, he came to this place, and it was a big bakery, but overtaken by the Poles. [tape pause] So, they said to him, "Go back. You have nothing to do here. This belongs to us." Of course, he didn't want to go back right away, and he was standing there after and it—until it got dark, then he went into a shed, to sleep, overnight there. And at night, they killed him. Couple days later, a brother is—was survived. He also came, and he came to this hometown, and he has heard about it that they killed his brother, he was running there over—and he went only to his funeral. After the funeral, he went back, to Germany. From there he looked away, to go to the United States, or to Israel or some other places, I don't—I didn't hear from him anymore.

Then I didn't want to listen about all these stories what the girls are telling me, I asked them, "Did you see—Miss Zylberberg, from home? She is Zylberberg, and she is Spiegelman, fr—uh, she's my—sh-she's my wife, maybe she—you saw her? How long were you in Sosnowiec? Oh, you were there three weeks." These girls, they came also from concentration camp. But they came to look for relatives. But they didn't find, and they heard what a misery is going on there in Poland she [sic] ran back to Germany and she came to this liberation camp. One said, "Yes, I said [saw] her, on Modz—Modrzejowska Street—I saw her! I saw her, she's alive!" I really didn't want to believe.

And then, she told me, the number what she has on the hand. She was a very good friend of her, they were together in camp. And she told me the number what I remembered, exactly—of course I don't remember exactly now—but I remembered the name, if I—remembered the number, but if I have heard the number, and she told me how she looks, and this—"Oh! she is—so she is alive."

"She is looking for you to come. She told me that we made an agreement during the war, that if somebody will be alive from us, you, me, or—or anybody from the family, we have only to come to the hometown to find each other." Of course, she came first, because she got liberated on the Russian side. And the Russian side, uh, from the Russian, people got liberated earlier than from the American side, because we went very deep, deep, there into, to German. And my liberation took, uh, maybe a couple months longer, and beside this, I was very sick, of the—of the typhus fever, and I was laying a few weeks that I couldn't still go. And I figured later, once I can go now, and before I am leaving for Sosnowiec, to my hometown, I remembered that we made such an agreement, I will still go from one camp to another, maybe I will find somebody, until I came to this camp where I found the girls. And the girls told me about my wife, that she's alive, of course I was very happy, and I changed my trip, everything, to go only back to Sosnowiec.

Minding about the number what she told me—that uh, I have forgotten to tell you about

my number. I am going back now when I came the first day to Auschwitz. I came out from the place where they took away my clothes and everything. A priest is observing me. All the time. And then he approached a little closer to me and started talking to me. "When did you come to Auschwitz?" "Oh, I came just today morning." "Why are you so sad?" "Why? I have to be happy! Did I come to a carnival? That I have to be happy here?" Then he looked at me and he looked at my hand. And he has seen my number. "I guarantee you that you will be alive. I don't know what will happen to me, but you will be alive."

Talking about the numbers, I want to tell you that numbers, in the very beginning, when Auschwitz started, they put a number, in the ver—a letter in the very beginning, A, A one, A two, A three. That it went very sky high. I came to Auschwitz much, much later. And the numbers went maybe to millions—to hundred thousand or a million, and they didn't want to have a record of such high numbers. So they stopped this number all of a sudden, and they started giving—starting again from number one, without the A. And I came it was one seventy-five thousand, one hundred thirteen. So it was the numbers. I didn't know it in the very beginning, but I noticed that friends of mine, they have with the number A, so they explained me, how it was.

Well, going back to the story, from uh, the two girls what I said, so I was very excited and I packed everything and I was on the way, to come—to Poland, to Sosnowiec. This was a trip what it took a very long time, because there were no trains, no planes, people went by foot, people went—uh, they—wherever they wanted to go it was no s—station, no—it was not a place to buy a ticket and to go to some place. But they were such—it were—they were, crossing from one place to another, such, uh, they were freight trains. Different places going, but not, uh—but they couldn't go straight, because some tracks were destroyed, and they stopped, and you could stop you see one day one night, and so . . .

"When I came the first day to Auschwitz, a priest started talking to me. 'When did you come to Auschwitz? Why are you so sad?' Then he looked at me and he looked at my hand. And he has seen my number. [He said,] 'I don't know what will happen to me, but you will be alive.'"

Of course, I went with my friend. Who's, uh, my friend what I told you that, uh, that we got liberated. His name was Shivek, and—we were together, he said, "If you are going to Poland now, I am also going to Poland." He was nearby, the place was Będzin. And Będzin was maybe ten—ten, uh, miles from Sosnowiec. So he said, "I will go with you." All right, so we went together. But once we came to one place, and we didn't have any water. And I told him—and this, and the train stopped, and it was standing there hours, hours, hours. We had a little belongings, what we took together a little clothes. And even I took a, a nice—uh, uh, a nice uh, little fur coat, for my wife. And some dresses because I figured, maybe she's—will not have anything to put on, and if I will come, I will bring her this presents. I exchange it also for food, I had always much more food than some other people, I was speaking English, and I—I was in, in close contact with the American, and they always gave me chocolate and conserves, and other things, and this I exchange, with, for d—for dresses, for, for suits and therefore I had it.

And we had a nice little baggage, a few trunks. And I told him, "You sit, and watch the trunks. I will go down and look for water. If I will go, I will bring water."

Of course, he was waiting, and I have made a note, a sign, where I am, in order to come back here. I went down, and I was maybe an hour or two, but I brought water, whatever we had, canteens, different canteens, I took everything, and I brought water. I came back with the water but I didn't see anymore the train, I didn't see anymore my friend and the luggage. Cause they—they change—they changed the—the train, on another track, it was changing, and I couldn't find him anymore.

Of course, that time I didn't have any more than water, I didn't have even a piece of bread, I didn't have anything to change, I was only in a little thin shirt and a pair of slacks. And so I was dressed, and nothing more.

Well—I will not go to look for him now, and I will not go back to the place where we started. Because I don't know whether I will find him, I don't know where he is, I will continue my trip. So I started walking around through the tracks and finding out which track is going in the direction

> **"Mother wouldn't go through all this without me and I kept her till the last moment and she survived."**

to Poland. Until I found a, a train, they said, "This train is going in the direction—how far, and how long it will go we don't know, because we don't know how the tracks are." I went up on this, uh, uh, on train, and was going, going, going a little, maybe a few hours, and then it stopped. I had to go down and to ask whether they are, uh, whether they are changing it to go back, or some, and this way I—combined this way it took me maybe three or four weeks until I came to Pole.

And finally I came to my wife's hometown, Sosnowiec. When only I came to the town, I looked—I have seen very little people, very little Jews. I have seen mostly Poles. But where to go, whom to look, and where to see? I went to the Jewish community, it was—I asked for the Jewish community. When I came in, some—girls were there working, and they recognized me. "Oh, you came! Your wife is here! She is looking for you, she is coming here every day and asking—oh, how happy she will be!" "Where is she, where is she?" I ask. "Oh, she is now here, and—she was here, and she went down now to the street, in this and this street maybe you will meet her." Of course, I went down, and looking for her, going up and down, until finally I found her. The rest I don't need to tell you—[cough] Sorry. Because we both were very happy.

And that's the story what I had in my past, in my lifetime. And I, and my wife, we only survived. Later on we were looking around. She lived in a little room, I was together with her, and I ask her, "What did you find out till now? Who is still alive, who is here?" "Yes, our nephew is alive, Lolek—Lolek is alive. And he is here."

Lolek, he was also to-together with us in Auschwitz, and he ran away—when they liquidated Auschwitz, Lolek ran away and was hiding, and he was also free. He got free soon after the German came over to Poland—after the German left Poland. And he was in the underground, together with the Poles, working, and he was a soldier there, and if they had s—the Poles, if they had some Jews on the underground, they send them out on the worst places, in order that they will get killed. But he survived.

And, if the war was over, he came also to Sosnowiec, because this was his address to reunion. And he met my wife earlier than me, but I didn't s-see him there in, because his parents left Poland in 1939. They went to the United States, to the exhibition in Chicago [*sic*], it was a big exhibition, and they left their two children with us. The younger sister—the younger sister perished together with my s—previous son—on an *aktion* [operation] when they caught children. And he was a little grown up, I kept him together with me, and then he came to a working camp, where he survived.

But [Lolek's] father took him—wanted to take him of us, with Red Cross, straight to this United States, but he couldn't, so he took him over to Sweden. And from Sweden he took him over to the United States on a preference visa, like a, a son to a father. His—his father was a brother of my wife. Later on, the father heard that we both survived. He sent us such visas, from the United States to Sw—to Sweden, and took him [*sic?*]

also in Sweden. And there, in Sweden, we waited for the quota, and, after five years, it was a 1950, October 15th, 1950, we came to the United States. And this is my story.

This was all my story, folks. This was the story from me and my wife and by miracle we both survived. Mother wouldn't go through all this without me and I kept her till the last moment and she survived. So long. Let's hope that this will not repeat, in no century, neither for the Jewish people or for other people. Such a disaster what was that six million people, six million Jews, and twelve million people were destroyed and burned in the gas chambers. That's it.

Anja, Art, and Vladek. Stockholm, 1949.

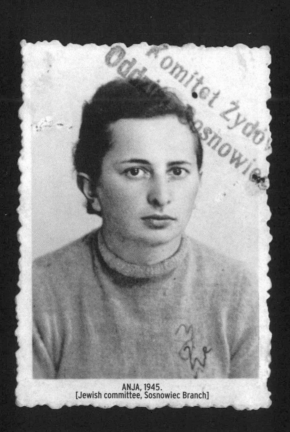

ANJA, 1945.
[Jewish committee, Sosnowiec Branch]

SEARCHING FOR MEMORIES OF ANJA.
INTERVIEWS WITH WOMEN WHO KNEW ANJA IN THE CAMPS AND AFTER

(NOTES FROM 1986–1991 *MAUS* NOTEBOOKS)

CONVERSATION WITH RENYA OSTRY (11/29/87)

Lived next door to Anja in Sosnowiec, 6 or 7 years younger than Anja.

Her father-in-law was a close friend/business associate of Vladek.

Lived with Anja in Srodula.

Knew Anja in Birkenau—had bed across from her
—also was transferred to camp extension.

Also in Ravensbrück.

Renya went to Auschwitz (December 13, 1943?)—
quarantine barracks.

January 12 to working area.

On Yom Kippur 1944 (Sept.) transferred to camp extension.

Women hanged—she says on day she was transferred.

[A.S. note: According to my references, Yom Kippur was Sept. 27, 1944.
According to Auschwitz museum documents, the women from Sosnowiec
who revolted were hanged on Jan. 5, 1945.]

After, as a "treat" taken to block 1 or 2 in Auschwitz to see a movie
(Marlene Dietrich film)—she wandered off—in one room she met a
Greek woman badly cut up from medical experiments.

Worked nights at Union Werke factory.

Renya was badly beaten that night... Anja was never beaten.

Vladek brought Anja a salami.
It was very rare. No men saw the women—maybe somebody they met there;
but not a husband and wife!

Anja never had an appetite—never hungry.

"She called me 'Katchka' (duck); I called her Goose."
"On a selection in front of Mengele I had typhus—I had it twice—My friend said:
'Well. today you and tomorrow me...'"

"I never pushed—I didn't have a position—I never tried to survive."

Your father fathered Anja. He always protected her.

...Renya marched out of Birkenau to Grossrosen. Train to Ravensbrück.
No food very crowded.
I left with a transport from where Mala was—GLEIWITZ—went to Neushtalgaber[?]
The Russians were coming.

After 3 or 4 days we realized nobody was there, the war was over.

[Art:] The Russians liberated you? "Nobody liberated us. The war ended."

We had to run from the Russians. As a Jewish Russian officer told us: "You're at the front. The men are hungry. You'd better run." For 5 weeks I ran—didn't take my clothes or shoes off—I was with 3 girls and 2 men. When the men saw the raping that was going on they ran and rightly so—they would have been shot. I was lucky nobody raped me.

In Ravensbrück Renya took her dress off for the night. It was stolen.
A friend was wearing two dresses—gave her one.

Went back to Sosnowiec. "2 Russian women of ill-repute were living in her house and a janitor that had stolen her possessions [clothes] during the war. That house was where my [Renya's] mother was shot. I saw it once. Didn't stay."

Remembers Anja and Vladek's 25th Anniversary:
I [Art] was drawing a caricature of a woman there at the table who already wasn't pretty —she was all fatness and a big jaw—but you made her a monster.
Your mother was so upset—but what harm, the woman didn't see the drawing.

RENYA OSTRY (MARCH 20TH, 1989)

On Jan 18 or 19, on a train out of Auschwitz, then we got off a train and walked and walked and walked. Cold overtook my hunger. Then in Gross Rosen only one or two, maybe three days. Gross-Rosen wasn't a camp. It was... like a farm... a field with a large shack, like an airplane hangar... a very dim light near the entrance—it was night—it was already very crowded, there were a lot of men there already. It was hard to find a place to sit...they didn't give us anything to eat. I saw something—I don't know if I ever told anyone this 'cause they wouldn't believe me—I saw a man sucking a dead man's finger. At first I didn't know what it was but that's what I saw. I was in shock.

CONVERSATION WITH BLANCA THURM
(BLIMA MANDELBAUM) (12/8/87)
[Contacted via Renya Ostry. She was Mandelbaum's daughter.]

In Bielitz prison with Anja, Vladek, and Marisha Shubert.

Doesn't remember transport to AUS with Anja and Vladek.

Vlad's memory about Mandelbaum's nephew, Avraham, differs:

Liba Eibschutz—Mandelbaum's niece—made the contact for the trip to Hungary... Avraham was a Jewish policeman who turned them in.

Liba met Avraham, a cousin (?) who worked before on the Jewish Police and people didn't say such good things on him, and he made the connection to Hungary. Liba went first and she made arrangements to send a letter back in Yiddish, a letter phrased in a very specific way, as a CODE—if everything was OK.

And the letter came back the wrong way, but my father [Blima's] wanted to go anyway.

BLANCA THURM CONTINUED (HANUKAH, 12/15/87)

To go to Aus we always had time—hiding in the shoe shop then looking for place to hide in Sosnowiec. My cousin (Father's niece) Mother, Father + I we were chased by Poles in the street. But a Polish man took us in for no money...

My Father [Blima's] was restless. My cousin looked around for somewhere to go, met Avraham, a relative of our family.

RENYA OSTRY (12/15/87)
[AT BLIMA'S HOUSE]

Renya left Poland after Kielce Pogrom, May 1946.
Blima: "My child doesn't know Yiddish. It's like another language."

When Renya was under 10—"I overheard the senior class was all communists... You know what kind of communists they are—they all eat red caviar." (rich)

I remember walking to Auschwitz from Birkenau, to work with a girl who was very sick, weak, depressed, I almost had to carry her. Tried to cheer her up... reminded her of her boyfriend— boyfriend, hah! He said he loved her. He only waved to her from a distance, he couldn't come closer—I thought if only I had something to give her to cheer her up... and I bent over to pick her up when she fell, and I found a man's ring, cracked on the ground, and kept it...

At work, I worked in the Union Werke factory, they called me the monkey because I climbed on the machine, high to turn the handles, I worked with men—and I showed one the ring and he gave me something for it—a lot—half a loaf of bread, three sardines and something else.

And we ate, and ate, and ate.

I worked on the night shift, and that's what saved me— the worst things went on during the day.

Blima: I got my father's beard brush from someone in Auschwitz. He didn't have a beard there, but he still had the brush somehow (when we arrived some women from Sosn. who were there earlier told us to give them our things because they'd be taken away by the Germans; they would keep the things and give them to us after. I gave my shoes and some photographs of the family—the shoes I never saw again; I got two left shoes or something like that but I got the photos.) and they told me what happened to my father (Alter Mandelbaum).

He was caught in a selection, but somebody hid him. The truck left. They noticed his number was missing and they came back for him. This always bothered me. It was even worse to go alone....

(Asking Blanca how many women slept in a cubicle—)
About 6 and sometimes 6 on top of that facing the other way.
(I express astonishment:)
We just saw those cubicles when we were in Poland.
How could you fit 12 people into one cubicle?
Blanca: Well we were skinnier then.

Renya—Once a Polish woman in the kitchen gave me an onion.

CONVERSATION WITH MARYSIA WINOGRON (2/8/87)
[PHONE CALL TO NJ]

Related to Anja (second cousin)

I was in Birkenau before Anja—she was in Birkenau, I was in Auschwitz
but we always saw each other.
I worked at night at the Bomb Factory sorting little things at tables.

And when we were moved to the new buildings, in Auschwitz, we were together.

I loved your mother, we were very close. She was such a fine person—not many people knew
her as well as I did—she was wonderful.

I was on the same block as Hanka Sucher (Hanna Heron) in Birkenau. We were bunkmates.
We shared everything.

When I was with Anja she was very sick—running to the bathroom always—I gave her the
little piece bread what I had. She couldn't eat the soup... "You're so good" she said to me—
but I said, "it's okay. I'll eat the soup you can't eat and you'll eat the bread"
—we burned the bread in the oven to make a toast so she could eat.

Anja with Marysia Winogron, postwar.

We were together going
after Auschwitz and we
escaped together.

A Russian woman named
Mala, your mother, and me.
The Germans were taking
us from place to place... This
was after a number of places,
including Ravensbrück—I
think it was Malhoff that
we escaped. Mala investi-
gated and we followed. It
was in Germany... A Polish
man who was working for a
German woman took us in.
We had in the stable in the
hayloft Germans came below
us, searching, it was no fun...

Two Russian soldiers came to
see us. They brought vodka.
They were mercenary—the
Russians were crazy for sex.
They wanted to...be with us. Mala explained in Russian to one of them, he was Jewish, that
we weren't regular girls, we couldn't do anything, we were from camps. He got his friend very
very drunk on vodka and, thanks God, took him away.

(Marysia had a stroke recently)—can't remember some things too well—I forget names and
places, but I remember numbers—was just at the hospital for tests yesterday... wants to give
my number to David(?), her son, he cares about family. He's the one that showed MAUS to
her. She was surprised I hadn't called before this to talk about Anja...

A CALL FROM MARYSIA WINOGRON (12/18/87)

(I had called back, as arranged, on Sunday 12/13/87. She had to go out,
I called again Monday—no answer. Tonight, 12/18, she called me…)

ESCAPING FROM MALHOFF, GOING BACK TO SOSNOWIEC:

My memory is no good. I can't remember if we were in Lelhoff or Malhoff in Germany after
Ravensbrück. We were in both, I don't know which one we were in when we escaped.
I wasn't afraid from horses, there were some horses and wagons; the Russian soldiers gave me
a wagon with horses—I can't remember if it was 1 or 2.

It was in May that we escaped. I was afraid, but Mala—not your Mala—a Russian girl, said
we have nothing to lose, and Anja said come Marishka.

We left. It was the middle of the day; nobody stopped us.

It was very near the end—they were afraid for themselves, the Russians were coming. They
didn't have dogs anymore…

In Malhoff—or Lelhoff—we didn't work… we just counted straw and talked about veg-
etables we didn't have—we pretended the straw was carrots.

We met a Polish man, a "worker" for a big German "Jadzic" (Polish word, meaning
Farmer/landowner?) "I don't have words… I have other languages in my head"
—He hid us in a stable, in straw.

Two German soldiers came in. We were frightened; didn't make any noise
—they were frightened too, they were hiding from the Russians in the same barn.

At night Mala went down to them and gave them margarine (or sold them, I don't know).
We shared food with them.

Next day the Polish man let us come to his room and use it, two single beds.

Two Russians came and threw him out. One was not so nice, the other was a Jewish Russian.
Mala spoke to him in Russian: "We're not certain girls, we're just out of the camps, sick and
hungry. You shouldn't treat us this way." The Jewish guy got the nasty one drunk and took
him away.

Next morning—the Jadzic was gone, we looked around for something to eat. I found some
marks and gave some to the other girls. Maybe they could be worth something. Later, in
Poland we were able to use them.

We had the wagon. I remember the horse ran away, I found them (it?).

We picked up two Poles with suitcases, men, not Jewish, also from camps. They rode
with us.

We heard about two girls we knew in Auschwitz who were together; in Litunstadt they were
molested by Russians; one tried to get away and they killed her.

Some other Russians took our wagon away eventually.
(We had talked our way out of an earlier group of Russians taking it away.)

We took a coal train back to Sosnowiec, I don't know where Mala went.

Anja found friends in Sosnowiec who took her in. She said, "Marisha you can always go in with me," but I had to look for my people. When I needed to sleep I stayed there.

Whenever I organized, a pillow or something, I brought her...

POSTWAR, MEMORIES OF ANJA, MEMORY...

I'm a Zylberberg. Anja's father and my father were cousins. We were second cousins. I lived in Anja's mother's house for a long time. Anja was older than me, there was quite a difference in our ages—she went to Gymnasium; I never did. She was much better educated.

I had the stroke 4 years ago. I can't remember things—I remember phone numbers—I remember my number was 74421. I was there earlier than your mother. What was her number? ("I don't know, I wish I did...")

I forgot everything, but I didn't forget Anja... I may have some letters; I'll try to look.

After the war I went from Sosnowiec to Germany with my husband—I knew him before the war, we got married after—it's a long story... My husband [Michael?] worked for the United Jewish Committee helping Jews, we arrived in NY in 1950.

I was in New York, without Language (couldn't speak English). Anja wrote to me—I went to see her in Norristown right away when Anja came to the U.S.

I even moved to Norristown for 1.5 years—3 years? See—I forget—Anja spoke to Herman and he gave my husband a job. It only lasted a short while but we met other people there—Italians—and he got other work.

I was at your house when Anja died. You remember? ("No...")
I slept over with Hela, in the same bed ("I vaguely remember that, now that you mention it...")
They gave me a tranquilizer, but it kept me awake...

Art: "Did you know about my mother translating Communist documents?"
Marysia: "No—from your book I learned this.
Maybe grandparents didn't want anybody should know."

ON MAUS:

Can I say something? Don't be angry on this. Your book made me a little angry. I don't like dirty wash being cleaned in the open. I know your mother. She was a wonderful generous warm person, your father I knew as a nice man...

Davy (my younger son, the other is Lenny...) explained that younger people aren't the same as in my day, that many people are reading it. I'll have to read it again...

AUSCHWITZ-BIRKENAU

Anja was a very good-hearted woman. She shared with everyone. But till me—she never said this to me, but to my husband—till me, nobody shared with her.
Even before the war she had no appetite, she didn't eat well. Anja's mother always struggled with her to eat. Here in camp, maybe she would eat, but she didn't have anything...

In Birkenau we were going with stones back and forth.
Throw stones and bring them back and forth.
Also worked in potato field—I brought potatoes back in my pants.

AUSCHWITZ-BIRKENAU: AUSCHWITZ EXTENSION

I saw Anja in Birkenau in her barrack—I always saw Anja—on Sundays we could exchange
rooms if somebody didn't notice. You risked your life but you could always do something.

I never got beaten by the Germans.
But by the Czech girls, kapos, I got a bloody nose when I fell asleep while working.
Anja didn't get beaten either.

...When we moved to Auschwitz, there was a woman—she was friends with Anja too—she
lived in Atlantic City till they started building casinos—she got beaten.
She stuck her tongue out through the window and made "fingers with her hand" arguing.
They took her out and beat her.

The Czech block commander was Jewish, the kapos at work were German girls.

The Czech girls had earlier numbers.
The Czech blockowa would throw us down from the wood planks for the Appel.

SELECTIONS—

At first time they looked at you undressed, after the shower. Later, near the end they didn't
even take first the girls from the hospital—they took the sick ones— Just every night at the
Appel, it was something 1, 2, 3, 4, 5—the 5th to burn.
"Sometimes they took the 10th one. It depended how high they could count."
They took the whole women's camp to Auschwitz.

(Art: "Everybody?")

It wasn't so many anymore. The leftovers. Lucky from the selections.

We worked making bombs. You gathered little things at tables and got them together by
size. I was on the night shift. Your mother—? I was with Hankah Zucker (Hanna Heron).
Your mother, I doubt she worked at the machines, they took bigger ones for that work.
She was too small—

My memory. I don't remember any music when we were marching; just boomp, boomp,
boomp, marching, but other people remember—I don't know if it's the stroke
—I never remembered, maybe I was frightened.

RAVENSBRÜCK-MALHOFF:

In Ravensbrück we were—I don't know—was it two weeks. No food. On straw
—sometimes they threw bread—they didn't have.

I had typhus. I could go to the kitchen—maybe I worked there—I stole out margarine, jelly,
whatever I could, and took it out and shared it with the two girls.

"We were on cattle cars and packed like cattle so I don't remember being cold…"
Maybe I'm lucky I don't remember. Anyway, it was so many years ago. Other new things, a new life, new struggles. You wanted to forget, to be like everyone else, not meshugah…

CONVERSATION WITH ITA AND DAVID KRACAUER, 4/15/91
[HALLENDALE, FL] ART'S GODPARENTS.

David, born March 10, 1908 (Vladek was 3 yrs older)
Ita born June 16, 1916

[Became close with Vladek and Anja postwar, in Sweden]

Ita: We came to Auschwitz/Birkenau Oct '44…
"We came late."

David: I was a tailor before the war. In the beginning of war I ran to Lvov, the Russians were there.
Sept–Feb '40… I was a tailor and got work (went to a design school)

[Art:] Did you know what was happening in Auschwitz?

"A friend with Aryan papers brought news and bread."

Ita: We came to Birkenau late, then to Dachau-Lanzburg.

David: Two months after liberation, May 2, we were 30 sick people left—they were supposed to kill us—the graves were made—but we had a German doctor who said,
"Bring me legalization papers or I can't give you…"

Americans came and liberated.
[David looks in wallet for picture of himself in uniform stripes] I tailored it myself.

I was in Poland in Aug. 1945. Back to Sosnowiec.
I stayed with a friend, a furrier, who knew Anja. After 6 months Ita came back from Sweden.

Ita: This friend wrote to a girl who was through the whole war with me.
I was working in a stocking factory in Sweden—they were wonderful to us
They emptied out a house for us, schools etc.
a few more women were there—we insisted, we wanted to work.

The friend woke me up—I got a letter from David. I didn't believe it—I got so excited.
I sent a telegram with a paid return… I didn't even wait for the answer.
I was already on my way from Sweden…
I went to a port city in Sweden, Malmer, and a ferry took the train to Gdansk
and I took the train to Katowice—
He (David) said: "Why did you come?"
A lot of people were leaving. The Russians were there…

It took five years to get a transit visa.

David: I started working as a tailor again. A woman, a customer came in through Gutcha, Miloch's wife, who could get me to France—not Sweden… but her boyfriend was best friends

to the Attaché from Sweden... He could do it if someone in Sweden could put up $700, and we got a passport.
The Polish Attaché to Sweden was my customer.

Herman [Anja's brother in the US] got visas for Vladek and Anja to go to Sweden

Sweden to America—we made reservations together a year in advance—
Vladek and Anja waited four months to go on the same boat.
Ita and David moved to boardinghouse in Sweden with Vladek and Anja in Oct '46.
In boardinghouse 7 or 8 months. Polish refugees in house.

Vladek worked in a store—ENKO—but he was (at first) a plain worker opening boxes, carrying things... He was a hard worker.

Then we got an apartment for a year together...
He got your mother a [cleaning] girl for a year.
Then he got a big apartment...
Herman made him a representative to sell stockings from America.
He opened a store—No...
[Vladek became a "partner" at ENKO, dealing black market stockings]

They started to arrest people—
Sweden didn't have a black market. The Jews started one.

David: Anja was in a store—she overheard a little girl talking to her mother.
"Why does that lady have such a long nose?..."
Two operations to fix it.
I went to V and said: "Vladek—wouldn't you like Anja should be happy with her looks?"
and I talked him into it. It took a long time to convince him to spend.
In 1947, Katz [owner of the ENKO Department store] helped Vladek get a good apartment.
Katz got it for him him without key money...
Vladek was a rich man by the time he left Sweden.

David and Ita Kracauer, Sweden, 1949.

Anja had two miscarriages before Art was born...
"She was so happy when you were born—you couldn't buy for no money."

Moved to US in Oct 1950... Kracauers moved to Ft. Tryon Park in Manhattan in June.
At the end of '51, Vladek and Anja moved there.

Ita tells me about going back to Poland in '48 and through Miloch Spiegelman getting down quilts, silverware etc, a lot, in a big wicker trunk and smuggling it back to Sweden.
At Anja's request she got two of everything—one for Anja...

Ita had to pay American dollars.
[When she returned to Sweden] Vladek wanted to reimburse at a lower exchange rate.
Ita didn't want... said she could resell for a profit.
V and A returned home with an empty suitcase, then paid.

Anja only went to the movies maybe once a month in Stockholm—
we all went two, three, four times a week.
Ita: Vladek stood on line for 1½ hrs for the tickets.
David paid 10 cents more but had the tickets ordered by phone and waiting.

Anja, David, and Ita went to Florida on vacation...
Vladek gave the money for her trip to David:
"I thought he was crazy. Figured out to the penny!"

Anja wanted to bring Vladek back a gift, a wallet,
but I wouldn't give her money for a gift for him. For a gift for you I gave...

Anja, Art, and Vladek, Sweden, c. 1949.

Last cruise together with my beloved wife March, 1968.

Died May 21-st 1968.

TIME FLIES
[A MAUS CHRONOLOGY]

1906

Oct 11. Vladek Spiegelman born in Dąbrowa, a village in Silesia, Poland.

1912

Mar 15. Anja Zylberberg born in nearby Sosnowiec.

1917

March 22. Mala Kurland born in Sosnowiec.

1933

Jan 30. Adolf Hitler named chancellor of Germany.

March 22. Dachau, first of more than 1,000 Nazi concentration camps, established in Munich.

1935

Sept 15. Anti-Semitic Nuremberg laws passed in Germany.

Dec. Vladek and Anja meet.

1937

Feb 14. Vladek and Anja wed.

Oct. Richieu, their first son, born.

1938

Winter. Vladek and Anja first see Nazi flag while traveling to Czech sanitorium by train.

1939

Aug 24. Vladek drafted into Polish army.

Sept 1. German army invades Poland. World War II begins.

Sept 1939. Vladek taken as war prisoner by German Army.

Oct. Sosnowiec annexed into German Reich. Jewish Council (Judenrat) formed in Sosnowiec; all Jewish businesses put in hands of Aryan overseers.

Nov. Sosnowiec Jews required to wear armband with Jewish star in public.

1940

Feb 8. First major Jewish ghetto established in Lodz, home of Zylberberg family hosiery factory.

Mid-Feb. Vladek released as POW.

1941

Apr. (Before Passover) Jewish community of nearby Oswiecim relocated to Sosnowiec while Auschwitz concentration camp built.

May 31. Nuremberg laws enforced in Sosnowiec.

June 22. Germany invades Russia.

Sept 5 (Rosh Hashanah). Yellow star sewn on garments replace armbands.

Autumn. First gassing experiments with Zyklon B at Auschwitz.

Dec 7. US enters war.

By end of December, Zylberberg family household forcibly relocated to Stara Sosnowiec district of city.

1942

Jan 20. Wannsee Conference convened to coordinate Final Solution.

March. Jews hanged in center of Sosnowiec for black market trading.

May. Anja's grandparents transported to Auschwitz. Systematic deportations begin.

Aug 12. Jahn Street Stadium selection. Approximately 11,000 Jews of the 26,000 in Sosnowiec taken away.

1943

By Spring, Zylberberg household is moved to ghetto in Srodula, a small suburb.

Family sends Richieu to Zawiercie ghetto for greater protection.

June 19. Moniek Merin and leaders of Srodula Judenrat deported to Auschwitz.

July 31. Germans begin liquidation of Srodula ghetto. About 10,000 Jews, including Anja's parents, deported.

Aug 3. Small group, including Vladek and Anja, remains to work in Braun's shoe shop (600 official workers plus about 1,000 others).

Aug 26. Zawiercie ghetto liquidated; Tosha Zylberberg poisons children in her charge, including Richieu, and herself.

1944
Jan 13. Srodula ghetto totally liquidated. Vladek and Anja go into hiding.

Mar 16. Vladek and Anja arrested in Bielsko while trying to reach Hungary; taken to Auschwitz.

Mar 17. Hitler orders the occupation of Hungary.

Apr or May. Vladek begins to work in Auschwitz tin shop.

May 2. Hungarian Jews begin to arrive in Auschwitz en masse.

May. Vladek meets Mancie, who arranges for him to see Anja in Birkenau.

Aug or Sept. Vladek works as shoemaker.

Oct or Nov. Vladek taken to hard labor.

Oct 7. Several hundred Sonderkommandos blow up Crematorium IV and kill several guards before being captured.

Oct 10. Anja transferred from Birkenau to camp extension in Auschwitz I.

Nov 26. Himmler orders gas chambers and crematoria dismantled as Soviets advance; Vladek put to work dismantling crematoria.

1945
Jan 6. Four women prisoners, friends of Anja from Sosnowiec, publicly hanged for smuggling explosives to Sonderkommando.

Jan 18–Jan 27. Prisoners begin death march from Auschwitz to Gross-Rosen, about 165 miles away.

Jan 27. Sosnowiec and Auschwitz liberated by Red Army.

Jan 28–Feb 4. Vladek transported in cattle car from Gross-Rosen to Dachau.

Vladek contracts typhus in Dachau.

Late Apr. Vladek put on passenger train to Switzerland in prisoner exchange.

Apr 29. US troops liberate Dachau.

Early May. War ends.

Summer. Vladek and Anja reunited in Sosnowiec.

Vladek and Anja move to Sweden on transit visa where Vladek finds work with NK (EnKo) department store.

1948
Feb 15. Art Spiegelman born in Stockholm.

1951
Spiegelman family emigrates to US, moving first to Norristown, PA, then NYC, finally settling in Rego Park, Queens in 1955.

1955
Oct 24. Françoise Mouly born.

1961
Adolf Eichman, "architect of the Final Solution," caught in Argentina, put on widely televised trial.

1963–1965
Spiegelman attends High School of Art and Design in Manhattan. Commissioned in 2008 to design a stained-glass window for its new building in 2012.

1965–1968
Studies art and philosophy at Harpur College (now SUNY Binghamton); writes "Master Race: The Graphic Story as an Art Form," for an art history class.

1968
Put in Binghamton State Mental Hospital for one month; ends university studies.

May 21. Anja Spiegelman commits suicide.

1969
Oct. Vladek and Mala wed.

1972
First taped interviews with Vladek.

"Maus" published in *Funny Aminals #1* by Apex Novelties.

1973
"Prisoner on the Hell Planet" published in *Short Order Comix #1*.

1975
Moves back to NYC after four years in San Francisco; meets Françoise Mouly.

1977
Breakdowns: From Maus to Now published by Belier Press.

July 12. Art and Françoise wed.

1978
Begins work on *Maus* book.

1979
Travels to Poland to research *Maus*.

July. Mala leaves Vladek in the Catskills.

1980
Spiegelman and Mouly launch *RAW*. Issue #2 contains first chapter of *Maus*, which continues to be published as an insert up through its penultimate chapter, in 1991.

Sept. Mala returns to Vladek; they sell home in Rego Park and move to Florida.

1982
Aug 18. Vladek Spiegelman dies.

Maus in progress receives Yellow Kid Award from International Comics Festival in Lucca, Italy.

1985
May 26. "Cats, Mice and History—The Avant-Garde of the Comic Strip," an essay about *Maus*-in-progress by Ken Tucker published in *NYT Book Review*.

Spiegelman begins to see therapist Paul Pavel, an Auschwitz survivor, after completing Chapter 6 of *Maus*.

1986
July. "Contemporary Artists: Jewish Themes," The Jewish Museum, NYC.

Sept. Pantheon publishes *Maus I: A Survivor's Tale: My Father Bleeds History* as a trade paperback.

Maus nominated for National Book Critics Circle Award in Biography/Autobiography.

Joel M. Cavior Award for Jewish Writing.

1987
Research trip to Poland with German film crew for ZDF/BBC documentary on *Maus*.

May 13. Nadja Spiegelman born.

1988
Maus I receives Alfred Award for Best Foreign Album in Angoulême, France.

Profiled in *Comic Book Confidential*, a documentary history of comics.

1990
Guggenheim Fellowship for continuing work on *Maus*.

1991
Maus II serialized weekly in *The Jewish Forward*.

Nov. Pantheon publishes *Maus II* in hardcover; appears on *NYT* bestseller list.

Dec 17–Jan 1992. "Making Maus" exhibit at Museum of Modern Art, NYC.

Maus II nominated for National Book Critics Circle Award in Biography/Autobiography.

Dec 29. Dashiell Spiegelman born.

1992
Special Pulitzer Prize for two-volume *Maus* series.

LA Times Book Prize for Fiction.

"The Road to Maus," solo exhibition, Galerie St. Etienne, New York. (Travels through 1996 to museums in Fort Lauderdale, San Francisco, Amsterdam, St. Louis, Paris, Düsseldorf, Canton, and Philadelphia.)

Eisner Award, Best Graphic Album.

July 14. Paul Pavel dies.

1993
Maus II receives Alph-Art Prize for Best Foreign Album, Angoulême, France.

1994
Voyager releases *The Complete Maus* CD-ROM.

"La Scrittura di Maus," touring exhibition travels through 1997 (Genova, Rome, Modena, Forte dei Marmi, Trieste, Turin, Brussels, Basel, and Denver, Colorado).

Cultural Achievement Award from the National Foundation of Jewish Culture.

1995
Spiegelman awarded Honorary Doctorate of Letters by SUNY Binghamton.

NY Public Library centennial exhibition includes *Maus* as one of the "100 Books of the Century."

1996
On the tenth anniversary of *Maus I,* Pantheon issues the two volumes as one book, *The Complete Maus.*

1998
Edits and designs *Comix, Essays, Graphics & Scraps: From* Maus *to Now to* MAUS *to Now,* catalog for an international traveling retrospective of his work.

1999
Inducted into Will Eisner Hall of Fame.

2004
"Art Spiegelman: MAUS," Jewish Museum of Australia, Victoria. Travels to Migration Museum, Adelaide, Australia.

2005
France awards Spiegelman a Chevalier de l'Ordre des Arts et des Lettres.

Time magazine names Spiegelman one of the "Top 100 Most Influential People" in the world.

"Masters of American Comics," group exhibition, Museum of Contemporary Art and UCLA Hammer Museum, LA.

2006
Inducted into the Art Director's Club Hall of Fame, NY.

2007
Spiegelman plays himself on "Husbands and Knives" episode of *The Simpsons,* alongside Dan Clowes and Alan Moore.

Art Spiegelman: Conversations published by University Press of Mississippi.

July 7. Mala Spiegelman dies.

2008
Pantheon republishes *Breakdowns* with new introductory work, "Portrait of the Artist as a Young %@&*!"

2009
"Art Spiegelman," solo exhibition, Galerie Martel, Paris, France. Travels to Galleria Nuages, Milan.

2010
Awarded Honorary Doctorate of Fine Arts by Rhode Island School of Design.

ARTE European television documentary, *Art Spiegelman, Traits de Memoire.*

•

INDEX

Page numbers in *italics* refer to images. Page numbers in ***bold italics*** refer to short works by Art Spiegelman.

O

P

R

S

Thanx to the following collectors who allowed access to their original Maus sketches for use in this book and on the accompanying DVD: Lorna Bieber, Andy Breslau, Tom and Harriet Burnett, Josh Cramer, Cecily Langdale Davis, Kevin Goodman, Peter Kuper, Elizabeth Marcus, Dr. Bonnie Maslin and Yehuda Nir, David Neidhart, Suzanne Pavel, Archie Rand, Eric Sachs, Michael Shankman, and Neil Wilson.

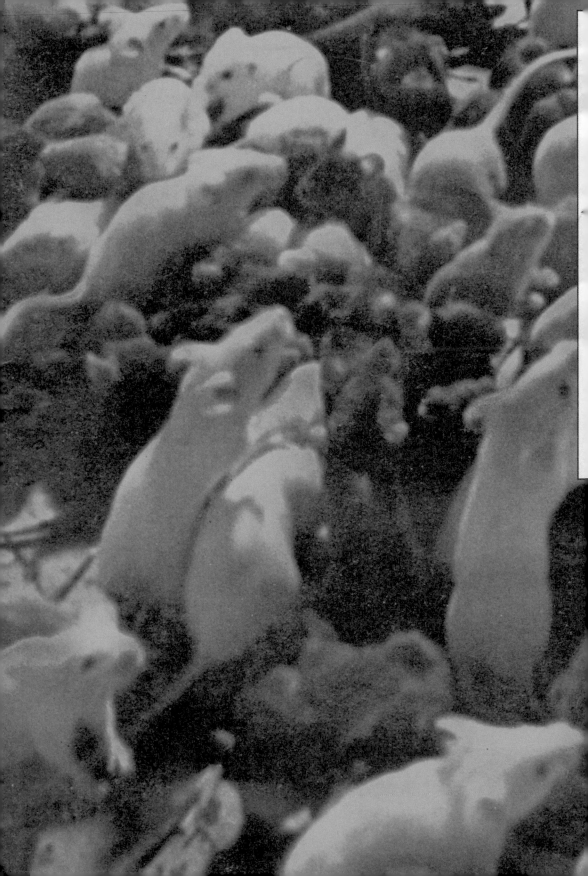